How to Do
Everything™

Windows® 8

About the Authors

Mary Branscombe has been a technology writer for over 20 years, writing for numerous websites, magazines, and daily newspapers like the *Financial Times*. She's fascinated by the how, the what, and the why of technology—how and why it works (and why it works that way), why anyone would use it, and what it does for you. You can currently find her work on *TechRadar* and *ZDNet*, where she co-writes the *500 words into the future* blog with her writing partner, Simon Bisson. Together, they are the authors of *Windows 8: What Your Business Needs to Know*. With a smartphone in one hand and a Windows tablet in the other, Mary is rarely away from computers entirely, but when she's not working, you can find her on a road trip, with her nose in a book, or knitting something complicated.

Simon Bisson is an IT journalist and technology strategy consultant. He has written for many publications, from the *Financial Times* to *ZDNet*. In a varied career outside journalism, Simon has worked on tools to help design electromagnetic launchers and other exotic weapons, helped build the world's first solid-state high-power HF transmitter, was CTO of one of the U.K.'s first national ISPs, and consulted on the development of some of the most recognizable websites. Outside work, Simon walks, travels, takes photographs, and reads a lot. He occasionally reviews science fiction and has had some of his own fiction published. He regularly confuses the TSA by presenting them with a passport from the original Jersey.

Eric Butow is the owner of Butow Communications Group (BCG) in Jackson, California, which offers online marketing ROI improvement services for businesses. He has written 21 books, most recently *How to Succeed in Business, Second Edition* and *My Samsung Galaxy Tab 2*. Eric also developed and taught networking, computing, and usability courses for Ed2Go, Virtual Training Company, California State University–Sacramento, and Udemy.

When he's not working in (and on) his business or writing books, you can find Eric enjoying time with friends, walking around the historic Gold Rush town of Jackson, and helping his parents manage their infant and toddler daycare business.

About the Technical Editors

Iain Thomson has been a technology writer for most of the past two decades, making Windows 8 the seventh Microsoft operating system launch he's covered. British-born, Iain has had spells working on *PC Magazine* and *V3.co.uk*, set up *IT Pro*, and currently covers Microsoft (amongst other topics) at *The Register*. He currently resides in Berkeley with his wife and their small nervous black cat, who is paradoxically called Boo.

As the founder and editor of www.Windows8update.com, **Onuora Amobi** is a leading authority on Microsoft's newest operating system, Windows 8. A former Microsoft MVP for the Windows Desktop, Onuora has more than 16 years of enterprise IT, management consulting, and online marketing experience. He is currently a leading expert and consultant in the areas of strategic analysis and ROI evaluations for organizations looking to move to Windows 8.

How to Do
Everything™

Windows® 8

Mary Branscombe
Simon Bisson
Eric Butow

New York   Chicago   San Francisco   Lisbon
London   Madrid   Mexico City   Milan   New Delhi
San Juan   Seoul   Singapore   Sydney   Toronto

Cataloging-in-Publication Data is on file with the Library of Congress

How to Do Everything: Windows® 8

1234567890 QFR QFR 109876543

ISBN   978-0-07-180514-8
MHID   0-07-180514-1

Sponsoring Editors
Megg Morin, Wendy Rinaldi

Technical Editors
Onuora Amobi, Iain Thomas

Production Supervisor
George Anderson

Editorial Supervisor
Jody McKenzie

Copy Editor
Bill McManus

Composition
Cenveo® Publisher Services

Project Editor
Rachel Gunn

Proofreader
Nancy Bell

Art Director, Cover
Jeff Weeks

Acquisitions Coordinator
Stephanie Evans

Indexer
Ted Laux

Cover Designer
Jeff Weeks

To friends and family, online and everywhere.
—Mary Branscombe and Simon Bisson

For my family.
—Eric Butow

Contents at a Glance

Contents

Acknowledgments

It's been a pleasure working with Megg Morin and Stephanie Evans at McGraw-Hill and the rest of the editing and production team, who displayed grace under pressure; and we never miss an opportunity to work with Iain Thomson.

We owe thanks to the many members of the Windows team who helped us learn about Windows 8 (and came up with a great operating system for you to use), and to friends and colleagues who helped us out with information, testing, and checking how different parts of Windows 8 work around the world. Special thanks to Claudette Moore for timely advice.

—Mary Branscombe and Simon Bisson

First, I want to thank Megg Morin and Stephanie Evans at McGraw-Hill for shepherding this book from inception to completion. I'd also like to thank Onuora Amobi for his valuable technical input, as well as all the copy editors, indexers, and layout professionals who helped make this book a reality. And my thanks wouldn't be complete without a shout out to the best literary agent on the planet, Carole Jelen.

I also want to thank my family and friends for their endless support, and thank you for choosing this book to help you use Windows 8 to its full potential.

—Eric Butow

Introduction

Meet Windows 8. It's fast, it's fun, it's connected—and it's different.

It works just as well on a super-thin tablet like the Microsoft Surface as it does on an all-in-one computer with a big touchscreen, or a notebook you can use on the couch or carry to the coffee shop. It has a new Start screen with tiles that are all about you—showing you what your friends are up to and showing off your favorite photos and websites, as well as apps from the Windows Store, which look great and are easy to use. It comes with a powerful new version of Internet Explorer, a starter set of Windows Store apps, and extras like free streaming music. But Windows 8 still has the familiar Windows desktop where you can run your favorite programs and be as productive as ever—or even more so, as Windows 8 is faster and more secure than ever.

It's the best of both worlds, PC and tablet, and we're going to show you how to make the most of what Windows 8 has to offer.

What Does This Book Cover?

There are so many things you *could* do with Windows 8 that no one book could cover all the possibilities. What we've concentrated on is everything you *need* to know to get the most out of this new version of Windows, from the minute you turn on your computer and discover a new way of working. If you have a Windows tablet or a PC with a touchscreen, we'll show you how to use your fingers to tap, drag, and swipe your way through the new interface, but we also show you how to do everything with a mouse and keyboard. Here's a quick look at everything you'll learn:

- Chapter 1 introduces you to Windows 8 and helps you get set up and signed in. (If you're upgrading from an older version of Windows, we'll help you choose the right edition of Windows 8 and get it installed.) You'll learn how to use the new Start screen and Charms bar, how to get to the desktop and back, and how to use two applications at once. If you have a new touchscreen PC, you'll learn the gestures that take you where you need to go.

- Now that you have Windows 8 running and you're confident about how to get around the new interface, Chapter 2 explains more of what you can do in the Windows 8 interface and dives into the new features in the upgraded File Explorer. You'll learn how to pin tiles to the Start screen, how to pin icons to the taskbar, and how to make your computer look really personal.

- In Chapter 3 we take a look at some of the other settings on your PC that you might want to change to make it work the way you want. You'll learn where to find all the different options you can tweak, from changing your password to keeping your family safe online.

- Chapter 4 shows you how to work with files and documents in Windows 8. Even if you're familiar with File Explorer, there are some handy new options to make your life easier. You'll learn how to back up personal files with File History, how to sync files to the cloud with SkyDrive, and how to sync your Windows settings to other PCs you use.

- Sharing information through the cloud is very convenient, and Chapter 5 shows you how to get online, but if you have several PCs at home, you can share files more quickly if you connect them together in a network. We'll also show you how to set up a homegroup to share photos, media, and other files with any other computers you have at home.

- Chapter 6 introduces the new browser in Windows 8, Internet Explorer 10. We explain why there are two versions of Internet Explorer and show you how to browse multiple websites in different tabs, how to search, and how to protect your privacy online.

- Chapter 7 shows you how to set up your printer, and how to print from the new Windows Store apps. You'll also learn how to set up other peripherals, like keyboards, mice, scanners, and more.

- In Chapter 8 we introduce you to the Windows Store apps that come with Windows 8, starting with the Mail and Calendar apps. You'll learn how to set up your email account, whatever service you use, and how to stay on top of meetings and appointments with reminders.

- When email isn't fast enough, send a more instant message. In Chapter 9 we show you how to chat with your friends using the new Messaging app.

- Sometimes you need to say what you feel rather than writing it down. Chapter 10 shows you how to use the new Windows Store Skype app to stay in touch via phone and video calls.

- In Chapter 11 we put all your social networks together. We explain how signing in with a Microsoft account puts your friends in the People app, and how to keep your favorite people at your fingertips on the Start screen and share what you care about.

- All the music you love—and free music you'll fall for, played the way you want it. In Chapter 12 we'll show you how to make the most of the Xbox Music streaming service (which comes free with Windows 8) to enjoy your favorite artists or build smart playlists that help you find new music you'll like. We'll also show you how to organize your own music library and burn CDs in Windows Media Player, and how to play music from your PC on other devices, like your Xbox.

- Get more from the new Photos app; sign in with a Microsoft account and you can bring together the photos on your PC with all the images you have stored online in Facebook, Flickr, and SkyDrive. In Chapter 13 we'll teach you how to fix your photos, how to use them to personalize Windows 8, and how to take advantage of all the different ways to share and enjoy them.
- The way you watch TV, movies, DVDs, and your own videos changes in Windows 8. In Chapter 14 we'll show you how to install Windows Media Center if you want to watch (and record) live TV or play a DVD, how to use the new Video app to stream music from the Xbox video store, and how to watch videos from the Web on your big-screen TV.
- Chapter 15 covers the other useful Windows Store apps that come with Windows 8. You'll learn how to scroll, swipe, and search PDF documents, how to navigate with Bing Maps, and how to search the Web and stay on top of news, sports, and finance with the beautiful new Bing apps.
- Useful as they are, the apps that come with Windows 8 don't do everything you need, but you can get thousands more Windows 8 apps and games from the Windows Store. In Chapter 16 we'll show you how to search the Windows Store and install more apps and games, as well as how to control your Xbox 360 with the SmartGlass app.
- Windows 8 is designed to fix itself and not to slow down after you've been using it for a while, but there are still some things you can do to keep your PC running smoothly. In Chapter 17 you'll learn how to check for problems Windows is warning you about and how to customize advanced options for power, screen settings, and combining disks to get more storage space.
- If anything does go wrong, Chapter 18 teaches you how to use the built-in tools for finding and fixing problems, with Windows 8 itself or with your PC and peripherals.
- It's easier than ever to reset Windows so it works the way it did when you first bought it; Chapter 19 shows you exactly how to do that without losing your files. And if the problem is a serious hardware fault or a PC that's just not what you need, you'll learn how to transfer your information to a new computer, ready to enjoy Windows 8 again.

Conventions Used in this Book

As you read this book, you'll see we've highlighted some information that we think will help you get up to speed with Windows 8. Notes have useful ideas and concepts you need to know about, Tips help you get the most out of Windows 8 with handy shortcuts, and Cautions warn you about potential pitfalls. Keep an eye out for "How To…" sidebars that walk you through specific tasks. "Did You Know?" sidebars give you more in-depth information and other ways of getting things done in Windows 8.

1

Get to Know Windows 8

HOW TO...

- Explore the four versions of Windows 8
- Install or set up Windows 8
- Log in to get started
- Use the Start screen
- Run Windows Store apps
- Switch between Windows Store apps and desktop programs
- Use the Windows desktop
- Work with gestures if you have a touchscreen PC

Welcome to Windows 8! This is a brand new operating system with lots of exciting features and powerful tools that make it easier than ever to get the most out of your PC. In this book we're going to show you what you can do in Windows 8—and how you do it.

As you start using Windows 8, keep in mind that you're using a completely redesigned version of Windows. Some things have changed (and some of those changes are controversial), and under the hood there are a lot of improvements that make Windows 8 faster and more secure than ever. Equally, there are many places Windows 8 will feel familiar, especially if you've been using Windows 7 or even Windows Vista.

Since Microsoft released Windows 1.0 in 1985, the operating system has gone through several major changes, so this isn't the first time we've seen a new look for Windows or a new way of working with the features. Back in 2001 when Microsoft released Windows XP, it was a big shift from Windows 95. The look and feel evolved in Windows Vista and Windows 7, but in Windows 8 you have the next leap forward in operating systems at your command.

Why is Windows 8 such a leap? What's so different? It's not just that the Start menu is gone. It's replaced by a full-screen Start screen that combines popular features from the taskbar, like pinning your favorite apps, with the innovative design and "live" tiles of the Windows Phone operating system that keep you up to date at a glance. But those

1

apps might also be very different from the desktop programs you use today (although you can still run most of those as well). These new apps come from the Windows Store, they run full screen (or snapped into a small side window) rather than on the desktop, and they're designed to work just as well, or even better, on touchscreens as with a mouse.

Over the past few years, smartphones and tablets have become extremely popular. They're thin, light, and fun to use, they have long battery life, and they let you browse the Web and run apps that are powerful enough to let you do a lot of what you want and need to do, from gaming to online banking to sketching to making music. However, *a lot of* what you want and need to do isn't *everything* you want and need to do; for example, you can't run Office or an image editing program with the full power of Photoshop, or even look at a website that uses Flash.

The success of the iPad means you might find yourself choosing between the convenience of a tablet and the power of a PC. Microsoft saw an opportunity to combine the two in Windows 8, and to make versions of Windows that run on something very different from the PCs and laptops we've been using for years.

Add in cloud services like SkyDrive and Dropbox that let you share files and photos between different devices, and devices like tablets (which are designed to always be connected) become the ideal companion device. PCs will always have more power and they aren't going away, but smartphones and tablets are an integral part of our lives now. With Windows 8, you can have the best of both worlds. You can have a traditional Windows PC or notebook, which might have a touchscreen as well, or you can have a Windows tablet that gives you a real alternative to an iPad. You can click with a mouse or tap on the screen. You can run the same apps and do the same things on both—and that's what this book will show you how to do. We'll also explain the differences between Windows 8 and Windows RT; if you have a Windows RT device, a lot of what's in this book applies to your device as well.

If you've bought a new desktop, notebook or tablet with Windows 8, you're ready to set up your account and start exploring. If you're upgrading to Windows 8 from an older version of Windows, we'll help you work out which edition of Windows 8 is right for you and show you how to install it.

As you start to discover Windows 8, we'll explain how the new Start screen works and the ways you navigate the new features like the Charms bar and control Windows Store apps. Plus we'll show you how to get to the desktop and back. If you have a new PC with a touchscreen, we'll show you the touch gestures that make Windows 8 easy to use; and if you have a mouse and keyboard, we'll show you the most important shortcuts for those as well.

Compare the Four Versions of Windows 8

Windows 7 came in six different editions, and sorting out the differences between them was confusing. Microsoft has pared this down to four editions in Windows 8, and the differences are much clearer. If you haven't purchased Windows 8 yet or you're going to upgrade other computers as well and you want to understand which edition is best for you, here's what you need to know.

Which Editions of Windows 8 You Can Upgrade To

If you want to keep the programs you already have installed and not have to worry about copying your files somewhere safe and then moving them back onto your PC, you need to have Windows 7 already and you need to make sure you get an edition of Windows 8 that you can use for a direct upgrade. You can run the Windows 8 Upgrade Assistant from the Microsoft website to determine whether any programs you have installed need to be uninstalled because they won't work with Windows 8 (or whether there are any peripherals you won't be able to use). Windows 8 will do the same check when you start to install it, but it's useful to know in advance.

If you're happy to reinstall programs and transfer files (or if you have Windows XP or Vista), you can pick the edition that suits you and do a "clean" installation on your PC. Remember, this deletes your previous version of Windows, including your programs and all your files, so you should back up your files and collect together the installation media for your software. Windows 8, Windows 8 Pro, and Windows 8 Enterprise all come in both 32-bit and 64-bit versions. You only need to worry about the difference if you have 64-bit hardware that you're currently running a 32-bit version of Windows 8 on and you want to change to 64-bit Windows 8 (for example, so that you can use more memory). In that case, you'll also need to do a "clean" install. Either way, the Windows 8 installer will take care of everything for you.

Windows 8

The "regular" edition of Windows 8 is just called Windows 8 and is designed for home users. If you have Windows 7 Home Premium, Home Basic, or Starter edition, then you can upgrade to Windows 8. If you have Windows 7 Ultimate or Professional, you can't upgrade directly to plain Windows 8—you need to remove Windows 7 from that computer and install Windows 8 from scratch (the Windows 8 installer will help you do both of those) or upgrade to Windows 8 Pro.

Windows 8 Pro

Windows 8 Pro contains all the features in Windows 8 and also includes several more tools that are designed for power users and businesses. For example, Windows 8 Pro supports Group Policy, which manages user and computer accounts, and DirectAccess, which enables you to connect remotely to a work network. If you want to use Windows Media Center, you also need to have Windows 8 Pro. You can upgrade to Windows 8 Pro from any version of Windows 7 (except the Enterprise edition), and you can also upgrade from the standard version of Windows 8 later on if you decide you need the extra features.

Windows 8 Enterprise

The Windows 8 Enterprise edition isn't something you can buy in a store; it's for businesses and organizations who deal with Microsoft as enterprise or Software Assurance customers. (The term *Enterprise* in the edition name means it's designed for large organizations, including businesses and government entities that buy many copies of software at the same time.) The Software Assurance program includes extra tools, support, and upgrades for organizations that run Windows (or other Microsoft applications like Office) on five or more PCs. The Enterprise edition includes special features, including Windows To Go, which allows you to install Windows 8 on a removable device such as a USB drive and then run Windows directly from that removable device. You can only upgrade directly to Windows 8 Enterprise from Windows 7 Enterprise, or from Windows 7 Professional as long as it uses a volume license.

Did You Know?

What You Get to Keep in an Upgrade

How much you get to keep from your current version of Windows depends on which version of Windows that is. If you're still on Windows XP, as long as you have Microsoft's Service Pack 3 installed, you can keep the files you have on your PC but not the programs you have installed or the settings you've chosen in Windows. If you upgrade from Windows Vista, you can keep both files and settings but, again, not applications. When you upgrade from Windows 7, as long as you upgrade directly rather than doing a "clean" installation, you can bring along your Windows settings, personal files, and programs.

Upgrading from:	Personal Files	Windows Settings	Applications
Windows XP SP3 and later	Yes	No	No
Windows Vista	Yes	No	No
Windows Vista SP1	Yes	Yes	No
Windows 7	Yes	Yes	Yes
Windows 8 Preview releases	No (Saves data in Windows.old folder)	No	No

Windows RT

Windows RT is a new version of Windows that runs on computers that are powered by an ARM chip. The desktop and notebook PCs you're familiar with have processors inside from Intel or AMD, which are also known as x86 or x64 chips. Smartphones and tablets like the iPad (and now Windows RT tablets) use ARM chips, which have less processing power than x86 CPUs but also use less power to run apps. That means you can have a smaller battery in a thinner, lighter device and still get a longer battery life than most notebook PCs offer.

You can't go out and buy a copy of Windows RT; it comes preinstalled on the only computers that can run it. Initially these are tablets from PC makers like Asus and Samsung, as well as Microsoft's own Surface RT, many of which have detachable or dockable keyboards that turn them into mini notebooks. In the future we expect to see Windows RT on thin and light notebooks with touchscreens and even on some all-in-one desktop PCs.

Windows RT has the Windows desktop, with Windows Explorer and familiar tools like Notepad and Paint. It also includes a special version of Microsoft Office Home and Student Edition 2013, which gives you Word, Excel, PowerPoint, and OneNote. (You don't get Office included when you buy Windows 8, but your PC maker might choose to bundle it on some systems.) Apart from Office, Windows 8 RT will only run the apps you download from the Windows Store, not any existing desktop programs. (You'll learn more about the Windows Store in Chapter 16.)

If you're shopping for a Windows tablet, you need to decide whether you want a thinner, lighter, and possibly cheaper tablet with a longer battery life, in which case you'll want to purchase a Windows RT tablet, or you need to run desktop programs as well, in which case you'll want to purchase a Windows 8 tablet that uses an Intel or AMD x86 chip. Many PC makers offer both tablet versions, with very similar model names, so check the details carefully when you shop. If the description says you can't run desktop programs, it's a Windows RT device.

Install Windows 8

You can buy a boxed copy of Windows 8 or get the software online and download it, in which case instructions for copying it onto a DVD or USB drive are included. Installing Windows 8 is much simpler and faster than for previous versions of Windows, and there are only a few choices to make. The first thing to remember is that after you install Windows 8, you can't uninstall it and get your older version of Windows back, even from the recovery partition. If you think you might want to go back to the older version, make sure you create a backup before you install Windows 8. You can use the Windows Backup and Restore tool in your current version of Windows for this; for example, in Windows 7, open the Control Panel, choose Back Up and Restore, and click Create a System Image in the left panel. You'll find full instructions for doing this in Windows 7 at http://windows.microsoft.com/en-US/windows7/Back-up-your-programs-system-settings-and-files, which also has links to how to make backups in earlier versions of Windows.

You should also keep your old Windows media. If your PC didn't come with a DVD to reinstall Windows, start your PC using the recovery partition (look in the manual that came with your PC to find out how to do this, or look in the support section of your PC maker's website). You will find tools here to create a disc that you can use to reinstall your current version of Windows. Make sure you do this before you install Windows 8.

If you want to upgrade to Windows 8 and keep your files and as many of your programs and settings as possible, turn on your PC as usual and then run the Windows 8 installer. If you want to do a "clean" installation from scratch, turn your PC off and put the Windows 8 DVD in the drive before you turn it on, or start your PC from the USB drive with the Windows 8 installer that you downloaded.

There are only a few steps to installing Windows 8. You pick which language you want to install (see Figure 1-1), accept the license, and then choose whether to upgrade your existing version of Windows or start afresh.

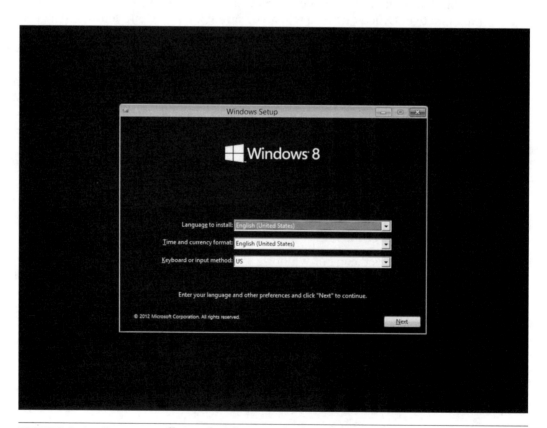

FIGURE 1-1 Begin installation by choosing languages and keyboard type.

It's worth reading the new Windows 8 license. Microsoft has rewritten it in a Q&A-style format to make it easier to understand, so you can see exactly what you're allowed to do and understand what Microsoft does with any information you provide (for example, by submitting problem reports).

If you're upgrading and keeping programs, the installer will check for compatibility; if there are programs that won't work, you can uninstall them and restart the installation automatically. Be patient if you have a lot of applications installed, as this can take 15 to 20 minutes to scan your system and then an hour or more to transfer files and programs to finish the installation. A fresh install will take as little as 15 minutes (see Figure 1-2 and 1-3).

At this point, you go through the same steps to set up Windows 8 that you'll see the first time you turn on a PC that has Windows 8 preinstalled.

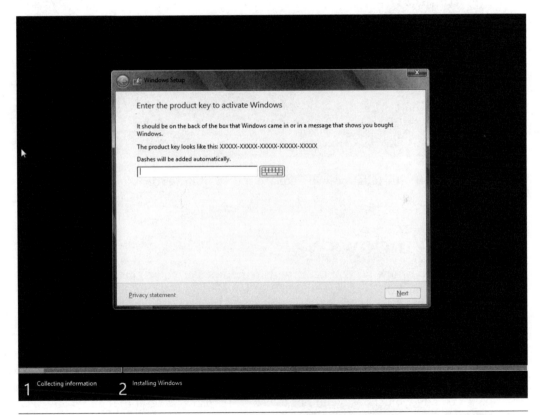

FIGURE 1-2   Enter the Windows product key. Windows 8 will be automatically activated as it installs.

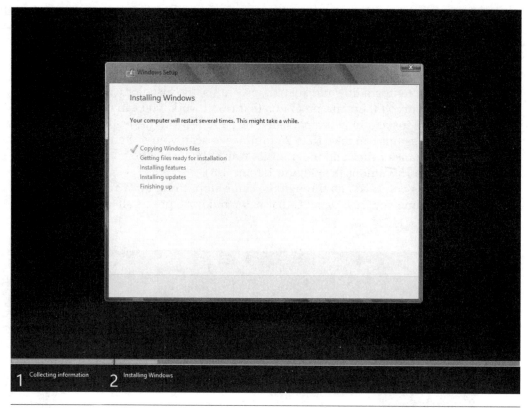

FIGURE 1-3   Installation will take around 15 minutes on a new PC.

Set Up Windows 8

If you have a new PC that came with Windows 8 or you've just installed Windows 8, the first time you turn on your computer, you'll go through these brief steps to set up Windows 8.

First you pick a color scheme to customize your PC with, as shown in Figure 1-4 (we'll show you how to change that in Chapter 2), and then you connect to your Wi-Fi network. You can accept the Express Settings or make your own choices about whether to allow Microsoft to collect anonymous information about how you use Windows and whether to turn on the Do Not Track setting in Internet Explorer.

Finally, you choose whether to use a Microsoft account to log into your PC (which we recommend) as shown in Figure 1-5, or create a local account. After that, Windows displays a short tutorial showing you how to access the new Charms bar by moving your mouse into one of the corners on the right side of the screen; if you have a touchscreen, the tutorial also shows you how to swipe with your fingers. We'll show you how to do both in this chapter.

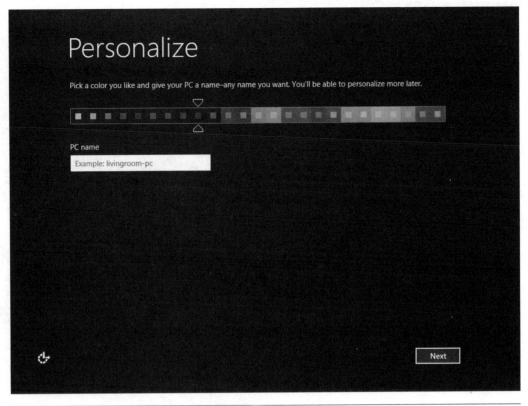

FIGURE 1-4   Pick a color scheme for Windows 8

Why You Want a Microsoft Account

Although you can still create a local account on Windows the way you have before, with or without a password, there are advantages to using a Microsoft account for Windows 8. A Microsoft account is an online account; if you have a Windows Live ID, a Hotmail or Outlook.com address, or an Xbox gamer tag, you can use that, with the same username and password, or you can set up a new Microsoft account as part of setup.

If you choose a local account with a password, that password will apply only to your computer, whereas if you use a Microsoft account, many of your Windows 8 settings will be saved in that Microsoft account. This is very convenient if you use multiple computers because you won't have to re-create your preferred Windows settings on each computer. You'll get the same color scheme and the same desktop background, and even your Internet Explorer history and Wi-Fi hotpot logins will sync to the other PCs you use. Plus, using a Microsoft account gives you a head start on getting your PC set up. Windows will fill in your Hotmail details in the Mail and

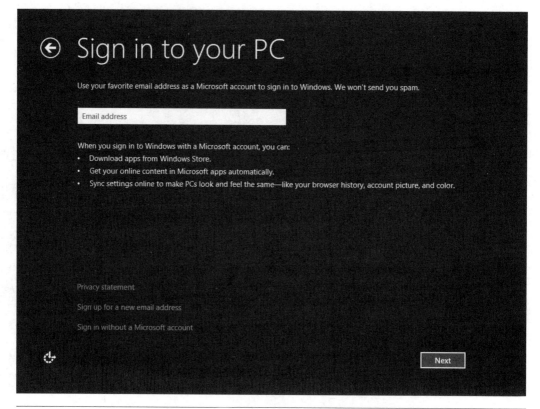

FIGURE 1-5　Set up Windows 8 to log in with your Microsoft account.

Calendar apps, grab your Hotmail and Windows Messenger contacts for the People app, and include your SkyDrive photo albums in the Photos app, along with any other services and social networks you already have linked to your Windows Live ID, like Facebook or Flickr.

Log In to Get Started

When you turn on your PC for the first time after setting up Windows 8, you see the new Lock screen, which stops other people from seeing what you're working on and shows you the same kind of useful information as the lock screen on a smartphone. We'll show you how to pick what image you see on this screen in Chapter 2; you can choose from the built-in images or use a favorite photo.

The Lock screen shows you the date and time with a row of notification icons below, as shown in Figure 1-6 (in which only one icon is present). We'll show you how to choose some of the icons you see here in Chapter 3; others depend on what kind of

(1)
(2)
(3)

FIGURE 1-6   The Windows 8 lock screen shows you what's going on your PC before you even open Windows, such as (1) current time, (2) current date, and (3) notification icons.

computer you use and whether you're connected to a network. The first icon shows the status of your network connection. If you're running Windows 8 on a notebook or a tablet, the next icon shows whether it's plugged in or, if not, how much battery life you have left. You may also see icons telling you how many unread email messages you have, how many times you've been mentioned on Twitter, or whether you've missed a Skype call. If you have a meeting or a birthday reminder scheduled in the Calendar app, you'll see that next to the date.

Use PC settings to control the Windows 8 Lock screen, as shown in Figure 1-7. Unlike past versions of Windows, what you don't see on the Lock screen is a box to enter your password so that you can log in and use Windows 8. So how do you access the login screen where you type in your password? Just click or tap on the picture and drag it up and off the screen, or press any key on the keyboard. The login screen appears.

There are two versions of the login screen, depending on whether you only have a text password that you type in or you have a touchscreen and you've created a picture password (see Chapter 3) that you draw on screen as gestures. Both screens show your account picture; if you're using a Microsoft account, this is your profile picture, while if it's a local account, you can choose an image. The login screen also shows your username (and your email address if you're using a Microsoft account).

If you have a picture password set up, you see the picture, ready to draw your gestures on; if you're using a text password, the Password box is under your username as shown in Figure 1-8, ready for you to type into. Type in the password for your local account or for your Microsoft account and press ENTER, or click or tap the right arrow button to the right of the Password box.

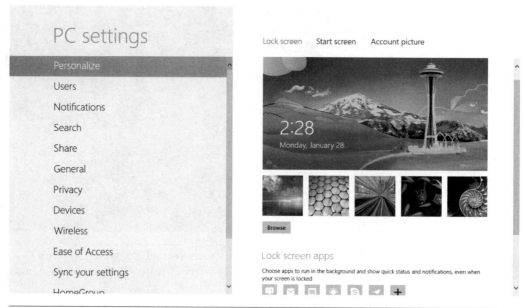

FIGURE 1-7 Configure your Lock screen from PC settings (covered in Chapter 3).

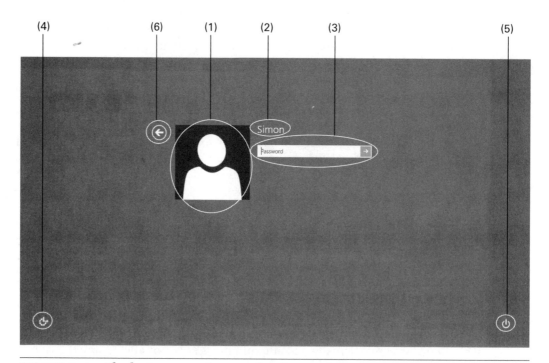

FIGURE 1-8 The login screen is more than just a place to type your password. It has a place for (1) your profile picture, (2) your username, (3) type your password, (4) Ease of Access menu, (5) Power menu, (6) Go back to switch accounts.

If you want to log in with a different account, click or tap the arrow to the left of your profile picture to see all the accounts that are set up on your PC. We'll show you how to change your password and set up a picture password in Chapter 3.

 If you don't enter a password within a minute or two, the Lock screen reappears. You'll have to move the picture off the screen or press a key again to access the login screen.

Shut Down Your Windows 8 Computer

In Windows 8, you don't turn off your PC by clicking the Start menu and choosing the Shut Down option. Now, there are several different ways to shut down your machine. The easiest way is always from the Charms bar (or you can just use the power button on your PC). In the lower left corner of the screen, click or tap the Power icon to open the menu shown in Figure 1-9. (This is the same icon you'll also find in the Settings charm.)
     You may see up to four options in the Power menu:

- **Sleep**   Click or tap if you want to save power but have your PC wake up quickly when you need it.
- **Hibernate**   Click or tap to put your computer in low power mode. This option doesn't appear by default. In Chapter 18 you'll learn how to add this option to the Power menu.
- **Shut down**   Click or tap to shut down Windows and turn off your computer.
- **Restart**   Click or tap to shut down Windows and restart your computer.

FIGURE 1-9   The Power menu

If you change your mind while you're still starting up your PC, you can turn it off right from the Lock screen as well.

Explore the Start Screen

After you type in your password in the login screen, the Start screen shown in Figure 1-10 appears. If you've used Windows Phone or recent versions of the Xbox dashboard, you may recognize the interface (the style is called the Microsoft Design Language, although it's been referred to as Metro in the past). The Start screen is where you'll come to launch apps and programs, to check the weather and the news headlines, to check for messages, or to see the latest stock prices. Like the Lock screen, the Start screen takes concepts you're probably familiar with on your smartphone and brings them to Windows to give you a new way of navigating your PC.

Unlike the various versions of the Start menu that we've been using since Windows 95, which put programs and Windows features on a hierarchical menu that popped up over the desktop upon clicking the Start button, the Start screen in Windows 8 takes up the entire screen. And now, instead of lists of programs and files, you have rectangular buttons called *tiles*.

A tile can open a Windows Store app like Mail or People, a desktop program like Word or Windows Media Player, or even a Windows feature like File Explore, Control Panel, or the Run dialog. Or a tile can link to a specific feature inside a Windows

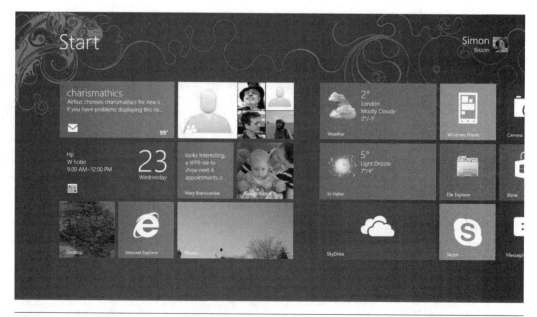

FIGURE 1-10 The tiles on the Start screen link to the apps and programs you want to open quickly, or even to specific tools and people.

Store app, like a single note in OneNote for Windows 8, or your best friend from the People app.

The Start screen contains a variety of tiles for different apps and Windows features by default. As you install more Windows Store apps and desktop programs, tiles for them will be automatically pinned to the Start screen, and you can choose to pin, move, or unpin tiles for the various apps and programs you have on your PC. The colors of the tiles for Windows Store apps differ from the color of the tiles for desktop programs, and some of the Windows Store app tiles are larger to make room for more information, like a detailed weather forecast, the details of your next appointment, or the first line of a new email message. We'll show you how to experiment with pinning the tiles you want, moving them around, and changing tile sizes in Chapter 3.

 You can tell whether a tile opens a Windows Store app or a desktop program by the color of the tile and the style of the icon on it. Tiles for desktop programs all use the accent color for the color screen you've chosen and have the same icon you'll see for the program on the Windows desktop or in the taskbar. You can't make the tiles for desktop programs bigger.

Windows 8 always puts more tiles on the Start screen than fit onto your PC screen at once. Seeing the edges of the tiles on the right side of the screen is meant to show you that there are more tiles beyond the edge of the screen, as you can see in Figure 1-11.

When you move your mouse pointer, you'll see a scroll bar at the bottom of the screen shown in Figure 1-12 so you can scroll right and see the rest of the tiles. If you

FIGURE 1-11   Tiles appear truncated on the right side of the screen. Scroll or swipe sideways to see the rest of the tiles on the Start screen.

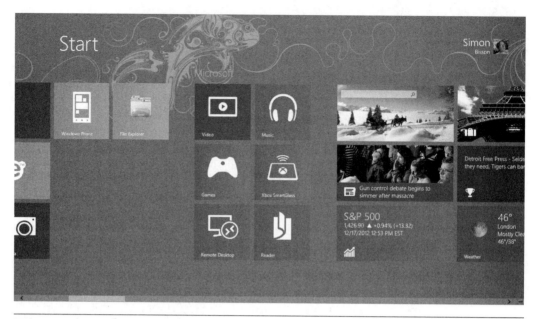

FIGURE 1-12 The remaining tiles in the Start screen appear after you scroll to the right.

have a touchscreen, you can just drag your finger across the screen to see the rest of the tiles. To zoom out and see all the tiles at once (called Semantic Zoom), either pinch with your fingers (on a touchscreen), click the minimize button in the bottom right corner of the scroll bar that appears when you move your mouse, or hold down the CTRL button and press the – key. You can also right-click or swipe over the top or bottom edge of the screen to see the All Apps list, which includes programs and apps you don't have pinned to the Start screen.

Access the User Menu

In the upper right corner of the Start screen, you'll see your username and the profile picture for your account. Click or tap your name or picture to view the User menu shown in Figure 1-13.

You can select from one of four options in the menu:

- **Change account picture** Click or tap to jump straight to the PC Settings option to select a new account picture (or take a photo with your webcam).
- **Lock** Click or tap to lock your computer and show the Lock screen if you're going to walk away from your PC and you don't want anyone to see what you're doing or use it while you're gone. You'll have to type in your password or draw your picture password to unlock your computer and continue working where you left off.

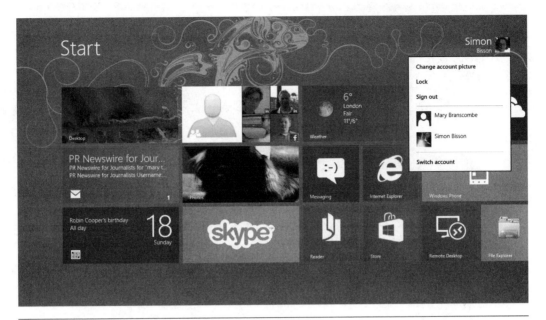

FIGURE 1-13 The User menu

- **Sign out** Click or tap to sign out of your current Windows session. This doesn't shut down Windows or restart your PC; it just signs your account out and takes you back to the Lock screen, where you can sign in again or sign in with a different account.
- **Account name** You'll see the name of your Windows account here. If you have other accounts set up on your computer, you can log in with another account without signing out first by clicking or tapping the account name here. If you don't share your PC all the time, you might still have a Guest account that you let visitors use. Choose Switch account to access an account that's already logged in.

View the Charms Bar

Many of the tools you'll use frequently for controlling Windows 8, from searching or opening the Control Panel, to connecting to Wi-Fi or turning your PC off, are tucked away in a menu called the Charms bar, shown in Figure 1-14. (You might find that the five icons on the bar remind you of a charm bracelet or perhaps a certain breakfast cereal.) A bit later in this section, we'll explain what each icon does, starting at the top of the screen and working down.

To open the Charms bar on a touchscreen, you swipe in from the right edge of the screen and tap the icon you want. You can use a similar gesture on some notebook

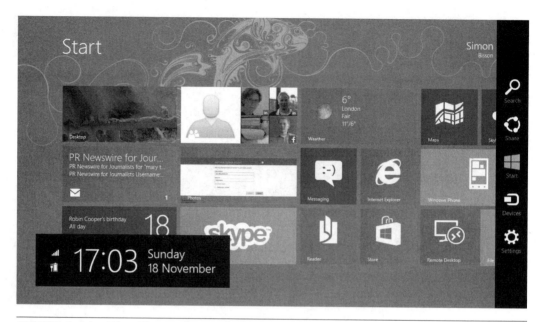

FIGURE 1-14 The Charms bar with the panel shows the date and time.

trackpads or if you have a mouse with a touch surface, and recent keyboards have buttons for each of the four main charms. You can also press WINDOWS KEY-C on your keyboard.

If you're using a mouse, just move the cursor to the top or bottom corner on the right side of the screen. That brings up outlines of the five icons on the Charms bar (see Figure 1-15).

Because you might have moved the mouse into the corner by accident, the white icons shown in Figure 1-15 show up as hints to tell you the charms are there. If you want to use the charms, just move your mouse toward them and the full Charms bar appears on screen, along with a panel showing the time and date plus your power level and network connectivity (as shown in Figure 1-14).

Note If you didn't mean to open the Charms bar, you don't have to do anything to get rid of the white icons. If you don't move the mouse pointer toward the icons to activate the Charms bar, then after a couple of seconds they disappear.

FIGURE 1-15   Move the mouse pointer into the upper or lower right corner of the Start screen to see the white Charms bar icons.

Search

The ability to search is built right into Windows 8, and you can search directly from the Start screen for all the apps and programs you have installed, for settings in the Control Panel, for files on your PC, and for items in any Windows Store apps that are designed to work with Search, or even for websites. You can search all of these in the same way, by selecting the Search charm.

When you click or tap on it, the Search charm opens the Search pane, shown in Figure 1-16. Start typing what you're looking for (you don't need to click in the Search box first), and the results appear in the main screen. If you start your search from the Start screen, the results you see are for the Apps category (which also includes desktop programs). You can see results from the Settings category (which includes the Control Panel), the Files category, or any of the apps on the Search list just by clicking or tapping its name or icon in the list.

  If you are on the Start screen and you start typing, the Search pane appears automatically, showing the characters you typed in the Search box and any matching apps or programs as results. This automatic search works only in the Start screen—not when you're on the desktop. If you're on the desktop, you have to select the Search charm first.

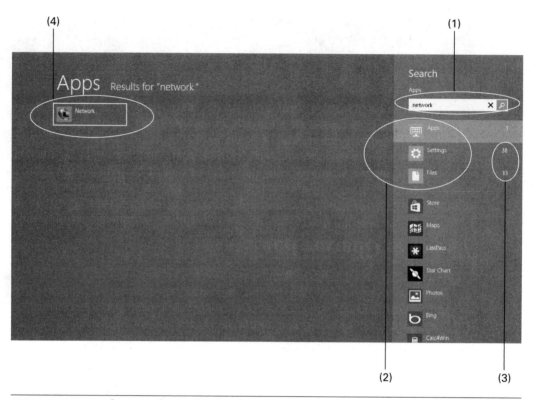

FIGURE 1-16 The search results for the term "network" in the Apps category. (1) search box, (2) search categories, (3) search results in each category, (4) search results list in the Apps category.

In this example, we searched for the word "network" and the search results for Apps show the Network control panel. You can also see how many settings and files match the search term. When you click or tap Settings, the Settings search results screen shows the list of control panels, tools, utilities, and topics in PC Settings, as you can see in Figure 1-17.

For example, when you click or tap the Connect to a Network link in the list of results for Settings, this opens the Start screen Networks pane, as you can see in Figure 1-18. You'll learn more about setting up your network and changing network settings in Chapter 5. If you're looking for a document with the word "network" in, click or tap Files instead. To search for other things, choose apps from the list in the Search pane; for example, choose Bing to repeat your search on the Web.

Share

Like the search functionality, sharing information such as a picture you like, the music you're listening to, or a link to an interesting website is built into Windows 8 and works with any Windows Store app that is set up to support sharing. Again, you always share using the Share charm. For example, in Figure 1-19 we're sharing a link

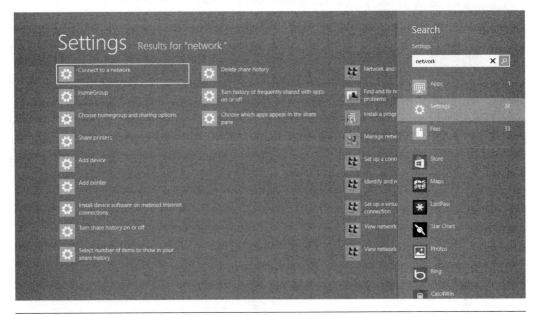

FIGURE 1-17   The Settings search results appear to the left of the Search pane.

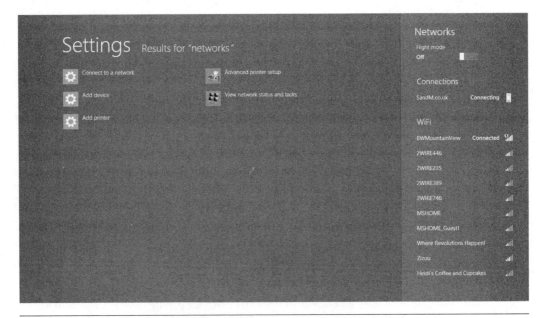

FIGURE 1-18   The Networks pane allows you to change network settings.

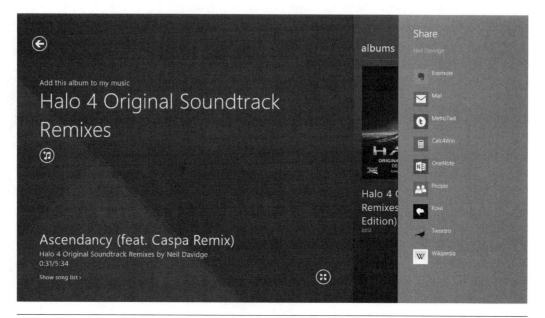

FIGURE 1-19 Sharing the link to an album in the Music app

to an album in the Music app. In the Share pane, you have the option of sharing the link in an email message through the Mail app or on a social network like Facebook or Twitter through the People app. You can learn more about sharing in Chapter 5, and we'll explain how to share with specific apps as we cover them.

What you see in the Share pane depends on what app you're using. Some apps, such as Calendar, can't share information at all. Some apps let you share from them (like Internet Explorer), some apps let you share to them (like Mail), and some apps let you do both (for example, a Twitter application might let you copy a tweet to a mail message or share a photo from another app to send it as a tweet).

Start

The Start screen charm opens the Start screen or, if you're already on the Start screen, switches you back to the last app or program you were using—including the desktop. Pressing the WINDOWS key on your keyboard works in the same way; the first time you press it, it opens the Start screen, and when you press it again you go back to the previous program or app.

Devices

Click or tap the Devices charm to open the Devices pane, shown in Figure 1-20, to use devices that the app you're running can work with, which could be anything from your printer to a second monitor or an Xbox console. We'll look more at how you use devices in Chapters 7, 12 and 14.

FIGURE 1-20   Click or tap the Devices charm to use peripherals connected to your PC. Icons for devices that are connected to your PC work with the running app, like a second screen and an Xbox 360.

Settings

The last charm on the Charms bar is the Settings charm. Like the Search and Share charms, the Settings charm works in almost every app, but the Settings charm is context sensitive. That is, the options you can get to with the Settings charm depend on which app you're running or where you are in Windows. For instance:

- Wherever you are when you open the Setting charm, you'll always find a link at the bottom of the Settings pane that opens marked Change PC Settings (see Figure 1-21), which opens the PC Settings tool (described in detail in Chapter 3). You'll use the PC Settings tool to make changes to Windows settings that you're likely to use more often than the more complex tools in the Control Panel.
- If you're in a Windows Store app, the Settings charm brings up the various options and settings for the Windows Store app.
- In the Mail app, you use the Settings charm to add accounts.
- In the People app, you use the Settings charm to choose options like whether to sort by first name or surname.
- If you're on the desktop, the Settings charm has links for the Control Panel, Personalization, PC Info, and Help.

FIGURE 1-21 Open the settings pane from the Settings charm to change options like volume, brightness or settings for Windows or the current app.

Run Windows Store Apps

Running a Windows Store app is simple: just click or tap the tile. For example, when you click or tap the Mail app, the Mail app opens on screen. And if you click or tap on the Internet Explorer tile, the Internet Explorer app opens, but this time things are a little more complicated. We'll look at this in detail in Chapter 8, but Windows 8 comes with two versions of Internet Explorer so you can have two different tiles for Internet Explorer on the Start screen. There's the familiar desktop Internet Explorer with the address bar and the title and tabs and other tools at the top of the page, and that has a desktop-style tile with a small icon. But there's also the Windows 8 version of Internet Explorer, shown in Figure 1-22, which doesn't show any of those tools while you're browsing, leaving more room on screen for the website you're looking at. To open that, you use the Windows 8-style tile which has a large icon.

Windows Store apps usually have a very clean look and what you want to do most of the time will usually be right there on screen. But there are always more tools and options, and you can find them on the app bar and in the Charms bar.

When you want to see the list of tabs or the address bar in Internet Explorer, you open the app bar by right-clicking (or swiping over the top or bottom edge of a touchscreen). And when you want to change options inside a Windows Store app like Internet Explorer, you open the Charms bar and choose the Settings charm. To search, you use the Search charm; to print, you use the Devices charm. Although the features and options you get will be different in every Windows Store app, you always use the app bar and the Charms bar to get at them.

FIGURE 1-22   The Windows 8 version of Internet Explorer has a much simpler interface.

Switch Between the Start Screen, Windows Store Apps, and the Desktop

Windows Store apps are new and different. They're simpler than desktop programs. They're better designed for use on tablets and touchscreens. They're more secure because of the way they're designed, and they use less power because they don't run in the background the way desktop programs do.

But the Windows Store apps don't do everything you need. There are still thousands of powerful, useful, and fun programs for the desktop, and Windows 8 includes the familiar Windows 7–style desktop to give you the best of both worlds. If you have programs that you already use on Windows 7, they should run without any problems on Windows 8 (although some utilities and system tools will need to be updated, as will your security software). If you're using Windows Vista or XP, you should check the Windows 8 Compatibility Center at www.microsoft.com/en-us/windows/compatibility/win8/CompatCenter/ or the software vendor's website to find out whether the program will run on Windows 8 or you need to upgrade it.

When you're using Windows 8, the desktop functions like just another app that you can access by clicking or tapping the Desktop tile, which appears on the Start screen as a live tile with your current desktop background, as shown in Figure 1-23.

So how do you access the Start screen and Windows Store apps and then switch back to the desktop? You can always go to the Start screen and click or tap the Desktop

FIGURE 1-23 The Desktop tile on the Start screen. Click or tap this tile to open the Windows desktop.

tile every time, but there are several other ways to open the Start screen or to switch between running apps and programs:

- Press the WINDOWS key on your keyboard (or tap the Windows button on your tablet) to switch back to the Start screen from any application. If you're using a keyboard that doesn't have the WINDOWS key, press CTRL-ESC.
- Open the Charms bar and click or tap the Start screen charm; you can open the Charms bar when you're inside an app or using the desktop (as well as from the Start screen).
- Move the mouse pointer to the lower left corner of the screen. When you see the Start button shown in Figure 1-24, click or tap it.
- Move your mouse to the top left corner of the screen. When you see the thumbnail for the next open app, move your mouse down a little and the Start button will appear, as well as a list of all running apps and programs. We'll show you how to see the same list on a touchscreen in the next section.
- Press WINDOWS KEY-TAB to see the same list of running apps and programs with the Start button at the bottom.
- Press ALT-TAB to see the familiar task switcher; keep pressing TAB to switch to the next program in the list. This includes individual desktop programs and Windows Store apps, but not the Start screen itself.
- Use the gestures we explain at the end of this chapter to split your screen between two apps at once; either of those can be the desktop.

FIGURE 1-24   The Start button appears in the lower left corner of the screen when you move your mouse there. Click or tap this thumbnail view of your Start screen to open it.

Quickly Change Settings and Options

In previous versions of Windows, the Start menu included shortcuts to useful Windows features like the Control Panel and the Command Prompt (for entering text commands). The desktop in Windows 8 contains a hidden menu where you can access many of these functions quickly that's even more convenient.

Move your mouse into the lower left corner of the screen as if you were going to click the Start button when it appears; instead, click the right mouse button. This opens the menu of utilities and power tools shown in Figure 1-25. Optionally, you can press WINDOWS KEY-X to open the menu from the keyboard (use the on-screen keyboard on a touchscreen).

For example, you can view the list of devices installed on your computer by clicking or tapping Device Manager, and you can open Task Manager to view a list of programs and processes that Windows is running. Close the menu by clicking or tapping anywhere else on screen.

FIGURE 1-25 Open the Advanced tools menu by right-clicking on the Start screen thumbnail, or by typing WINDOWS KEY+X.

Work with Gestures

Many PCs designed for Windows 8 have *touchscreens*, which are monitors that recognize gestures you make with your finger. Windows 8 tablets have touchscreens as the primary input method (some also have an active pen that lets you write smoothly on screen to produce digital "ink" that you can keep as handwriting or have Windows 8 turn into text). All-in-one PCs, where the computer is built into the screen, making them convenient to use in the kitchen or den, often have touchscreens, and you can get touchscreen monitors to use with desktop PCs. Some notebooks, especially ultrabooks, have touchscreens as well.

In this book we don't assume that you have a touchscreen; we'll tell you how to use Windows 8 using a mouse (and the most important keyboard shortcuts). But Windows 8 is designed for touchscreens and tablets as well as for notebooks and desktops, so we also explain how to control your PC by touching it. Mostly that's as simple as tapping the screen rather than clicking with a mouse but there are also special gestures you can use to control Windows 8. You can use the same gestures on some larger touchpads, especially on notebooks designed for Windows 8, and on mice with touch surfaces (like the Microsoft Touch Mouse) or external touchpads you plug into a desktop PC.

Swipe

The term *swipe* describes holding your finger down next to one edge of the screen and then dragging your finger right, left, up, or down toward the center of the screen to open a feature such as the Charms bar.

- **Right edge**   Open the Charms bar by swiping from the right edge of the screen. The right edge is for controlling your PC.
- **Left edge**   Swipe from the left edge of the screen to switch to the next app that's already running (the desktop counts as another app when you're swiping). The left edge is for swapping between apps.
- **Swipe from the left and then back quickly**   Use this gesture to open the list of thumbnails for all the apps that are currently running. For each app, you see a thumbnail that you can tap to open that app on the screen.
- **Swipe from the left edge and then slowly back**   When you swipe to drag the next app on screen and then drag it slowly (and you may need to experiment to find out how slowly you need to drag on your PC) back a little toward the edge of the screen instead of dragging it on top of the one you're using, you can drag it next to it and have two apps snapped side by side. You'll see a vertical bar in the accent color of your color scheme appear between the apps, showing how much of the screen each app will fill—one app gets a quarter of the screen and the other app gets three-quarters of the screen. This only works if your screen resolution is high enough (at least 1366 by 768).
- **Top and bottom edges**   When you're in an app, you can open the app bar with handy commands at the bottom of the screen by swiping from either the top or bottom edge. If you want to close the current app, drag your finger down from the top of the screen until the app vanishes. If you only want to open the app bar by swiping from the top of the screen, then swipe your finger just a short distance down the screen.
- **On a Start screen tile**   Swipe down on a Start screen tile to select it and open the app bar at the bottom of the screen. You'll learn more about using the app bar with Start screen tiles in Chapter 2.

Drag and Slide

You can hold your finger down on a location in the screen and then drag or slide your finger to perform certain tasks.

- **Drag down to close an app**   When you have an app open on the screen, you can close it by holding your finger down at the top of the app screen and then dragging it toward the bottom edge of the screen.
- **Drag to scroll**   Scrolling down through a long page or list by dragging your finger up and down the screen is obvious. But you can also scroll through a horizontal list (for example, a list of currently open websites in Internet Explorer) or scroll through the different groups of tiles on the Start screen by holding down your finger on the screen and dragging it to the left or right.

- **Drag to jump backward and forward in Internet Explorer** When you're in the Windows 8 version of Internet Explorer rather than the desktop version, you can swipe your finger to the left and right on the page to jump back a page or load the next page. You'll learn more about using Internet Explorer in Chapter 6.

Tap and Press

Tap on an object, such as a tile on the Start screen, to open it as if you were clicking with your mouse. To access context menus on the desktop or pop-up menus in Windows Store apps, tap and hold on the screen until you see the menu appear (like right-clicking with your mouse).

Pinch and Stretch

If you find that something is too small for you to see clearly or takes up too much space, you can shrink or widen the view (called *zooming in* and *zooming out*) using two fingers at once. To zoom in, place your thumb and index finger on the screen and then bring them both together in a pinching motion. If you want to zoom out, place your thumb and index finger close together on the screen and then move them apart at the same time in a stretching motion. On the Start screen and in some apps, this will change the view to show you less detailed information (like a month view instead of individual days); that's called Semantic Zoom.

Rotate

If you are using an app that allows you to rotate objects such as images, you can rotate them using your fingers. Place your thumb and index finger on the object and then turn both in the direction in which you want to rotate the object.

2

Learn How to Get Around Windows 8

HOW TO...

- Use the Windows 8 user interface
- Customize, move, and group tiles on the Start screen
- Pin icons to the taskbar
- Change the look of the Start screen, Lock screen, and desktop

Now that we've given you a tour of the Start screen, it's time to pull back the curtain a bit more and dig into how you work with the new Windows 8 user interface (UI) in more detail. First we'll show you how to put the apps and programs you want to use often on the Start screen or on the taskbar on your desktop. Then we'll show you how to have two Windows Store apps open on screen at once and explain how to work with the new File Picker in Windows Store apps. Finally, we'll show you how to personalize your PC by changing the colors, styles, and images that you see on the Start screen and the desktop.

Use the Windows 8 User Interface

The Start screen is, appropriately enough, where you start to use Windows, and it's also where you see the new Windows Store apps. Some of these are installed automatically with Windows 8, like People, Mail, Calendar, Messenger, and Photos. There are thousands of other apps that you can download from the Windows Store; we'll cover that in more detail in Chapter 16. The Start screen is also where you get to the desktop from, and you can pin tiles to the Start screen that open your favorite desktop programs.

There are two types of applications you can run on Windows 8. To keep things clear, throughout this book we'll refer to *Windows Store apps*, which run in their own window on screen, and *desktop programs*, which run inside the familiar Windows desktop. Windows Store apps are often simpler; they're designed to do one or two things and they have an interface that works well on a touchscreen if you have one. Desktop programs are the applications we've been running on Windows for years.

The Start screen is very personal; once you start working with Windows 8, your Start screen will quickly look different from the Start screen on anyone else's PC. That's one reason why you don't see all the different Windows features and desktop programs you have installed on your PC on the Start screen (it would also make things very cluttered). There's an easy way to see all your apps and programs though: the All Apps screen. If you have a touchscreen, swipe over the top or bottom edge of the screen. Otherwise, use your mouse to right-click on any blank area in the Start screen (click anywhere except on a tile). At the bottom of the screen you'll see the app bar; unless you've selected a tile from the Start screen first, the app bar only has the All Apps icon at the far right of the screen as shown in Figure 2-1.

Click or tap the icon to open the All Apps screen shown in Figure 2-2. You'll have more tiles than can fit on screen for all the different apps, desktop programs, and Windows features on your PC, so move the mouse pointer to the bottom of the screen to use the scroll bar to scroll through all of them (or swipe across the screen using a trackpad or touchscreen).

FIGURE 2-1 The All Apps icon in the menu bar

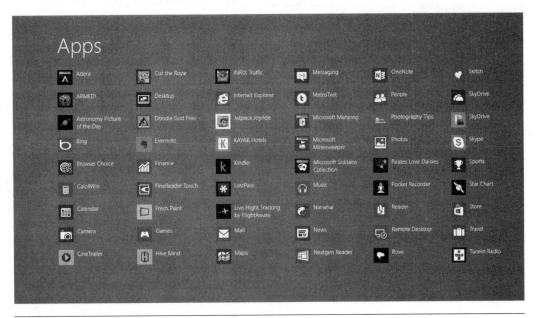

FIGURE 2-2   Windows Store apps are listed first.

If you have a lot of Windows Store apps installed, they'll be split up into alphabetical groups, as shown in Figure 2-3. At the end of that list of Windows Store apps are your desktop programs, arranged alphabetically by the name of the program, with your Windows accessories and system tools in their own groups.

If you have a lot of programs and apps installed and you want to look through them quickly, use Semantic Zoom to see tiles for the letters of the alphabet and the program groups, as in Figure 2-4. Zoom out by pinching your fingers together on a touchscreen, holding down the CTRL button while you scroll your mouse wheel, or pressing CTRL and the – key on your keyboard. Click or tap one of the alphabet or group tiles to see the tiles inside it or spread your fingers apart on a touchscreen, hold down CTRL and scroll the mouse wheel in the opposite direction or use CTRL and the + key to zoom back in. You can also use Semantic Zoom to move around the Start screen more quickly.

Practice finding programs you're familiar with. Look on the right side of the screen for the Windows System tools like Control Panel, Task Manager, and File Explorer. You can zoom in and out of the All Apps screen to look at other groups or you can simply scroll to the left and right to view all the apps. Remember, you can also jump straight to the app or program you want by typing the first few letters of its name when you're on the Start screen.

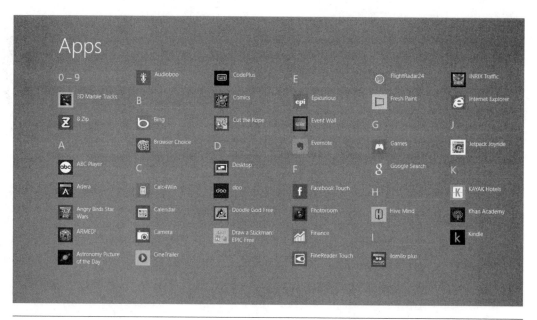

FIGURE 2-3 Groups of tiles on the All Apps screen, with Windows Store apps grouped alphabetically by name

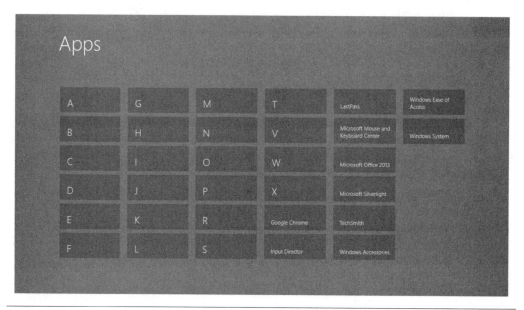

FIGURE 2-4 Semantic Zoom on the All Apps screen organizes Windows Store apps and desktop groups alphabetically.

Customize Tiles on the Start Screen

You can choose which tiles you have available on the Start screen and how they're organized. You can also make some choices about what the individual tiles look like.

First you need to select the tile you're going to work with. Right-click the tile (or swipe your finger up over the tile if you have a touchscreen) to open the app bar. A check mark appears in the upper right corner of the tile to show that you've selected it, as you can see on the tile for the Photos app in Figure 2-5, and the app bar appears at the bottom of the screen.

As always when you have the app bar for the Start screen open, the All Apps icon appears on the far right of the bar in case you want to look at the list of installed apps and programs. But the tools for choosing how your tile looks or working with the app or program the tile opens are on the left side of the bar, as shown next. Which icons

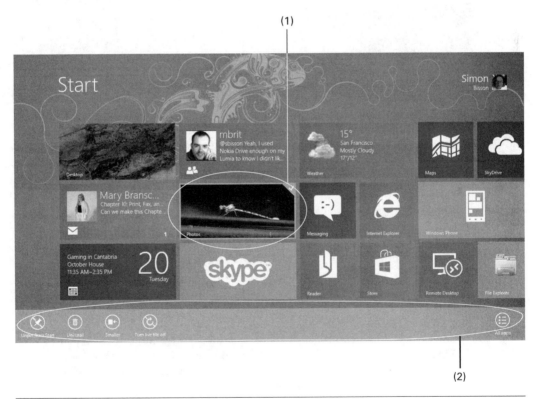

FIGURE 2-5 (1) The selected app has a check mark in the upper right of its tile and (2) the app bar appears at the bottom of the screen.

you see here depends on what the tile you've selected opens, because they're different for Windows Store apps, desktop programs, and pinned websites.

- Click or tap Unpin from Start to remove the tile from the Start screen. You'll always see this icon when you select a tile, and it's the only option you'll see for a tile that opens a pinned website. If you unpin a tile, you can always pin it back to the Start screen later, but it will appear at the end of the Start screen rather than where you had it pinned before. You can move it to where you want it by following the instructions in the next section.
- Click or tap Uninstall to uninstall the app or program from Windows completely. If the tile is for a Windows Store app, Uninstall removes it straight away. If it's a desktop program, Uninstall takes you to the Control Panel and opens the uninstaller wizard for the program. You won't see the Uninstall option for pinned sites (because there's nothing installed) or for Windows 8 features like the desktop and File Explorer.
- The Larger and Smaller icons change the size of the tile. If it's a small tile, you can click or tap Larger to make it twice as wide; if it's a large tile, you can click or tap Smaller to make the tile smaller. You can see in Figure 2-6 that the Photos tile is a large tile and the Messaging tile next to it is smaller. You can't enlarge tiles for desktop programs or pinned websites.
- Some apps have animated live tiles to show you more information as it arrives. The Photos tile can display a slideshow of your images, the Mail tile will show new messages, and other Windows Store apps can show weather forecasts, news headlines, messages from your friends, and other useful information. Usually, the live tile is turned on by default, so in the app bar you'll see the Turn Live Tile Off icon, which puts the icon for the app back on the tile instead. If you want to see the animated information again, click or tap Turn Live Tile On.

- For desktop programs, you will see more icons on the app bar. If the program is pinned to the desktop taskbar as well as the Start screen, you'll see the Unpin from Taskbar icon. Once you get used to using the tiles on the Start screen to open apps and programs, you might not need to keep as many icons pinned to the taskbar. If a program isn't already pinned to the taskbar, click or tap Pin to Taskbar to add it.
- If the desktop program is already running and you want a second copy, click or tap Open New Window. This is useful if you want a second copy of a document open on screen, or if you need two File Explorer windows open to make it easier to move files.
- Some desktop programs have extra functions and commands if you run them when you're logged in as an administrator (we'll explain the details of administrator accounts in Chapter 3). To use those, start the program by clicking or tapping Run as Administrator.

If you decide not to make any changes to the tile, then right-click or swipe up on the selected tile again or press ESC. The check mark in the corner of the tile disappears.

You can select more than one tile at once by right-clicking (or swiping up) on each tile in turn. But the only action you can take when you select more than one tile is to remove them all from the Start screen at once so you will see only two options in the app bar (aside from All Apps): click or tap Unpin from Start to remove all the selected tiles, or click or tap Clear Selection if you didn't mean to select multiple tiles. Unpinning more than one tile at a time is most useful after you install a new desktop program. Windows 8 puts tiles on the Start screen for all the different applications and utilities in your new program, but you probably won't want to keep all the tiles it adds. Select all the ones you don't want and then unpin them all at once by clicking or tapping Unpin from Start.

 It's easy to tell which tiles open Windows Store apps and which open a desktop program. Only Windows Store apps have live tiles and even if they only have an icon instead of a live tile, it's larger. The icons on tiles for desktop programs are always a smaller size, and you can't change the size of the tile (except for the Desktop tile—because it's so useful and because it has an image of your desktop background rather than a small icon, you can make it larger).

Move Tiles on the Start Screen

You can move and rearrange tiles easily. All you have to do is move the mouse pointer over the tile, hold down the mouse button, and drag the tile to a new position on the screen. It's even easier with a touchscreen; you just press your finger down on the tile and drag it to where you want to see it. To make sure Windows knows you're trying to move a tile rather than just selecting it or scrolling through the screen, you need to drag it firmly with your finger; the easiest way is to drag it up and out of the group and then back into the position you want.

If you move the tile into the middle of a group of tiles, Windows 8 will move the other tiles out of the way to make room, although that might mean you'll see empty

FIGURE 2-6 The Camera tile we moved is now above the Mail tile, leaving a gap between the Camera and People tiles.

spaces in the group, such as in Figure 2-6, as Windows adjusts the layout of larger and smaller tiles.

If you want to move the tile to a location in the Start screen that's off the visible screen, you can drag the tile toward the right edge of the screen. The Start screen starts scrolling to the right so you can see the other tiles and groups, and you can drop the tile when you get to the group where you want it. A faster way to move tiles a long way across the Start screen is to drag the tile all the way up to the top of the Start screen. That turns on Semantic Zoom so you can see more of the groups of tiles at once. Drag the tile back down into the group where you want to put it.

Group Your Tiles

Tiles on the Start screen are arranged in groups. When you first start using Windows, you get a couple of groups just to space the tiles out across the screen, but you can make your own groups and use them to organize your apps, programs, and favorite websites.

To make a new group, drag the first tile you want to put in it until it's between the groups on either side and hold it there until you see a grayed-out bar appear on screen. That tells you Windows will make a new group when you let go of the tile. Now you can drag other tiles into the new group.

When you drag tiles, you can only move one tile at a time. Even if you have two or more tiles selected, as soon as you start moving one of them, you lose the other tiles you had selected and only the tile you're dragging moves. The only way to move more than one tile at once is to put them in the same groups and move that. To move a group of tiles, use Semantic Zoom. Zoom out (by pinching your fingers together on a touchscreen, holding down the CTRL button while you scroll your mouse wheel, or pressing CTRL and the – key on your keyboard) and then drag the whole group (either with your mouse or with your finger on a touchscreen) to the new position.

While you're in Semantic Zoom, you can also name the groups on the Start screen. You don't have to name all of them, but once you have a lot of groups on the Start screen, you'll want to name at least some of them to help you keep things organized and be able to find what you're looking for. Select the group you want to name by right-clicking on it in Semantic Zoom, or by swiping up over the group on a touchscreen, shown in Figure 2-7. You'll see a check mark and an outline around the group you've selected, and the app bar appears at the bottom of the screen; click or tap the Name Group icon on the app bar, type the name you want into the dialog box that pops up, and then click the Name button.

Run Two Apps at Once

Just as in previous versions of Windows, you can run several programs at the same time on the desktop, and you can rearrange the program windows any way you want. You can have one program on top of another one, or you can drag a program window into the bottom left or right corner to "snap" it into place and fill exactly half of the screen.

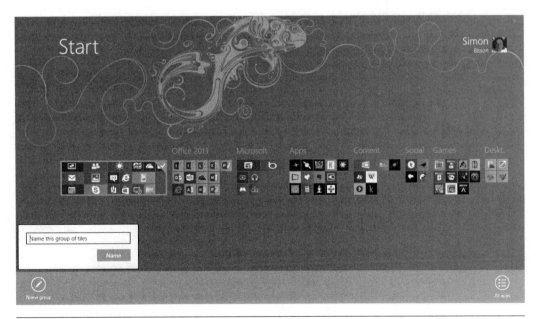

FIGURE 2-7   Labeling groups in Semantic Zoom

Windows Store apps don't work the same way. You can have several apps running at once, but usually one app fills the whole screen so you can't see the other apps. In Chapter 1 we explained the different ways to switch between the apps you have running, but you can also have two Windows Store apps on screen at once (or one app and the desktop, with all the desktop programs you have running).

Open the first app you want to run from the Start screen, then press the Windows key on your keyboard (or use the Start charm, or move your mouse to the lower left corner of the screen and click the Start button when it appears) to go back to the Start screen and open the second app. Remember, either of these can be the desktop or a desktop application.

On a touchscreen, drag your finger in from the left edge of the screen and hold it still a short way in from the edge. The app that's already on screen will move over a little to make room for the app you're selecting; when you see that, let go of the thumbnail you're dragging, and the second app will appear, "snapped" into a narrow window beside the first app, as shown in Figure 2-8. If you want to make the second app bigger, drag the bar between them across the screen. If you only want to see one app again, drag the bar all the way to the edge of the screen until you push the app on that side off screen.

With a mouse, move the cursor to the top or bottom corner on the left side of the screen and leave it there until you see a thumbnail appear in the corner. Instead of clicking the thumbnail to open it, move the mouse down or up a little, so you're moving it toward the middle of the edge, and you'll see thumbnails for all the apps you have running. (You can get the list of thumbnails on a touchscreen by swiping your finger in from the left edge of the screen and then back a little.)

FIGURE 2-8 Windows 8's snap view lets you run two Windows Store applications at the same time.

With your finger or the mouse, drag the thumbnail for the second app you want to see on screen a little way onto the screen and then move it a short way back toward the edge. That snaps it into place next to the first app, and again you can drag the bar to change which window is larger.

When you have a Windows Store app in the smaller window on screen, it will usually change its layout to fit. You might get a vertical list of tiles or headings instead of the full content. When you have an app in the larger window, it will look the same, just a little smaller. That's what happens if you have the desktop in the larger window as well. But when you put the desktop into the smaller window, you see thumbnails of all your open programs and documents in a list you can scroll through. When you click or tap one, the desktop automatically resizes to the larger window size so you can see the program you've chosen.

Add and Rearrange Icons on the Desktop

You can pin both Windows Store apps and desktop programs to the Start screen as tiles, but you don't have to go back to the Start screen every time you want to open a desktop program. You can put icons on the desktop or pin them to the taskbar in the same way as in Windows 7.

You Can Add and Remove Icons on the Desktop

Some programs automatically add an icon to the desktop so you can find them easily, and you can also add icons for your favorite programs to the desktop, but remember that when you have windows open, they cover the icons up. When you pin icons to the taskbar, you can use jump lists and thumbnails to work with your files as well.

If you no longer want to see an icon that's already on the desktop, just drag it into the Recycle Bin. If you want to add a new icon, you can create a shortcut to a program. If you know where on your computer the program file is, right-click or tap on a blank area on the desktop and then choose New | Create Shortcut in the pop-up menu. Click or tap the Browse button to open the Browse for Files and Folders window, browse to the folder that contains the program file, select the file, and then click or tap the OK button. Click or tap Next, type a name for the shortcut, then choose Finish.

If you don't know where to find a program file, use the All Apps screen to search for the program. Right-click or swipe up on the tile to select it, then choose Open File Location from the app bar. This opens Windows Explorer with the program file selected. Click or tap the New item menu in the New section of the ribbon and choose Shortcut to start the Create Shortcut wizard. Look ahead to Chapter 4 for more details about the Windows Explorer interface.

Pin Icons to the Taskbar

The taskbar across the bottom of the Windows 8 desktop shows icons for all the programs you're running, but when you first open the desktop, you will also see icons for the desktop version of Internet Explorer and for File Explorer, even though they're not running. These icons are *pinned* to the taskbar, so they're always visible and they're always in the same order. You can pin icons for your own favorite desktop programs to the taskbar, and you can also pin your favorite websites.

As we've already mentioned, you can pin a desktop program to the taskbar from the app bar in the Start screen or from the All Apps screen. Right-click or swipe up on the tile for the program and choose Pin to Taskbar as shown in Figure 2-9, and Windows will add an icon for it to the end of the taskbar.

You can also pin any program that's running on the desktop. Right-click or press and hold with your finger on the icon in the taskbar to see the jump list. Click or tap Pin This Program to Taskbar. And if a program you've just installed puts an icon on the desktop, you can drag that onto the taskbar to pin it there instead.

To pin a website to the taskbar, drag the tab from Internet Explorer down onto the taskbar and you'll see an icon with the logo for the website.

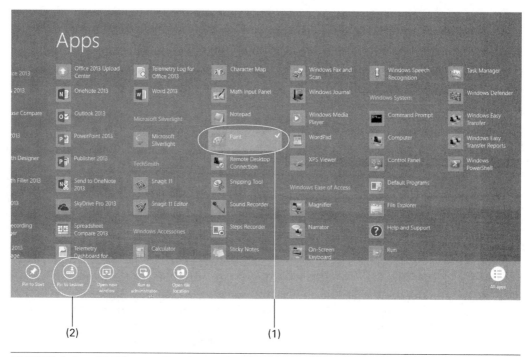

(2)   (1)

FIGURE 2-9   (1) The application we're going to add to the taskbar from the All Apps screen. (2) Click or tap to pin the selected app.

Once an icon is pinned to the taskbar, you can drag it to another position on the taskbar and it will stay there until you unpin it, even when the program isn't running. You can also right-click or press and hold on the icon to see the jump list.

For most programs, this gives you a list of handy tasks and links. For Word and Excel, you get a list of recent files, for File Explorer it's a list of the folders you open most, and for Internet Explorer it's a list of the websites you visit frequently, any of which you can pin to the jump list using the pushpin icon that appears when you hover your mouse over the list. A pinned website might have links to useful pages and tools; if you pin Outlook.com, the jump list has links for writing a new email or going straight to your calendar. If you pin Amazon.com to the taskbar, you can jump straight to the Kindle Store, check your latest order, or see what's in your shopping cart.

Some pinned websites update the icon on the taskbar to tell you about changes on the website; if you pin Hotmail, the icon will tell you how many new email messages you have. You get similar notifications for some websites when you pin them to the Start screen, but you only get jump lists on the taskbar.

Change the Look of the Start Screen and Desktop

Windows 8, just like previous versions of Windows, allows you to customize the look and feel so your PC feels like it's yours. You have to change the Start screen and desktop look and feel settings separately, so you can have a different color scheme for each of them or make them match if you prefer.

Change the Start Screen

Although you probably picked a color scheme for your Start screen when you first set up Windows 8, you can also change the background design (or pick a different color scheme) by using the new PC Settings tool.

Open PC Settings from the Charms bar by clicking or tapping the Settings charm. When the Settings pane opens at the side of the screen, click or tap Change PC Settings at the bottom of the pane. Personalize is the first section in the PC Settings navigation bar on the left side. On the Personalize page, click or tap the Start Screen heading on the right.

You can pick from 20 different background designs for the Start screen that go from subtle to wild and wacky. As you click or tap a design from the rows of boxes showing the patterns, the large sample image of the background changes to show you a preview. Some of the patterns have designs and decoration that change color, so you may want to try out a few of the color schemes to see the difference. The last design has no background design at all, just a solid color.

Figure 2-10 shows an example of how the Start screen looks in the preview with a particular color scheme and background selected from the options below the preview.

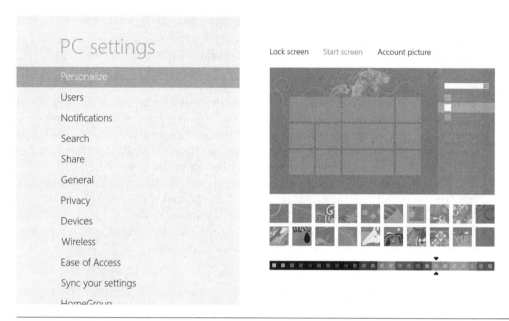

FIGURE 2-10 PC Settings shows a sample image of the Start screen to help you pick the design and colors you like best.

Below the row of patterns is a row of boxes showing the 25 different color schemes you can choose from. Each box shows two colors; the outer color shows what your background color will be, and the inner color shows the color that will be used to highlight things like your selection in a menu or the Start button on the Charms menu. Each color scheme uses shades of this highlight color for elements like tiles on the Start screen that open desktop applications, so you get a range of matching or contrasting colors throughout the interface.

When you've made all your choices for how you want the Start screen to look, press the WINDOWS key or use the Windows button on the Charms bar to open the Start screen and view your new color scheme.

 If you use the same Microsoft account to log in to more than one Windows 8 PC, the color scheme and background you choose for the Start screen will apply to all your other computers as well, unless you turn off that sync option in PC Settings.

Change the Lock Screen

You'll see the Lock screen every time you turn on your PC and whenever you go back to your computer after not using it for a few minutes (see Chapter 7 if you want to change how long it takes for your screen to turn off). If you don't like any of the built-in images, you can use your own photo as a background for the Lock screen, or use the Bing app to choose the current Bing image. Open PC Settings, choose the Personalize section on the left, click or tap Lock Screen on the right, and then choose the Browse button. This opens the new File Picker, which you will see in a lot of Windows Store apps when you need to select a document or image to work with. This has the same colorful design and tiled layout as the Start screen, rather than the familiar File Explorer interface, and it's designed to be easy to use with your fingers, although you can still use it with a mouse, of course.

As you can see in Figure 2-11, when you're selecting a new Lock screen image, the File Picker opens to your Pictures library. If you see the image you want to use for your Lock screen, click or tap on it, and a highlighted border and check mark will appear; click or tap Choose Picture to use this image. You can also choose to pick from the Photos app (covered in Chapter 13), which lets you use images stored on SkyDrive, Facebook, or Flickr.

If you want to open a file that's in a subfolder, click or tap the tile for that folder and then click or tap the tile containing the image you want to use. Go up to the folder above the current one by clicking or tapping Go Up. If you have a lot of photos, you can arrange them in date order rather than alphabetically by clicking or tapping Sort by Name and then choosing Sort by Date in the menu.

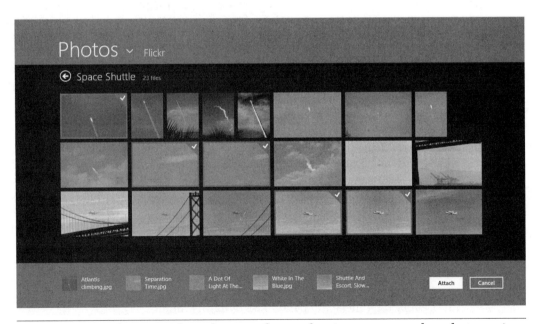

FIGURE 2-11   The new File Picker interface makes it easy to see what photo you're selecting.

The File Picker is a way to navigate more than just the same files you can see in Windows Explorer on the desktop. Click or tap the Files heading at the top of the screen and you will see a list of the different libraries on your computer (and you can browse the other folders on your computer, or even other computers on your home network). But when you scroll down the list, you will also see the names of apps like SkyDrive and Camera. Pick an app to use that app to select the image you want, whether that's taking a new photo with the Camera app or using a photo you have stored in the cloud on SkyDrive (we'll cover the SkyDrive cloud service in more detail in Chapter 4).

Depending on which Windows Store apps you have installed, you might see other apps listed here, like Bing. The Bing search app you can download from the Windows Store works with the File Picker, so you can search for an image you like online straight from the File Picker (instead of having to open a web browser, save the image, remember where you saved it and what you called it, and then navigate back there to select the image again).

Change the Desktop

Windows 8 has a new desktop wallpaper with a daisy blowing in the breeze. If that's not your look, you can choose a different background, pick a theme that gives you a slideshow of images, and even opt to see a new photo every day. You can choose from dozens of high-quality themes that are free from Microsoft, including blockbuster movies, games, seasonal selections, and some stunning photography of the natural world. Themes can include images for the desktop background, the color of the title bar for different windows, a sound scheme, and sometimes a screensaver as well.

If you're used to Windows 7, then changing the look of the desktop is exactly the same. Open the Personalize menu by right-clicking on a blank area in the desktop and then clicking Personalize in the pop-up menu. If you're using a touchscreen, press and hold your finger on a blank area in the desktop until you see a square outline and then release your finger to open the menu. Next, tap Personalize in the pop-up menu.

The Personalization window shows you any themes you already have installed, and the built-in themes (you might have to scroll down to see them all). There are three Windows Default Themes (the Windows daisy, Earth, and Flowers) and four High Contrast Themes that can make the screen easier to read, especially if you have poor eyesight. If you don't like any of the default themes, click or tap the Get More Themes Online link shown in Figure 2-12.

The Themes page on the Microsoft website will open in your browser, showing a list of the newest themes (see Figure 2-13). There are dozens of themes to choose from, with new ones added frequently. Some themes automatically download new pictures every day; these are called RSS dynamic themes.

 If you have more than one screen attached to your computer, Windows 8 will stretch the desktop over both displays. Choose one of the panoramic themes to get images that are wide enough to fill both screens.

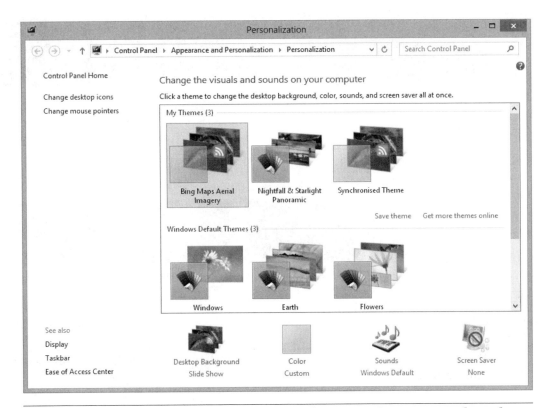

FIGURE 2-12   Get more desktop themes from the Personalization control panel.

See what images are in a theme by clicking or tapping the Details link for it. Click or tap the Download Theme button on the details page or the Download link on the Themes page. When you browser asks what you want to do with the file, choose Open to save the theme to your PC and set it as your new desktop look.

Make Your Own Theme

You can also individually customize the desktop background, window color, and the different sounds Windows plays when an event occurs (such as when a device connects to Windows successfully), and select a screen saver. Use the links at the bottom of the Personalization window to change each of these (refer to Figure 2-12).

When you click or tap the Desktop Background link, the Desktop Background page appears. This shows all the images in the current theme, how they are arranged on screen, and how often the background image will change.

 You can choose multiple images as your desktop background. Windows will change which image is displayed every 30 minutes by default. If you're using a laptop, the image won't change if your laptop isn't plugged into an electrical outlet, to save on battery life. Any time you feel like a change, just right-click or press and hold on a blank spot on the desktop and choose Next Desktop Background.

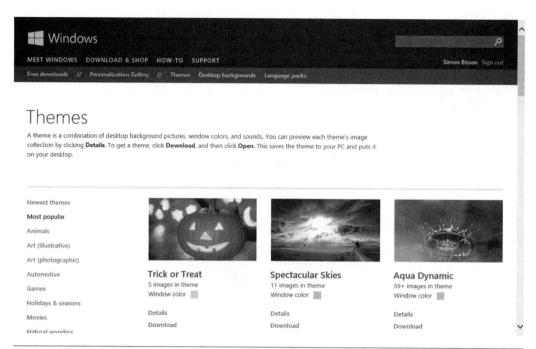

FIGURE 2-13 There's a large selection of desktop themes online, including new multi-monitor themes designed for Windows 8.

Click or tap the Picture Location drop-down menu to choose what kind of background to use. You can select from Windows Desktop Backgrounds, your own Pictures Library, Top Rated Photos, or Solid Colors if you want a plain background. If you're looking for suitable images, there's a Desktop Backgrounds section on the Themes website (click or tap Get More Themes Online in the Personalization window and then click the Desktop Backgrounds link at the top of the web page).

After you select your color or picture, click or tap the Save Changes button. The desktop background color appears above the Desktop Background link in the Personalization window. You can change the window border and taskbar colors by clicking or tapping Color and picking a shade in the Window Color and Appearance page shown in Figure 2-14.

Select the color you want to use by clicking or tapping on the color sample. The default color is Automatic, which changes to match the desktop background image. If you want a slightly different color from the 15 standard colors, you can move the Color Intensity slider to the left to make the color lighter or to the right to make it darker.

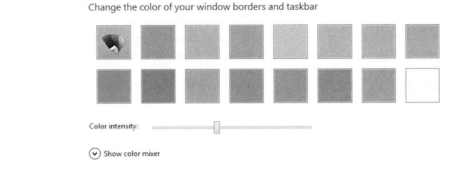

Change the color of your window borders and taskbar

Color intensity:

Show color mixer

Save changes   Cancel

FIGURE 2-14   The Window Color and Appearance page

You can also create a new color by clicking or tapping the down arrow next to Show Color Mixer and then moving the Hue, Saturation, and Brightness sliders to set those color component levels. As you make your changes, the color of the window border and taskbar change so you can see how your new color will look. But the color doesn't permanently change until you click or tap the Save Changes button, so if you don't like the result, you can choose Cancel instead.

Use Your Own Images to Create New Wallpaper

If you have a favorite photo, you can use that as your desktop background. (You can't use an image file as the Start screen background, but you can make your photo the Lock screen image, as previously discussed, or even your picture password, as described in Chapter 3.)

Like choosing a theme, you start by right-clicking or tapping on a blank area in the desktop and then selecting Personalize in the pop-up menu. In the Personalization window, click or tap Desktop Background. Instead of using the Picture Location drop-down list, click or tap the Browse button to open the Browse For Folder dialog box.

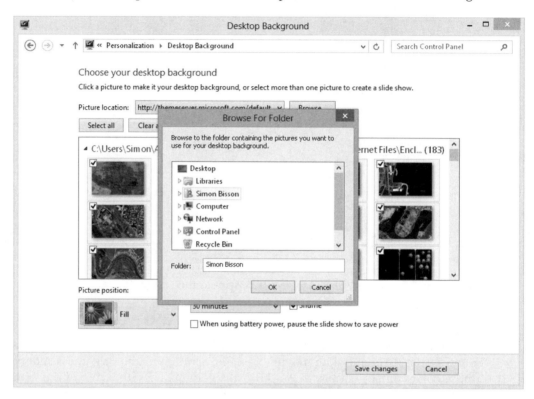

In the Browse For Folder dialog box, find the folder that contains the image file that you want to use as the background. When you find the folder, select it and then click or tap the OK button. Windows will preview your image as the desktop background, so you can decide how well it works. If there is more than one picture in the folder you chose, you'll see them all listed here. You can click or tap on a single picture if it's the only one you want to use; if you'd like to have a slideshow of several images, make sure the check box is selected for all the pictures you want to use. You can preview the other images by right-clicking or pressing and holding your finger on a blank spot on the desktop and choosing Next Desktop Background. When you're happy with your selection of images, click or tap the Save Changes button.

3

Make Windows 8 Your Own

HOW TO...

- Change Windows settings
- Explore the Control Panel
- Change your password
- Set up Family Safety

Now that you know how to use the Start screen and customize the way Windows looks, it's time to learn how to change your settings and how to work with different user accounts. First we'll look at some of the most useful settings that control the way Windows 8 works straight from the Settings charm. We'll also explain where to look for different settings, now that there are two places to set preferences: in the new PC Settings area, and in the Control Panel.

Change Common Options with the Settings Charm

Windows 8 has a new, simple tool called PC Settings for changing the options and settings you'll use the most, but the controls you need most frequently, like volume and power, are also easy to find because they're in the Settings pane (which you access from the Settings charm). As we explained in Chapter 1, the Settings pane always lets you change settings and options for whatever you have on screen at the time, whether that's the Windows Store app you're using or the Start screen itself. There are also some settings you can change directly that apply to everything on your PC.

If you want to adjust the volume or the brightness of your screen, connect to a different Wi-Fi network, use a different keyboard layout, turn off app notifications for a while, or turn off your PC, just click or tap the Settings charm and the controls are right there on the Settings pane (see Figure 3-1).

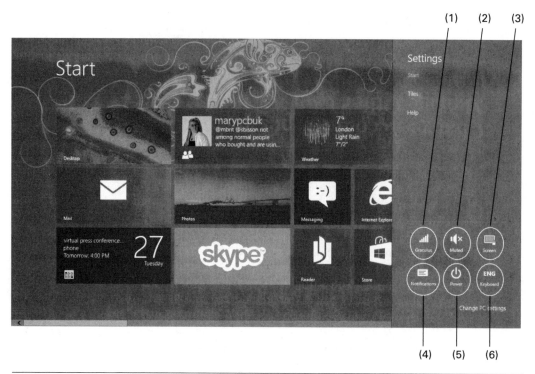

FIGURE 3-1 The Settings pane with (1) Network, (2) Volume, (3) Screen, (4) Notifications, (5) Power, and (6) Keyboard

Choose Network Settings

Tap or click the Network icon to see a list of the Wi-Fi access points you can connect to; pick the one you want from the list and Windows will connect to it automatically. If you need to fill in a password, you'll see the dialog to do that here as well. You can also put your PC into Airplane mode here, which turns off all the wireless radios in your PC (a good idea if you're on a plane or you just want to save power on your laptop); drag or swipe the bar at the top of the list of Wi-Fi networks to turn this setting on or off.

 If you connect to the wrong Wi-Fi network, right-click or tap and hold on the name of the network and choose Forget This Network from the menu that appears.

Once you're connected to a Wi-Fi network, you'll see the name of it on the network icon. If you have an Ethernet network (where you plug a cable into a port on your PC to get connected), you don't need to select anything; the name of the network should appear automatically.

Change the Volume

Tap or click the Volume icon on the Settings pane to change the volume of all the applications on your PC at once by dragging up or down on the volume bar. You can also tap or click the button at the top of the volume bar to mute or unmute your speakers.

Change Screen Brightness and Rotation

Tap or click the Screen icon on the Settings pane to change the brightness of your screen by dragging up or down on the brightness bar. If you have a tablet or a monitor with a stand that rotates, you can change whether the screen rotates automatically by tapping or clicking the button at the top.

Hide Notifications

If you use the Mail app, you'll see a small notification in the top right corner of the screen for every email that arrives; the Calendar app reminds you about appointments in the same way, and other apps can give you similar notifications for incoming instant messages, Skype calls, or tweets that mention your name. If you don't want to see notifications while you work on something important, click or tap the Notifications icon on the Settings pane and choose whether you want to hide notifications for one hour, three hours, or eight hours. If you don't want to see them at all, you can turn them off in the individual apps one at a time, or on the Notification page of PC Settings (we'll cover that later in this chapter).

Turn Off Your PC with the Power Menu

You might recognize the Power icon from the Lock screen. The menu you see when you click or tap the Power icon on the Settings pane is the same. Choose Shut Down when you want to turn your PC off; choose Sleep or Hibernate if you want to save power but still have your apps, programs, and documents waiting for you when you come back (we'll cover setting up the Hibernate option in Chapter 18). If you're having a problem with your PC or you want to apply an update straightaway, choose Restart.

Choose Keyboard Settings

If you write in more than one language, you can tap or click the Keyboard icon on the Settings pane to switch to a different keyboard layout, like Spanish or French. You can also use the Keyboard icon to open the onscreen keyboard if you're using a PC with a touchscreen. Usually the onscreen keyboard opens automatically when you tap anywhere that you can type, but if you want to search the Start screen, for example, you need to open the keyboard by tapping the Keyboard icon.

Did You Know? **You Can Choose Different Touch Keyboards**

If you have a Windows 8 tablet and you use the onscreen keyboard, you have several different layouts to choose from, which you change by tapping the icon in the bottom right of the keyboard. The default keyboard has the biggest buttons for the letters and numbers but does not display as many of the secondary keys; if you want a function key, just tap the Keyboard icon and pick the keyboard layout that has function keys. You can also switch to the split keyboard, which puts the keys close to the corners so you can hold a tablet in both hands and type with your thumbs, or use the handwriting panel. You don't need a special pen for that; you can write with your finger, and Windows will recognize your handwriting. You can also close the keyboard from this icon.

Change PC Options in PC Settings

The Settings pane is also a quick way to get to the settings you'll change most frequently in Windows, which are now in a new, simple interface called PC Settings. Click or tap the link at the bottom of the Settings pane that says Change PC Settings, as in Figure 3-2.

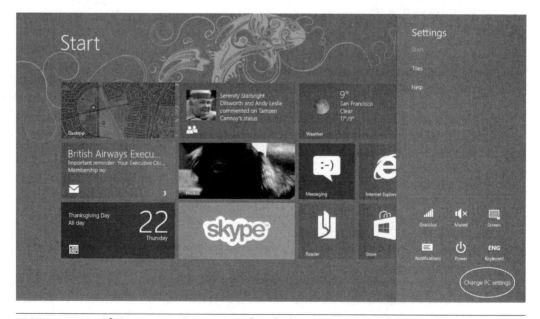

FIGURE 3-2 Change your PC settings by clicking or tapping Change PC Settings in the Settings pane.

This opens the PC Settings tool, which has 13 sections as you can see in Figure 3-3. Chapter 2 already discussed some of the options you can change in the Personalize section in PC Settings, like picking the look you want for the Start screen, and in Chapter 18 we'll go into more details about some of the sections you probably won't need to use as often, like Ease of Access. In this chapter, we'll first explain the purpose of each section, and then we'll cover the following useful options in more depth:

- Changing your password
- Changing your user picture
- Setting up multiple accounts on one PC

FIGURE 3-3   Choose the PC Settings you want to adjust.

Personalize Your PC

The Personalize section is where you choose what you see on the Lock screen, Start screen, and desktop, as covered in Chapter 2. You can also change the picture for your account; we'll show you how to do that later in this chapter.

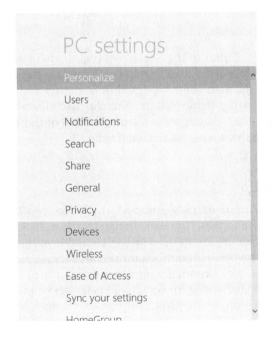

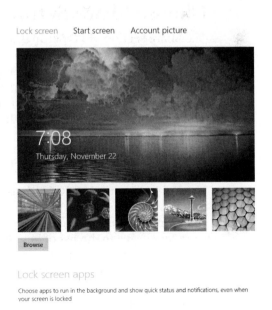

Manage User Accounts

The Users section is where you change the password for your user account, create a picture password, or add accounts for other people who will also use your PC.

Configure Notifications

We've already mentioned how you can temporarily turn off notifications from apps by clicking the Notifications icon in the Settings pane. If you want to see notifications from some Windows Store apps but not from others, you can use the Notifications section to set which apps can show you a message. For example, you might want to get reminders for appointments but not get notifications when it's your turn in a multiplayer game. Or you can turn off all notifications completely here. You can also add a notification sound if you want to hear when new messages arrive.

Choose Search Settings

The Search section of PC Settings is where you choose what you see on the Search pane when you open the Search charm. You might not want to see the list of every Windows Store app that supports the Search pane, so you can turn off individual apps here. You can also choose whether to save searches so you can easily repeat them, choose to delete your search history if old searches are getting in the way, and choose whether to put the apps you search in the most at the top of the list in the Search pane.

Choose Share Settings

The Share section of PC Settings is very similar to the Search section. If there are some Windows Store apps you have installed that you don't want to see on the Share pane when you click or tap the Share charm to send information from one app to another, you can turn off those apps' sharing features here. You can also choose how many of the apps from which you share information show up at the top of the list, which can make it easier to find the one you want to use each time.

Change General Settings

The General section of PC Settings has a mix of tools, some of which take you to the relevant Control Panel settings to make changes. You can change which time zone you're in, change language settings if you use more than one keyboard layout, add more languages to the list of keyboard layouts, set options for the onscreen touch keyboard and the way spelling mistakes are corrected automatically, and turn off the ability to run two Windows Store apps side by side on screen. This is also where you'll find the tools for refreshing or resetting your PC if you have problems with Windows. We'll come back to these options in Chapter 19.

Choose Privacy Settings

Some Windows Store apps can use your physical location (which Windows can work out from the details of what network you're connected to, if your PC doesn't have a GPS sensor in), for example to find restaurants that are nearby or to show you a local map. Each Windows Store app that uses location must request permission to do this when you install it; if you decide you don't want any apps to use your location, you can turn off location tracking in the Privacy section of PC Settings. You can also tell apps not to share your account picture or the anonymized information the Windows Store wants to collect about websites (this is used to track the web content Windows Store apps load, to protect you against apps that link to malicious sites).

Add Devices to Windows

Usually, all you need to do to set up a peripheral is to plug it into your PC; Windows takes care of finding and configuring the drivers you need automatically. If your peripheral connects by Bluetooth or Wi-Fi rather than with a cable, click or tap the Add a Device button in the Devices section to get started. You can also see a list of which devices are already set up and whether they're connected and ready to use.

Change Wireless Settings

Most of the tools you need to work with wireless network connections are right in the Settings pane. The Wireless section of PC Settings has the same slider for putting your PC into Airplane mode, but it also has options to control the individual wireless radios in your PC. If you have Bluetooth, NFC, or GPS radios in your laptop or tablet, you can turn them on and off here.

Choose Ease of Access Settings

Windows 8 has built-in tools to magnify the screen and read aloud the information that's on screen. These are useful if you find dialog boxes hard to read, for example. We'll go into more detail about the options in the Ease of Access section of PC Settings in Chapter 18.

Sync Your Settings

If you use more than one PC with Windows 8 and you sign into them all with the same Microsoft account, you can sync settings such as what color the Start screen is, which websites you've visited, and the passwords for the Wi-Fi hotspots you connect to. That can be very convenient, especially on a new PC, because you don't need to fill in information more than once. If you prefer, you can use the Sync Your Settings section to turn off any of the categories of settings that Windows 8 can sync.

Choose HomeGroup Settings

If you have more than one PC at home, you can share files easily by using a simple network called a homegroup; we'll show you how to do this in Chapter 5 but this is where you choose what to share.

Configure Windows Update

There are more detailed options for Windows Update in the Control Panel; the Windows Update section in PC Settings is a quick way to see when you last installed new updates or to check for any critical updates you don't have yet.

Change Your Password

Now that you know what the different sections in PC Settings are for, let's look at the options you might want to change more often, starting with your password. It's always a good idea to require a password to access your PC, to protect the personal information you have on there, and you should immediately change your password if you think someone has discovered it. You do that in the Users section of PC Settings, as shown in Figure 3-4; click or tap the Change Your Password button.

In the Change Your Password window (or the Change Your Microsoft Account Password window, shown in Figure 3-5, if you're using a Microsoft account), type your old password in the Old Password box. Then type the new password in the

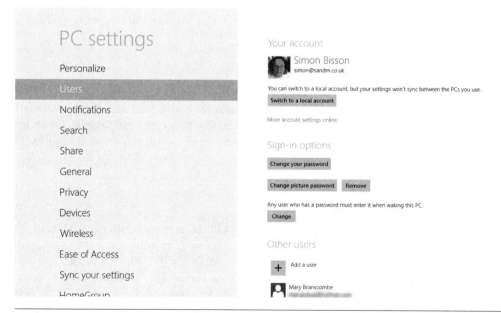

FIGURE 3-4 Users section of PC Settings

FIGURE 3-5   Change Your Microsoft Account Password window

New Password box. Windows asks you to type the new password again in the Reenter Password box in case you made a mistake when you typed it first.

Note   If you're using a Microsoft account to log in to Windows 8, you can still change the password here, as long as you're online. Just remember that doing so changes the password for any other Windows 8 computers you use the same account with, as well as for the services like Hotmail or Outlook.com that you use the account for.

When you're finished, click or tap the Next button. After Windows processes the new password, it will tell you that you've changed your password. Click or tap the Finish button to close the window and return to the Users page.

Make a Picture Password

If you have a touchscreen computer, you can always type a text password in using the onscreen touch keyboard, but that's awkward if you've made a secure password with capital letters, numbers, and punctuation marks in it (that kind of password is harder to guess but also harder to type). You could just set a PIN (like the number you type to use your debit card at the store), but obviously that's not as secure as a complex password. Windows 8 has another option called a picture password that's easier to use on a touchscreen but still secure.

You choose one of your own pictures and then choose three gestures to draw on the picture; you can draw any combination of straight lines and circles or just point to a particular part of the picture. The order in which you make the gestures matters too. Windows 8 records the gestures you make, including the direction you draw the line or circle, and the next time you turn on your PC, you can draw the same gestures instead of typing your password.

 Don't worry about someone guessing your password by looking at your finger marks on the screen. Using a picture password is secure because once you unlock your PC, you carry on touching the touchscreen to do other things, thereby disguising the gestures for your password with other finger marks on the screen. But you should still pick your picture and gestures carefully. For example, if you choose as your password to touch the faces of three people in a picture, choose an image with more than three people in it—or choose to touch three places on one face.

To add a picture password, click or tap the Create a Picture Password button in the Users section of PC Settings. You first have to type in your current password, to prove you have authority to change password options, and then Windows 8 shows you an example of a picture password in action. When that tutorial finishes, click or tap the Choose Picture button; you can use a picture on your computer, an image you have on SkyDrive, or even a picture you find by searching on Bing. This uses the new File Picker interface introduced in Chapter 2.

Once you see the picture full screen, you might not like it as much, so Windows gives you the chance to change your mind and click or tap Choose Another Picture. If you're happy with your selected picture, then click or tap the Use This Picture button. Windows 8 makes you draw the gestures twice, as shown in Figure 3-6, just like it requires you to type a new text password twice.

FIGURE 3-6 Creating a picture password

You can go back and change the picture you use or the gestures you draw at any point by clicking or tapping the Change Picture Password button in the Users section of PC Settings. And if you ever forget what gestures you've set, you can click the Replay button to get a reminder. Use the Remove button (shown in Figure 3-4) if you want to get rid of your picture password. When you're signing in to Windows, click or tap the Switch to Password button on the picture password screen to use your text password instead.

Change Your User Picture

If you use a Microsoft account to log in to Windows 8, the user picture for your account is the one you've set for Windows Messenger, Hotmail, or the other Microsoft services you use that account for. If you have a local account, Windows uses a placeholder image for your user picture until you add your own. If you want to add your own photo (or change the image for your Microsoft account), or just add a picture that you like, you can go straight to the Personalize section of PC Settings, or you can change it from the Start screen.

On the Start screen, click or tap your username at the top of the screen and then click or tap Change Account Picture in the menu to open the Personalize section of PC Settings, as shown in Figure 3-7.

Click or tap Account Picture at the top of the page to change your account picture.

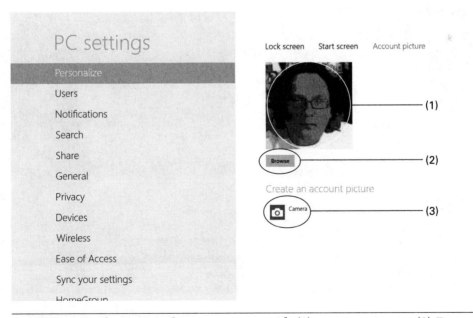

FIGURE 3-7   The Personalize menu page with (1) account picture, (2) Browse button, and (3) Camera icon

The Account Picture page shows the account picture you already have; if you haven't previously chosen an image, you'll see the standard placeholder image here.

If you have a webcam and you want to take your own picture using the Camera app, click or tap the Camera icon. After you take the photo, it appears on the Account Picture page automatically.

If you have a photo you want to use, find it on your computer by clicking or tapping the Browse button. This opens the same File Picker that is used to find an image for the picture password (we also used it to change the Lock screen in Chapter 2). What you see initially are the files and folders in your Pictures library. Click or tap the tile showing the image you want to add; you can also open folders to see the pictures stored in them. If the picture isn't on your PC, click or tap the Files heading at the top of the screen to see a list of other libraries as well as apps that you can use from the File Picker, like the Photos app shown in Figure 3-8 where we're choosing a photo from Flickr.

Once you choose the picture you want, a check mark appears in the upper right corner of the tile. Click or tap the Choose Image button to change your account image to the selected one, which will now appear on the PC Settings screen's Account Picture page.

The next time you go to the Start screen, you'll see your image next to your username in the upper right corner of the screen. You'll also see the image next to your name every time you log in.

FIGURE 3-8 Access the Photos app from the File Picker to use your online photos in Windows.

Add a New Account

If you're not the only person who uses your PC, you can create separate user accounts for each person. This enables each user to maintain the privacy of their own files and choose their own colors, background images, and other settings. To add a new account, click or tap Add a New User at the bottom of the Users section of PC Settings (where you can see any other accounts that are already set up). This opens the Add a User wizard shown in Figure 3-9.

As with your own user account, you can create local accounts for other users by clicking or tapping the Sign In Without a Microsoft Account link at the bottom of the wizard, but using a Microsoft account for the other users on your PC gives them the same convenient synchronization of settings and passwords.

To use a Microsoft account, type the email address for that user in the Email Address box, and then click or tap the Next button. (If they don't have a Microsoft account already, click or tap the Sign Up for a New Email Address link at the bottom of the wizard.) In the next step, if the account you're creating is for a child, then click or tap the Is This a Child's Account? check box under the email address or username. This turns on the Family Safety feature, which lets you limit how the child can use the PC and provides you with regular reports about your child's computer usage. (We'll go into the details of Family Safety settings in the next section.) Click or tap the Finish button to create the account, which you will now see in PC Settings.

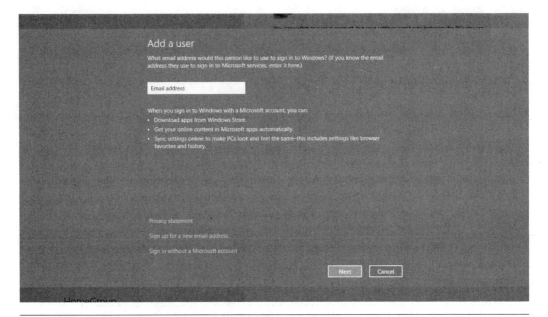

FIGURE 3-9   Add a new account in the Add a User wizard.

How to... Log In with a Different User Account

Usually, Windows shows the last account you logged in with on the login screen, and you can click the arrow next to your username to see the other accounts on the system if you want to log in to one of those instead. After you add a new account to Windows, the next time you log in to Windows, you'll see all the usernames and photos in the login screen instead. Click or tap the photo to select the user account with which you want to log in to Windows. Then you can enter the password for the user account.

Change Settings in the Control Panel

The Control Panel is where you can view and change a much wider variety of system settings. These settings are grouped into the following eight categories, as shown in Figure 3-10. If you've used Windows 7 or Windows Vista, you'll find the Control Panel very familiar, although some items have changed or moved. If you're used to the Windows XP Control Panel, having settings organized into categories is new.

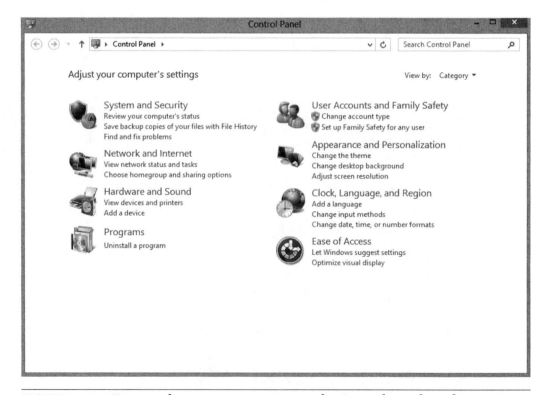

FIGURE 3-10 You can change system settings in the Control Panel window.

- System and Security
- Network and Internet
- Hardware and Sound
- Programs
- User Accounts and Family Safety
- Appearance and Personalization
- Clock, Language, and Region
- Ease of Access

There are several ways to open the Control Panel. If you're already in the Windows desktop, open the Charms bar either by moving your mouse to the upper or lower right corner of the screen, pressing WINDOWS-I, or, if you have a touchscreen, swiping your finger in from the right edge of the screen; click or tap the Settings charm, and then click or tap Control Panel.

You can also open the Control Panel from the shortcut menu that appears when you press WINDOWS-X (whether you're on the desktop or on the Start screen). Or you can open it from the Start screen. Just start typing *control panel* and a tile will appear in the search results. And if you open the All Apps list, by right-clicking or tapping on a blank area in the Start screen and then clicking or tapping the All Apps icon in the app bar (or by swiping up from the bottom or down from the top of a touchscreen), you'll find Control Panel in the Windows System Group. Refer to Chapter 2 if you need a refresher on the All Apps screen.

There are so many different options in the Control Panel that covering them all could fill an entire book. For each of the eight categories, you can click the blue links under the category name to jump straight to common tasks, or you can click the category name to see all the settings and tools in that category, including advanced and low level options you won't often need to change.

If you need to find a particular tool, you can browse through the categories or you can just type what you're looking for into the Search box in the top right corner to see a list of matching tools and options. We'll come back to some of the advanced options in Chapters 18 and 19; for now, we'll show you the basics of managing user account options that aren't available in PC Settings. You can monitor how a child is using the computer with the Family Safety feature and have Windows warn you when you're about to make changes to important Windows settings.

Change Account Types and Manage Other User Accounts

In addition to the options in PC Settings for making simple changes to your own account and creating other accounts, Windows 8 offers a lot more options to choose how user accounts work on your PC. Like other system tools you won't need to access as often, these additional options are located in the Control Panel, under User Accounts and Family Safety.

To change what type of account someone has or remove an account for someone who no longer uses the computer, click the links listed under the User Accounts heading, shown in Figure 3-11. You can change your own account and, if you have a special kind of account called an administrator account, change the settings for other accounts as well. You'll learn more about the two different types of accounts and how to change them next.

Change Your Account Type

There are two types of accounts you can use in Windows 8: *standard* and *administrator*. (You can also create a *guest* account to let a friend use your PC temporarily without being able to see all your files.) Most of the time a standard user account is sufficient to accomplish all you need to do in Windows, and spending most of your time in Windows logged in as a standard user is safer; that way, you can't accidentally change important settings, and any malware that tries to trick you into running it can't change those settings either.

When you're logged in with a standard account, you can still change system settings, but only ones that don't affect other users or Windows security. You can change the time zone, the screen resolution, or the default printer, for example, but not whether someone can connect to your computer remotely or whether Windows warns you when you make changes that affect security. A user who is logged in with an

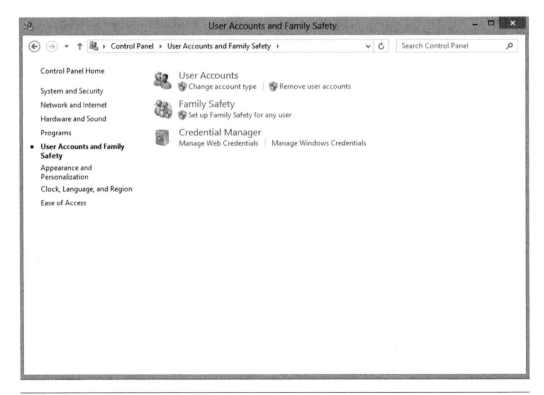

FIGURE 3-11 Change account settings in the User Accounts page.

administrator account has full control over the computer and can access all files and settings. Every PC must have at least one administrator account so that secure settings can be changed if necessary, but you don't need to use the administrator account all the time. If you want to make a change that only an administrator can make, Windows 8 will ask you to enter the password for the administrator account first.

Click or tap Change Your Account Type under the User Accounts heading. If you are logged in as an administrator, you can make changes to any other accounts on your computer; in that case Windows will ask you to choose which account you want to change on the Manage Accounts page, shown in Figure 3-12. You then can click or tap the Change the Account Type link on the Change an Account page.

Choose the Standard or Administrator radio button to set the account type, and then click or tap the Change Account Type button. If there is only one account on the computer, that account is required to have administrator privileges and you can't change the account type to Standard.

Manage Another Account

If you are logged in as an administrator, you can manage all the other user accounts by clicking or tapping Manage Another Account on the User Accounts page. Again, you can choose the account you want to change by clicking or tapping on the username in the list of users.

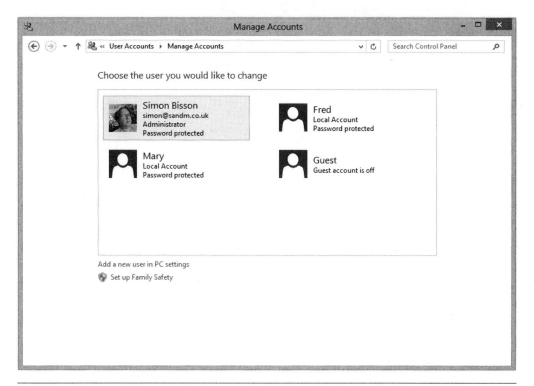

FIGURE 3-12   Pick a user account to change on the Manage Accounts page.

For each account, you can see details like the username, the email address the user uses to log in (if this is a Microsoft account rather than a local account), and if the account is password protected. If the user is an administrator, then the word Administrator appears under the username or email address, as you can see in Figure 3-11. Click or tap the links on the Change an Account page to change the name of the account, add or change the password, set up the Family Safety options for children's accounts (which you'll learn about next), change the account type, or delete the account if the person no longer uses this PC.

Set Up Family Safety

If you share your computer with your children, or you're setting up the PC they will use, you can give each of them their own account and set up Windows' built-in Family Safety feature to control and monitor what your children do. On the User Accounts and Family Safety control panel, click or tap Set Up Family Safety for Any User.

This opens the Family Safety page, where you can click or tap the name of the user account that you want the Family Safety features to apply to. On the User Settings page that opens, shown in Figure 3-13, click or tap the On button to turn on Family Safety, and then choose which controls and reports you want to use for this account, as described next.

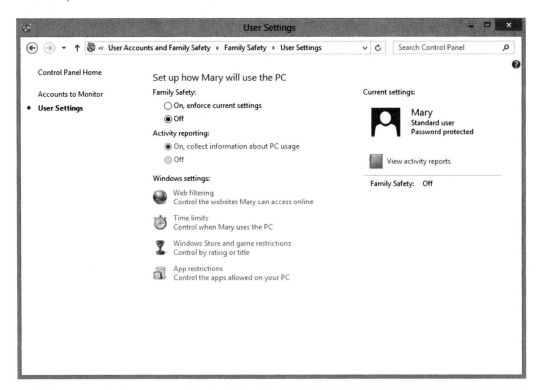

FIGURE 3-13 Set up Family Safety options on the User Settings page.

You can only apply Family Safety to standard accounts, not to administrator accounts. And to make Family Safety effective, you have to set up a password for all the administrator accounts on your computer; otherwise, anyone could log in with an administrator account and bypass all the Family Safety settings.

By default, Family Safety collects the computer activity details of users who are protected by Family Safety. You can see which programs they use most, which websites they visit most, which websites they attempt to visit that have been blocked by the Family Safety features, and at what times they've used the PC in the last week. You can also get a much more detailed report that includes a record of all the websites they've visited, which files they've downloaded, and which apps they've installed from the Windows Store. To do so, click or tap the View Activity Reports button, which takes you to the Family Safety website.

 You can log in to the Family Safety website from a computer other than the one Family Safety is protecting, which enables you to not only monitor how your children are using their computers when you're away at work, for example, but also remotely change settings and allow or block specific web pages.

You can use Family Safety to protect an account without tracking how that account is used if you don't feel the need to monitor it. Turn tracking off by clicking or tapping the Off button under Activity Reporting. You can also set how the various limits and restrictions that Family Safety turns on are applied. For each of the following four options under Windows Settings, you can turn restrictions on or off and choose what the limits are:

- **Web filtering**   You can choose which websites the user can open, either by setting a specific list of allowed sites or choosing one of several different filtering levels (such as only sites that are designed for children, general interest sites, or online communication sites, which include social networking sites such as Facebook and common email sites). Turning on filtering also blocks adult images and websites in the results the user will see on the main search engines. With most of the filtering options, all sites with adult content are blocked, but you do have the option to turn on a warning for adult sites and let the user choose whether to look at the site after they've seen the warning. You can block all file downloads as part of web filtering if you choose.
- **Time limits**   You can choose when and for how long the user can use the computer. You can set the number of hours and minutes per day the user can use the computer (and you can opt to give the user more computer time on weekends). You can also set a curfew if you want to control whether the user can use the computer after bedtime or in the middle of the day. You can set a time allowance, a curfew, or both. For the curfew, select on which days and during which times the computer is off limits.
- **Windows Store and game restrictions**   You can control which games and apps the user can view and download from the Windows Store and also control which

games and apps the user can run. You can allow or block specific games and apps, or you can use the Entertainment Software Rating Board age rating assigned to the game. For example, you can restrict the games the user can download and use to only those games rated Everyone or pick an appropriate ESRB age rating. You can also choose whether the user can install and play games that don't have a rating.

- **App restrictions** You can control which of the Windows Store apps and desktop programs installed on the computer the user can run. For example, you may not want your children to be able to use Windows Media Player so they can't watch videos while they're supposed to be doing their homework, or you might just want to prevent them from accidentally running an uninstaller that removes a program or changes its settings. This option also lets you control apps from the Windows Store that don't have age ratings.

Whatever Family Safety settings you choose, you'll want to have a discussion with your children about how they use their computers, what they should and shouldn't do, how to protect themselves online, and which websites and programs you feel are appropriate for them. You might want to show your children how you're setting up Family Safety on their account, so that they understand the decisions you're making and what you will be able to see in the activity reports, if you choose to keep tracking turned on.

Change User Account Control Settings

As you've been looking at the Control Panel, you may have noticed the blue and yellow shield icons next to some of the tools and tasks. That shield tells you that the tool or task you're about to click or tap will make a change that could potentially harm your system. These are tasks such as installing or uninstalling an app, changing a user account type, and viewing or changing another user's files and folders. It also includes some tasks you might think are safe, like changing the system clock, but being able to change the time on your PC is something a virus can exploit to make it harder for your security updates to download when they're supposed to. Windows 8 won't stop your making these changes as long as you have an administrator password, but it will make sure you know that you're making a change that could cause problems.

These shield icons represent a feature called User Account Control (UAC), which was first introduced in Windows Vista. When you click a link with a UAC shield next to it, or an icon or button that has the UAC shield on it, Windows will dim the screen and show you a dialog box that tells you that performing the task could cause harm to your computer and asks if you want to proceed. Click or tap the Yes button in the dialog box to proceed with the task.

You can determine when UAC notifies you about potential changes to your system by clicking or tapping Change User Account Control settings on the User Accounts page. In the User Account Control Settings window, shown in Figure 3-14, the default selection for the slider bar is to notify you only when apps try to make changes to your computer.

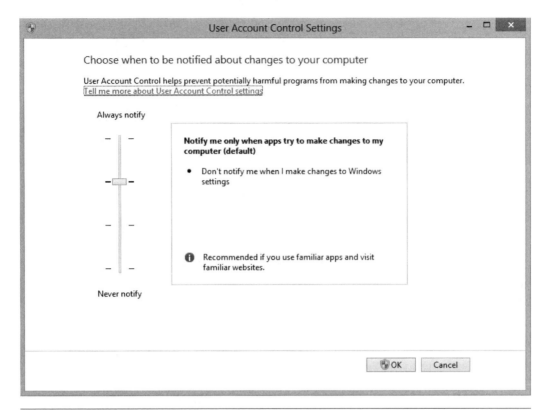

FIGURE 3-14 Make changes to your UAC notification in the User Account Control Settings window.

If you move the slider all the way up to Always Notify, the maximum setting, UAC will always notify you when apps try to make changes to your system and when you are about to make changes to Windows settings. If you move the slider down one notch, UAC will still notify you when apps try to make changes to your system, but it won't dim the desktop, so the notifications are easier to miss. If you move the slider all the way down to Never Notify, UAC won't warn you at all when apps make changes or you make changes to Windows settings. This setting isn't recommended, and it's much better to leave UAC turned on. If you want the most protection, move the slider up to Always Notify; otherwise, you can leave it on the default setting.

Click or tap the OK button when you're finished. The OK button has a UAC shield on it, so as you'd expect, when you select it you will see the UAC dialog box asking if you want to make the changes to your system. Proceed by clicking or tapping the Yes button.

4

Manage, Back Up, and Sync Your Files

HOW TO...

- Navigate File Explorer
- Delete files and folders
- Back up files with File History
- Copy files to CDs and DVDs
- Work with files on SkyDrive
- Sync your music, video, and images to other devices
- Sync your settings between PCs
- Make your computer a Trusted PC

These days, many of us use a wide range of different gadgets and devices—from traditional desktop and laptop computers, to smartphones and tablets, to digital cameras—and we want to create and access files and photos on all of them, without worrying about how we took a photo or which computer a document started life on. With this in mind, Microsoft set out to make it easier than ever in Windows 8 to store all your documents, photos, and other files in one place and share them among all your devices.

As with previous versions of Windows, Windows 8 enables you to share files and folders across a network of several computers, so you can access your photos or your accounts from any of your PCs (we'll look at creating a homegroup in Chapter 5), and now it's easier than ever to keep backups of your most important files with File History. Windows 8 also works with SkyDrive, Microsoft's online file sharing and storage system, to sync files to other devices—including smartphones and tablets. You can still work with files and folders in File Explorer on the desktop and copy files by hand, and we'll cover the new features you get in Windows 8, but that's no longer the only way to get files on and off your PC.

Navigate File Explorer

As with past versions of Windows, when you want to find, view, edit, delete, and manage files in Windows 8, you do that in File Explorer. File Explorer (Explorer for short) is part of the Windows 8 desktop, and you'll find an icon for it pinned to the Windows taskbar. You can also open it directly from the Start screen if you pin a tile for it there (refer to Chapter 2 for instructions). See Figure 4-1 for details.

 From anywhere in Windows, you can open Explorer quickly by pressing WINDOWS-E.

Use the Ribbon Bar

Many features of Explorer will look familiar if you've used previous versions of Windows, especially Windows 7. However, instead of menus, Explorer in Windows 8 has a "ribbon" bar of commands at the top of the window, as you can see in Figure 4-1.

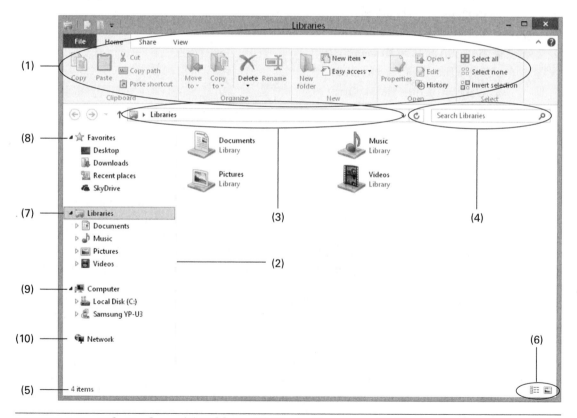

FIGURE 4-1 File Explorer (1) Ribbon, (2) Navigation pane, (3) Navigation bar, (4) Search bar, (5) Status bar, (6) Switch views, (7) Libraries, (8) Favorites, (9) Computer, and (10) Network.

If you've used any recent version of Microsoft Office (2007 or later), then you're already familiar with the ribbon bar concept. In Windows 8, Paint and WordPad also have a ribbon. If you haven't used a ribbon before, it's easy to get started; the tools you need the most are arranged in logical groups and split between several tabs so they fit on screen more easily.

The top of the ribbon in File Explorer has several tabs. Initially, you'll see four: File, Home, Share, and View. Each is described in turn next.

To the left of the title in every Explorer window is a group of smaller icons, called the Quick Access Toolbar. Right-click any tool on the ribbon and choose Add to Quick Access Toolbar to put tools from the different tabs together in one handy place. Click or tap the drop-down Customize menu at the end of the toolbar to add useful tools directly.

File

The File tab is highlighted in blue, so it's always easy to find. Although it looks like a ribbon tab, when you click or tap on it, the File menu opens as shown in Figure 4-2. It's split into two sections: on the left are commands that are always the same; on the right is a Frequent Places list of the ten folders you've opened most often. The list will change as you use Windows 8, but you can click or tap the pushpin icons to make sure

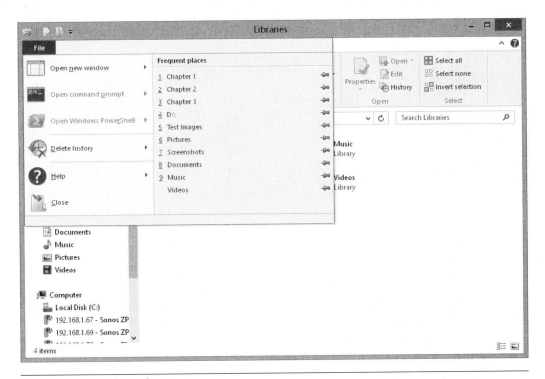

FIGURE 4-2   The File menu

your favorite folders are always on the list. This is the same list of recent and pinned folders that you see on the jump list when you pin the Explorer icon to the taskbar, as explained in Chapter 2.

Despite the name, the File menu isn't where you work with files (the commands you use most are on the other tabs of the ribbon), and most of the commands in the left panel are advanced tools. Open a new window showing the current folder by clicking or tapping Open New Window. If you're an advanced Windows user and you want to manage your files by typing commands rather than using the tools on the ribbon bar, click or tap Open Command Prompt to open a command-line window pointing to the folder you were looking at in Explorer. (If you prefer the PowerShell command interface, click or tap Open Windows PowerShell.) In both cases, you can choose to open the command interface as an administrator, if the commands you're going to use require more access.

You can also click or tap Delete History to delete the file locations in the Frequent Places list if they're not useful any more. Click or tap anywhere else in the Explorer window to close the File menu when you're finished. Only choose Close if you want to close the Explorer window itself.

Home

The Home tab is the section of the Explorer ribbon with the commands you'll use the most frequently, which is why it's the tab Explorer displays by default when you open Explorer. As shown in the following illustration, the tools on the Home tab are grouped into four areas: Clipboard, Organize, New, Open, and Select.

Clipboard The following are the tools in the Clipboard area of the ribbon you'll likely use most frequently:

- **Copy** Click or tap to copy files or folders to the Clipboard and then paste those copies in another folder.
- **Paste** Click or tap to paste cut or copied files or folders from the Clipboard to another file or folder.
- **Cut** Click or tap to cut files or folders to the Clipboard—that is, delete a file or folder from its current folder and paste it into another folder.

You can also copy a shortcut to the location of a file or folder (Copy Path) and then paste that shortcut (Paste Shortcut), which gives you a link to the original file or folder rather than a second copy of it.

Organize In the Organize area, you can move, copy, delete, and rename files or folders.

New   In the New area, you can create a new folder and create blank documents and other new files. You'll also find some useful tools for navigating folders on the Easy Access menu:

- Use Pin to Start to pin to the Start screen a tile that opens Explorer and takes you straight to the current folder.
- Libraries are an easy way to organize folders without moving them. For example, if you have music tracks stored in several different places (including on other computers elsewhere in the house), you can include all of them in your Music library so you can see them all at once without moving them. Files in libraries are also backed up by File History (described later in the chapter). Add the current folder to a library by picking the library name from the Include in Library menu (which also enables you to make a new library to put the folder in).
- Put folders you use often in the Favorites list at the top of Explorer's Navigation pane so you can jump straight to the folders you use most; you can also see this list in dialog boxes for some desktop programs like Office, so you can find and save files in the right place more easily. Choose Add to Favorites to add the current folder to this list.
- If you have a homegroup network, you can make disk drives on other computers look as if they're connected directly to your PC by giving them a drive letter. Use Map as Drive to do that. We'll cover setting up a homegroup in Chapter 5.

Open   In Explorer, you can see a preview of almost any document by selecting the file, and you can open a file in the program or app associated with its file type by double-clicking it. The Open area gives you more options for working with files:

- **Properties**   Click or tap to find details about a selected file, such as when you first created it, what resolution a photo is, what album a music track is from, and lots of other information.
- **Open**   Click or tap to choose which program or app to open a selected file with.
- **Edit**   Click or tap to open and edit the selected file in the default program or app.

Did You Know?

You Can Take Network Files Offline

Depending on which version of Windows 8 you have, you may also see three commands in the Easy Access menu for working with files from a network server even if you're not connected to the network (you would use this to bring files home from work on a notebook computer, for example). When you mark a file as Always Available Offline, you will see a local copy of it in Explorer even when you're not on the network; use the Sync command when you're back on the network to make sure changes are copied to and from your PC. Choose Work Offline if you want to see your local copy even if you're connected to the network.

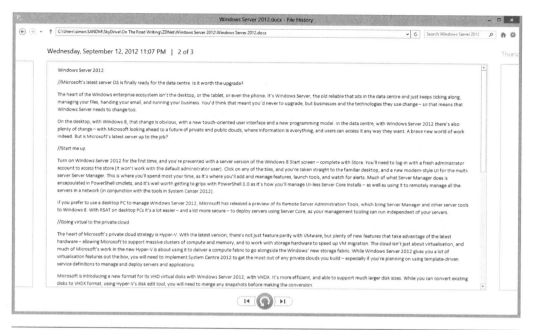

FIGURE 4-3 Different versions of a file in File History

- **History** Click or tap to see the changes that you've made to a file that's protected by File History. You can step back through all the different versions of the file that have been saved by File History until you find the one you want (see Figure 4-3). Click the green Restore button to recover that version of the file so you can work with it. (We'll explain how to set up File History later in this chapter.)

 If you just need a line or two from an older version of the file, you can copy and paste that material from the preview.

Select When you need to work with more than one file at a time, use the tools in the Select area. These are particularly handy on a touchscreen, where it's harder to select multiple files accurately.

- **Select all** Click or tap to select all the files in a folder.
- **Select none** Click or tap to make sure you don't have any files selected.
- **Invert selection** Click or tap to invert your selection. Suppose you want to select everything in the folder except one or two files. It's quicker to select the one or two files you don't want to include and then click or tap Invert Selection; Explorer switches the selection to give you everything except your initial selection.

 A quick way to cut, copy, or paste a file or folder is to use keyboard shortcuts. Just select the file (or folder) in Explorer and then press CTRL-X to cut or CTRL-C to copy. Navigate to the folder where you want to paste the file or folder, and press CTRL-V to paste.

Share

The Send area of the Share tab brings together tools for sending files by email, compressing files into a Zip file, burning files to an optical disc, and printing or faxing files. The Share With area has options for setting permissions for sharing files over a network. The Share tab also has an Advanced Security option for setting file and folder permissions. Click or tap the Share tab to open these tools in the ribbon.

Send   The tools you'll use the most on this tab are in the Send area:

- **Email**   Click or tap to attach selected files to an email message.
- **Zip**   Click or tap to or compress selected files into a Zip file so that they take up less space.
- **Burn to disc**   Click or tap to copy selected files and folders to a CD or DVD; we'll explain the different options for burning optical discs later in this chapter.
- **Print/Fax**   Click or tap to print or fax selected files.

Share With   If you share your PC with other people or your PC is connected to a homegroup or network, you can use the Share With tools to choose which of them can view or edit specific files. You'll see a list of accounts on your computer, as well as options for letting users in your homegroup view or edit the selected files. Depending on how your computer is set up, you might also see the Advanced Sharing option, which lets you set up more complex permissions for how people can change files. If you no longer want to share the selected file or folder, click or tap Stop Sharing.

You will rarely, if ever, need to click or tap the Advanced Security option and use the Advanced Security Settings window, shown in Figure 4-4; they let you change permissions for how different accounts work with folders on your computer.

View

The View tab collects together the options for choosing the information Explorer shows about your files. It includes four areas: Panes, Layout, Current View, and Show/ Hide, and Options menu on the right.

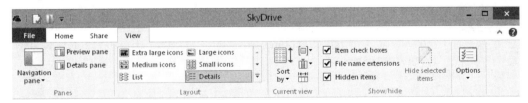

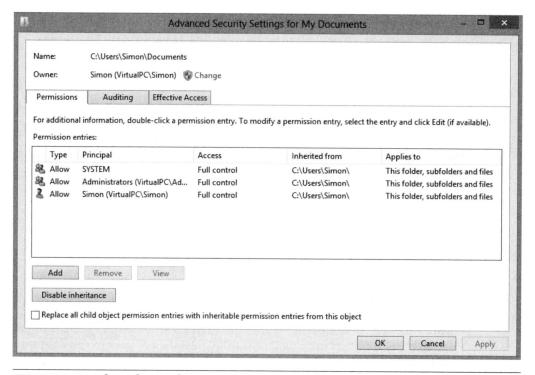

FIGURE 4-4 The Advanced Security Settings window

Panes Click or tap the Navigation pane drop-down menu to see options for the layout of the Explorer window. You can turn the whole Navigation pane on the left on and off; clear the checkbox next to Show favorites to hide the list of Favorite folders. You can also choose whether the Preview pane or the Details pane is displayed when you select a file.

Layout Use the Layout options to choose how files are listed in Explorer windows. The default view is Tiles, which shows a thumbnail view of the file as well as the file name, type, and size. Other views range from Extra Large Icons, which shows large thumbnails and the file name (handy for looking through your images), to Details, which shows a detailed list of each file that includes the file name, creation date and time, and file size (useful when you want to sort by date or size).

 If you open the Options menu at the right end of the View ribbon and turn on the Status Bar option, not only can you see details about the file you have selected without switching to the Details view, but you get two handy controls in the bottom right corner of Explorer to switch instantly between the Details view and Large Icons view.

Current View Use the Sort by drop-down menu in the Current View area to choose how to sort the list of files in Explorer, so they're arranged by date or size, so you see the most recent files first, or the largest ones first. You can also put files and folders into groups, based on different file properties. If you're in Details view, you can also add extra columns of information, such as a column for the resolution of images. Once you have a lot of columns, you might need to resize them so you can see them all at once with Size All Columns to Fit.

Show/Hide   Use the options in the Show/Hide area to turn features on and off or hide files you don't want to change by accident.

- **Item check boxes**   Check this box to see a small check box next to each file name in Explorer. This makes it easier to select multiple files at once, particularly on a touchscreen. Using check boxes to makes selections enables you to click or tap the check box to select a new file without unselecting the files that are already selected.
- **File name extensions**   Check this box to see the extension at the end of a file name that tells you want kind of file it is (such as .jpg for the photos you take with your digital camera, or .docx or .doc for Word documents). Explorer hides extensions by default, but you may find it useful to see what kind of files you're working with.
- **Hidden items**   Check this box to see the important files that Explorer hides from view, such as Windows system files. Explorer hides these by default so that you don't accidentally move, rename, or delete the files Windows needs to run properly. If you're looking for a system file, such as during a call to technical support, click or tap the Hidden Items check box so that you can find it; but remember to hide the files again once you're done, to keep them safe.
- **Hide selected items**   You can protect your own sensitive files in the same way as the hidden items are protected, by selecting them and clicking or tapping Hide Selected Items; just remember that you won't see them in Explorer until you select Hidden items.

How to...   Select Multiple Files or Folders

You don't have to select files or folders one at a time. If you want to select nonconsecutive files or folders in a list, using the check boxes in Explorer is one option, and it's the easiest one on a touchscreen. If you're using a mouse and keyboard, you can also select multiple nonconsecutive files by holding down the CTRL key and then clicking on each file (or folder) that you want to select in the list.

If you want to select a group of consecutive files, click or tap the first file you need, hold down the SHIFT key, and then click or tap the last file you want to select. You can also select multiple consecutive files using just your keyboard; navigate to the first file or folder that you want to select, and then hold down both the CTRL and SHIFT keys as you press the down arrow key to select more files and folders.

Options   Click or tap Options and choose Change Folder and Search Options to change a range of settings in Explorer. As you can see in Figure 4-5 the Folder Options dialog box that opens has quite a few options; we'll describe the ones that are most useful.

The Folder Options dialog box opens with the General tab displayed (see Figure 4-5). The most useful options on the General tab are located in the Navigation Pane section:

- **Show favorites**   Clear this check box to hide the list of Favorite folders in the Navigation pane in Explorer if you don't find the list useful.
- **Automatically expand to current folder**   Check this box if you always want to see the current folder in the Navigation pane; you'll have to scroll further to get to other areas on your computer, but you'll be able to see quickly where you are in the folder tree as well as on the address bar.

If you don't like any changes you make on the General tab, click or tap the Restore Defaults button to put things back the way they were.

The Advanced Settings list on the View tab of the Folder Options dialog box has a long list of options, including some you can also set on the View tab of the ribbon, like hiding extensions and system files, as in Figure 4-6. You can always get back to the

FIGURE 4-5   The Folder Options dialog box

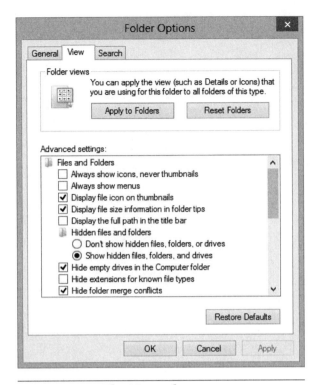

FIGURE 4-6   The View tab

initial settings by clicking or tapping the Restore Defaults button. These are some of the most useful settings to change:

- Explorer in Windows 8 by default shows only the name of the current folder in the title bar. If you'd rather see the full directory path as the title of the window, such as C:\Users\Pictures\, check the Display the Full Path in the Title Bar check box.
- If you want to see more of the system files that are on your computer, you can change the Hidden Files and Folders setting to Show Hidden Files, Folders, and Drives. That will still hide the files that make up Windows itself; if you really need to see those files, clear the check box next to Hide Protected Operating System Files (Recommended).
- If you want Explorer to take you back to the last folder you were working in before you shut down Windows, check the Restore Previous Folder Windows at Logon check box. This will automatically open any Explorer windows you had open at the end of your last Windows session.
- Choosing Show status bar uses a little extra space at the bottom of the Explorer window, but it lets you see things like the size of a file without switching to Details view.

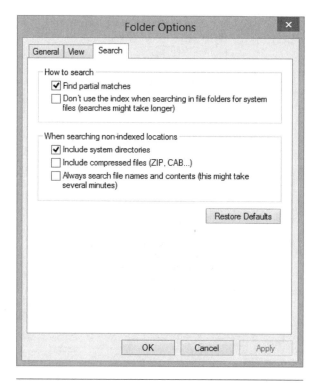

FIGURE 4-7   The Search tab

- By default, when you type a letter on the keyboard when you're working with Explorer, Explorer jumps to the first file that starts with that letter, so, for example, you can type S to jump straight to files starting with S. If you prefer to start a search as soon as you start typing (instead of clicking the Search box first), change the When Typing into List view option to Automatically Type into the Search Box.

You can change more options for conducting searches on the Search tab of the Folder Options dialog box.

To speed up searching, Windows creates an index, which is a database of information about what's in the files on your computer. Windows indexes the most common locations where your files will be located, including your libraries, apps on your Start screen, and even the history of websites you've visited in Internet Explorer. You can search in folders that haven't been indexed, though it's slower, so the defaults on the Search tab are set to make those searches as fast as possible while still being comprehensive. If you don't need to find files that are part of Windows itself, such as files within the C:\Windows folder, you can speed up searches slightly by clearing the Include System Directories check box. If you want to get better results when you're searching in a folder that hasn't been indexed, even if it takes longer, you can change the following options on the Search tab:

- **Always search file names and contents** Select this radio button to search both file names and the contents of the file for your search terms. Searching the contents of files will make searches take longer because Windows has more data to search through, but you're more likely to find the file you need.
- **Include compressed files** Check this box to search inside compressed files, such as those with the .zip file extension.

More Ribbon Tabs

Depending on which folder you have open or which files you have selected in Explorer, you may see other tabs appear in the ribbon.

Library Tools Tab If you're looking at a folder that's included in a library, you'll see the Library Tools tab, which lets you manage which folders are included in the library, which folder new files are saved in by default, and what kind of files the library is optimized for.

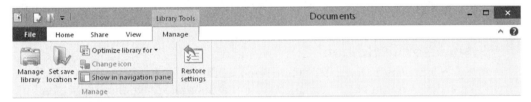

Picture Tools Tab If the library is optimized for Pictures or you've selected an image, you'll see the Picture Tools tab, which has options to rotate images, play the images in the folder as a slide show, and use images as the desktop background.

Music Tools Tab If it's a library optimized for music or you select music tracks, you'll see the Music Tools tab with controls for playing tracks and creating playlists.

Note The Picture Tools tab and the Music Tools tab both have a Play To control, which lets you play music, video, and photos on devices on your network, such as other PCs, a streaming music player, an Xbox, or a connected TV. We'll explain more about how to do this in Chapters 12, 13, and 14.

Manage Tab If you're looking at a USB drive, a CD or DVD, or the top level of a disk drive in Explorer, you'll see the Manage tab with various drive tools, including Format. Optimize defragments the disk to make the free space more efficient. Cleanup removes temporary files, out-of-date error messages, and other system files you no longer need for running Windows 8. There are special tools here for working with CD and DVD drives as well, which we'll look at later in this chapter.

 Sometimes, some of the icons in the ribbon will be grayed out. For example, if you don't have a file selected, then most of the icons in the Clipboard area of the Home tab are grayed out because there's nothing to copy or cut. Similarly, if you haven't already selected and copied or cut a file, the Paste and Paste Shortcut icons are grayed out because there is nothing to paste.

Manage the Ribbon

You might want to have the ribbon open all the time so that you can see your tool choices, or you might prefer to collapse the ribbon to leave more space on screen to view files and folders. By default, Explorer collapses the ribbon; click or tap the down arrow icon in the menu bar to open it. If you want to hide the ribbon again, click or tap the up arrow icon. You can open individual tabs by clicking or tapping the name of the tab—when you do that, you can pin the ribbon open by clicking or tapping the pushpin icon in the top right corner.

 When you shut down Windows, Explorer remembers whether you left the ribbon open or closed, and that's the status of the ribbon you'll see the next time you use Windows.

The Help icon is next to the pushpin control for showing and hiding the ribbon; click it to learn more about using File Explorer.

Navigate Your Files

Use the Navigation pane on the left side of the Explorer window to navigate your computer and the other devices you're connected to.

You can expand the libraries, drives, and folders shown by moving your mouse pointer over and clicking or tapping the arrow icons that appear to their left. A darker arrow indicates the item is expanded to show you what's inside it; a white arrow means there are more levels inside it that you can expand.

For example, as shown in Figure 4-8, when you open Libraries and click or tap the Documents library, you'll see the My Documents and Public Documents folders inside the Documents library (and any other folders you've added to the library). With the Documents library open, you'll see dark arrow icons next to the Libraries and Documents levels and lighter arrows next to the folders inside Documents, like My Documents.

There are five areas in the Navigation pane:

- **Favorites**   Enables you to jump straight to the folders you use most frequently. When you first start using Windows 8, Favorites includes by default entries for the Desktop, the Downloads folder, which is where Internet Explorer puts files you download, and the Recent Places folder, which shows you folders in which you've saved files recently, so you can locate them easily. You can drag links to folders you use often into the Favorites area, and if you install the SkyDrive desktop software, you'll see a link to your SkyDrive library here (we'll look at SkyDrive later in this chapter).

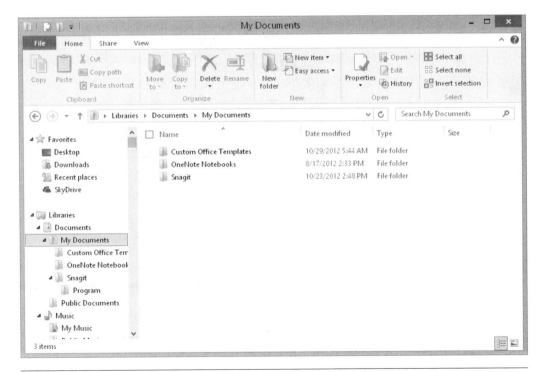

FIGURE 4-8   The folder tree in the Navigation pane

- **Libraries** Includes links to the Documents, Music, Pictures, and Videos libraries as well as any libraries you create to organize your folders. Once you get used to using libraries, you can quickly jump straight to the files you need to work with.
- **Homegroup** Lists other computers that you share files with, when they're turned on and connected to the homegroup. We'll explain how to set up your homegroup and share files in Chapter 5.
- **Computer** Shows all the disk drives, removable drives, and devices connected to your computer. If you plug in a USB drive or connect your MP3 player, you'll see it listed here (along with any devices you can use Play To with, which we cover in Chapter 12). If you map drives from your network, you'll see those as well.
- **Network** Shows any computers that Windows can see on the network you're connected to. We'll cover setting up a network and sharing files in Explorer in Chapter 5.

As well as clicking and tapping in the Navigation pane to find the folder you want, you can also use the navigation bar shown here or you can search for files.

The navigation bar works a little like the address bar in a web browser. Use the Back and Forward buttons to step backward and forward through the folders you've already opened. Use the Up button to jump up a level in the folder hierarchy. You can also click the drop-down arrow between the Forward and Up buttons to see a list of recent folders, as shown here.

For example, if you open the Libraries area, then open the Pictures library, and then choose a folder of images, when you click or tap the Back button, Explorer moves back to the Pictures library. Click or tap Forward and Explorer opens the folder you were just looking at.

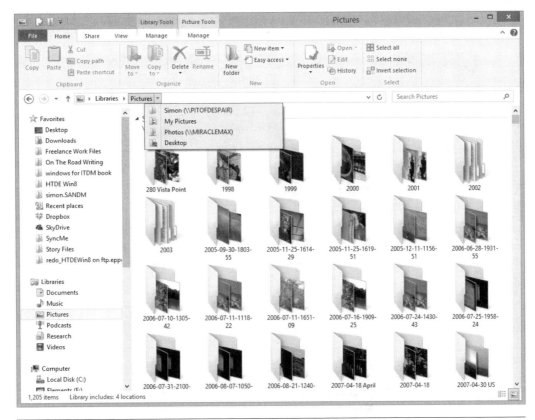

FIGURE 4-9   The list of folders in a library appears below the library's name in the address bar.

As you navigate your computer, the address bar shows you where you are with a mini version of the folder tree that's in the Navigation pane. You can click a folder name in the heading to jump straight to that folder in Explorer, and you can click or tap the arrow after each heading to see a drop-down menu of the other folders inside it, as in Figure 4-9. The icon at the beginning of the address bar changes to show which of the different sections of the Navigation pane you're in, and when you click or tap the icon, you can navigate to those sections and to some other special places on your computer as well, including the Desktop, the Control Panel, and the Recycle Bin.

Search For Files

If you don't remember which folder a file you need is in, you can search for it. If you can narrow the search down to a set of folders, the search will be faster. Select the folder or area in which you want to search and then type some words from the document you're looking for into the Search box in the top right corner of the Explorer window. As soon as you stop typing, Explorer will start to display a list of files with file names or contents matching those words, as shown in the following example, where we searched for "microsoft".

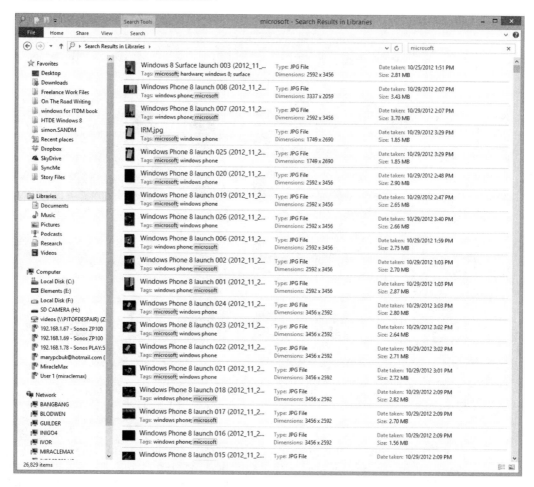

If you want to search for an exact phrase, put quote marks around it. Searching for "Windows 8" will find only the files that contain those words next to each other, and exclude files that contain both "Windows" and "8" but not "Windows 8."

Depending on how large the folders you're searching are, Explorer may take a little time to display all the results. Explorer highlights in yellow the words in the file name and the document preview that match your search. If Explorer can't find any matching results, you'll see a message in the file list pane that says, "No items match your search." Use the tools on the Search tab to refine your search if you need to narrow down the results to a particular kind of file or one created after a specific date.

When you find the file you want, you can also right-click or press and hold on a file to see more options as shown in Figure 4-10 (including extra tools added by other desktop programs that you've installed).

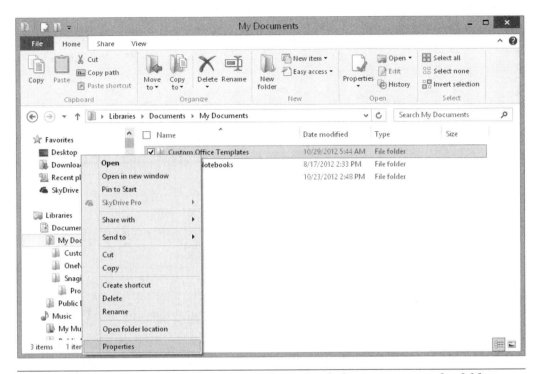

FIGURE 4-10   Click or tap Properties in the right-click menu to view the folder properties.

Delete (and Recover) Files and Folders

When you no longer need a file or folder, it's easy to delete it. Click or tap to select the file and then click or tap the Delete icon on the Home tab in the ribbon, shown next (or press DELETE or CTRL-D on your keyboard). If you want more control, click or tap the drop-down arrow below the Delete icon to see extra options.

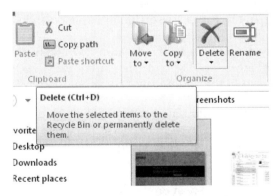

Usually, when you delete a file, Windows automatically puts it in the Recycle Bin, which gives you an opportunity to restore it in case you change your mind. If you want to make sure that happens, choose Recycle from the Delete drop-down menu. If you delete a file from a removable or network drive, however, the Recycle option isn't available; the file won't move to the Recycle Bin and you can't get it back if you change your mind.

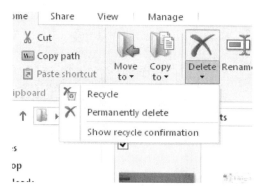

If you know you won't need a file again and you want to free up its space on your disk drive straightaway, click or tap Permanently Delete. This option doesn't put the file in the Recycle Bin, and you can't change your mind after you permanently delete a file or folder, so use this option with care.

If you want to see a message from Explorer confirming that it has put the file or folder you're deleting into the Recycle Bin, click or tap Show Recycle Confirmation in the menu. When you look at the menu again, you'll see a check mark next to Show Recycle Confirmation, and when you delete files, you'll see a confirmation dialog box.

Open the Recycle Bin

If you need to restore a file that you've deleted, check the Recycle Bin. Unless you chose to permanently delete a file or it was too large to fit in the Recycle Bin (you'll get a warning about that when you delete it), then your file will still be there.

There are several ways to open the Recycle Bin:

- Open it from the All Apps menu or by searching from the Start screen.
- Open Desktop in the Favorites section in Explorer and you will see the Recycle Bin as one of the options.
- Open the Recycle Bin icon on the desktop (to quickly access the desktop from an open program, press WINDOWS-D or click or tap the Aero Peek area to the right of the time and date in the bottom right corner of the screen).

When you see the Recycle Bin icon on the desktop, if the picture of the wastebasket has papers in it, then the Recycle Bin contains deleted files or folders you can restore. Double-click or tap the Recycle Bin icon to open the Recycle Bin.

Recycle Bin

Right-click or press and hold on the Recycle Bin icon and choose Properties to set how much disk space is allocated to deleted files. If you have more than one disk drive on your PC, you can choose the amount of space for each drive here, or even turn off the Recycle Bin for a drive where you don't need to protect files.

Restore a File or Folder

As you can see in Figure 4-11, the Recycle Bin looks like any other Explorer window, with its own Manage tab in the ribbon. Any files or folders that you've previously deleted appear in the file list; you can see the name, type, and size of the file, and if you need more information (like which folder a file used to be in), you can right-click or press and hold and choose Properties. If you only need some of the files, select them in the file list as normal and then click or tap Restore the Selected Items in the ribbon. If you want to keep all the files and folders in the Recycle Bin, you don't have to select any of them in the list—just click or tap Restore All Items in the ribbon.

When you restore a file or folder from the Recycle Bin, Windows puts it back in the original location you deleted it from.

 If you can't find the deleted file you're looking for in the Recycle Bin, use Explorer to check File History for the folder it used to be in. If it was in a library, you will usually be able to get the file back from the File History window even after it's no longer in the Recycle Bin. File History is discussed in the following section.

Empty the Recycle Bin

The files in the Recycle Bin do take up space on your PC. If there are a lot of files in the Recycle Bin and you're sure you don't need them any more, click or tap the Empty Recycle Bin icon in the Manage ribbon (or right-click or press and hold on

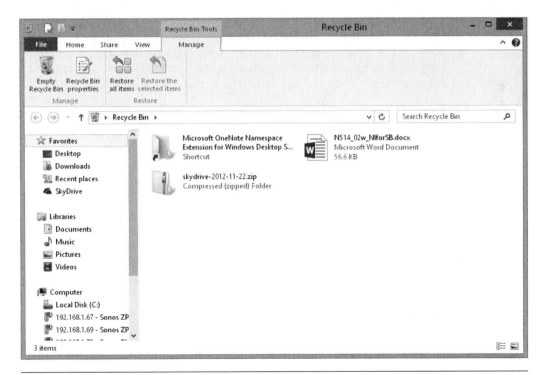

FIGURE 4-11   The Recycle Bin window

the Recycle Bin icon on the desktop and choose Empty Recycle Bin) to remove them all permanently. In the Delete File dialog box that appears, click or tap Yes to confirm that you want to delete the files and you understand that you can't get them back later.

When there are no files in the Recycle Bin, the file list is labeled "This folder is empty" and the Recycle Bin icon on the desktop doesn't have any papers in it.

Back Up Files with File History

One of the most important things to remember about computers is that no matter how easy to use and reliable they become, hardware does fail. Whether it's a disaster, a power failure, or simple wear and tear, the disk drives in your PC won't last forever. Fortunately, in Windows 8, it's easier than ever to keep important files safe by automatically backing them up to another drive using the File History feature.

The File History service built into Windows 8 is rather different from the Backup and Restore utility you may have used in Windows 7 (which shows up in Windows 8 as the Windows 7 File Recovery tool, in the Control Panel). They both save copies of your files and folders to another drive—Windows recommends backing up to an external device such as a USB drive—so you can restore those files and folders in case of an emergency.

 You should also keep a backup that's physically removed from your computer, so that if, for example, you suffer a disaster like a house fire, then your backups won't be lost along with your computer. Because you need to leave your File History drive connected to your PC so that Windows can save new versions of your files regularly, consider creating a separate backup on a drive that you can take to work or leave at a friend's house, or using an online service for backup.

File Recovery can save specific files and folders or make a copy of your entire Windows system, but a full backup is slow to create and not always easy to recover files from. With new tools in Windows 8 that make it much easier to reset your copy of Windows to deal with any problems (we'll look at these tools in Chapter 19) and the option of storing key settings on SkyDrive so they're backed up and restored automatically (discussed later in this chapter), saving copies of just the files you care about most is much faster, and this new and simpler tool may be all you need.

File History creates multiple copies of files as you make changes to them, and it only keeps as many copies as you have space for on your File History drive. It also backs up only the files that are in your libraries (and some special folders), not everything on your PC.

File History backs up all the files in specific folders, which include the following:

- Contacts
- Desktop
- Favorites
- All the libraries you have set up, including the built-in Documents, Music, Pictures, and Videos libraries, and any other libraries that you create

You can't add any other folders to the File History backup (except by including them in a library), and you don't need to do anything to have your libraries backed up once you've turned on File History and chosen your backup drive.

Set Up File History

Open the File History window by opening the Control Panel and then clicking or tapping Save Backup Copies of Your Files with File History, under the System and Security heading (you can also find it by searching the Start screen for File History, under Settings, as explained in Chapter 1).

When you first look at the File History window, it shows you that the service is turned off by default, as shown in Figure 4-12. That's because File History can't back up any files until you've told it where to save them. Even if Windows has found a drive that's suitable for File History, it won't turn the service on until you confirm that's the drive you want to use.

Before you turn on the File History service, you need to connect to your computer the external drive that you want to copy files and folders onto, or choose a drive that's connected to your network. If it's the only drive that File History will work with, you'll see it listed as the drive to which Windows will copy files, as shown

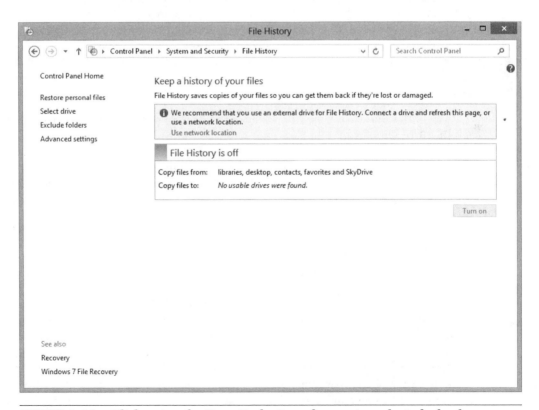

FIGURE 4-12   Click or tap the Turn On button after you've selected a backup device.

You Can Suggest Which Drive to Use for File History

If you're part of a homegroup (a simple network Windows 8 can create for sharing files with the other PCs you have at home, which you'll learn more about in Chapter 5) and you're the first person in the homegroup to turn on File History, you'll be asked if you want to suggest the same drive you're using for File History as a good place for other people in the homegroup to use to save their own File History. As long as they can see the drive as well (meaning it's shared from your computer to the homegroup or available on the network), they'll automatically see it listed as one of the drives they can select to use with File History.

in Figure 4-12. If the drive shown there isn't the one you want to use, click or tap Select Drive in the list of commands on the left of the File History window, choose the correct drive in the list, and then click or tap OK.

To choose a drive that's on your network for File History, click or tap the Add Network location button in the Select Drive window. This opens a dialog box in which you can navigate to the drive you want to use; click or tap Select Folder once you've found it.

If you don't have any external or network drives to back up to, the Turn On button is disabled.

When the File History window shows the backup drive you want to use, click or tap the Turn On button.

Once you've turned File History on, it will create a copy of all the files in the folders it's protecting. After that it runs at regular intervals (we'll show you how to change how often that happens a bit later in this chapter). If you've just finished some important work, you can go into File History and click or tap Run Now to create a backup straightaway.

Use Different Drives for File History

You can switch to using a different drive for File History, if you run short of space on the current drive or you get a larger or faster drive you want to use instead. When you choose the new location in the Select Drive window, File History will ask if you want to move to the new drive the files you've already backed up to the previous File History drive (as long as it's still connected to your PC).

File History can recognize drives that already have a File History backup stored on them. If you choose a drive that's been used for File History before (or is already being used for File History on another PC, with the same account name that you're logged in with), you can choose to either add your new backups to the existing backup or create a new backup.

File History Checks For Network Drives Regularly

If you're backing up to a network location but you haven't connected to the network recently, File History will turn itself off and warn you that it can't see the drive to back up to. The same thing happens if you're using a removable drive and you disconnect it. You'll see the drive you were using still listed in the File History window, and if you reconnect it and click or tap Turn On, File History will start backing up to it again.

If the drive is a drive you've used before on the same computer with the same user account, File History shows you the backup you previously used and enables you to select that. If it's a drive you used with a different computer, File History doesn't show the details of the backup, in case it's connected to another user, but you can select the I Want to Use a Previous Backup on This File History Drive check box to start your backup and keep those files. If it's a drive you're using for File History on another PC, don't select this check box or else you'll get two separate backups.

Exclude Folders from Backup

File History protects all the libraries on your PC automatically, and the only way to add a folder to File History is to include the file in a library. If a library has some folders in it that you don't need to protect with File History, like podcasts that you can easily download again, click or tap Exclude Folders in the navigation bar of the File History window. In the Exclude Folders window, shown in Figure 4-13, click or tap the Add button to open the Select Folder dialog box, browse to the folder you want to exclude and select it, and then click or tap the Select Folder button. The selected folder appears in the list of excluded folders in the Exclude Folders window. (Confusingly, Windows will let you exclude folders that File History isn't protecting anyway, so remember to only pick folders that are in a library.)

Change File History Settings

You can choose how often File History saves a copy of your files, how much disk space it can use, and for how long it keeps the saved versions of your files. Click or tap Advanced Settings in the navigation bar of the File History window if you want to change these settings (which are shown in Figure 4-14).

If you've been using File History for a while and you don't need the oldest versions of the files you're backing up, click or tap the Clean Up Versions link to remove older backups. You can choose how far back to delete old versions or choose to just keep the most recent backup.

If you change your mind about having other people in your homegroup use the same drive, clear the Recommend This Drive check box; they can still use it but it won't be the default for new users. You can also look at the File History event logs if you want to see if there have been any problems with your backup.

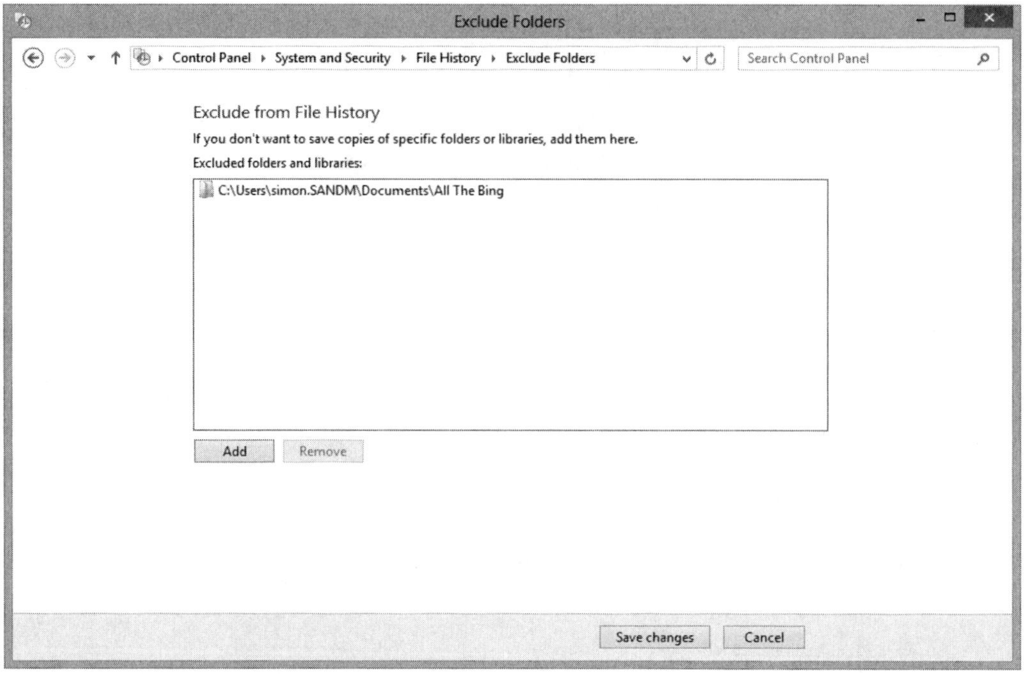

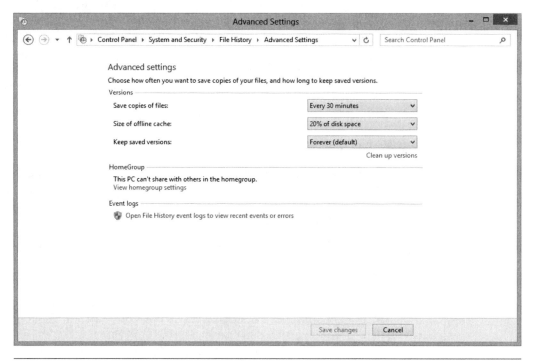

FIGURE 4-13 Exclude folders from File History.

FIGURE 4-14 Use the Advanced Settings window to configure File History.

Restore Files

The easiest way to restore a file that you've been backing up with File History is to open in Explorer the folder it's stored in. If the file is still there, select it and click or tap the History button in the Open section of the Home tab to see all the versions that File History has saved, as shown in Figure 4-15. Click or tap the arrows at the bottom of the screen to see earlier versions; when you find the one you want, click or tap the green Restore button at the bottom of the window to put the file back in the same folder.

If the file you want to restore has been deleted or if you will want to restore more than one file at once, select the folder the file used to be in and click or tap the History button on the Home tab to see a list of files and folders that File History has backups for. Use the arrow buttons to go back until you see the file you want to restore.

If it's easier to find the file you want by date rather than by starting in a specific folder, or if you want to see all the folders and files protected by File History, click or tap the Restore Personal Files link in the navigation bar of the File History window. This opens the File History interface shown in Figure 4-16. You can navigate back to the date and time you're interested in using the arrows at the bottom of the window and then select the folder you want, or select a folder and look through the different dates you have backups for. You can also open a single file by double-clicking or tapping it in File History and look at the different versions to find the one you need.

To restore specific files or folders to the original locations, select them in the File History window and click or tap the green Restore button at the bottom of the window. If you want to restore all the files in a folder, or even all the files and folders from a specific date, click or tap the green Restore button without selecting anything first.

FIGURE 4-15   See all the previous versions of a file in File History.

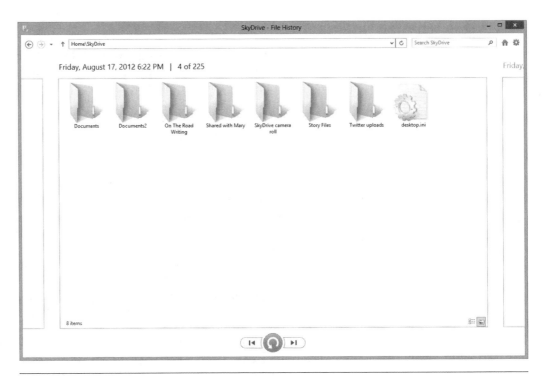

FIGURE 4-16 Choose the folder from which you want to restore files in the File History window.

 If you want to choose where to put the file you're restoring, right-click or press and hold on the file and choose Restore To from the context menu that appears.

Copy Files to CDs and DVDs

If you want to use CDs or DVDs to back up your files, Windows Explorer makes copying your files and folders to an optical drive as easy as copying to any other folder.

Insert into your computer's optical drive the CD or DVD disc you want to copy files to. The first time you do this, you'll see a notification in the corner of the screen asking you to choose what to do when you put this disc into your PC; click or tap the notification to see your options. If it's a blank disc, unless you have other disc-burning software installed, the choices are to burn files to the disc in Explorer or to do nothing.

 If there are already files on the disc, the choices are to open the disc in Explorer or to take no action. Choose Open in Explorer, and every time you insert this disc into your PC, Explorer will open a window showing the drive, enabling you to drag and drop files into it just like any other folder.

FIGURE 4-17   Set CD or DVD formatting
options in the Burn a Disc dialog box.

Choose Burn Files to Disc to open the Burn a Disc dialog box, shown in Figure 4-17. First you need to choose how you want to format the disc. There are two options:

- **Like a USB flash drive**   Choose this option if you want to be able to save, edit, and delete files on the disc. This is the default option, and you should use it if you're backing up data. You'll be able to use it in most recent computers.
- **With a CD/DVD player**   Choose this option if you're going to burn a movie file or music files to a disc that you want to put into a CD or DVD player. This will prepare the disc so you can also read it on something that isn't a PC (this is called *mastering* the disc) as well as on different computers, but you won't be able to delete the files you put on it.

Windows gives the disc the current date as a default title; if you want to call it something else, type that into the Disc Title box. Then click or tap the Next button. Windows formats the disc and opens an Explorer window so you can drag files onto the disc. You can also select the files in another Explorer window and click or tap the Burn to Disc button on the Share tab of the ribbon.

When you're finished, click or tap the Eject button on the Manage tab, and Windows will make sure the disc is ready to use on other computers.

 Although you'll see the standard file copying dialog box when you drag a file onto your disc or use the Burn to Disc button, on some discs that have been formatted on other computers, you'll need to complete an extra step. If you see a message from Windows that you have files waiting to be burned to a disc, click it to open the disc in Explorer. On the Manage tab in the ribbon, click or tap Finish Burning.

You can delete files from rewriteable CDs and DVDs by clicking or tapping the Delete button on the Home tab of the Explorer ribbon as usual. If you want to remove all the files on a disc, click or tap the Format icon on the Manage tab in Explorer.

Sync and Share Files with SkyDrive

As well as copying files back and forth between computers on USB drives and CDs the way you're used to, you can store your files in *cloud* services on the Internet so they're easy to access from different computers and devices. Windows 8 includes a Windows Store app for working with Microsoft's own cloud file-storage service, SkyDrive.

If you log in to your PC with a Microsoft account, you're ready to use SkyDrive; if not, you can log in to the SkyDrive app with a Microsoft account. Either way, you get 7GB of free storage that you can access from most smartphones, tablets, notebooks, as well as desktop computers (both Macs and PCs) and your web browser, so you can access and use your files on whatever device you're working on.

Open SkyDrive by clicking or tapping the SkyDrive tile on the Start screen. You then see the files and folders in your SkyDrive account, as shown in Figure 4-18. You can view any files you already have stored on SkyDrive and open them on your computer (if you don't have Microsoft Office installed, Office documents from the SkyDrive app will open in the corresponding Office web applications). You can search for your files using the Search charm, or navigate through the tiles for the different folders.

FIGURE 4-18 Viewing cloud-stored files from the Windows 8 Start screen with the SkyDrive app

You can also create new folders and upload files from your computer in the SkyDrive app.

The advantage of using the SkyDrive app rather than just visiting the SkyDrive web site is that the app enables you to open or save files on SkyDrive directly from other Windows Store apps. Anywhere you see the File Picker, just click or tap the Files heading and choose SkyDrive from the drop-down menu, then pick the folder you want on screen.

Did You Know?

There Are Two SkyDrive Applications For Windows 8

The Windows Store SkyDrive app is installed automatically in Windows 8 (and Windows RT) and lets you view files that are already in your SkyDrive account (including files other people have shared with you) or upload individual files. The desktop SkyDrive program lets you choose SkyDrive folders to sync to a SkyDrive library on your computer so that you can work with your files even if you're not connected (your changes are uploaded automatically when you're online again).

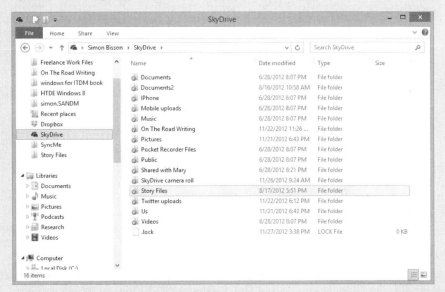

You can upload files just by putting them in your SkyDrive library. But you can't see files other people have shared with you on SkyDrive using the desktop program; you have to use the Windows Store app or go to SkyDrive in your web browser.

(Continued)

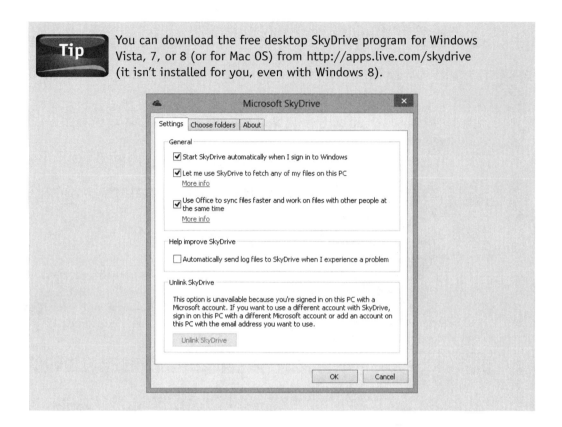

Tip You can download the free desktop SkyDrive program for Windows Vista, 7, or 8 (or for Mac OS) from http://apps.live.com/skydrive (it isn't installed for you, even with Windows 8).

Upload Files to SkyDrive

In the SkyDrive app, navigate to the folder where you want to upload your files. Right-click (or swipe over the top or bottom edge of a touchscreen) to open the app bar where you can switch between thumbnails and details view, create a new folder, and upload files (using the File Picker introduced in Chapter 2). The File Picker opens to the Documents library on your computer; click or tap Go Up To or use the Files drop-down menu to navigate to other libraries or folders on your computer, or to access files in other Windows Store apps. Click or tap to select the files you want to upload to SkyDrive, and then click or tap the Add to SkyDrive button to upload them.

Note You can upload a file or picture to SkyDrive from any Windows Store app that uses the Share charm. In the Share pane, pick SkyDrive as where you want to share to, and then pick which folder to upload into.

Share Files on SkyDrive

Using the SkyDrive app, you can put files on SkyDrive to share with your friends and family, and you can see files and folders that people have shared from their own SkyDrive accounts.

To share files with people, just upload them into a folder that you've already shared; SkyDrive creates a Public folder for you that shares files with everyone, or you can use the SkyDrive web page to set the sharing options for other folders or even for individual files.

Once you've uploaded a file to a shared folder on SkyDrive, use the Share charm to send an email or share a link on Facebook or Twitter to tell people where to find the file. Select the file in the SkyDrive app, open the Share charm, and pick the app you want to send the message with from the list on the Share pane (shown in Figure 4-19).

See Files Shared with You on SkyDrive

You can access files people have shared with you on SkyDrive in the SkyDrive app. It's similar to choosing another library in the File Picker. Click or tap on the name of your own SkyDrive account at the top of the screen and choose Shared from the menu

FIGURE 4-19   Sharing a file on SkyDrive from the SkyDrive app

---

Did You Know?

You Can Use SkyDrive On Other Devices

There are SkyDrive apps for iOS, Android, and Windows Phone (and you can use the SkyDrive.com website on most smartphones). These apps don't sync files to your phone, but they do let you view and sometimes edit the files on SkyDrive from your phone, and you can save files into SkyDrive from apps like Camera Roll on the iPhone. The mobile apps for SkyDrive also let you see the files that other people have shared with you.

---

that appears. You'll see all the various files and folders that different people have shared with you on screen.

Sync Your Music, Video, and Images

Want to copy files from your PC to your MP3 player or tablet automatically? If you connect a device that Windows can treat as if it were a removable drive (for example, an MP3 player or an Android tablet like the Samsung Galaxy Tab), you can sync music, videos, and image files to it using Windows Media Player.

When you first plug in a device that lets Windows 8 "talk" directly to its storage, you'll see a notification in the upper right corner of the screen that asks you to click or tap to choose what you want to do with the device. When you click or tap the notification, a menu appears that includes the option to sync digital media files to your device using Windows Media Player.

When you click or tap Sync Digital Media Files to This Device in the menu, the Windows Media Player window appears with the Sync tab displayed, as shown in Figure 4-20, so you can choose which files you want to copy to your device. You can drag and drop individual music files onto the Sync tab if you want to pick specific tracks, or you can drag and drop an album, an artist, or a playlist (including auto playlists that sync different content each time, like music you've downloaded recently). Click or tap Start Sync in the toolbar to transfer files to your device the first time; the sync will happen automatically the next time you plug in the same device.

FIGURE 4-20   Drag and drop music files to the Sync list so you can sync the files by clicking or tapping Start Sync in the toolbar.

 If you connect a device that has more than 4GB of storage and all the music you have in your Windows Media Player Library will fit onto the device, Windows Media Player will automatically sync all of your files once you choose to sync media to it.

You'll learn more about using Windows Media Player in Chapter 12, including setting up auto playlists.

Sync Your Settings Between PCs

If you log into your PC using a Microsoft account, by default Windows 8 will save many of your settings in SkyDrive and sync them with other PCs on which you use the same account. This is very convenient if you use more than one PC because you can have the same browser history and favorites on all your computers, making it easier to get back to a web page you were looking at even when you're away from the computer you used to open it. You can also sync passwords for websites and Wi-Fi hotspots, and for your homegroup, instead of having to type them in on every PC you use.

 If you need to restore your PC or switch to a new computer, syncing your settings enables you to get the computer up and running much faster.

Settings sync is turned on by default. The only thing you need to do is confirm that you trust your computer to synchronize passwords for websites, Wi-Fi hotspots,

Windows Store apps that support settings sync, and your homegroup. But if there are some settings you don't want to sync, you can turn off syncing for them in PC Settings (open the Charms bar, click or tap Settings, choose Change PC Settings, and then click or tap the Sync Your Settings section). If you have multiple computers, you can sync settings between some of them and not others; just turn off settings sync on the PCs where you don't want to have your settings be the same.

If you don't want to sync any settings at all, change the Sync Settings on This PC option to Off. You can also turn sync on or off for these groups of settings for this PC:

- **Personalize** Syncs the color scheme and design you choose for the Start screen, the picture you choose for the Lock screen, and your account picture. If you want your Start screen to be green on one PC and blue on another, turn off this setting.
- **Desktop personalization** Syncs the images you choose for your desktop background and the colors and other choices you make for the desktop theme and taskbar. If you have two displays connected one of your computers and but your other PC is a small tablet, you might want to have different desktop backgrounds on each PC; if so, turn off this setting.
- **Passwords** Syncs the sign-in details for websites, Wi-Fi hotspots, Windows Store apps that support settings sync, and your homegroup.
- **Ease of Access** Syncs Ease of Access tools like Magnifier. If you have these tools turned on for one PC, you probably want them on your other computers.
- **Language preferences** Syncs the languages you have installed, which language Windows uses for menus and windows, and which keyboard layout you're using. If you want to use one language on one PC and a different language elsewhere, don't sync these settings.
- **App settings** Syncs for some Windows Store apps (like games) the options you choose, your high scores, and items you buy inside the game (extra levels, for example).

Did You Know?

Windows 8 Knows Mobile Data Is Expensive

Some notebooks and tablets have a mobile broadband connection that enables you to be online wherever you are (you can also plug in a broadband dongle or, sometimes, your smartphone). Windows 8 refers to these as *metered* connections because you have a limited amount of data on most carrier plans and you might even be charged for the amount of data you use (particularly if you exceed your data plan). By default, Windows 8 doesn't download large files like updates but it will sync settings over metered connections (except when you're roaming abroad) because they're small files (except for desktop backgrounds), but you can turn that off here as well.

- **Browser**   Syncs your browser history and favorites between the different computers you use, and syncs Internet Explorer settings.
- **Other Windows settings**   These include whether you have the ribbon visible in File Explorer and how you have the mouse set up.

Make Your Computer a Trusted PC

There are two places in PC Settings where you can make your computer a Trusted PC so that it syncs passwords: the Users section and the Sync Your Settings section. In either section, click or tap Trust This PC.

Your account

Simon Bisson
simon@sandm.co.uk

Your saved passwords for apps, websites, and networks won't sync until you trust this PC.

Trust this PC

You can switch to a local account, but your settings won't sync between the PCs you use.

Switch to a local account

This opens Internet Explorer and asks you to sign in to your Microsoft account, as shown in Figure 4-21, after which it takes you to the Security Info page for your account. If you already have extra security information, like a second email address or a mobile phone number, associated with your Microsoft account, you can pick which one Microsoft should use to send you a message asking you to confirm that you trust your new PC.

If you choose an email address, you will receive an email message with a link you can click or tap to mark your PC as trusted; click or tap the Confirm button in the message.

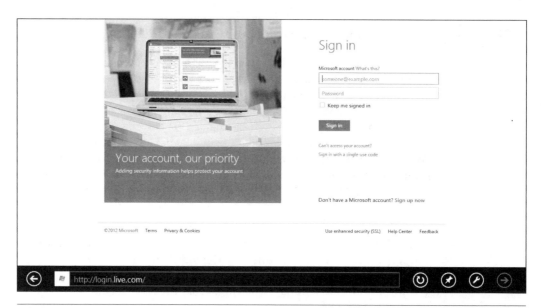

FIGURE 4-21 You'll need your username and password to log in to your Microsoft account.

If you choose a mobile phone number, Microsoft will send a confirmation code to you by text message. Click or tap OK on the Microsoft account web page you have open in Internet Explorer and it will take you back to the Security Info page, which will now show the name of your PC with links underneath to Confirm or Delete. When the text message arrives, click or tap the Confirm link, enter the code from the message, and click or tap the Submit button. A new web page will open confirming your computer is now a trusted PC. If you go back to the Account Info page, you'll see the name of your PC listed under Trusted PC further down the page.

Microsoft account   Simon Bisson

Trusted PC

BLODWEN
Delete

OfficeNext
You're currently using this PC.
Delete

BuildTablet
Delete

Ivor
Delete

SimonSurface
Delete

5

Share Files Among Computers with a Windows 8 Homegroup

HOW TO...

- Understand different type of network connections
- Set up an Internet connection
- Connect to a wireless network
- Use Airplane mode to save battery
- Fix problems with your network connection
- Set up a homegroup between your computers
- Share files in a homegroup
- Change your homegroup password

Your PC can do a lot more when you connect it to other computers. If you have more than one PC at home, you can connect them together with a network cable or a Wi-Fi access point and share files, enabling you to view your photos or watch a video on one computer even if the folder or file is stored on a different computer. When you connect your computers, you can share peripherals as well. You can use the same external hard drive to back up all your computers using File History (described in Chapter 4) and you can share the same printer rather than having to buy a separate printer to use with each PC. This interconnection of computers and peripherals is called a *network*, and in Windows 8 a network that you use at home is called a *homegroup*.

Something else you can share among all the computers you have at home is your Internet connection. That's another kind of networking, but because the connection works in a similar way to a network, you'll find several of the tools to manage your online connection grouped together with the other network tools in Windows 8.

Understand Different Network Connections

There are three main ways you can connect your computers together to form a network:

- **Use Ethernet cables** If you want to connect only two computers together, you can connect them directly with an Ethernet crossover cable. If you want to connect more than two computers together via Ethernet cable, or if you want to connect two or more networked computers to the Internet as well as to each other, then you also need to connect them to a *router*. A router is a device that forwards (routes) the information you send and receive to the right place, from computer to computer or out onto the Internet (so, for example, you can use the same cable both to access a website and to stream music from one computer to another in your home). If you have a broadband modem for connecting to the Internet, it may already have a router built in so you can connect multiple computers to it; if not, you can connect a separate router to your modem to share your Internet connection. A router also has a built-in firewall, so it provides another layer of protection against viruses and other malware (in addition to the Windows Firewall that we'll be looking at in Chapter 18). Many notebook and desktop PCs have a built-in Ethernet port in which to insert the Ethernet cable; if yours does not, you can buy an Ethernet adapter that connects to a USB port or uses an expansion slot inside a desktop PC.
- **Use your existing power wiring** You can buy HomePlug adapters for each computer and connect them to a power outlet in each room (you'll need a HomePlug adapter for your broadband modem or router as well). HomePNA is a similar technology that uses the phone jack instead of a power outlet.
- **Use a wireless connection** If you don't want to have cables running between your computers, you can connect them with a *wireless* network, using a Wi-Fi access point (which also acts as a router to send data to the correct destination, so these devices are sometimes known as *wireless routers*). Again, some broadband modems have a Wi-Fi access point built in so you can also get all of your computers online wirelessly; if your modem does not, you can use an Ethernet cable to connect the Wi-Fi access point to your modem. All modern notebooks and tablets have Wi-Fi capability built in; Wi-Fi capability is less common in desktop PCs, but again, you can buy a Wi-Fi adapter that connects to a USB port or fits into an internal expansion slot inside the PC case.

Set Up an Internet Connection

If you haven't yet set up your broadband modem, router or Wi-Fi access point, refer to the manual that came with your hardware to do that. The Microsoft Support website has a helpful guide to setting up network hardware at http://windows.microsoft .com/en-US/windows-8/connect-to-the-internet. Once it's plugged in and working, connect your computer by following the instructions in the next section and then try opening a web page; often, the modem will connect automatically. If not, you can use Windows 8 to configure it. Right-click or press and hold on the network icon in the taskbar and choose Open Network and Sharing Center (you can also find the Network and Sharing Center in the Control Panel under Network and Internet).

In the Network and Sharing Center window, click or tap Set Up a New Connection or Network. In the Set Up a Connection or Network wizard that opens, choose the second option, Set Up a New Network, as shown next, and click or tap Next. Windows will scan your network for unconfigured routers or access points. Select your device from the list, click or tap Next, and then fill in the details for your Internet connection.

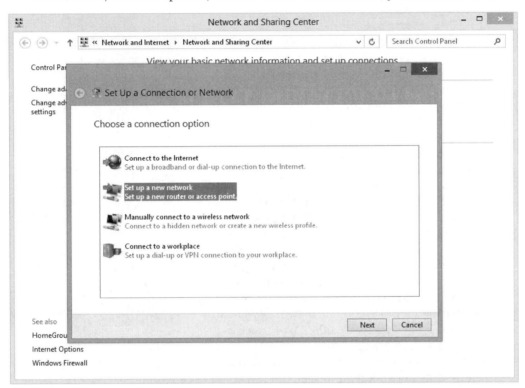

Connect to a Network

When you first installed or set up Windows 8 (as described in Chapter 1), if your Wi-Fi network was already up and running, with an Internet connection, you may have connected to it as part of setup. If so, Windows will remember the connection and carry on using it automatically. If you didn't connect to your wireless network during setup, or if you want to switch to using a different Wi-Fi network, we'll show you how to do that in this section.

Similarly, if your wired network is already set up, then all you need to do is plug an Ethernet cable from your router into your computer and Windows 8 will connect automatically. If your wired network is already set up to connect to the Internet, that's all you need to get online as well. To switch to using a new wired network, all you have to do is plug in the Ethernet cable for it.

Find Out Whether Your Computer Is Connected to a Network

You can easily see whether your computer is connected to a network in Windows 8. Here are three ways to do so:

- Open the Charms bar and look at the panel that appears on the left of the screen showing the date and time; if your computer is connected to a network, you'll see an icon for either a wired network (it shows a network cable in front of a computer) or a wireless network (it shows the signal strength as a number of white bars, like the number of bars on your mobile phone).
- Click or tap Settings in the Charms bar; you'll see the same network icon at the bottom of the Settings pane with the name of the network underneath it ("Graculus" in this example). Click or tap the network icon to open the Networks pane, shown in Figure 5-1, where you can see the network your computer is connected to (you'll see the word Connected after the name) and other networks you can connect to (if there are other Wi-Fi access points within range, or if you have a secure connection to your workplace).
- If you're on the desktop, the notification area on the right end of the taskbar shows the same network icon, which you can tap or click to open the Network pane.

If you see a triangle with an exclamation mark on the icon for a wired network, it means you're connected to the network but it's not working properly. If the wireless network icon shows a set of grayed-out signal bars and an asterisk, then there are Wi-Fi connections available but you're not connected to any of them; if there aren't any Wi-Fi networks in range, you'll see the same grayed-out icon with a cross in the corner.

Choose Whether to Share Devices on a Network

The first time you connect to a network, Windows may ask "Do you want to turn on sharing between PCs and connect to devices on this network?" If this is your home or work network and you want to be able to see other computers, share files, or connect to a network printer, choose Yes, Turn On Sharing and Connect to Devices. If you're using a public network in a coffee shop or airport, choose No, Don't Turn On Sharing and Connect to Devices; it's unlikely that there will be any devices you need to connect to, and turning on sharing will let other people on the same network see your computer.

You can change your mind about sharing later; right-click or press and hold on the name of your network in the Networks pane and choose Turn Sharing On or Off to see this question from Windows again. If you're having problems sharing files with your homegroup or connecting to devices such as your printer, make sure sharing is turned on for the network you're connected to.

Connect to a Wi-Fi Network

When you look at the Networks pane to see the list of Wi-Fi networks your computer can connect to (see Figure 5-1), you might see two different kinds of icons: one for secure wireless networks and one for open wireless networks.

The icon for a secure network displays just the bars that indicate how strong the signal from that network is (usually, the closer you are to the access point, the stronger the signal and the faster the connection). When you click or tap the name of a secure wireless network in the Networks pane to connect to it, you have to type in the password (unless you're using one of the automatic ways to connect to your router, covered a bit later). You'll also see the

FIGURE 5-1   See the available wireless networks from the Networks section of the Settings Charm. Note the mix of open and closed networks.

Connect Automatically check box; if you want to use this wireless network again, click or tap to select the check box and Windows will save the password and remember the connection. Click or tap Connect after you've entered the password. After a few seconds, the word Connected will appear next to the name of the network.

If you're syncing settings through your Microsoft account and you've made the PC you're currently using a trusted PC (as explained in Chapter 4), the passwords for wireless networks you've already used on other Windows 8 computers where you log in with the same Microsoft account will sync onto your PC. That means after the first time you connect to a network (when you will need to know the password to get online and sync), you won't have to type in passwords for wireless networks you've already connected to, even if it was on another computer. So when you take a new Windows 8 notebook someplace where you've previously connected to a network, it might connect without you having to do anything—very convenient.

Any wireless network for which you don't have to type in a password to get connected is an *open* network. That means anyone in range can use it; the Wi-Fi networks in coffee shops and airports are usually open networks. If you leave your wireless network at home open, any of your neighbors could use it—meaning less bandwidth for you, and also possibly leaving you liable if they download illegal content over your connection. It also means a hacker could be using the wireless network and running a tool called a *sniffer* that can look at information passing over the network, such as any passwords you type in on sites that aren't protected by their own encryption. If a website address starts with the word https instead of http, it's a secure connection protected by encryption; if not, a hacker on an open wireless network with the right tools would be able to see anything you type into that site.

Because of the risks of using open wireless networks, Windows 8 marks them with a special icon: a shield with an exclamation mark next to the signal bars. When you click or tap the name of an open wireless network in the Networks pane, Windows also warns you that other people might be able to see information you send over the wireless network.

Some open wireless networks still require a password, but you have to enter it into a web page rather than in the Networks pane. If that's the case, Windows will usually open Internet Explorer automatically and load the web page where you enter the password. If your browser doesn't open automatically but you see the word Limited rather than Connected next to the name of the wireless network in the Networks pane, open a browser window yourself and try to load a new page like Bing.com. If you need

How to... Connect with Wi-Fi Protected Setup

There's an easy way to make a secure connection to Wi-Fi access points that support a standard called Wi-Fi Protected Setup (WPS), or Microsoft's Windows Connect Now (WCN) technology. The first time you connect to a WPS Wi-Fi network, Windows 8 will ask you to press the button on the Wi-Fi access point to make a secure connection (or you can type in the PIN that's printed on the access point). That means you don't have to create a password for the wireless network and type that in on your PC. It's particularly useful if you're connecting devices like wireless printers and cameras, where typing in a password is more awkward because you don't have a keyboard.

to type a password, the page where you enter this should now load. (If it doesn't, take a look at the troubleshooting steps later in this chapter.)

An open wireless network where you type the password into a web page doesn't protect you the way a secure wireless network does because the network traffic isn't encrypted, but it does stop people who don't know the password from connecting.

Use Your Smartphone to Get Online

Your data plan may let you use your smartphone like a modem, to connect your notebook or tablet to the Internet when there isn't a Wi-Fi access point to use (you will usually have to pay an extra fee to your mobile carrier to use this feature). When you turn on the Internet sharing or *tethering* option on your phone, it will appear in the list of wireless networks like any other Wi-Fi access point and you can connect to it.

Because mobile data is expensive and you may have a limited amount of bandwidth, you should mark it as a mobile connection so that Windows doesn't use it to download updates. Right-click or press and hold on the name of the network in the Networks pane and choose Set as Metered Connection. You can also see how much bandwidth you've used on this network; right-click or press and hold on the name of the network in the Networks pane and choose Show Estimated Data Usage.

Turn On Airplane Mode

At the top of the Networks pane is a slider that lets you turn on Airplane mode. When you activate Airplane mode, Windows turns off your Wi-Fi radio (and any other radios in your computer, like Bluetooth or GPS) to comply with U.S. Federal Aviation Administration (FAA) regulations. Unless you're flying on a plane that offers Wi-Fi service, you can only use your notebook or tablet after takeoff if you've turned off Wi-Fi and any other radios. Airplane mode gives you one convenient place to turn all your radios off at once. If you want to turn different radios back on individually

How to... ## Connect to a Hidden Wireless Network

If the wireless network you want to connect to isn't visible in the Networks pane, it might be a hidden network that doesn't broadcast its name. If you know the name of the network and the password for it, you can still connect to it. Start the Set Up a New Connection or Network wizard from the Network and Sharing Center, choose Manually Connect to a Wireless Network, and click or tap Next. On the next wizard page, fill in the network name, the security type and encryption type that it uses, and the security key, then click or tap Next.

Hidden wireless networks aren't actually any more secure than a standard secure wireless network, because even though Windows can't see them, the kind of network tools a hacker users will find them easily. You might have to use a hidden network that someone else has set up, but don't make your own wireless network hidden.

(just Wi-Fi and not Bluetooth, for example), you do that in the Wireless section of PC Settings. You can also use Airplane mode to turn off Wi-Fi if you want to save battery power while you're using your notebook if you don't need to be online, or if you know you can't use any of the available wireless networks.

Troubleshoot Your Network Connection

If you find that your network connection isn't working correctly, the Network and Sharing Center includes a set of troubleshooting tools that will try to find and automatically fix problems. If you have the desktop open, right-click the network icon in the notification area of the taskbar and choose Troubleshoot Problems to look for problems with the network you're currently using. This opens a troubleshooter wizard that tests your network connection by seeing if some common websites are accessible; if not, it checks various settings, changes any that don't match what it expects to see, and tries to connect to those websites again. If it can reach them after the changes, the wizard asks if it has fixed your problem. If it still can't connect, it will offer some suggestions for checking and repairing the network connection at your router or access point.

If it can reach the test sites straightaway, the wizard offers you two choices: to get help reaching a particular website or network folder that you can't access, or to see other network troubleshooting options.

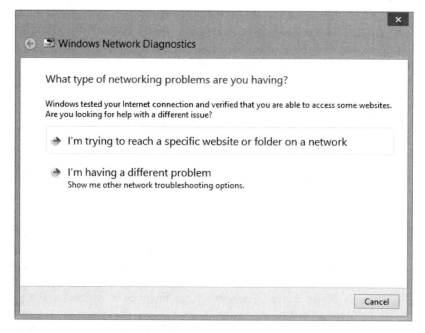

If you choose the second option, I'm Having a Different Problem, you are given a choice of three more troubleshooter wizards that can help with network problems: allow other people to connect to your PC remotely, connect to a work network using DirectAccess, or check the settings for a specific network adapter in your computer.

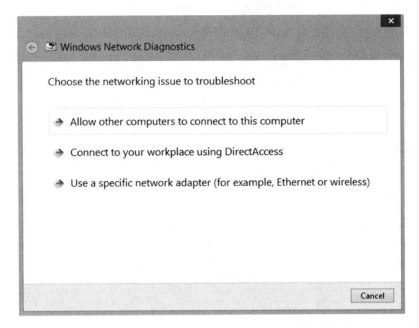

If you want to jump straight to the list of the different troubleshooting tools, open the Network and Sharing Center and click or tap Troubleshoot Problems. This offers you some of the same troubleshooters (Incoming Connections has more detailed tools for solving problems with remote connections), plus one for dealing with problems in a homegroup. Pick the one that looks closest to your problem.

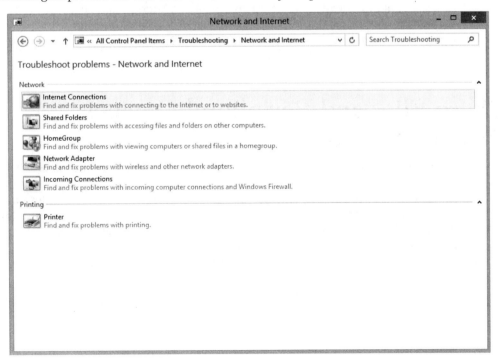

If all the settings are correct and none of the suggestions for fixing your network work, the wizard will tell you that it can't identify the problem. Often this means the problem is not with your PC. If you're at home, you can check with your ISP to see if there is a fault; if you're traveling, contact the person who runs the network you're trying to connect to. Click or tap the View Detailed Information link at the bottom of the wizard to see which tests the troubleshooter has run and what the results are; they may be useful for the customer support team at your ISP.

If you find that you can use the network from another computer without the same problems, you can click or tap Explore Additional Options instead to get a list of ways you can get more help. (If you've opened the troubleshooting report click or tap Next to get back to the page of the wizard with the button to Explore Additional Options.) We'll cover these tools in detail in Chapter 19.

If you've tried to connect to a wireless network that doesn't get you online properly and you want Windows to stop trying to connect using that network, right-click or press and hold on the name of the network in the Networks pane and choose Forget This Network.

Change More Sharing Settings

If you're having a problem seeing other computers on a network or sharing files with them, and just turning sharing on from the Network pane doesn't help, open the Network and Sharing Center and click or tap the Change Advanced Sharing Settings link in the navigation pane on the left. This lets you control the settings for network discovery, automatically setting up any devices Windows detects on the network, and file and printer sharing, on the current network and any other network you connect to. For security reasons, it's best to only turn on sharing for *private* networks that you trust, like your home and work networks.

Share Files and Peripheral Devices in a Homegroup

If you have several computers at home, once you have them all connected to a wired or wireless network, you can also share files between them by setting up a Windows homegroup. If you use a network to share files at work, that puts your files on a *server*, a specific computer that stores files centrally and manages services (like shared printers) and sometimes even programs that everyone can use over the network. A homegroup doesn't need a server. Your files stay on the same computer they're already on, but all the PCs in the homegroup can access them, so you can view or edit a file stored on one computer from a different computer.

If you like to take the photos off your digital camera on your desktop PC where you have a large, removable drive to store them and a larger screen for viewing and editing them, when you set up a homegroup you can also view them when you're sitting on the couch using a Windows tablet, for example (as long as your desktop computer is turned on). Or if you've bought a music album and downloaded it to one computer, you can play the same tracks on another computer without having to copy the files across.

Your homegroup is protected by a password, so you can control who can connect to it and see your files. You choose the folders and libraries you share in the homegroup. You can also decide whether to let other users only see your files or edit them as well.

 To join a homegroup, your PCs need to be running Windows 7, Windows 8, or Windows RT. If you have a PC with Windows XP or Windows Vista, you can still share files with them over a network, but it's not as easy as setting up a homegroup.

Set Up Your Homegroup

When you set up a PC with Windows 8 on it, a homegroup is automatically set up for you (unless there's already one on your home network), but no files are shared and no connections are made until you tell Windows you want to use the homegroup. Open PC Settings, click or tap the HomeGroup section, click or tap Create on the HomeGroup page (see Figure 5-2), and then select the libraries and devices you want to share from the list that appears.

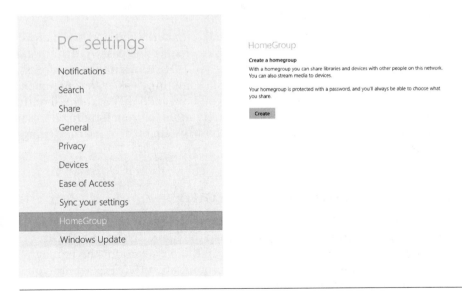

FIGURE 5-2   Create a new Homegroup from inside PC Settings.

If you have a Windows RT device, you can join the homegroup and see files that are on other computers, but you can't share files from Windows RT (which would run down the battery too quickly).

- Under Libraries and Devices, you can choose to share the files that are in the Documents, Music, Pictures, and Videos libraries. You can share one library and not another; just swipe or drag the slider for the library you want to share so it changes from Not Shared to Shared. The other people in your homegroup can only view the files in these libraries; if you want to let them edit some or all of your files or to share other files, we'll show you how to change those sharing settings in Explorer in the next section.

 When you share a library, that shares all the folders that you've included in the library, even if they're on a removable drive. That means you don't have to unplug the drive and connect it to another PC when you want to see those files. The more you use libraries to organize your files, the more useful your homegroup will be.

- If you have a printer or other peripherals like a scanner connected to your computer, you can share them with the homegroup by moving the Printers and Devices slider to Shared. That way, each computer doesn't have to have its own printer; you can connect a printer to one PC and enable everyone else in the homegroup to use it.
- The libraries you share through the homegroup are available on the other PCs in the homegroup. But if you want to stream media files like music and movies to devices such as a connected TV or a game console that's connected to your network but can't actually join the homegroup, then move the slider in the Media Devices section to On.
- Anyone who wants to join your homegroup needs to know the password (and be on the same network as you). Windows creates this password automatically, and you can see it in the HomeGroup area of PC Settings under Membership (see Figure 5-3). If you want to change it to something easier to remember, you have to go to the Control Panel (we'll show you how to do that at the end of this chapter).
- If you don't want to share your files any more, or you don't need to see files on other computers, you can leave the homegroup by clicking or tapping the Leave button in the Membership section.

Join an Existing Homegroup

On your other PCs, you join a homegroup in the same way you set it up on the first PC. Open PC Settings and click or tap the HomeGroup section. Instead of the Create button, you'll see a space to type in the password for the homegroup. If you're syncing settings using your Microsoft account, any other PCs where you sign in with the Microsoft account will already have the password, so you don't need to type it in again (as long as you've made the computer a trusted PC; see Chapter 4 to learn

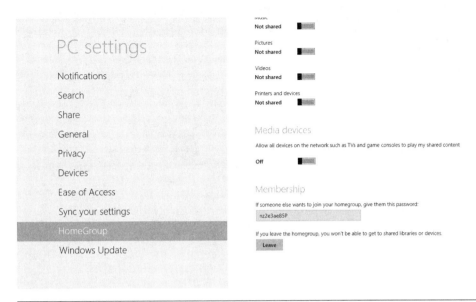

FIGURE 5-3   Windows creates a complex password for your homegroup that other people need to know before they can join it.

more about this). Select any libraries and devices you want to share from this PC and set whether media devices on your network can stream your files in the same way you did when you created the homegroup.

If you want to join a homegroup from a PC that's running Windows 7, type the word **homegroup** into the search box on the Start menu to find the HomeGroup control panel, where you can make the same choices about which libraries and devices to share and whether to let media devices stream your files. Click Join Now to join the homegroup.

Open Files from Your Homegroup

Once you've joined a homegroup, you'll see it listed in the Navigation pane in File Explorer and in many file dialog boxes in desktop programs. You can also use your homegroup in the File Picker when you're looking for a location to open or save a file in a Windows Store app; click or tap the arrow next to Files at the top of the screen and choose Homegroup.

When you look at the homegroup, you'll see the name of the homegroup and then the names of all the computers inside the homegroup; click or tap the name of the computer to see the shared libraries and folders (see Figure 5-4). You won't see any PCs that are turned off, hibernating, or asleep.

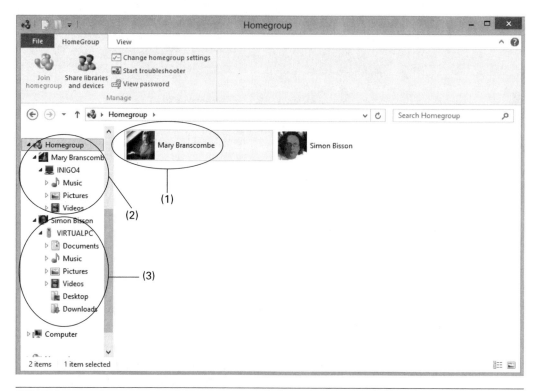

FIGURE 5-4 Homegroup (1) User view, click to see PCs and files, (2) Mary's PC and libraries in the navigation pane, (3) Simon's PC and libraries.

 Tip To use a printer that's shared through a homegroup, use the print command in your program or app as normal and the homegroup printer will be listed automatically. The PC that the printer is physically plugged into has to be switched on for you to print to it.

Choose How to Share Files and Folders with Your Homegroup

The libraries that you share let other people in your homegroup look at or listen to your files, but not change them. If you want to let other people in your homegroup change some of your files, or if you want to share files that aren't in the four libraries that you can share directly from the HomeGroup section in PC Settings, or if you want to stop people in your homegroup from seeing a particular folder in one of your shared libraries, you can do that in File Explorer.

To share a file or folder that's not in one of the four libraries (or a library you've created yourself) or to let other people edit specific files or folders in the shared libraries, select the file, folder, or library in Explorer, click or tap the Share tab on the ribbon, and then select how you want to share it with the homegroup (or who else you want to share it with) from the Share With list. You can choose:

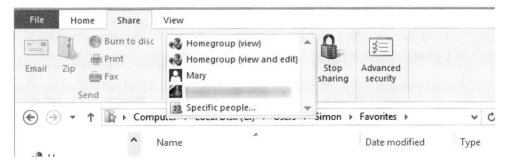

- **Homegroup (view)**   Choose this option if you want to allow all homegroup users to be able to see and open the file, folder, or library but you don't want them to be able to make changes to it. This is the default option for any libraries you've already included in the homegroup.
- **Homegroup (view and edit)**   If you want everyone in your homegroup to be able to edit this file, folder, or library, this is the option to choose.

 If you let other people edit your files, they can also delete them. File History will let you get files from your libraries back if someone deletes them by accident, so make sure you've turned it on (see Chapter 4 for details on how to do that).

- *Username*   The Share With list will show the names of other users who have accounts on your PC, as well as the names of other users in your homegroup. To share the file, folder, or library with one specific person but not let them make changes to it, click or tap their name in the list.

 If there are several people you could share a file with, there will be too many names to fit in the ribbon, so you can scroll through the list or use the arrow at the bottom to see the whole list at once.

- **Specific people**   Choose this option if you want to share a file, folder, or library with someone and let them make changes. If you're part of a network as well as a homegroup, you will also see their names in the File Sharing dialog box that opens so you can share files with them. Select the name of the person you want to share with from the drop-down list and then click or tap the Add button; if there are a lot of names, you can start typing the name you want and Windows will jump to the first matching name. When you add the person, you'll see their name in the Name list with details in the Permission Level column of what they're allowed to do to your files. By default, they can only see files, not change them, so the permission level is Read. If you want to let them edit your files, click or tap anywhere on their name or the permission level and change Read to Read/Write, as shown in Figure 5-5. If you no longer want to share the file, folder, or library with the person, choose Remove instead. When you've set the permissions the way you want them, click or tap the Share button.

- If you don't want to share a file, folder, or library any more, or there's a specific file or folder in a shared library you don't want to share at all, select it in Explorer and then click or tap Stop Sharing on the ribbon.

If you prefer, you can right-click or press and hold on a file, folder, or library in Explorer and choose Share With on the context menu that appears, offering the same options you see on the ribbon.

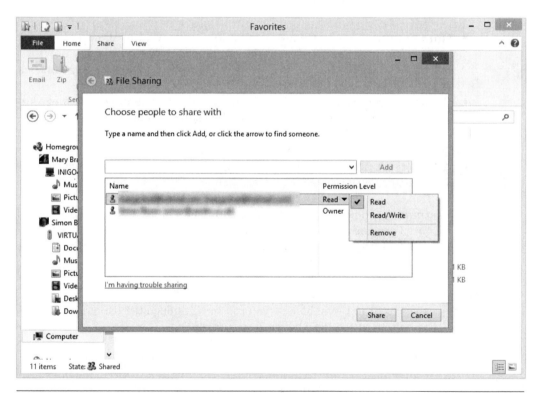

FIGURE 5-5 The Permission Level column in the File Sharing dialog box allows you to choose what specific people you share files with can do with the files you share.

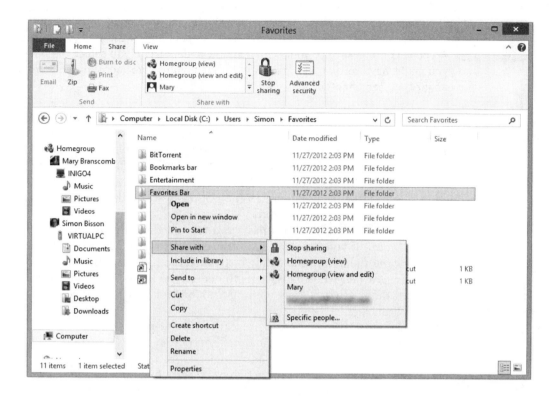

Change the Homegroup Password

The password that Windows 8 creates for your homegroup is complex enough to be very hard for anyone to guess, but that does make it hard to remember. You can always go back to the HomeGroup section in PC Settings to see the password again, but if you prefer you can change it to a simpler password (just remember that also makes it easier to guess). You can also ask Windows to create a new complex password for you, if you think someone outside the homegroup has found out the password or if you decide to block someone who already has access to your homegroup from using it anymore.

Because changing your password isn't something you need to do often (and something you shouldn't do without a good reason, because it means everyone who uses the homegroup has to enter the new password before they can share files), you have to do that in the Control Panel. Open the Control Panel (you can do that quickly from the Settings charm when you're in the desktop) and, under Network and Internet, click or tap Choose Homegroup and Sharing Options. In the HomeGroup control panel, click or tap the Change the Password link.

The Change the Password link has a UAC shield icon to remind you that you're changing an important setting in Windows. Depending on the way you have User Account Controls set up, your screen might go dark when you select the link or you might have to type in a password for an administrator account. To learn more about UAC, see Chapter 3.

It's best if you have all the computers in your homegroup turned on when you change the password because you can only enter the new password on a homegroup computer if there's another computer already using the new password that's turned on at the time. Having all your computers on also makes it easier to go around and change the password on all of them straightaway, so they get access again. You'll see a reminder of that in the Change Your Homegroup Password dialog box. When you're ready, click or tap Change the Password.

Windows creates a new, complex password for you (click or tap the two arrows on the refresh button if you want to get a different password), or you can type the password you want to use into the dialog box. Once the password has been changed, you will see the new password on screen; you can write it down or click or tap on the link to print out the password along with instructions for how to change the password on other computers.

Now you can enter the new password in the HomeGroup section in PC Settings or in the Homegroup control panel on the other computers.

When you open the HomeGroup section in PC Settings or the Homegroup control panel on your other computers, you'll see the name of the person who changed the homegroup password; that way, if they haven't given you the new password, you know who to ask.

6

Browse the Web

HOW TO...

- Understand the new Windows 8 version of Internet Explorer
- Search inside web pages
- Manage multiple web pages in tabs
- Pin a website to the Start screen or your taskbar
- Print web pages from the Devices charm
- Set your home page or have multiple home pages
- Work with Internet Explorer on the desktop
- Manage add-ons, plugins, and ActiveX controls
- Stay safe while you browse the Web

Windows 8 includes a new version of the familiar Internet Explorer web browser. In fact, it includes two new versions. There's the latest desktop version of the browser, Internet Explorer 10 (often called IE 10), which has all the features of the Windows 7 version, like pinned websites, plus better performance, better support for the standards used to make the latest cool websites, and new tools to protect your privacy and security online. But you also get a Windows 8 version of the IE 10 browser that looks a lot like other Windows Store apps, with an interface that's easy to use with your fingers on a touchscreen and leaves more space on screen to see the web page you're looking at. In this chapter, we'll look at the differences between the two versions of IE and how to get the most out of both of them.

 Note There are some tasks you can only perform in the desktop version of IE even though they affect both versions of the browser, like changing settings; we only cover these once in this chapter so be sure to look in both sections.

Understand the New Windows 8 Version of IE

Open the Windows 8 version of IE by clicking or tapping the Internet Explorer tile on the Start screen.

If you prefer to use a different browser, like Chrome or Firefox, you can download and install another browser and make that the default for viewing websites. Both Chrome and Firefox are expected to have versions that have the same option of opening web pages either in a desktop browser or in a finger-friendly version. If you do make another web browser the default on your system, clicking or tapping the tile for the Windows 8 version of IE will open the desktop version of IE instead.

By default, when you open IE, the home page is a version of Microsoft's MSN website specially designed for Windows 8. The design matches the look of the Windows 8 Start screen, and the layout is optimized for the wider screens that are common on new Windows 8 PCs. But just like any other browser, you can set your own home page instead.

If you sign in to Windows with a Microsoft account, your home page will sync to your other Windows 8 PCs, along with the list of your favorite websites and saved usernames and passwords for the websites you log in to.

When you first open a web page, the app bar with the address box appears at the bottom of the screen automatically, as shown in Figure 6-1. As the web page is loading, if you decide that you don't want to see that particular page, you can stop it by clicking or tapping the cross icon that appears to the right of the web address (in place of the Refresh icon shown in Figure 6-1). If a web page that you *do* want to see doesn't load completely, click or tap the Refresh icon to the right of the address box to attempt to reload it. Click or tap Back to go back to the previous page. Click or tap Pin to Start to pin the current page as a tile on the Start screen. Click or tap to open the Page Tools menu. Click or tap Forward to move to the next page.

Once you start scrolling or swiping your way down a web page to see more of its content, the address bar hides itself. You can make it reappear, like any other app bar, by right-clicking or swiping up from the bottom of the screen or down from the top. Those actions also open the tab area at the top of the screen. We'll explain how to work with tabs later in this chapter, but first let's look at how you browse to web pages you want to visit.

Open a Web Page

You can open a different web page from the one you're currently viewing either by following a link on the web page you're looking at, by typing the address of the web page into the address box, or by searching using your default search engine

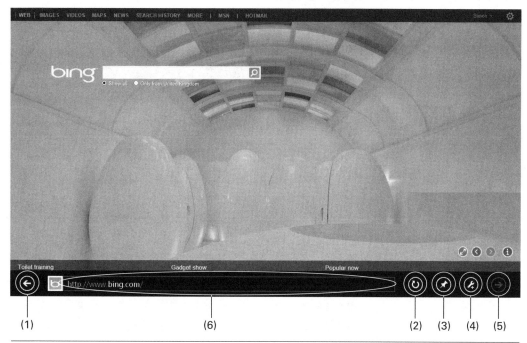

FIGURE 6-1   (1) Back will go back to the previous page; (2) Refresh will reload the page; (3) Pin to Start will pin the current page as a tile on the Start screen; (4) Page Tools menu; (5) Forward will move to the next page; (6) Start browsing the Web by typing a website address in the address box.

How to... Choose Which Version of IE to Open

When you click or tap a web link in an email message or in a message from one of your friends on a social network that you see in the People app, or when you click or tap a pinned website on the Start screen, the web page opens in the Windows 8 version of IE. If you'd rather have such actions open the web page in the desktop version of IE, open the desktop version now by clicking or tapping View on the Desktop in the Page Tools menu, choose Tools | Internet Options, and click or tap the Programs tab in the Internet Options dialog box.

If you want to change the IE version in which websites pinned to the Start screen open, check the Open Internet Explorer Tiles on the Desktop check box. If you want to change settings for all websites, do that from the Choose How You Open Links drop-down menu (when this is open it hides the checkbox). Choose Always in Internet Explorer to open all links in the Windows 8 version of IE, or Always in Internet Explorer on the Desktop to open all links in the desktop version of IE. Some web pages work better in the desktop version of IE; if you want to always use the Windows 8 version

(Continued)

of IE except in cases where the website has content that only works on the desktop, choose Let Internet Explorer Decide.

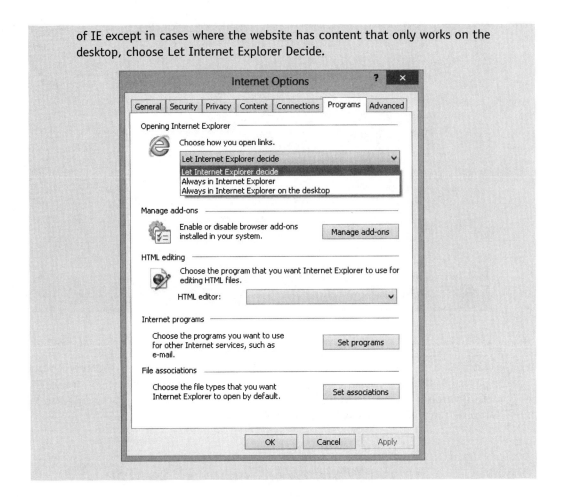

(as described in the next section). You can also go straight to websites you've visited before; as soon as you click or tap in the address box to enter a new web address, IE shows you tiles for websites that that you've pinned to the Start screen (we'll explain how to do that later in this chapter). Swipe or scroll to see the Frequent set of tiles, which includes the eight websites you visit the most often, shown in Figure 6-2. Swipe or scroll across further to see your Favorites; this is the same list of bookmarked websites you see in the desktop version of IE.

Right-click or press and hold on a tile in the Pinned, Frequent, or Favorites list to open a menu where you can open the website in a new tab or delete it from the list. You can do the same with links on the web pages you visit; right-click or press and hold the link and then choose Open in New Tab.

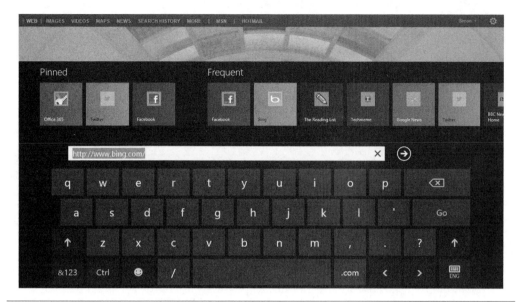

FIGURE 6-2   The tiles for websites you visit often show the icon for the website and are color coded to match that icon.

If you don't see a tile for the website you want to visit, just start typing the name of the website. When you type the first letter, IE will suggest websites you've been to before that start with that letter, as well as Favorites, Pinned websites, and Frequent websites. IE fills in the address box with the address for the first website on the list; if that's the website you want to visit, simply press ENTER on the keyboard (or click or tap the Go arrow to the right of the address box) to open it. If the website you want to visit is one of the others in the Results area, click or tap its icon.

You Can Swipe or Flip to the Next Page on a Touchscreen

If you're using Windows 8 on a tablet or a computer with a touchscreen, instead of tapping or clicking the Forward and Back buttons in the address bar to navigate to web pages you've previously visited, you can just swipe your finger across the screen. Swipe to the right to go back a page; swipe to the left to go to the next page.

And if you turn on the Flip Ahead feature, you can swipe to the next page even if you haven't already opened it. Open the Settings charm and choose Internet Options; under Flip Ahead, drag the slider to turn the feature from Off to On. Now when you have a page of search results open or you're on the first page of a news story that's split over multiple pages, you can swipe ahead and IE will figure out which page you want to go to and open it. This doesn't work on all web pages, but when it does it's very useful.

As you type more letters, IE narrows down the list of websites in the Results area. It's okay to include spaces when you're typing; IE will match what you're typing to the titles of pages rather than to their addresses.

If IE can't find any websites that match what you've typed, it will tell you that no previously visited pages match your search. If you know the address, you can type it all in by hand and then press ENTER or click or tap Go to open the page.

Search the Web

You don't have to type a web address in the address box to visit a website. You can search the Web very quickly using Microsoft's Bing search (or your favorite search engine) just by typing in the address box the search terms you're looking for. IE will keep showing you pages you've visited in the Results area if they match what you're typing, but when you press ENTER or click or tap the Go button, the search results page on Bing will open.

Change advanced settings

There are only a few settings you can change from within the Windows 8 version of IE, like turning on Flip Ahead and setting the zoom level at which websites open (you can have them load at up to 400% zoom of the normal size, in which case you see a small portion of the web page greatly enlarged, or shrunk to 75% or even 50%, in which case you see much more of the web page but at a smaller size). You can also quickly delete your browsing history if you want to clear the pages you see in the Frequent list. Open the Settings charm in IE and choose Internet Options to do any of those.

If you want to change other options, you do that in the desktop version of IE; the changes you make there affect both versions of IE. In the Windows 8 version of IE, open the desktop version by clicking or tapping View on the Desktop in the Page Tools menu. After it opens, choose Tools | Internet Options to open the Internet Options dialog box, as shown in Figure 6-3. We'll cover the most useful settings you can change in this dialog box now and show you some of the more advanced options later in the chapter when we look at the features in the desktop version of Internet Explorer.

Change Your Default Search Engine

You can use Google, Yahoo, or other search engines in IE 10 by visiting their websites.

FIGURE 6-3 Customize your browser properties in the Internet Options dialog box.

If you want to make one of them your default search engine instead of Bing, you can do that in the desktop version of IE 10 (and it will apply to both versions). Click or tap the Tools icon in the top right corner of the desktop IE window (it looks like a cog) and choose Manage Add-ons.

In the Manage Add-ons window, shown next, choose Search Providers from the list of Add-on Types. If you see the search engine you want to use in the list on the right, select it and click or tap Set As Default. If you want to see suggestions as you type in your search, check the Search in the Address Bar check box; that sends what you type to the search engine before you finish typing so that the search engine can make suggestions about what you might be looking for, so you can select a suggestion instead of having to type it all in.

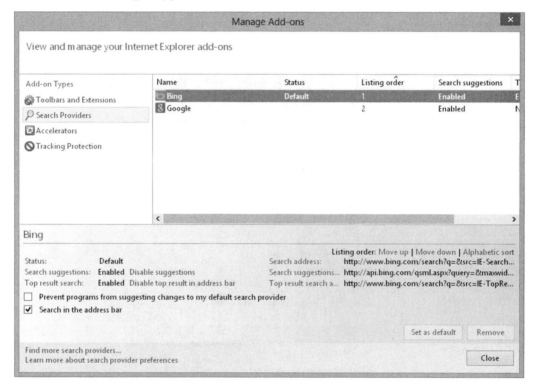

If you don't see the search engine you want to use as your default, click or tap Find More Search Providers at the bottom of the window. This opens the Internet Explorer Gallery website, shown next, where you can use the Search Providers section to add more search engines to the list. Choose Search in the list of topics on the left of the Gallery website to narrow down the list you see to just the main search engines.

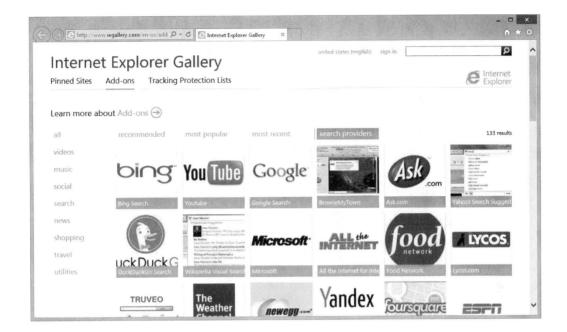

 Tip   You'll find more than just the big name search engines in the Internet Explorer Gallery; you can add search providers for Amazon, Facebook, and Wikipedia to search those websites straight from Internet Explorer.

Click or tap the icon for the search engine you want to add. If you want this to be your default search engine, select Make This My Default Search Provider in the Add Search Provider dialog box that appears. Click or tap Add.

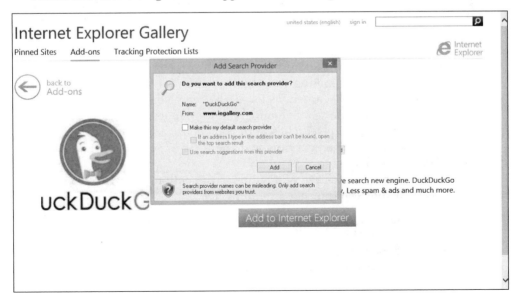

How to... **Stop Programs from Changing Your Default Search Engine**

If you install a browser toolbar (or even other programs), it might try to change the search engine that IE uses. If you want to do that, you can accept the change in the dialog box that IE displays. If you don't, and you don't want software you install to be able to suggest that you change the search engine you use, check the Prevent Programs from Suggesting Changes to My Default Search Provider check box in the dialog box that appears when a program suggests a change. You can check the same check box in the Manage Add-ons window.

☐ Prevent programs from suggesting changes to my default search provider
☑ Search in the address bar

Find more search providers...
Learn more about search provider preferences

You won't see the new search engine listed in the Manage Add-ons window straightaway, but it will be on the list of search engines when you start typing a search, and if you've made it your default search engine, that will apply immediately.

Use Multiple Search Engines

Once you've added more than one search engine to IE, you can choose which one to use for a specific search in the desktop version of IE. Type the words you're searching for into the address bar as usual, but don't press the ENTER key or click or tap the Go arrow to run your search. Instead, look at the menu pane that pops up; depending on what you've typed, this might show matching results from your Favorites and History as well as suggested searches from Bing. If you don't see this list of results, click or tap the Search button on the address bar or click or tap the Autocomplete arrow if you don't want suggestions from Bing. See Figure 6-4.

At the bottom of the list are icons for all the search engines you've added to IE; click or tap the icon for the search engine you want to use for this search. IE will keep using that search engine for searches until you choose a different icon or close all your browser windows. The next time you open IE on the desktop, you'll be restored to your default search engine.

You can also tap or click the Add button at the bottom of the results pane as a quick way of opening the Internet Explorer Gallery.

Search Inside a Web Page

If you're looking for something specific on a long web page, you can search for specific words. You might already know that the fastest way to do that in the desktop version of

IE is to press CTRL-F (you can also choose Tools | File | Find on This Page), which opens the Find bar under the address bar.

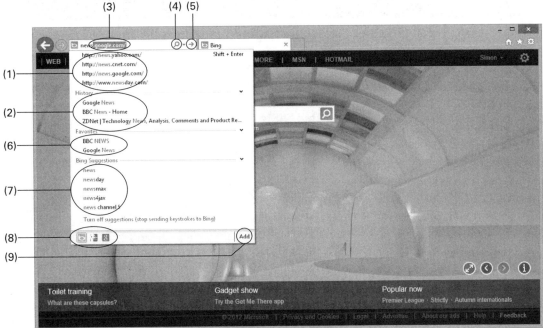

FIGURE 6-4   (1) Search results, (2) Browser history, (3) Autocomplete of most visited site from history, (4) Search button, (5) Go to the selected result, (6) Relevant websites from Favorites, (7) Suggestions from current search engine of possible search terms, (8) Switch search provider by clicking/tapping its icon, (9) Add additional search providers.

In the Windows 8 version of IE, you can also press CTRL-F or open the Page Tools menu and select Find on Page. This opens the Find bar at the bottom of the screen (in place of the address bar).

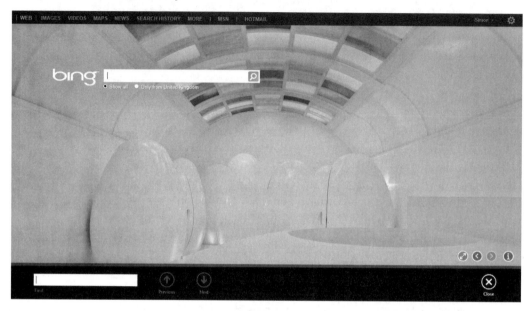

Start typing the words you're looking for and they will be highlighted in yellow on the page. Use the Previous and Next buttons to jump to the previous or next result.

In the desktop version of IE, the Find bar lets you choose to search for whole words (so searching for *transit* won't find *transition* as well, for example) or match the case of what you type (so searching for *Windows* won't find *windows* as well). Click or tap the Options button in the Find bar to change these settings.

Manage Multiple Web Pages with Tabs

Even though each web page you look at in the Windows 8 version of IE fills the whole screen, you can have more than one page open at a time in the browser. As in the familiar desktop browser, IE organizes these pages into tabs. But whereas those browsers display only small tabs containing the website names for the open pages not currently displayed (which the desktop version of IE still does), tabs in the Windows 8 version of IE are large thumbnails, as shown in Figure 6-5. They're easy to select with

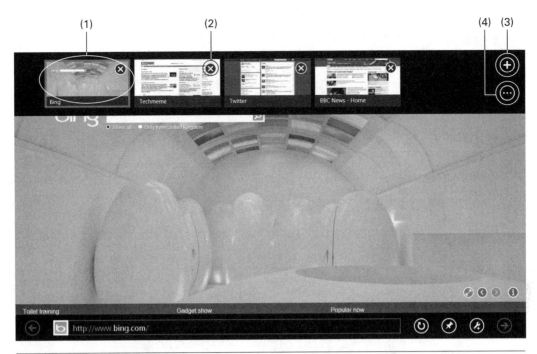

FIGURE 6-5   (1) Current tab will be highlighted, (2) Close the selected tab, (3) Click for a New tab, (4) Tab tools button, opens the tab menu.

your fingers on a touchscreen, and they show a preview of the web page so you can quickly spot the one you want. The tab area is closed while you're browsing, so you have more space on screen to view the website you're looking at. Open it along with the address bar like an app bar, by right-clicking on a blank area of the web page or swiping up from the bottom or down from the top of a touchscreen.

In the tab area, you can see all the web pages you already have open. The page you're looking at is highlighted by a blue frame around the thumbnail.

Switch to a different tab by clicking or tapping its thumbnail. Close any tab you don't need any more by clicking or tapping the × in the corner of the thumbnail. You can close all the open tabs by tapping or clicking the Tab Tools button (a circle with three dots) on the right side of the tab bar and choosing Close Tabs.

Open a new tab by clicking or tapping the plus-sign icon at the top right of the tab bar; this opens a blank tab with the address box and the list of Pinned, Frequent, and Favorite tiles already open. You can also open an InPrivate tab (where IE doesn't store any information about the websites you visit) from the Tab Tools menu. InPrivate browsing is described in the "Browse Without Leaving a Record" section later in this chapter.

When you're reading a web page and you want to open one of its links in a different tab, right-click or press and hold on the link and choose Open in New Tab.

Did You Know?

You Can Spell-Check What You Type in Web Pages

Internet Explorer 10 has a spelling checker built in; if you misspell a word when typing, you'll see a squiggly red underline to warn you about the mistake (a convention you may be familiar with from using Microsoft Word and other programs). IE can also correct some mistakes automatically and make typing on a touchscreen faster by making suggestions for the word it thinks you're trying to type, as shown next. If the suggestion is right, you can tap it rather than typing the rest of the word.

We'll look at the different options for working with tabs in the desktop version of IE later in this chapter.

Pin a Website to the Start Screen

The eight websites you visit the most often appear in the Frequent list, but if you want to make sure you always have a shortcut to a useful website (especially if you don't visit it often enough to keep it in the Frequent list), you can pin it to the Start screen as a tile. Open the website (and right-click or swipe up to display the address bar if you can't see it) and click or tap the Pin to Start icon to open the following dialog box. (You can also choose Add to Favorites from the same icon if you want to bookmark the website but not make a tile for it.)

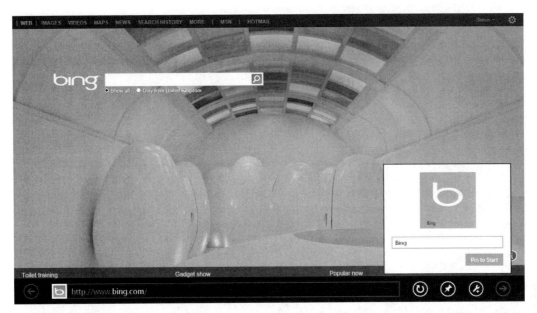

IE uses the predmoninant color of the website's icon as the color for the tile, and you can't change that color, but you can change the name you see on the tile in the dialog that pops up. Click or tap the Pin to Start icon to add the website to the end of the Start screen.

 Pinned websites are also synced between all your Windows 8 PCs if you log in with a Microsoft account.

You can also pin websites to the Start screen from the desktop version of IE: choose Tools | Add Site to Start Screen.

Print a Web Page from the Devices Charm

In the desktop version of IE, you print web pages by choosing Tools | Print (or Print Preview if you want to see what the page will look like first). In the Windows 8 version of IE (and in all Windows Store apps), you print by using the Devices charm on the Charms bar.

When you click or tap the Devices charm, you'll see any printers you have set up in the Devices pane (we'll cover setting up your printer in Chapter 7). Click or tap the printer you want to use and you'll see a print preview of the page right in the Devices pane, as shown in Figure 6-6. If there's more than one page, you can see the rest by clicking the arrows in the preview image, swiping the preview image to show the next page, or typing the page number you want to check in the box under the preview.

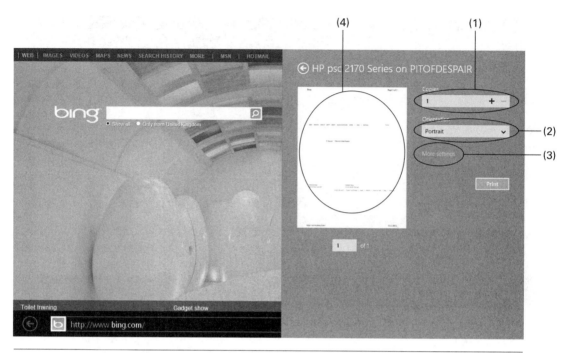

FIGURE 6-6 (1) Number of copies, (2) Set orientation: portrait or landscape, (3) Additional printer settings, (4) Print preview.

If the page looks better on wider paper, use the Orientation drop-down menu to change from Portrait to Landscape. Click or tap More Settings to change any other options your printer offers (for example, it might let you print on both sides of the page or print in black and white instead of color). When you've made any changes you want, click or tap the Back arrow at the top of the pane and click or tap the Print button.

 If you want to choose the headers and footers on printouts of web pages or turn on printing background colors and images (which are off by default because they can make printouts hard to read), do that from the desktop version of IE. Choose Tools | Print | Page Setup. The changes you make here apply in the Windows 8 version of IE as well.

If you want to email a link to a web page rather than printing it, send it to friends in your social network, or save it to the OneNote Windows Store app, you can do that from the Share charm. Open the Share charm from the Charms bar and choose in the Share pane how you want to share the page.

Change Your Home Page

You don't have to keep MSN as your home page, but you can't change it in the Windows 8 version of IE. Open the website you want to set as your home page, and if you're not already in the desktop version of IE, switch to it by opening the Page Tools menu and clicking or tapping View on the Desktop. In the desktop version of IE, choose Tools | Internet Options; the Home Page section on the General tab shows the address of the current home page (or home pages, if you've set more than one home page tab). Click or tap Use Current to make the website you have open your home page, as shown next, in which the home page has been switched from MSN to Bing. You have to close both versions of Internet Explorer before you see your new home page when you open a browser window.

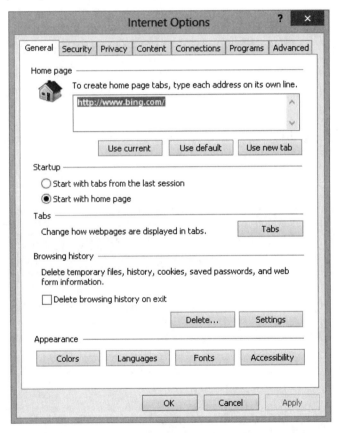

 If you want to go back to having MSN as your home page, click or tap Use Default in the Home Page section. If you don't want a page to load at all when you open the browser, choose Use New Tab and IE will open the new tab page instead.

How to... **Open Your Previously Used Tabs**

Instead of having a home page open when you start IE, you might find it more useful to open the tabs you were using the last time you used the browser. To reload all the tabs that were open when you closed your browser last, click or tap the Start with Tabs from the Last Session radio button in the Startup area of the General tab in Internet Options.

If you want to have several websites open every time you start your browser, in different tabs, type or copy and paste the additional website addresses into the Home Page box. Make sure you enter each one on a separate line.

Work with Internet Explorer on the Desktop

If you've used Internet Explorer 9 or other desktop browsers, the desktop version of IE 10 will look familiar, but if you're used to older browsers like Internet Explorer 6 or 8, the interface is much sparser.

When you first open the desktop version of IE, all you see are the Back and Forward buttons, the address bar, the tab for the web page you're visiting, and three icons in the top right corner (Figure 6-7).

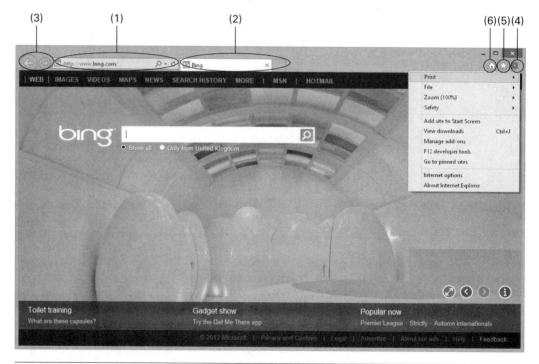

FIGURE 6-7 (1) Combined search and address bar, (2) Tabs, (3) Back and Forward buttons, (4) Tools menu, (5) Favorites, (6) Home.

Use the Home button to open your home page (if you have more than one home page, they will all open in separate tabs). Click or tap the Favorites button to open a pane with tabs for websites you've saved bookmarks for, *feeds* that tell you when websites you choose to subscribe to have been updated and the history of websites you've visited recently. Open the Tools menu to see most of the commands you'll use from day to day, including the link to change your settings in the Internet Options dialog box.

If you want to see the full set of Internet Explorer menus, press the ALT key on your keyboard or right-click or tap and hold on the menu bar and choose Menu Bar.

Manage Tabs and Tab Groups

If you want to open more than one website at once, you can do that using tabs. Right-click or press and hold on a link you want to open and choose Open in New Tab, or hold down the CTRL key as you click or tap the link normally. If you want to open a completely separate browser window, choose Open in New Window.

You can also open a new tab without loading a website; tap or click the blank tab at the far right of the list of tabs at the top of the browser window. You can also right-click or press and hold on any of the tabs and choose New Tab. Click or tap the × icon on a tab to close it.

If you close a tab and then change your mind and want to see it again, right-click or press and hold on any other tab. Choose Reopen Closed Tab to reopen the last tab you closed. Choose Recently Closed Tabs to see a flyout menu of the last few tabs you've closed. You can also open another copy of the current tab by choosing Duplicate Tab.

IE uses tab groups to help you organize the websites you have open. When you open a new tab by following a link, the new tab is put in the same group as the tab the link was in. If you open several links from a list of search results, they will all be put in the same tab group; if you make a new tab and start opening links into tabs from that website, IE will put those in a different tab group. Tab groups are color-coded to make it clear which ones are linked.

You can drag a tab from one tab group to another; the color coding on the tab changes to show that IE has put it in the new group.

If you drag a tab right out of the browser window, it opens in its own browser window.

Choose How Links Open

If you follow a link in an email message or another desktop application, you can choose whether that opens a brand new browser window or opens a new tab (if you already have a browser window open). Choose Tools | Internet Options, click or tap the Tabs button on the General tab, and make a selection in the Open Links from Other Programs In section.

When a link on a web page is set to open in a small new window called a pop-up, you can have Internet Explorer put it in a new tab instead. Choose which you prefer in the When a Pop-up Is Encountered section.

Close Tabs

When you click or tap the Close button (×) in the corner of the Internet Explorer window, if you have more than one tab open, you get the choice of just closing the current tab or closing all the tabs and your browser window.

Pin Websites to the Taskbar

In Chapter 3 we looked at how to pin to the taskbar the desktop programs you use a lot. You can pin your favorite websites to the taskbar as well and get the same useful jump lists. Some websites will even show notifications on the pinned icon, like the number of unread email messages waiting for you on Outlook.com, or add play and pause controls for music or videos you're playing on the website to the thumbnail you see when you hover your mouse over the icon in the taskbar. To pin a website to the taskbar, just open the website and drag the tab down to the taskbar.

The browser window will close and then reopen. The IE window for pinned websites is slightly different, as shown in Figure 6-8. The website icon appears to the

FIGURE 6-8   Pinned websites open in a special browser window with their own icon and no Home button.

left of the Back and Forward buttons, which change color to match the icon. There's no Home button in the window for a pinned website, because it always opens in the site you want. And if you have any toolbars or certain kinds of older add-ons installed, they won't load in the pinned website window, so that you can concentrate on the website you've pinned.

 To remove a pinned website from the taskbar, right-click or press and hold on its icon and choose Unpin This Program from the Taskbar.

Add and Organize Favorites

When you bookmark a website in the Windows 8 version of IE, the bookmark you save goes into the Favorites list, but you can't pick a folder to put it into. If you want to organize your favorites into folders or delete ones that you don't use any more, you can do that in the desktop version of IE.

Click or tap the Favorites icon in the top right corner of the browser window (it looks like a star) to open the list of all your favorites. To keep your Favorites open while you work, click or tap the icon on the left of the Favorites pane to pin the Favorites Center to the left of the browser window.

Right-click or press and hold anywhere in the Favorites pane and choose Create New Folder if you want to organize favorites into groups. Drag favorites into the folders you've made in the list.

 Use the History tab of the Favorites pane to find a website that you visited on a particular day.

Find Files You've Downloaded

When you click or tap a link that downloads a file to your computer, Internet Explorer will ask you whether you want to open the file straightaway (the button will say Open, or Run if you're downloading a program) or save it for later (Save). If you want to choose where to save the file instead of putting it in the default Downloads folder, click or tap the arrow next to the Save button, choose Save As, and then navigate to the folder where you want to keep it.

When the download finishes, another dialog box appears where you can open the file you downloaded, open the folder you put it in, or look at all the files you've downloaded.

If you don't know where you saved a file you downloaded, or you closed a tab while a file was still downloading and you need to check whether the download has finished, choose Tools | View Downloads. You can see recent downloads and open the files or the folders you saved them into.

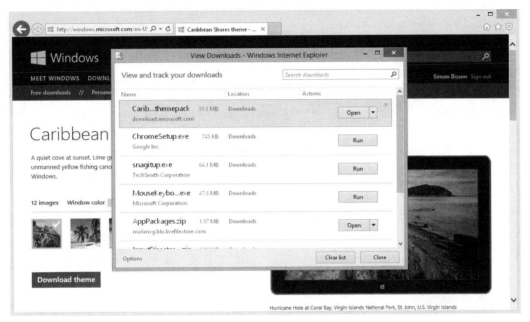

Manage Add-ons

You can add extra tools and features to the desktop version of IE by installing extra tools; toolbars like the Bing bar, plugins like Silverlight, and ActiveX controls are just some of the different kinds of add-ons for IE. These are useful, but badly written add-ons can make opening new tabs and downloading web pages slower, or even cause security problems. Choose Tools | Manage Add-ons to see which add-ons you have installed and to change their settings.

Look at the times in the Load Time column to see if any of the plugins you have installed are making your browser run slowly. To turn off an add-on that is slowing IE down, select it in the list and click or tap the Disable button.

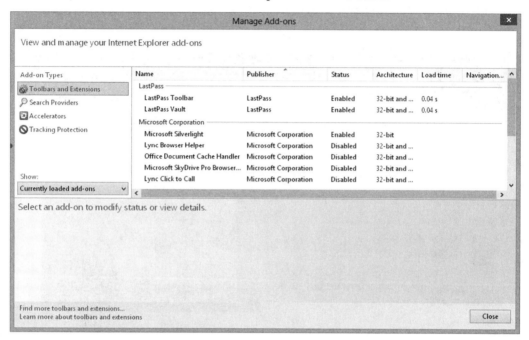

Flash Is Built into IE 10

Did You Know?

The only plugin you can use in the Windows 8 version of IE is Flash, which is preinstalled. It only works on a limited number of websites where the Flash content is easy to use with touch, but you can always click or tap View on Desktop on the Page Tools menu to switch to the desktop version of IE. The Page Tools menu will also show you if there is a Windows Store app you can use to view the content from this site; if Get an App for This Site appears on the menu, click or tap it to find out more about the app and download it from the Windows Store. If you already have an app, like the bundled Bing app, it'll offer an option to switch to that app.

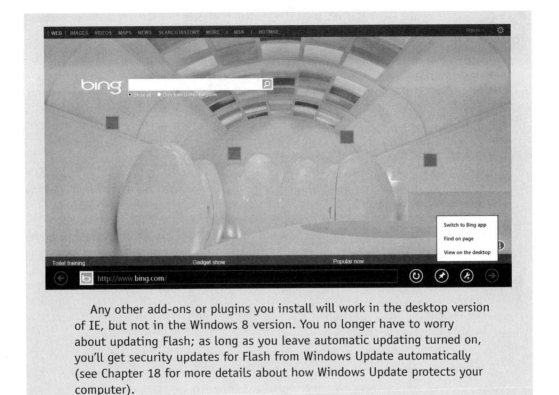

Any other add-ons or plugins you install will work in the desktop version of IE, but not in the Windows 8 version. You no longer have to worry about updating Flash; as long as you leave automatic updating turned on, you'll get security updates for Flash from Windows Update automatically (see Chapter 18 for more details about how Windows Update protects your computer).

Protect Your Privacy While You Browse the Web

When you visit a website and make choices about what you want to see, often the website saves a small file called a *cookie* on your computer so that it can remember your preferences the next time you visit that website.

For example, if you indicate on the CNN website that you prefer to read the U.S. rather than the international edition, the website stores that choice in a cookie on your computer. Thereafter, every time you return to the CNN website, it looks at the cookie, sees that you want the U.S. edition, and loads it, so you don't have to pick the edition you want to see every time you log in to the site. If you see your username already filled in when you return to a website that requires you to sign in, that means the website has probably stored your username in a cookie to save you time. Or, when you visit a retailer's website and add something to your shopping cart, a cookie might store what you have in your shopping cart while you continue to shop on the website.

Only the website that creates a cookie is allowed to look at it, so one website can't see what you do on another website.

Another kind of cookie stores information from multiple websites to help those sites show you advertisements that are more relevant to what you're interested in. These are called *third-party* or *tracking* cookies because they don't come from the website you're looking at; instead, they come from companies that put ads on different websites and they can track your behavior across those websites. For example, if you look at kitchen appliances on one website, when you go to another website that works with the same advertising company, you might see ads for the appliances you were looking at, because the advertising company can get that information from the cookie it saved on your computer when you were on the first website.

You can choose which types of cookies websites are allowed to save on your computer. You have to change this setting in the desktop version of IE, but, like the other options you can change in the desktop version of IE, it also applies to the Windows 8 version. Choose Tools | Internet Options and click or tap the Privacy tab, shown next. On the Privacy tab, you can move the slider up and down to choose between six different settings (from Allow All Cookies at the bottom to Block All Cookies at the top). You might want to change the setting from the default of Medium to Medium High, which blocks more tracking cookies, for example.

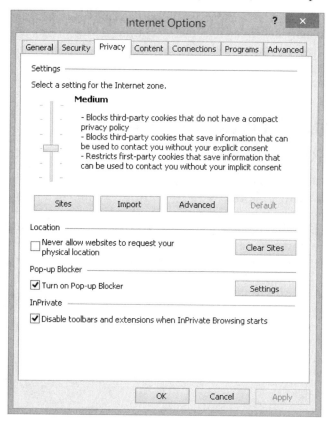

If you block or delete cookies, some web pages may not display correctly. If a website doesn't behave the way you expect it to, open the Tools menu in the desktop version of IE and choose Safety | Webpage Privacy Policy to see if your privacy policy is blocking any cookies that the site might need.

You can delete cookies along with the other information about your browsing history (such as saved website passwords, the list of websites in the Internet Explorer History list, data you type into web forms, temporary Internet files, and the list of the last set of tabs you had open, which IE saves in case you want to open them again). You might need to do this either for privacy reasons or if you're trying to fix a problem, but remember that this deletes a lot of useful information and could make browsing less convenient.

Open the Tools menu in the desktop version of IE and choose Safety | Delete Browsing History. In the Delete Browsing History dialog box, check any of the following check boxes to indicate the information you want to delete: Temporary Internet Files, Cookies, History, Form Data, Passwords, and/or Tracking Protection Data (we'll look at tracking protection in the next section). If you want to keep the information from the websites you have bookmarked as Favorites, check the Preserve Favorites Website Data check box.

Choose a Tracking Protection List

Internet Explorer 10 implements a controversial new standard for protecting your privacy online called Do Not Track (DNT). When you have DNT turned on (if you accepted the Express Settings when you first started using Windows 8, DNT is turned on automatically) and you visit a website that respects the DNT flag, you can opt out of being tracked. However, only a few websites support DNT so far, and how much protection using DNT will give you hasn't yet been finalized.

If you want to make sure you're not being tracked, you can install a Tracking Protection List (TPL) to actively prevent the websites you visit from automatically sending details about your visit to other sites that provide their content.

 A TPL stops content that tracks your browsing activity from loading at all, so some websites won't load properly if you're using a TPL.

To add a TPL, open the Tools menu in the desktop version of IE and choose Safety | Tracking Protection. This opens the Manage Add-ons window to show any TPLs you already have installed. Click or tap Get a Tracking Protection List Online to open the IE Gallery site and choose a list.

The different lists here don't come from Microsoft; instead, they're built and maintained by privacy groups. Some TPLs block advertising services that don't follow industry guidelines; others, like the TRUSTe list, make sure targeted ads from respected ad services aren't blocked. Click or Tap the Add button for the list you want to use and confirm the installation by choosing Add List.

You can see if any content on the website you're browsing is filtered by looking at the filter icon in the address bar; if it turns blue, some of the content on this site has been filtered out. Click or tap the filter icon and choose Turn Off Tracking Protection if you want to load everything on the website.

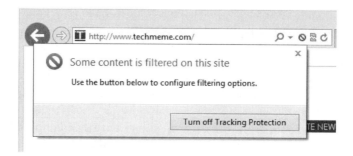

Browse Without Leaving a Record

When you open a new website in the current tab or in a new tab, IE keeps a record of the website in your History list so that you can find it again. If you don't want IE to store data about your web browsing, you can open an InPrivate tab to load specific pages. For example, if you share a computer and you don't want anyone else to see which websites you're visiting to do your holiday shopping, InPrivate browsing keeps your browsing activity private.

In the Windows 8 version of IE, you can open an InPrivate tab from the tab bar by clicking or tapping the Tab Tools button and choosing New InPrivate Tab. You'll see a message that InPrivate is turned on, and the address box also contains a small InPrivate icon.

In the desktop version of IE, you can click or tap the InPrivate browsing link at the bottom of the new tab window; again, you'll see a message from IE and the InPrivate logo in the address bar, as shown next. You can also choose InPrivate Browsing from the Safety section of the Tools menu.

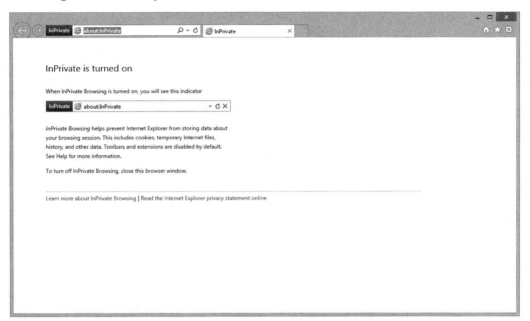

By default, IE disables all toolbars and extensions when you open an InPrivate tab because they might save information about your browsing behavior, but you can change this behavior by clearing the Disable Toolbars and Extensions when InPrivate Browsing Starts check box in the InPrivate section of the Privacy tab in Internet Options.

Hide Your Location

Some websites want to know where you are so they can give you more relevant information. For example, a mapping website can show your current location so it's easier to get directions, and the FedEx website can help you find the nearest FedEx office. IE will always ask you to confirm that you're happy to give a website your location. If you don't want any sites to know where you are, open Internet Options from the Settings charm in the Windows 8 version of IE and move the slider under Ask for Location from On to Off. You can also block all websites that you've already allowed to find your location by clicking or tapping the Clear button.

Manage Pop-up Windows

The Pop-up Blocker in IE does what it says: it blocks pop-ups from appearing when you visit a website that tries to open them. That means you don't see annoying ads that open on top of the website you're trying to look at, but it can cause problems if the banking or travel website you're using wants to open a new window.

The desktop version of IE notifies you when it blocks a pop-up; click or tap Allow Once to reload the page so you can open the link again to see the pop-up.

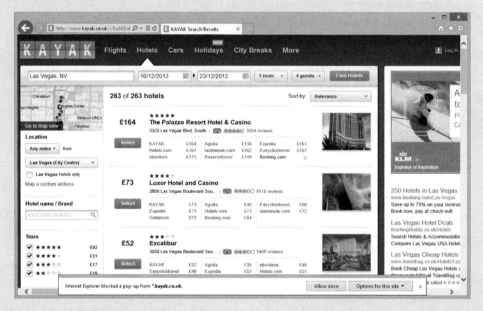

If you use the website often, choose Options for This Site and click or tap Always Allow; if you want to change how the Pop-up Blocker works, choose More Settings. Change the setting for Blocking Level to determine how many popups will be blocked or allowed.

Stay Safe While You Browse the Web

The default settings in Internet Explorer protect you from many threats on the Web. If you visit a website that asks you to turn off security settings, be careful; it might be a legitimate website that's not well written or it might be a website trying to compromise your PC.

Use SmartScreen

When you visit a website, IE checks to see if the address is for a legitimate, well-known website or if it's a *phishing site*, a deliberately similar address designed to trick you into visiting a suspicious site that might try to attack your computer. This SmartScreen Filter also checks every program file that you download to see if it's commonly downloaded software, known malware, or an unknown file that has the same name as a legitimate program.

If you visit a website that the SmartScreen filter doesn't detect as a phishing site but that you believe is illegitimate, choose Tools | Safety | Report Unsafe Website to send a report to Microsoft.

Use ActiveX Filtering

ActiveX controls are a type of Internet Explorer add-on that add extra features to the browser (like being able to copy clip-art straight from the Microsoft Office website into an Office document). The Flash plugin that's included in IE 10 is an ActiveX control. However, there are a lot of malicious ActiveX controls that try to load malware onto your computer, as well as badly written ones that can slow IE down or even make it crash.

You can turn off ActiveX from the Tools menu by choosing Safety | ActiveX Filtering. A check mark appears next to the menu entry to tell you it's selected. Now when you visit a website that tries to load an ActiveX control, IE will block the add-on, and the filter icon in the address bar will turn blue. This also blocks Flash, so if you're sure a website is safe, you can click or tap the blue Filter icon and choose Turn Off

ActiveX Filtering. IE will remember what you've chosen for each website in future browsing sessions.

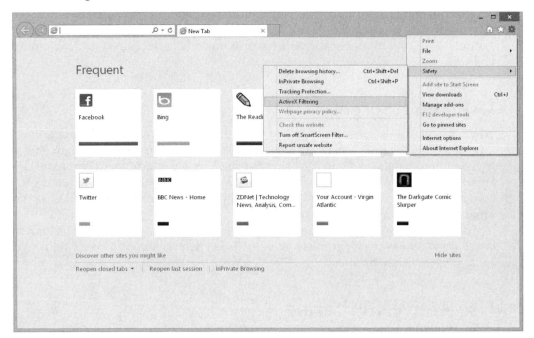

 If you find that IE isn't working properly, your "in case of emergency, break glass" option is to click or tap the Reset button in the Reset Internet Explorer Settings area at the bottom of the Advanced tab in Internet Options in the desktop version of IE. This will undo all the changes you've made, so only use it if you're having serious problems.

7

Print, Scan, and Fax with Windows 8

There are hundreds and hundreds of different peripherals you can plug into your computer, from mice and trackpads to webcams and external drives. You can plug in a digital camera to transfer photos, plug in a digital pedometer to download records of how far you've walked each day, or attach a broadband modem that lets you get online when there aren't any Wi-Fi hotpots nearby.

Whatever device you connect to your computer, Windows tries to automatically detect what it is and load the driver software Windows needs to control the device. This feature is called *Plug and Play*, because it lets you plug in your device and then play with it straightaway.

Some devices come with specific software that you need to run to get the most out of them, but the vast majority of devices will work as soon as you plug them in and Windows recognizes what the hardware is and downloads the driver from Windows Update (Windows 8 also includes drivers for many popular devices out of the box).

So, you can connect a printer and print out simple documents straightaway, but if you want extra controls to do things like print on both sides of the paper or see how much ink you have left, you will want to install the software that comes with the printer. If you plug in a mouse, you can move the cursor on screen with it, but if there are more than two buttons on the mouse, you'll need to install extra software so you can choose what the extra buttons do.

In this chapter, we'll look at the three common devices you can connect to your computer and use with Windows 8: printers, scanners, and faxes. But the same principles apply to almost all of the peripherals and devices you can plug into a PC.

Set Up Your Hardware

Before you can connect most devices to Windows 8, you need to make sure your hardware is set up first.

Plug your device into an electrical outlet (or, if it runs on batteries, make sure the batteries are charged) and turn it on. If it connects to your PC with a cable, make sure that's plugged into the right socket on the device (before you connect the other end to your computer, as instructed in the next paragraph). If it uses a wireless connection like Bluetooth, Wi-Fi, or RF (radio frequency), make sure that's turned on as well and put the device into "pairing mode" so it's ready to communicate with the PC (follow the instructions in the manual that came with your device). Make sure the same wireless radio is turned on in Windows; open the Settings charm and make sure you're not in Airplane mode. For RF devices (like wireless keyboards and mice), there will be a small adapter you need to plug into your PC to make the wireless connection.

Now plug the device into your computer using the cable supplied with it. For a wireless device, open PC Settings, click or tap Devices, and then choose Add a Device. You should see a notification that Windows is setting up the device, and then the device should appear in the Devices list, ready to use (see Figure 7-1).

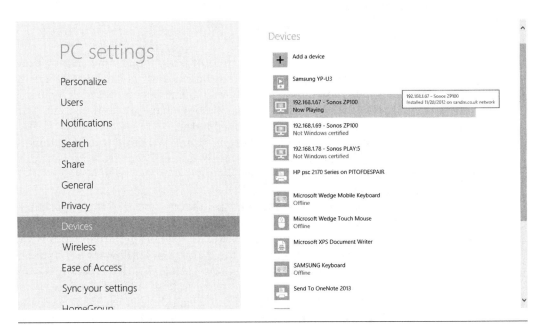

FIGURE 7-1 View and add devices in PC Settings.

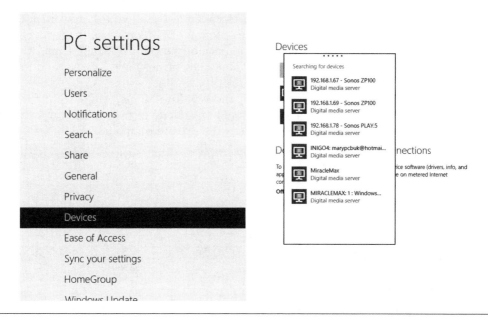

FIGURE 7-2 Tap or click Add a Device to add network devices or hardware that doesn't install automatically.

If you're connecting a device wirelessly, PC Settings may ask you to enter a code to confirm that you're allowed to use this device. For example, if you're connecting a Bluetooth keyboard to your Windows 8 tablet, you'll be asked to type a string of numbers and press the ENTER key. If Windows doesn't find your device automatically you'll need to add it by clicking or tapping the Add a Device button, and then select the hardware you want to install, as shown in Figure 7-2.

Add a Printer, Scanner, or Other Device by Hand

When you plug a peripheral like a printer or scanner into your PC, Windows usually will be able to detect and install it automatically. If you're on the desktop, the Device Setup window will open and you'll see a green progress bar in an icon that appears briefly on the taskbar while Windows is installing the device; the window and the icon will close automatically once your device is configured.

If the Device Setup window doesn't open to install your hardware automatically, and you can't add it from the Devices section of PC Settings either, you can add a device from the Hardware and Sound page of the Control Panel. Under the Hardware and Sound heading in the Control Panel, click or tap View Devices and Printers and then choose Add a Device in the toolbar.

The Add a Device wizard opens, and Windows scans your system and network for any connected devices that haven't been installed yet. When Windows has finished scanning, click or tap the icon for your device and then click or tap Next.

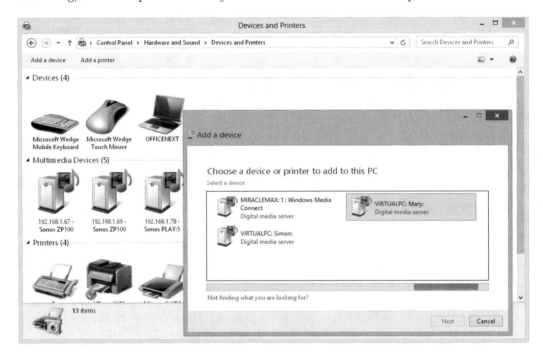

Windows will look online for drivers, download them automatically, and install the device for you to use. If you need to give any information, like a passcode to connect wirelessly, you'll be prompted to fill that in. If the installation finishes without problems, the Add a Device window closes automatically. Look in Devices and Printers to see your new device. If there are problems finding and installing devices, Windows 8 provides help and troubleshooters, as shown in Figure 7-3.

If you're adding a printer, you can choose Add a Printer from the toolbar instead of Add a Device and Windows will detect only printers that are connected to your PC or available on the network but not already installed. If you don't see your printer in

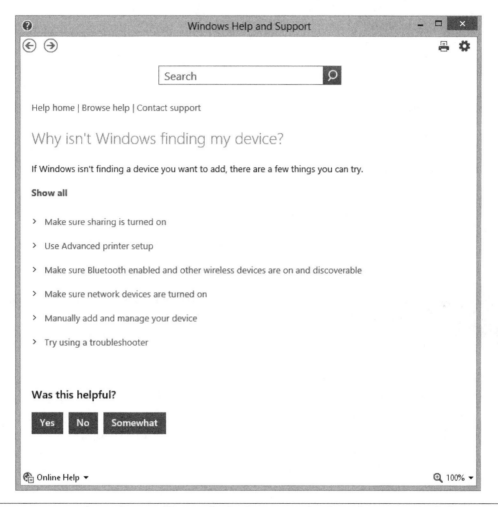

FIGURE 7-3   If Windows still can't find what you're looking for, you can click or tap Not finding what you are looking for? to use a troubleshooter to try to resolve the problem.

the Add Printer wizard click or tap The Printer That I Want Isn't Listed. The wizard will give you several options, including connecting a wireless printer and browsing your network to see shared printers.

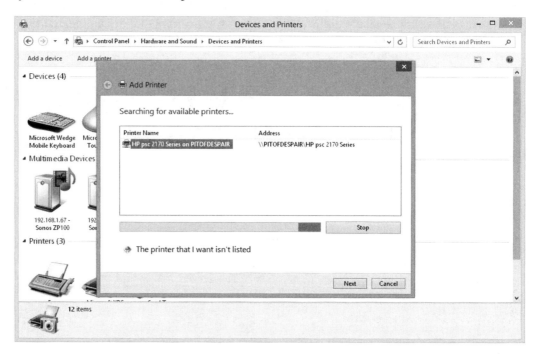

 Some peripherals have their own Windows Store apps; when you first plug them in, if you're online the Windows Store will open to show you details about the app so you can download it. Each time you plug that hardware into your PC, the Windows Store app will open so you can use it.

See More Details About Your Devices

PC Settings shows you some information about your devices. If your Xbox isn't turned on, you can see that it's Offline in the Devices section. If you have a streaming multimedia adapter like a Sonos wireless music player on your network, you can see if that's playing music. And you can see if your printer is printing documents. You can also hover over a device's icon with your mouse to see when you installed the device. But if you want to see more technical details and change settings for your hardware, you need to look in the Devices and Printers control panel.

In the Control Panel, click or tap View Devices and Printers under the Hardware and Sound heading. You'll see icons for all your hardware and devices in the Devices and Printers window, with any devices that are installed but not currently connected grayed out so you can see that you can't use them.

Click or tap a device to see more details about it, like the make and model, in the status bar at the bottom of the window. For a printer, you can see how many documents are in the print queue. If there's a problem with the device, you'll see a brief message about it listed as the Status.

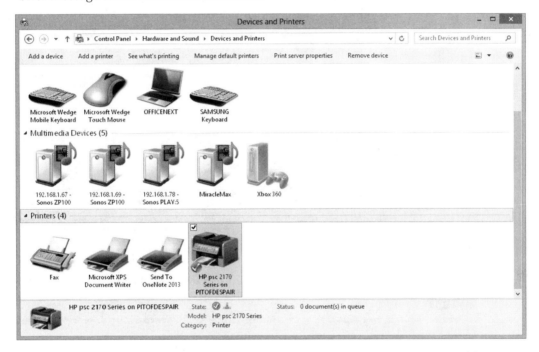

The functions in the toolbar at the top of the window always include Add a Device, Add a Printer, and Remove Device, but you may see extra tools as you select different devices. When you select your computer, for example, the toolbar includes

Browse Files (with a drop-down menu where you can select the different drives on your system). If you select a scanner, the toolbar includes Start Scan. When you select a printer, the toolbar includes See What's Printing, Manage Default Printers, and Print Server Properties (if you're sharing your printer with other computers in your homegroup, you can change who is allowed to print documents here).

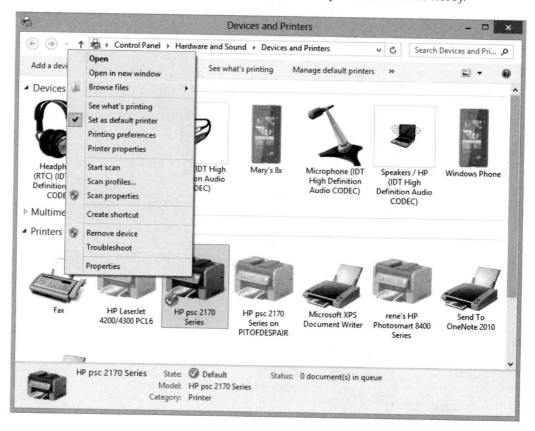

If you select a multifunction device, like a combination printer and scanner with a slot for storage cards so you can print photos directly, you'll see the tools for both printing and scanning in the toolbar, as well as the option to browse files from any storage card you have inserted.

If Windows has detected a problem with one of your devices you'll see the Troubleshoot button in the toolbar at the top of the Devices and Printer window when you select it.

You can see the same commands, and several more, when you right-click or press and hold on a device. Press and hold or right-click on the icon for your computer to see all the different components you can change settings for, like the mouse, keyboard, and display; there are also links to useful tools like System Properties and Windows Update.

If you right-click or press and hold on the icon for your printer, you see options to make it your default printer, set printing preferences, see the current print queue, and look at the hardware details in Printer Properties.

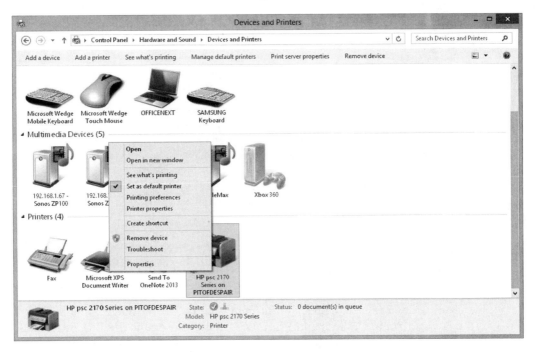

For a scanner, you can set Scan Profiles (default settings for what resolution and file size to use for scanning different types of documents), change what the buttons on your scanner do in Scan Properties, as well as start a scan. Most of the time you'll scan from within a software application, but you can always do it from here as well.

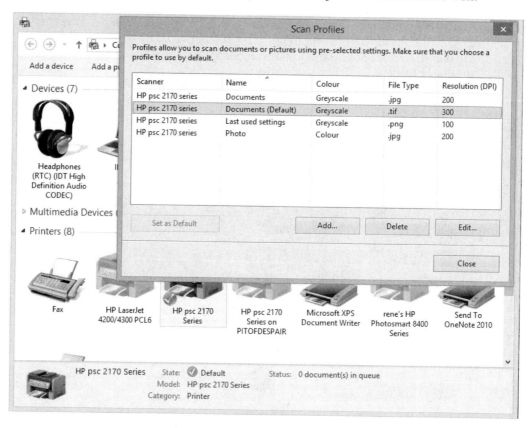

Some devices have a special interface called a Device Stage. Double-click or tap the device icon in Devices and Printers. Usually this opens the Properties dialog box for the device, but if there's a Device Stage, that will open instead (see Figure 7-4). Device Stage windows have links for useful tasks like running the software that comes

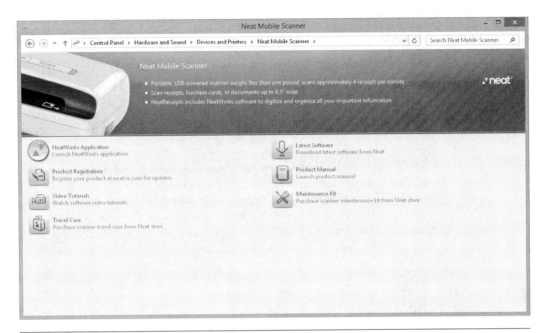

FIGURE 7-4 Device Stage views give you quick access to tools and information about your device.

with your device (and looking for updates), reading the manual for your hardware online, and accessing help content like tutorials. You might be able to register your device so you can get technical support, activate your warranty, or purchase spares and accessories for it (or ink for a printer).

Share Your Printer

If your computer is part of a homegroup, you can share any printers connected to your computer with other users in the homegroup. Follow the instructions in Chapter 5 to turn on printer sharing.

How to... Check If Your Hardware Is Installed Properly

If your hardware isn't working after you connect your device, first check that it's turned on and plugged in (or ready to connect if it's a wireless connection). If the problem still isn't solved, look in PC Settings to see whether the device is listed. If you can't find it there, and Windows doesn't see it when you choose Add a Device, look in Devices and Printers to check if Windows can see the device but can't operate it because you don't have the correct driver for it. That can happen if you initially connected your hardware when you weren't online, meaning Windows couldn't download a driver. If there's a device that Windows recognizes but that isn't working, the device icon will include a yellow warning icon, as shown next for the Neat Mobile Scanner. If the error isn't serious, you may only see it on the device context menu. See Chapter 19 for more help troubleshooting hardware problems.

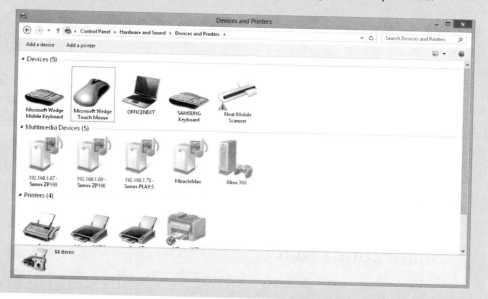

If you don't want to use a homegroup, you can still share your printer, but everyone who wants to use it will have to have an account on your PC, with a password, so they can connect to it. To share a printer without a homegroup, right-click or press and hold on the printer icon in Devices and Printers and choose Printer Properties. On the Sharing tab shown next, check the Share This Printer check box and give the printer a name people will recognize. Click or tap OK, and other people on your network will be able to see your printer and install it (as long as they have an account on your PC).

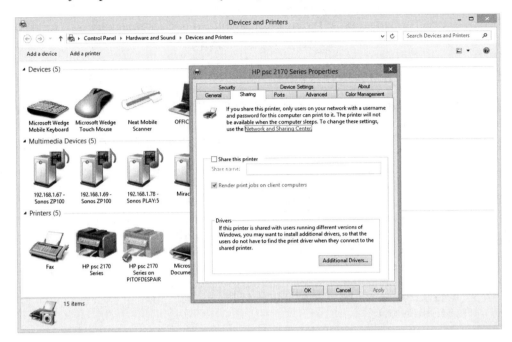

Make sure printer sharing is turned on by clicking or tapping the link at the top of the Sharing tab to open the Network and Sharing Center; click or tap Change Advanced Sharing Settings in the navigation pane on the left and, under File and Printer Sharing, select the Turn on File and Printer Sharing radio button if it isn't already selected.

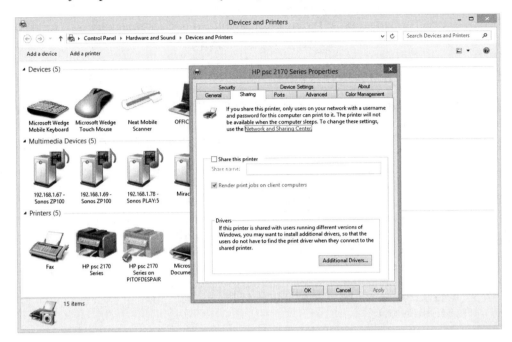

You can also open the Settings charm and tap or click the Network icon to see a list of networks; press and hold or right-click on the name of the network you're using and tap or click Turn Sharing On or Off. Choose Yes, Turn On Sharing and Connect to Devices. Other users on the network will need to do this as well.

Print a Document

Now that you have your printer installed and ready to use, you can print directly from within your software. In Windows Store apps, you print by opening the Devices charm and selecting your printer from the list. You'll see a preview of the page and options for your printer as shown in Figure 7-5.

In desktop programs, you can look for a Print button on the ribbon or toolbar or choose Print from the File menu. You can also print files straight from File Explorer; right-click or tap the file you want to print and then click or tap Print in the pop-up menu.

What you see next depends on the type of file you're printing and the software you're using. Every program has its own Print dialog box, where you can choose different options and preview what the pages will look like. For example, if you're printing images directly from File Explorer, the Print Pictures wizard lets you arrange multiple pictures on the same sheet of paper, as shown in Figure 7-6. You then click or tap the Print button to print the image.

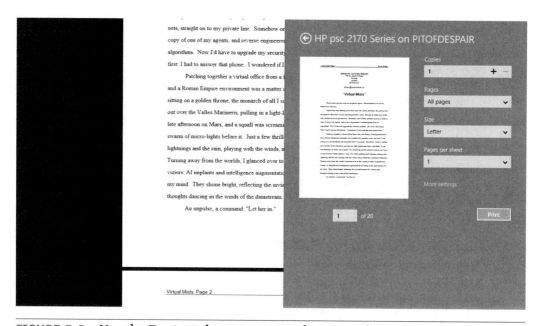

FIGURE 7-5 Use the Devices charm to print a document from the Reader app.

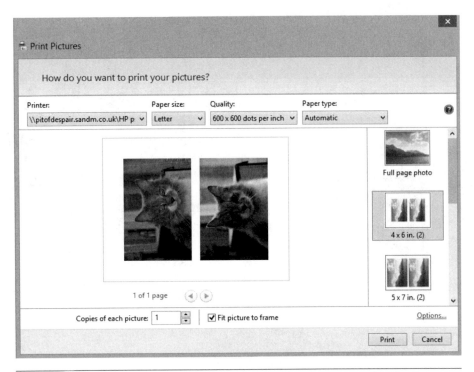

FIGURE 7-6   Change the settings in the Print Pictures window before you print the image.

Scan a Document

If you're scanning an image that you want to work with in your image editing software, you'll want to scan using the tools in that program. If you have Microsoft's free Windows Live Photo Gallery software installed, for example, you can click or tap Import on the Home tab of the ribbon, select your scanner in the Import Photos and Video dialog box, and then click or tap the Import button to open the New Scan window, shown in Figure 7-7.

If you're scanning documents such as pages from a magazine or your bank statements, your scanner may come equipped with software for organizing those documents. You can use the Windows Fax and Scan utility (you'll find this in the Windows Accessories section of the All Apps screen), which shows you documents you've already scanned and has tools for managing those documents. Or you can scan using the tools built into Windows 8. Select your scanner in the Devices and Printers control panel and click or tap the Start Scan button in the toolbar at the top of the window.

You may also be able to start scanning by pushing a button on your scanner.

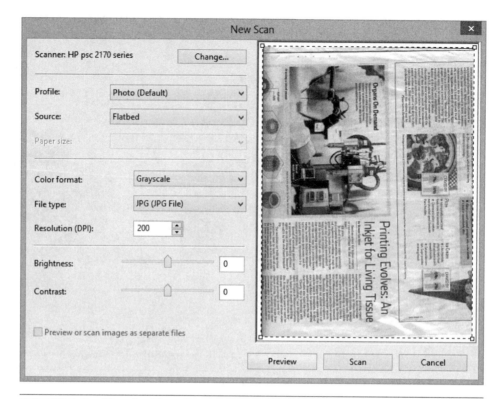

FIGURE 7-7 Use the New Scan window to control your scanner from Windows.

Again, the New Scan window opens. On the left are the settings that Windows will use to scan your document:

- **Change** If you have more than one device that you can use to scan with, click or tap Change to choose another device.
- **Profile** Use the drop-down menu to choose from your preset scanning settings for scanning documents or photos (pick Last Used Settings to use the same settings as your most recent scan), or change the settings individually.
- **Source** If you have an image scanner that can scan both photos and slides, make sure you have the correct scanning path selected.
- **Paper size** You may also be able to set the paper size, which tells the scanner what size of image you want to scan.

- **Color format**   Use the drop-down menu to choose whether to scan in color (for images), black and white (for black and white documents), or grayscale (a good option for documents that are in color that you don't need to scan in color, as it's clearer than black and white).
- **File type**   Choose which image file type you want to save in. A TIFF image is larger but gives you higher image quality if you want to use optical character recognition to convert text in your scan into a document. Save images as BMP if you want higher quality; save as PNG or JPEG if you want to create smaller files.
- **Resolution**   Changing the resolution affects both the physical size of the scan and the quality. The more dots per inch you scan, the larger the image area and the higher quality the scan. Only scan at 300 dots per inch (dpi) for documents that you need to be able to read clearly and recognize the text from; 200dpi scans will create perfectly good scanned images and photos.

Click or tap the Preview button to see what your scan will look like and to choose how much of your original document you want to scan. When the preview image appears on the right, drag the square handles in the corners of the dotted outline to mark the area you want to scan; the area that will not be scanned is grayed out. The smaller the area you scan, the quicker the scan will be and the smaller the file size will be.

If the image in the preview is too dark or too light, or both, drag the sliders to adjust the brightness and contrast.

When you're happy with the preview image, click or tap the Scan button. You'll see a progress bar while your original document is scanned, and then the Import Pictures and Videos dialog box will open.

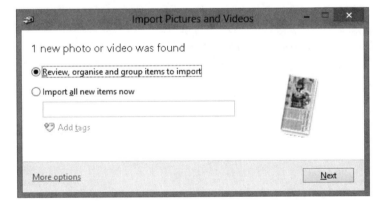

Click or tap Import and a second window will open where you can name the scan and add any tags that you use to organize your images. Windows will import the image using the same settings you use to import images from your digital camera.

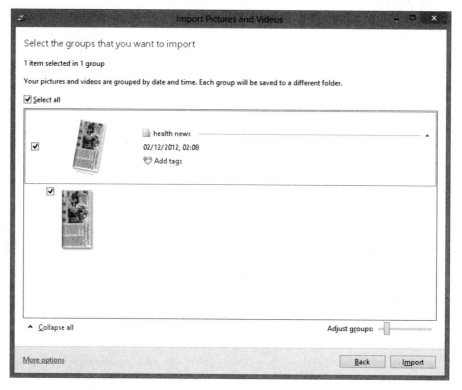

Click or tap More options to see which folder imported images are saved into and how the folders Windows creates for each new set of scans you import are named (if you want all your scans to go in a particular folder, set that in the Import Settings dialog).

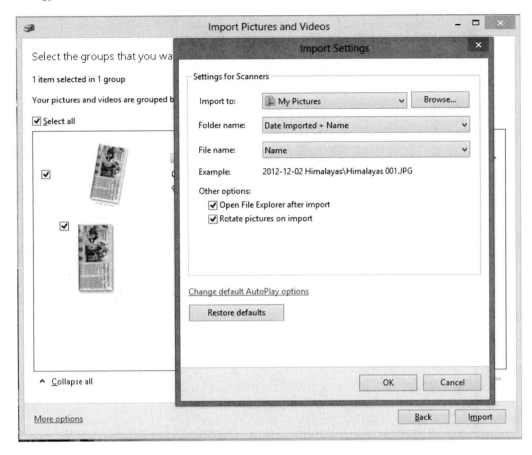

Click or tap Import when you're happy with the settings and name. Again you'll see a progress bar, and then File Explorer will open to show you your scan. If you don't want File Explorer to open, clear the Open File Explorer After Import check box in the Import Settings dialog box.

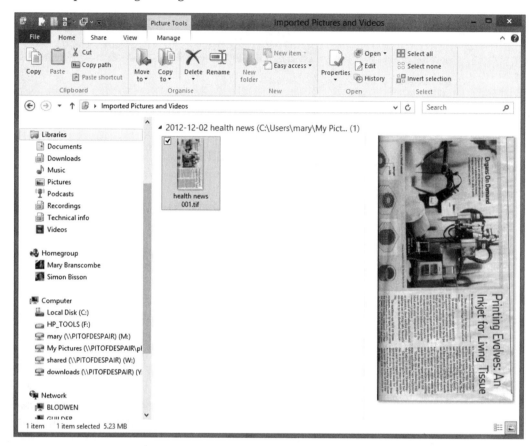

Manage Scans with Windows Fax and Scan

Scanning isn't just useful for storing digital copies of your old printed photographs on your computer. You can also use it to produce digital copies of paper documents that you need to keep, or to keep articles and recipes you clip out of magazines. That's more useful when you have a way of organizing and managing your scanned files. If your scanner didn't come with any document management software and you don't want to just look at your scans in File Explorer, you can organize the documents you scan with the Windows Fax and Scan tool, which you can open from the All Apps screen.

This is a tool that's been in Windows for some years, so the interface doesn't have new features like the ribbon, just menus and a toolbar of common commands. Click or tap New Scan in the toolbar to open the same New Scan window shown previously in Figure 7-7.

This time when you click or tap the Scan button, you won't see the Import Pictures and Videos dialog box and you don't get the chance to choose the file name. Instead, the scanned image appears in the Windows Fax and Scan window, shown next, and will be saved in the default Scanned Documents folder in My Documents when you save it. Every scanned file is called Image with a number after it, which doesn't make it easy to find the scan you're looking for. Right-click or press and hold on the name of the scanned file to choose Rename and give it a more memorable file name.

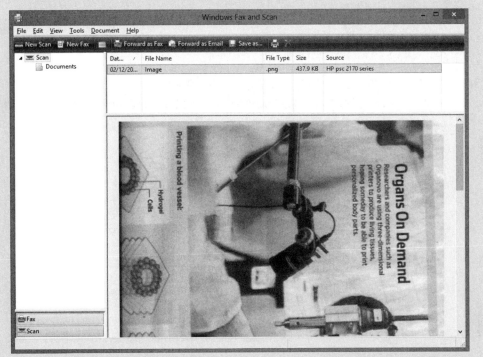

You can send the scanned file as an email attachment or fax it if you have a dial-up modem, and you can preview, print, and delete scanned files here too.

Fax a Document from Your Dial-up Modem

If you need to sign a document and send it to someone quickly, you can scan and email it. But sometimes it's still useful to send a fax. If you still have a dial-up modem connected to or installed in your computer, you can also use Windows Fax and Scan to send faxes (even if you normally use broadband); just connect the modem to your phone line.

Click or tap the Fax button in the folder pane on the left and you'll see the five folders your faxes are organized into: Incoming, Inbox, Drafts, Outbox, and Sent Items. Look in the Inbox folder to find a guide to using the Windows and Fax tool that's made to look like an incoming fax, as shown in Figure 7-8.

If you haven't already set up your fax modem, Windows will prompt you to do that the first time you click or tap the New Fax button in the toolbar. In the Fax Setup wizard, click or tap Connect to a Fax Modem. You can pick a different name for the fax modem if you want; otherwise, click or tap Next. Choose whether you want your

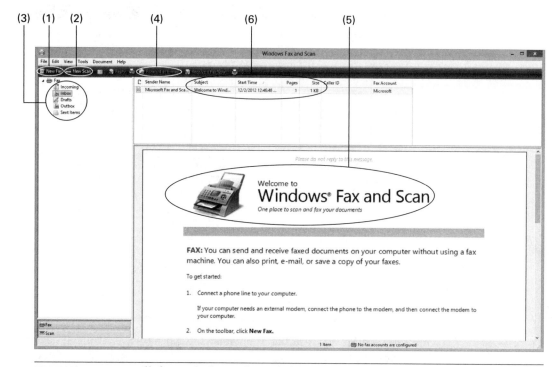

FIGURE 7-8 Scroll through the welcome document in the preview pane to get directions. (1) Send a fax, (2) Scan a document, (3) Default folders, (4) Forward a fax by email, (5) message in the fax inbox, (6) fax inbox.

computer to automatically accept incoming fax messages or to ask you every time (or tell Windows that you'll decide later).

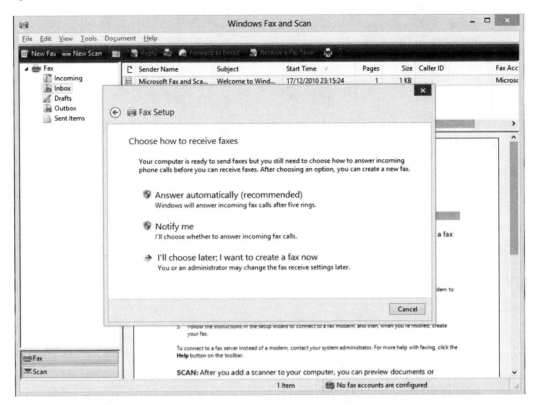

You may see a dialog box from Windows Firewall warning you that the fax service can only run on private networks; as you're most likely to use it when you're at home and connected to your phone line, that shouldn't be a problem, so click or tap the Allow Access button. Next, the New Fax window opens (see Figure 7-9), ready for you to compose a fax.

This is similar to writing an email message with a few differences:

- You can add a cover page to your fax by clicking or tapping the None drop-down menu to the right of the Cover Page label and selecting from one of four cover pages: Confidential, FYI, Generic, or Urgent.
- Type in the To box the fax number you're sending the message to. If you've saved the details of your contact, click or tap the To button to open the Select Recipients window and pick a saved contact.

You can also reply to a fax by clicking or tapping Reply in the taskbar.

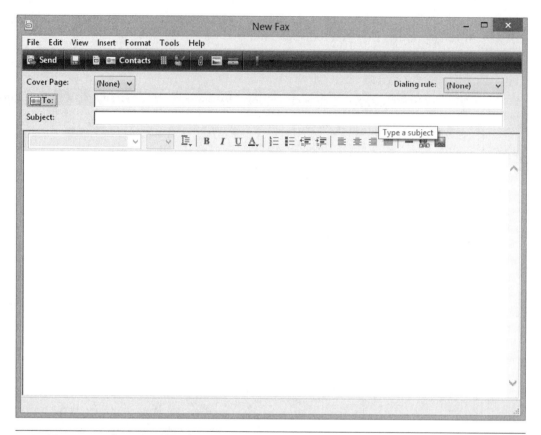

FIGURE 7-9 When you finish typing the recipient in the To box, the subject in the Subject box, and the fax message, send the fax by clicking or tapping the Send button.

Click or tap the Send button in the taskbar to send your fax straightaway. If you want to save it to edit later, click or tap the Save icon on the toolbar.

If you don't have a modem or you don't need to send faxes often enough to make it worth setting up, there are plenty of Internet fax services that let you send faxes via your email software for a monthly fee (usually around $10). They often have a free trial, but if you only need to send a single fax, sites like www.faxzero.com and www.sendafaxfree.com let you send a few free faxes from their websites.

8

Send and Receive Email

HOW TO...

- Set up email accounts in the Mail app
- Receive, send, and search email messages
- Manage email folders
- Stay in touch with friends in the People app
- Manage your calendar

If you've used versions of Windows prior to Windows 7, you may be familiar with the email tools that were included in those earlier versions of Windows, like Outlook Express and Windows Mail. Windows 7 didn't include a built-in mail client, but Live Mail was part of the free Windows Live Essentials suite. With Windows 8, the built-in email app returns in the form of the Mail app, which adds support for business email as well as personal email services like Outlook.com and Gmail.

The tile for the Mail app is pinned to the Start screen by default (it includes an envelope icon); if you've unpinned it, you can open Mail from the All Apps screen (introduced in Chapter 2). Tap the Mail app tile to open it.

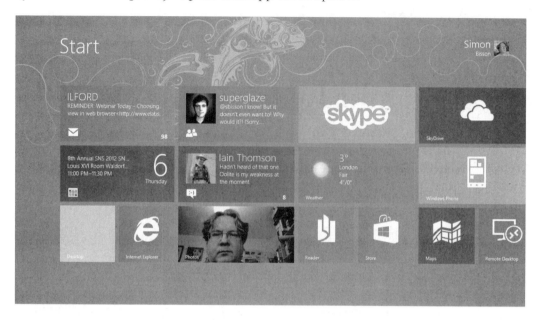

If you don't sign into Windows with a Microsoft account, when you first open the Mail app, it will prompt you to fill in the email address and password for your Microsoft account so that you can use it with the Mail, Calendar, People, and Messaging apps. Even if you don't use your Microsoft account for email, you have to sign in with a Microsoft account to use the Mail app with other email services like Gmail. If you don't already have a Hotmail, Outlook.com, Xbox Live, or other Microsoft account, click or tap the Sign Up for a Microsoft Account link to open Internet Explorer and create one.

Set Up Other Email Accounts

Once you sign in to Mail with a Microsoft account, you can continue to add other email accounts from web mail services like Gmail or Yahoo Mail, from the account provided by your Internet service provider (ISP), or from an Outlook account you have at work. You can also add another Microsoft account if you have more than one.

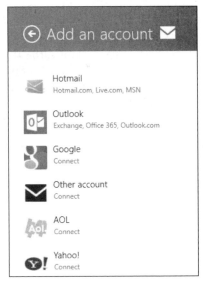

Open the Settings charm and choose Accounts to start setting up your other accounts; click or tap Add an Account to see the full list of options and choose the type of email account you have: Hotmail, Outlook, Google, AOL, Yahoo, or Other Account. We'll cover how to set up each of these in turn.

Set Up an Outlook Account

If you're using Microsoft's new webmail service, Outlook.com, you add that to Mail as an Outlook account. If you want to use an email account from the company where you work, it's likely to be an Exchange account (or possibly an account on Microsoft's Office 365 service), especially if you usually use Outlook to get your mail.

How to Get Mail from your ISP

There are two main protocols for receiving email from an ISP or email service provider: Internet Message Access Protocol (IMAP) and Post Office Protocol (POP).

Email servers that use POP download messages to your email app and then delete them from the server. After an email message has been downloaded to your PC, if you connect to your email account with a different computer, that message won't be downloaded again because it is no longer on the email server, and if you delete messages on your PC (or your PC fails), you can't get another copy. Windows 8's Mail app doesn't currently support POP.

Email servers that use IMAP keep the mail on the servers and synchronize it to your computer. If you read email from the same account on a second computer, you can read messages that have been stored on the server, but if you delete messages on one computer, they will be deleted on both computers and on the server.

If you have a webmail account using Microsoft Hotmail or Outlook.com, you'll be automatically set up with Microsoft's Exchange ActiveSync (EAS) protocol instead, which syncs your contact book and calendar as well as your email and automatically downloads new mail as it arrives. If you have an email account from your ISP or another service that doesn't use EAS, their setup instructions for email will tell you which protocol to use.

(You can also ask the helpdesk where you work what kind of account you have.) If so, you can add it as an Outlook account as well.

Click or tap the Outlook button in the Add an Account list to open the Add Your Outlook Account window shown in Figure 8-1.

Type your email address in the Email Address box and your password in the Password box. Often that's enough to find an Outlook account. If not and you need to enter more EAS mailbox information, click or tap Show More Details under the Password box. The Domain, Username, and Password boxes appear so you can type the email address, server address, domain, username, and password. Your helpdesk at work or your ISP can give you this information if you need it. Click or tap the Connect button to add the account.

Set Up an IMAP Account

If your email service uses IMAP, then click or tap the Other Account button in the Add an Account list. In the Add Your Email Account screen, choose IMAP, then click or tap the Connect button. If you set up a Gmail account, your mail will automatically be configured to work with IMAP without you needing to fill in all the details here.

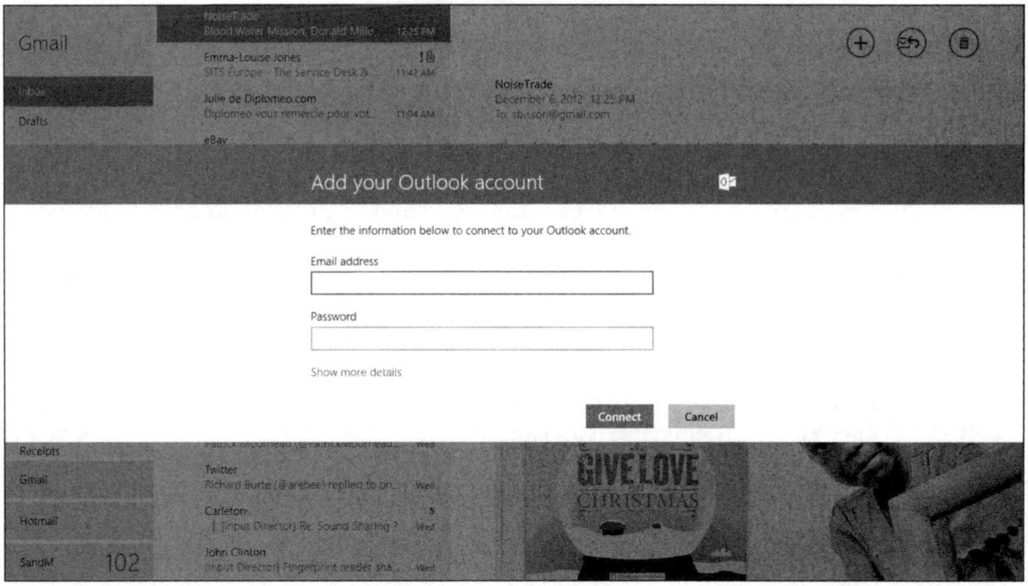

FIGURE 8-1   Add an Outlook account to Mail with just an email address and a password.

Caution   Although there is an option for POP accounts on screen, the Mail app doesn't work with POP email.

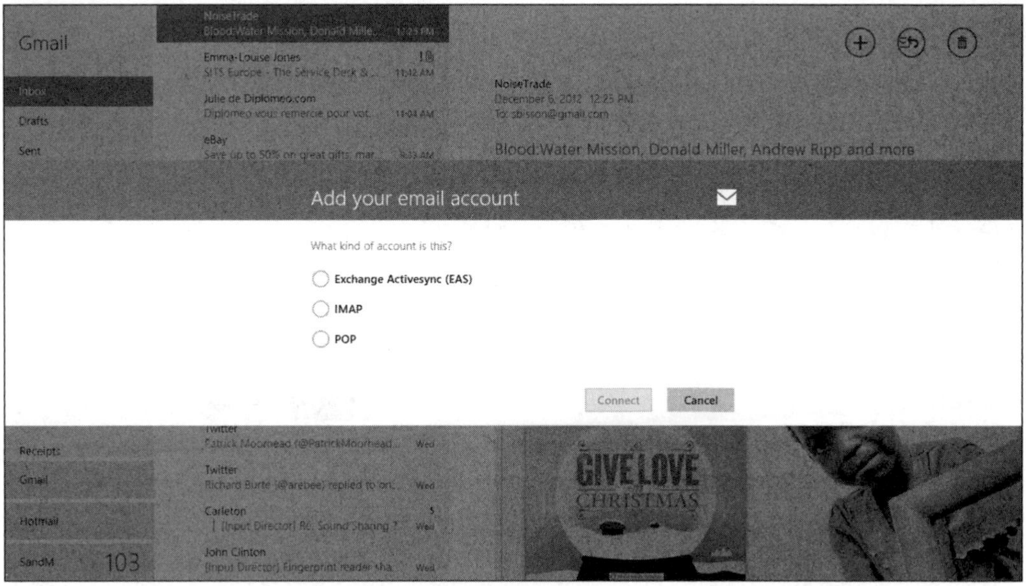

First, type in your email address and the password. For almost all IMAP systems, you will also need to enter more details about your account; click or tap the Show More Details link under the Password box and, in the expanded Add Your Other account screen, fill in these details (see Figure 8-2):

- **Username** This might be your email address, but not necessarily.
- **Password** Enter your password here (there's no need to do this again if it's already there).
- **Incoming (IMAP) email server** Enter the incoming email server name supplied by your email provider. You may also need to change the port number in the Port box to the right if the default port number doesn't match the details your email service provider sent you.
- **Incoming server requires SSL** Many mail services use SSL (Secure Sockets Layer) for transmitting data securely over the Internet, so this check box is checked by default; if the instructions from your email service provider tell you not to use SSL, clear the check box.
- **Outgoing (SMTP) email server** Enter the outgoing email server name supplied by your email provider. Again, if the default port number that the Mail app suggests in the Port box to the right doesn't match the information you have from your email service provider, type the new port number in the Port box.

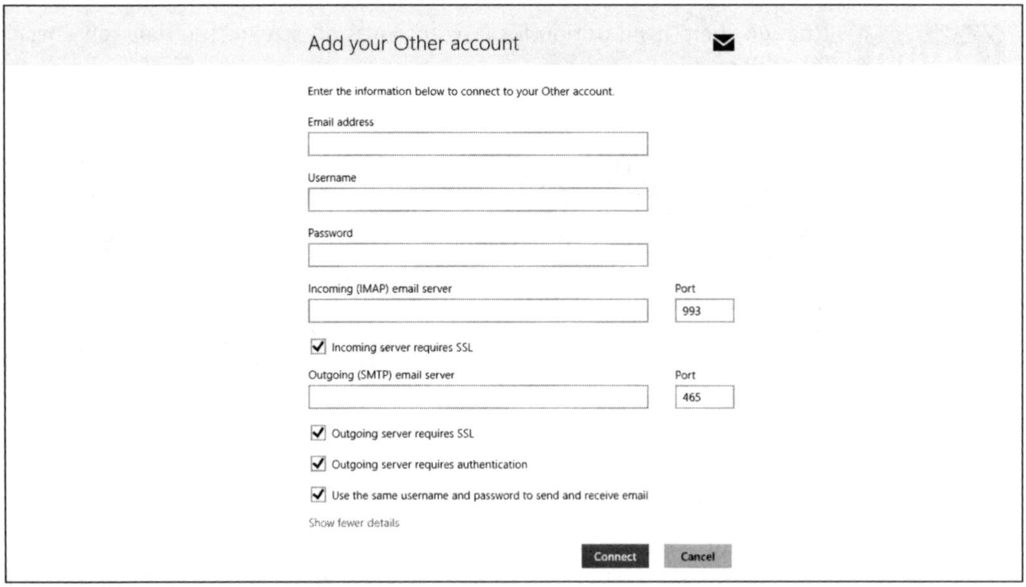

FIGURE 8-2 Expand the Add your Other Account view to enter specific email account information before you click or tap the Connect button.

The following three security settings check boxes at the bottom of the screen are all checked by default; only change these if your email provider tells you to.

- **Outgoing server requires SSL** This check box is checked by default to ensure that you send email securely. Only clear the check box if the instructions from your email service provider tell you not to use SSL.
- **Outgoing server requires authentication** Most email services allow you to send messages only if you have an account with the service, so this check box is checked by default. If your service allows anyone to send email using their servers, clear this check box.
- **Use the same username and password to send and receive email** Some email services allow you to have multiple email addresses, or you might collect messages from multiple services but send all your replies through one email service. In either case, clear this check box for and fill in the username and password you need to use for your outgoing email server.

When you've typed in all the details, click or tap the Connect button.

The Mail app tries to connect to your email account using the settings you entered. If one or more of the settings are incorrect, you'll see a warning at the bottom of the screen so you can make changes.

Set Up a Gmail, Hotmail, AOL, or Yahoo Account

Choose the type of email account you have from the Add an Account list, type in your email address and password in the screen that opens, and then click or tap the Connect button. Mail will automatically configure the appropriate options and set up your account.

If you're adding a Gmail account and you have two-step verification set up for your Gmail account, you will need to create an application-specific password for the Windows 8 Mail app in the Security section of your Google account at www.google .com/settings/account (look for the heading *Authorizing applications and sites*). Some older versions of the Mail app may offer check boxes to sync the contacts and calendar from your Gmail account; Google doesn't support this for personal Gmail addresses, so do not check these options unless you have a subscription to a paid Google Apps account.

Once you've added an account, the Mail app connects to the mail server and downloads your messages, as shown in Figure 8-3 for Gmail.

Set Up an EAS Account

There are some email services that use the EAS protocol but don't run Exchange, so you can't set up your account as an Outlook account. Choose Other Account from the Add an Account list, check the Exchange ActiveSync (EAS) check box, and then

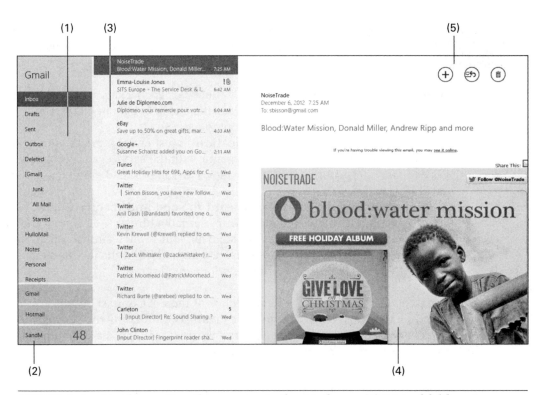

FIGURE 8-3 Read your Gmail messages in the Mail app. (1) List of folders in your mail account, (2) List of mail accounts, (3) Messages in the current folder, (4) Currently selected message, (5) Mail actions: new message, reply, delete.

click or tap Connect. Fill in your email address and password; click or tap Show More Details if you need to fill in other details like the server address, domain, or username (if you need this information, your email service provider will be able to give it to you). Click or tap Connect to add the account.

Set Up Another Email Account

If you want to add another email account at any point, open the Settings charm and choose Accounts (see Figure 8-4). Click or tap Add an Account and pick the account type you want to add.

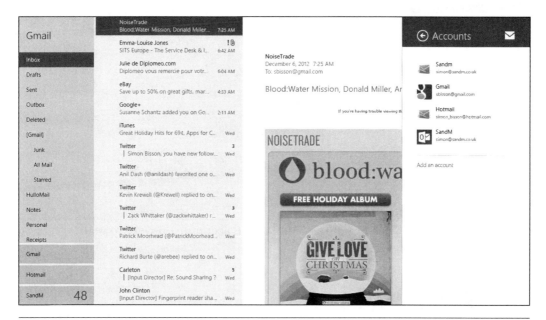

FIGURE 8-4   Click or tap Add an Account to add a new email account.

Switch Between Accounts

If you have more than one account, you can switch between them easily. In the folder list on the left side of the screen, shown in Figure 8-5, click or tap the name of the account under the folders list. After you click or tap the account name, the inbox folder for that account appears and displays the most recent message on the screen.

How to...   Delete Multiple Messages

If you want to delete the message you're reading, click the trashcan icon in the upper right corner of the screen. If you want to delete more than one message, right-click each additional message you want to delete (or swipe your finger left or right across the message in the message list on a touchscreen) to select it. Now when you click the Delete icon, all the selected messages will be deleted.

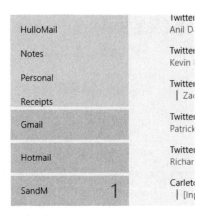

FIGURE 8-5 Click or tap the name of the account you want to read.

Receive Emails

By default, your email messages appear in your inbox as they arrive on the server, as long as you're using a service that uses EAS to send email; for IMAP you will need to set a download schedule. You can download content every 15 minutes, every 30 minutes, every hour, or manually.

If you want to check for new email messages without waiting for the Mail app to check automatically, or you want to check for email messages manually, right-click or swipe over the top or bottom edge of the screen to open the app bar at the bottom of the screen. Click or tap the Sync icon to check for new messages.

Send Emails and Reply to Emails

It's easy to create a new message or respond to the one you're currently viewing. In the upper right corner of the screen, click or tap the New icon (it looks like a plus sign) to write a new message or the Respond icon (with the envelope and arrow icon) to respond to the current message.

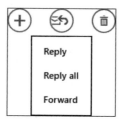

Write and Send an Email Message

When you click or tap the New icon to write a new email message, the new message screen appears. Click or tap the Show More link under the Cc box to see all the options shown in Figure 8-6. You enter the following information on the left side of

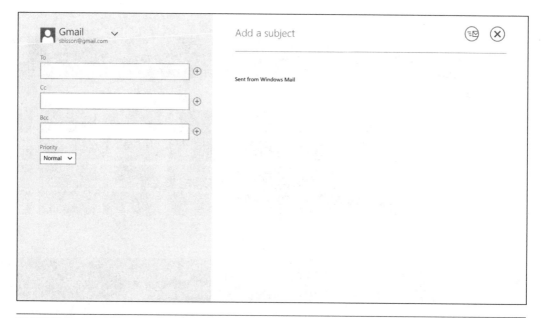

FIGURE 8-6   Choose who you're writing to and type your message.

How to... **Search for Email Messages**

There isn't a search button on the app bar in the Mail app, but that doesn't mean you can't search through your email. Just open the Charms bar, pick the Search charm, and then start typing the words or the name you're looking for; you'll see a list of matching messages in the current folder. To search another folder or another email account, select that first.

the screen, and you type the message and add attachments (as described later in this chapter) on the right side of the screen:

- **To** Type the email address(es) of the person or people to whom you're sending the message. Or, if you have an entry for the recipient(s) in the People app, you can click or tap the plus-sign icon to the right of the box to open the People app and choose the tile for their name (see Figure 8-7). Click or tap on as many names as you want before you choose Add.
- **Cc** If you want to send someone a copy of a message you're sending to someone else, type their email address in the Cc (carbon copy) box. As with the To box, you can add one or more names to the Cc box from the People app by clicking or tapping the plus-sign icon to the right of the box.

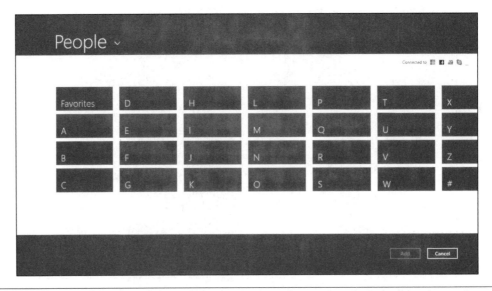

FIGURE 8-7 Add email addresses from the People app by clicking or tapping the plus-sign icon to the right of the To, Cc, or Bcc field.

- **Bcc** If you add people to the Bcc (blind carbon copy) box, using either of the methods previously described, they will get a copy of your message but the people in the To and Cc boxes won't know that.
- **Priority** Click or tap the drop-down Priority menu if you want to change from the default of Normal the priority level of the message. If it's an urgent message, change it to High Priority and it will appear in the recipient's inbox with a flag to make it stand out.

 If you have more than one email account set up, you can click or tap on the top left of the screen where your email address is shown to pick a different account to send the message from.

The Mail app puts placeholders in your new message to show you where to type. Click or tap where it says Add a Subject to add the subject for your message. Click or tap under the blue line where it says Add a Message to start typing your email.

By default, the Mail app includes a signature in every message that says Sent from Windows Mail. You can delete the Sent from Windows Mail text by selecting it and then pressing or tapping the DELETE key. If you don't want that signature on every message, we'll show you how to change it in the next section.

When you're typing your message, you can format it to make it look the way you want by right-clicking inside the message to open the app bar with formatting commands. If you're using a touchscreen, swipe your finger down from the top edge of the screen or swipe up from the bottom edge.

Use the commands on the app bar to paste text from the Clipboard, change the font color or make your text bold or italic, add emoticons and Emoji (described in Chapter 9), or click or tap the More icon to add bulleted and numbered lists or undo and redo your last changes. You can also use the app bar to save a draft of your message to finish later or to attach a file to the email.

If you want to edit what you've already typed, select the text with the mouse or your finger. The app bar of formatting commands opens automatically but with one change; you can also click or tap the Copy/Paste icon to copy the selected text to the Clipboard.

Attach a File

In the new message screen, right-click (or swipe over the top or bottom edge of a touchscreen) to open the app bar at the bottom of the screen. Click or tap the Attachments icon to open the File Picker.

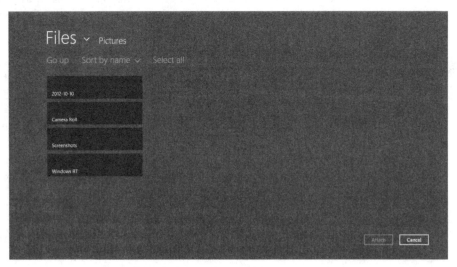

Refer to Chapter 2 for a reminder of how to use the File Picker interface. Click or tap folders to open them and use Go Up to go up the tree of folders. Click or tap the Files header in the upper left corner of the screen to navigate to a different library or location, including the Photos app, your SkyDrive account, or even Bing. Click or tap any files you want to attach to the message and then choose Attach. If you would rather put a copy of the files on your SkyDrive account and send a link instead of attaching the files to the email message, click or tap Send Using SkyDrive Instead.

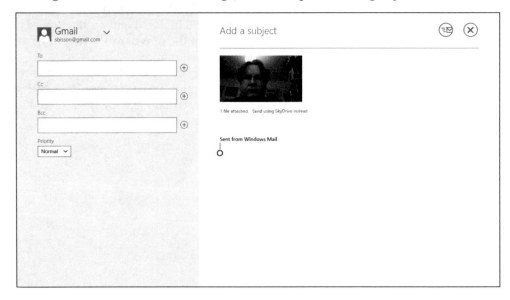

Send or Discard the Message

When you've finished writing your message, click or tap the Send button in the top right corner (it looks like an envelope). If you don't want to send the message straightaway, click or tap the Close button (it looks like an ×); from the pop-up menu, choose Save Draft if you want to save the message and come back to it later, or choose Delete Draft if you don't want to keep it at all.

Reply to a Message

When you want to answer an email, click or tap the Respond icon (which looks like an envelope with an arrow) and choose either Reply (to reply to the original sender only), Reply All (to reply to the sender and anyone else who was copied on the message), or Forward (to send a copy of the message to someone else) as in Figure 8-8.

If you click or tap Reply or Reply All, the Mail app fills in the email addresses for you automatically. When you forward a message, you need to enter in the To box the address of the person you're sending it to. Remember, you can click or tap the plus-sign icon to choose a name from the People app.

FIGURE 8-8   When you reply to a message, the original message appears in your reply for reference.

Edit an Existing Account

If you want to change the settings for any of your email accounts, open the Settings charm, choose Accounts, and then click or tap the email account whose settings you want to change, as shown in Figure 8-9.

You can change the following options:

- **Account name**   If you have two Hotmail or Gmail accounts, or you want to label your work email, you can change the name you see in the list of folders and accounts.
- **Download new email**   Use the drop-down list to choose how often Mail looks for new messages. The default is to download email when it arrives on the mail server, but if you have an IMAP account (or you don't need to see email straightaway), choose whether to look for messages every 15 minutes, every 30 minutes, once an hour, or only when you choose to check for messages.
- **Download email from**   If you want to change how much email you can see in the Mail app, use the drop-down menu to choose which messages will be copied from the server. The default is two weeks' worth of messages, but you can save space by just seeing three or seven days' worth of messages, or you can have messages for the whole month or even all the email you've ever received (you may need a lot of disk space for that).

FIGURE 8-9   The account information for a Yahoo mail account.

- **Content to sync**   Check or clear the Email, Contacts, and Calendar check boxes individually to control how much information you sync from this account.
- **Automatically download external images**   Tell the Mail app whether you want to download images in email messages automatically. For services like Hotmail and Gmail, the slider is set to On by default, which means images are downloaded. Set it to Off if you don't want to take the time to download images in email (this may also prevent advertisers from tracking whether the email they send reaches your inbox).

- **Use an email signature** The email signature that's automatically added to the bottom of your message is Sent from Windows Mail by default. With the slider set to Yes, you can replace that message with your own by typing a new email signature in the box. Move the slider from Yes to No if you don't want a signature at all.
- **Show email notifications for this account** If you want to see a pop-up message appear on the screen whenever you get a new message, move the slider from the default of Off (which means you don't get notifications) to On.
- **Remove account** Click or tap to remove the account from the Mail app if you don't want to see messages anymore; you can't remove the Microsoft account you use to log in to Windows from the Mail app, but you can remove any other email accounts.

Other options allow you to change your account details; you can change the username, password, or login details if they're wrong or need updating. You should change the password in your email account first before you change the password in the Mail app. While there is the option to change server details, this isn't recommended as this will stop you receiving mail.

Set Up Your Calendar

If you want to use Windows to keep track of your schedule, use the Windows Store Calendar app that's installed automatically. Launch the Calendar app by clicking or tapping its tile on the Start screen. This is a live tile that shows your next appointment.

If the email service you use has a calendar as well, this will be added automatically to the Calendar app when you set up that account in Mail (or if you log in to Windows with a Microsoft account). If you haven't already set up accounts in Mail, open the Settings charm and choose Accounts to add them directly to the Calendar app.

The Calendar app opens in month view, showing the current month with the current date highlighted. Right-click or swipe over the top or bottom edge of your touchscreen to open the app bar to change the view or create a new appointment.

 Calendar will show you appointments from all your linked accounts. However, it will not show you Facebook events; just birthdays for your Facebook friends.

Change the View to Month, Day, or Week

By default, the Calendar app displays the current month, so the Month icon is highlighted in white on the app bar at the bottom of the screen, as shown next. Click or tap the Day icon to see two days of appointments at a time (or just today's appointments if you have a screen you can rotate into portrait mode). Click or tap the Week icon to see appointments for the entire week. If you've been looking through your diary, click or tap Today to jump back to the current date (in the same view).

When you view your calendar by the day or the week, each day is divided into hours so you can easily see which appointments you have when. Month view shows up to two meetings or reminders per day. Swipe left or right, or click the arrows that appear in the top corners of the screen when you move your mouse, to see the previous or next day, week, or month.

 If you want the arrows to be visible all the time, open the Settings charm and choose Options; at the bottom of the list of calendars, drag the slider under Always Show Forward and Back Arrows from Hide to Show.

If you want to hide some of your calendars or pick how meetings from different calendars are color-coded, open the Settings charm and choose Options. Click or tap the drop-down menu of colors to pick a different shade, or drag the slider under a calendar from Show to Hide if you don't want to see those meetings.

Add a New Appointment

You can add a new appointment from any of the Calendar views. In Month view, click or tap the date of the appointment to open the Details screen, shown in Figure 8-10. In Day or Week view, you can click or tap on the time you want as well.

If you use several calendars, the default is the one for the Microsoft account you sign into Windows with. If that isn't where you want to save the appointment, click or tap the calendar name in the top left corner and choose the one you want to use from

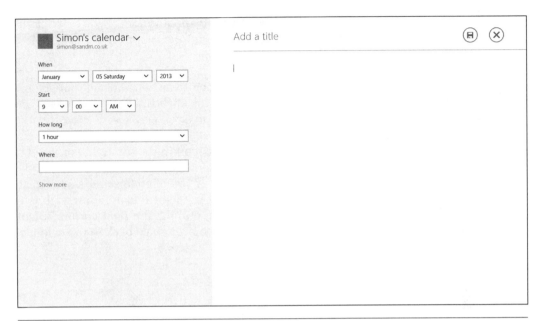

FIGURE 8-10   Set your appointment details in the Details area on the left; type the title and notes on the right.

the drop-down list. Fill in the details of the appointment on the left. Select the month, day, and year in the When drop-down lists, and select the time under Start. Set how long the appointment will last in the How Long drop-down list, and type in the location in the Where box.

Click or tap the Show More link if you want to set more options:

- **How often**   If you're scheduling something that you will do on a regular basis, change from the default of Once by choosing how often it will occur from the drop-down menu: Every Day, Every Weekday, Every Week, Every Month, or Every Year. It will then be added to your schedule appropriately.
- **Reminder**   By default, the Calendar app reminds you about appointments 15 minutes before they happen; click or tap Reminder and choose None if you don't want a notification, or choose anywhere from 5 Minutes to One Week beforehand.
- **Status**   If you aren't sure whether you're going to go to the appointment you're making, you can change your Status from Busy (the default) to Tentative or even Free. If you need to remind other people who look at your calendar that you'll be away, you can choose Out of Office so they know you'll be gone longer than the duration of the event.
- **Who**   If you want to invite someone else to join you, type their email address in the Who box or click or tap the plus-sign icon next to the box and choose their name from the People app. The Calendar app will mail an invitation to them, and if they have a calendar associated with that email address, the meeting will show up in their calendar too.

As with an email message, you can give the appointment a title by clicking or tapping the Add a Title placeholder and typing it in; click or tap the Add a Message placeholder to type in the details of the meeting.

 There isn't an app bar for adding information to an appointment, but you can use CTRL-V to paste in details you've copied to the Clipboard from another app, like an address from a website or directions from an email message.

When you're finished, click or tap the Save icon in the top-right corner of the screen (click or tap the Close button and choose Discard Changes if you decide you don't want to make the appointment after all). If you need to see the details later on or make changes, click or tap the appointment in the calendar. If you want to delete the meeting, click or tap the Delete Event button in the top right corner (it looks like a trash can) and choose Delete, or use the Close button to go back to the calendar view.

9

Send and Receive Instant Messages

HOW TO...

- Set up your IM account
- Sign in and out of the Messaging app
- Change your online status
- Invite people to your contacts list
- Send and receive instant messages
- Manage message threads
- Update your account settings
- Chat with Facebook friends

Email isn't always the fastest way to communicate, especially if you're just not getting your point across. If you need to talk to someone who's sitting in front of their computer (or even on their phone or tablet if they have the right messaging app installed), you can have a conversation in real time and get replies straightaway with instant messaging. The built-in Messaging app in Windows 8 lets you communicate with your friends whether they're using Windows 8, Windows Live Messenger, or even Facebook Chat. If you want to have a phone conversation with your friends or use your webcam for a video chat, you can do that in Skype; we'll show you how that works in Chapter 10. But if you want to type messages while you're doing something else on your PC at the same time, or you want to share a link to a website that's easier to copy and paste than read out, instant messaging is quick and convenient. We'll also show you how to avoid being disturbed by instant messages when you're busy.

Windows 8's Messaging app takes advantage of your Microsoft account to connect you to Microsoft's Windows Messenger service and to Facebook. If you log in to Windows 8 with a Microsoft account, you will be able to use Messaging as soon as you log in. If you don't, you'll need to add a Microsoft account the first time you run Messaging.

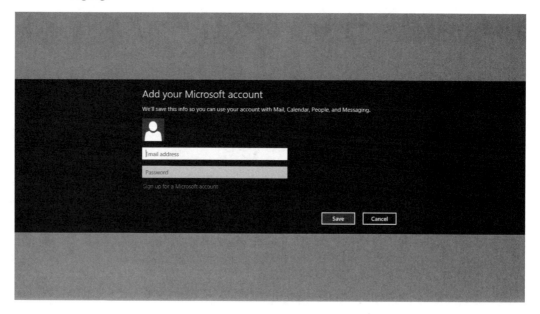

Launch the Messaging App

Open the Messaging app, shown in Figure 9-1, by clicking or tapping the Messaging tile on the Start screen.

The Messaging app screen is divided into three areas:

- A list of recent message threads appears on the left side of the screen. A *thread* is a group of messages about one topic. The Messaging app records each thread and makes each recorded thread available in the thread list so you can go back to the conversation later.
- The messages within the selected thread appear in the center of the screen.
- Any of your correspondents who are currently online are identified on the right side of the screen. The upper right corner of the screen displays an icon for each service to which you're connected.

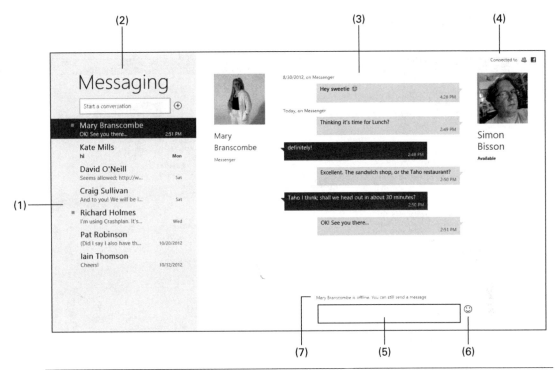

FIGURE 9-1   The Windows 8 Messaging app lets you chat with friends via Windows Messenger or Facebook. (1) Recent conversations, (2) Start a new conversation, (3) Your current conversation, (4) Your online status, (5) Type in a new message, (6) Add emoticons or Emoji, (7) Your contact's online status

Set Up Your Messaging Account

Your Microsoft account is also a Windows Messenger account, so you're able to chat with friends and contacts who are using Windows 8 or Windows Messenger (and now Skype when linked to a Microsoft account).

The first time you run Messaging, you'll see a helpful note in the lower left corner of the Messaging screen, stating that you should go to the Settings area and choose

Accounts to set up a new account or manage an existing account. Click or tap Ok to hide this note.

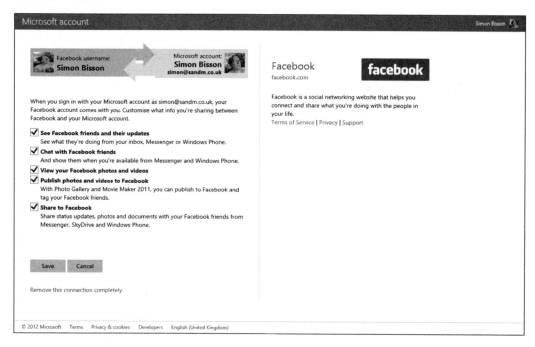

To add an account, open the Charms bar and then click or tap the Settings charm. In the Settings pane, click or tap Accounts. You can now add a Facebook account if you haven't previously linked one to your Microsoft account. Currently, Messaging only supports two accounts, one for Windows Messenger and one for Facebook. (If you want to use additional services or additional accounts, you'll need download a third-party app. You'll find several in the Social section of the Windows Store.)

To connect a Facebook account to your Microsoft account, go to http://profile.live .com and click Connect to choose connected social networks. To use Facebook Chat

Did You Know?

You Can Only use Messenger and Facebook

The Messaging app connects to the Windows Messenger service by default so that you can chat with other Windows 8 and Windows Messenger users. If you're already connected to both Windows Messenger and Facebook and you try to add a new account, you'll receive a message stating that "You've added all the accounts available for this app."

from Messaging, check the Chat with Facebook Friends check box and then click or tap Save. (The other options are described later in this chapter.)

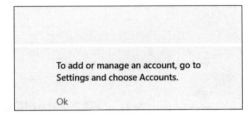

When you connect to Facebook from inside Messaging, you'll see a standard Facebook app authentication dialog box. Fill in your email address or phone number and your Facebook password. You may be asked to give your device a name for Facebook to use to remind you where you're logged in.

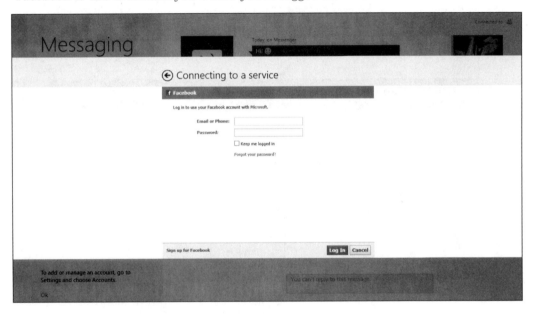

Change Your Online Status

When you start the Messaging app, it opens in the last conversation you were having, with the last message you sent. Messaging supports two status types: Available or Invisible. When your status is Available, anyone can send you messages, and can see that you're online. Setting your status to Invisible marks you as offline, though you can see your friends' online statuses.

To change your status, right-click in Messaging or swipe up from the bottom of the screen to open the app bar.

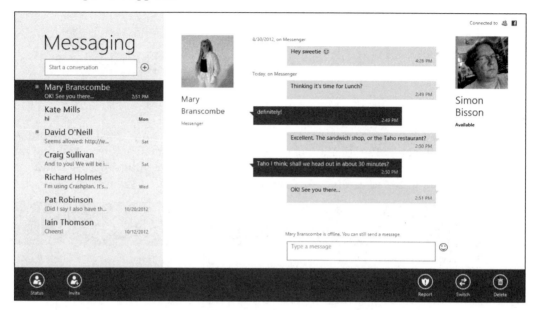

Click or tap the Status icon to open the Status pop-up menu. If you're online, then the Available option is checked. If you click or tap Invisible, you will remain online but your status will be shown as offline to everyone else.

Invite People to Your Contacts List

Windows 8 adds contacts associated with Windows Messenger to the People app, and you can use this to find who is online at any time. However, there may be occasions when you want to add someone to Messaging who's not in your contact list. To do so, you have to invite that person, as described next.

In Messaging, swipe up or right-click to open the app bar. Click or tap the Invite icon. This opens a web browser to a page in your online Microsoft account profile, Add Friends to Messenger. In the text box, type the email address of the person whom you want to invite to your contacts list. Click or tap Next.

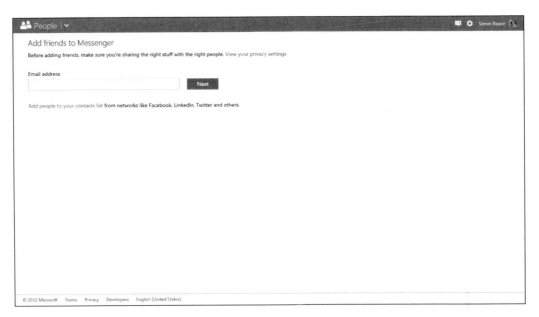

You'll then be prompted to send an invitation by email. The invitation, which can't be edited, includes your profile picture and a link to the Microsoft account website where the recipient can sign up for a Messenger account (if they don't already have a Microsoft account). Once they've accepted the invitation they'll then appear in your contacts list. Click or tap Invite to send the message.

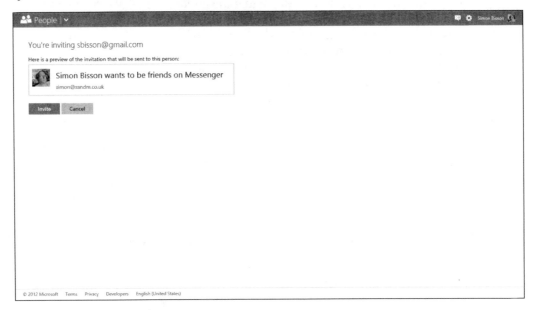

Close the browser and return to Messaging.

Set Permissions

In the Messaging app, open the Charms bar, click or tap the Settings charm to open the Messaging Settings pane, and click or tap Permissions to access the settings shown in Figure 9-2. Here, you can give the Messaging app access to your web cam so that you can use video chat, and allow the app to display notifications of incoming messages while you're using other apps. If you want to see a count of messages displayed on your Lock screen, then enable Lock screen support by setting the switch to On. This allows Messaging to run in the background and receive updates while your PC is locked.

Send and Receive Instant Messages

Once you're logged in to Windows 8 with a Microsoft account, you're able to receive instant messages from your contacts. There are three ways to start a conversation in Messaging: respond to a message from a contact, start a conversation yourself by picking a contact from the People app, or resume a previous conversation. This is very convenient because, like many instant messaging tools, Messaging keeps a record of conversations you've had in the past. You can pick up a conversation in Messaging days, or even weeks, after the last message was sent.

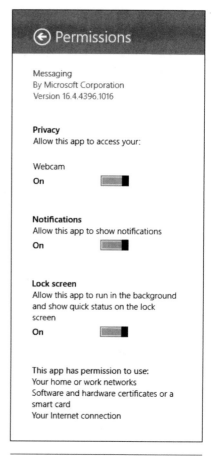

FIGURE 9-2 Choose whether you want to receive notifications and Lock screen status information.

If you no longer want to keep a conversation in your Messaging history, right-click or swipe up from the bottom of the screen to open the app bar and choose Delete. You'll probably want to do this with the sample message from Microsoft that's created when you open Messaging for the first time.

Create a New Message Conversation

Start a new conversation by clicking or tapping New Message in the upper left area of the Messaging screen. You can start typing a name into the text box, or tap or click the plus-sign symbol to use the People picker.

The People picker gives you a view of the People app's contact list, so that you can select the person you want to chat with. You can choose to see All or Online Only. Online Only gives you a dynamic view your online friends, as they log in and out of Facebook or Windows Messenger. Click or tap the name of the person in the list and then click or tap the Choose button.

This will start a new conversation and add the recipient's name to the list on the left side of the Messaging app. The most recent conversation appears at the top of the list, and the oldest appears at the bottom.

Your contact's profile picture (if available) and name appear in the middle of the screen,and you can begin typing a message to that person in the message box at the bottom of the screen (see Figure 9-3).

As you type your message, the Messaging app automatically identifies any spelling errors that it finds. Right-click or press and hold to choose a correct spelling, or to add a new word to the system dictionary. You can also choose to ignore the suggestions.

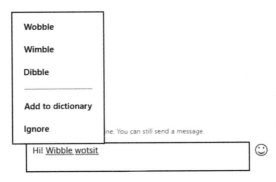

FIGURE 9-3 The selected message thread appears in the thread list, and you can type a new message in the message box.

If you want to add a quick shorthand for how you're feeling, you can use the smiley face icon at the side of the conversation text box to add an emoticon to your message. While you can type the familiar smiley or frowny faces, Windows 8 supports the more advanced Emoji character scheme that originated in Japan (see Figure 9-4). From the pop-up menu, you can pick a face that expresses an emotion, or any other icon, from a large selection. That large selection means you can use a graphical shorthand in your messages.

When you've typed your message, press or tap ENTER to send. You'll then see it at the bottom of the current conversation in a gray box. When your recipient is typing, you'll see "[Name] is typing..." just above the message box, where [Name] is the name of the friend you're talking to. After the recipient types his or her message, the response appears in a purple box (see Figure 9-5).

As you and the other person type messages back and forth, the conversation scrolls down and earlier messages in the conversation scroll off the top of the screen. If you need to scroll up and down in the conversation, move the mouse pointer to the right of the message boxes to open the scroll bar, or hold and drag the conversation up and down with a finger.

You'll also notice that the last response in the thread, either from you or your friend, appears just below the name of the person in the thread list. Unread messages are highlighted in purple.

FIGURE 9-4   Pick an Emoji symbol to insert a picture into your message.

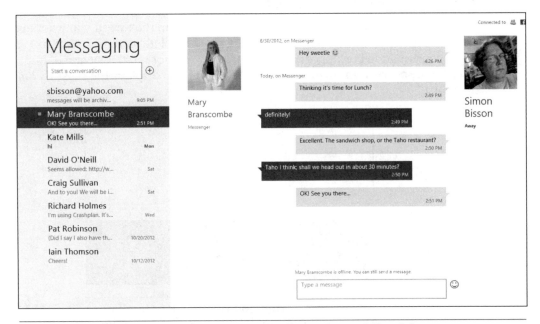

FIGURE 9-5   You can read the conversation down the middle of the screen. Gray speech boxes hold your messages, and purple boxes hold your contact's messages.

You Can See When Your Recipient Is Offline

If the person you're communicating with goes offline, the Messaging app lets you know right away by displaying a message telling you your contact is offline, but you can still send them a message.

Paste and Select Messages

If you have text on the Clipboard, such as a website address, that you want to paste into your message, right-click or tap the message box and then click or tap Paste in the menu. If you want to copy your entire message to the Clipboard for future use (or for another message), first right-click or tap the message box and click or tap Select All. Then, copy the selected text to the Clipboard by pressing CTRL-C or by clicking or tapping the selection and then clicking or tapping Copy.

Delete Message Threads

To delete a message thread in your list, right-click or tap the thread you want to delete, and open the app bar. You can then click or tap the Delete icon, as shown in Figure 9-6.

A confirmation box appears above the icon. Click or tap the Delete button. The thread disappears from the list and the Messaging app displays the most recent thread in the list.

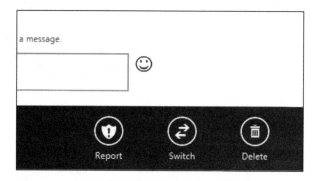

FIGURE 9-6 After you right-click or tap the thread you want to delete in the list, open the app bar and click or tap Delete.

If you want to switch between Messenger and Facebook, use the Switch icon to change accounts. You can also use the Report icon to let Microsoft know if a Messenger user has had their account hacked.

Update Your Account Settings

If you need to update your account settings at any time, open the Charms bar, click or tap the Settings charm, and then click or tap Accounts in the Settings pane. In the Accounts area that appears, click or tap the type of account you want to change. The Messenger account appears by default, and other accounts appear below it on the list.

Change Windows Messenger Settings

To change your Messenger settings, click or tap Messenger in the Accounts area to open the Messenger area, as shown in Figure 9-7. You can change the following options:

- **Account name**   The default name is Messenger. You can change this to a more memorable name.
- **Download new email**   Ignore this, as this is used by the Mail app.

Change Social Network Account Settings

If you have connected Facebook to the Messaging app and you want to change the account settings, click or tap the Facebook account in the Accounts list to view or change the account name and then click or tap Manage This Account Online.

Windows 8 manages all social network account information in your Microsoft account,

FIGURE 9-7   You can change the account name Messaging displays for your Windows Messenger account.

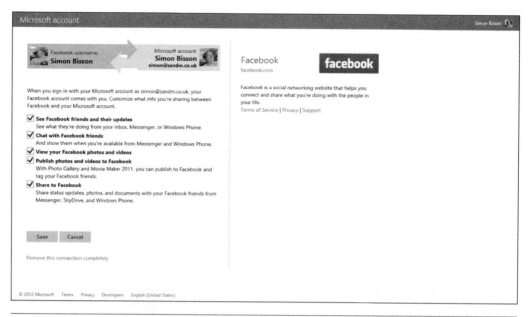

FIGURE 9-8 Customize the information you share between Facebook and your Microsoft account.

so after you click or tap Manage This Account Online, Internet Explorer opens and displays the Microsoft Account page, shown in Figure 9-8, where you can edit your social network account settings. Connecting to Facebook also lets Windows 8 work with Facebook photos and videos, as well as sharing to Facebook via the Share charm.

Use Facebook Chat from Messaging

Once you've connected a Microsoft account to Facebook, you can use Windows 8's Messaging app to chat to your Facebook friends, as well as to other Windows Messenger users. You'll also be able to see recent chat messages in the Messaging live tile.

To start a conversation, open Messaging. You can choose to continue an existing conversation from the history pane or start a new one. In the text box on the left of the screen, type a name. Windows will auto-complete names from accounts that are linked in the People app, so just tap or click a contact's name. Alternatively, you can open the People picker by clicking or tapping the plus-sign symbol. This automatically shows you friends who are online (you see a green bar on the right side of their profile picture). The People picker will dynamically update so you can see when new friends come online.

When you're in a conversation, you'll see which network you're using under your friend's name. Type messages into the textbox at the bottom of the screen and press or tap ENTER to send. Your messages will appear in gray speech bubbles, while your correspondent's will appear in purple speech bubbles. If you have several conversations running simultaneously, you can switch between them using the conversation history on the left side of the screen, which is sorted in date order.

Windows 8 supports a wide selection of emoticons and Emoji and they work in messages you send to Facebook friends as well. Tap the face icon by the text box to pick an appropriate icon. Icons are grouped by type, so if you're thinking of heading out for pizza, you can send a picture of a pizza!

 If you chat with a friend inside Facebook or on another PC, you may see some of their messages inside Messaging as well as some of your replies, but you won't always see all the messages in the full conversation.

10

Make Phone and Video Calls

HOW TO...

- Make Skype phone and video calls
- Add and manage favorites
- Save a phone number to your contacts list
- Configure Skype for Windows 8
- Use Skype for Windows on the desktop

Windows 8 contains two built-in tools that you can use to contact others, save contact information, and manage your contacts: Messaging and People. You can connect with friends on Facebook and Windows Messenger by using Messaging as an instant messaging tool, as described in Chapter 9. Online chat isn't the only way to talk to friends, especially if you want to talk to someone the way you would do on a phone or have video chats.

Microsoft recently bought Skype, an Internet telephony company, and has released a Windows 8 version of Skype's software that allows you to make phone calls and video calls, and send text messages, through your computer. Skype for Windows 8 runs on both Windows 8 and Windows RT, so you can also use it on a Surface tablet. Microsoft recently announced that Skype will replace Windows Messenger in 2013, and that Skype will become increasingly integral to both Windows 8 and Microsoft's other product lines.

Make Skype Phone and Video Calls

Start by opening the Windows Store and downloading the Skype app. The first time you launch Skype, you'll be asked to link any existing Skype account to your

You Can Get More Features with a Subscription

Skype comes in free and subscription versions. The free version allows you to make video and voice calls, call toll-free telephone numbers around the world, send instant messages, and connect with your friends. If you want to do more, Skype offers a range of different subscription services. These add features like unlimited calls to landline and mobile phones in countries around the world, text messaging, and adding incoming and outgoing phone numbers—so you can be called from land lines and mobile phones as well as from computers. Other premium features include group video and voice chat, as well as screen sharing. You can also register a business account, which lets you assign Skype call credit to groups of users.

Microsoft account. If you don't have a Skype account you can use it with your Microsoft account.

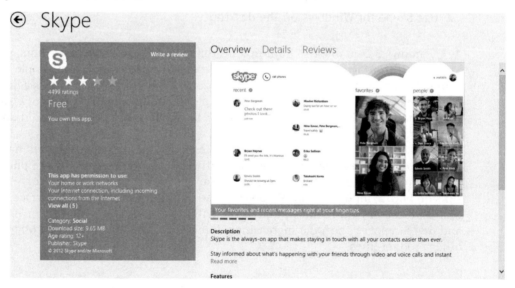

Skype also asks for access to your webcam and microphone for video calls. Choose Allow to enable voice and video. If you Block you will only be able to send text messages and use Skype chat.

Skype then requests to run in the background to show quick status and notifications of missed calls on your Lock screen. Choose Allow to receive call notifications. If you choose Don't Allow you will only receive call notifications when running Skype.

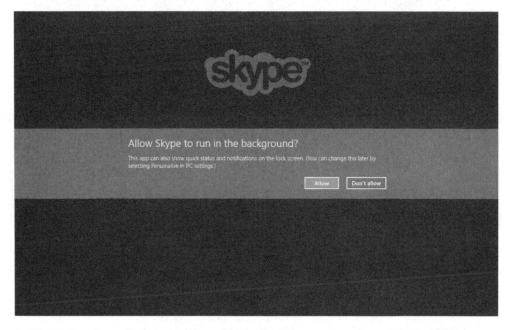

Skype then launches, connects to both the Skype network and the Windows Messenger network, and downloads your contacts to its People directory. It also links into the People app so that you can call and text people directly. If you've used the desktop version of Skype, you'll find that the new Windows 8 version is very different, as it's a touch-ready app that uses tiles and has all the user features you'd expect in a Windows Store app. It includes all the important features from the desktop version, but it's easier to use with your fingers. The new design means the things you want to do quickly, like calling frequent contacts, are right in front of you, just a click or tap away (see Figure 10-1).

The center of the Skype app shows a list of recent calls and contacts, as well as the text of the last chat message you've received. You'll see up to six calls on the main Skype screen. Click or tap Recent to see more of your call history.

Skype for Windows 8 takes advantage of Windows 8's background application and Lock screen features. You can set it as a Lock screen app in PC settings, to get quick notifications of missed calls when your screen is locked. The Skype tile is also a live tile, which shows your missed calls and messages on the Start screen.

Set Up Audio, Video, and Profile Settings

Skype for Windows 8 takes advantage of the new device management features of Windows 8 and automatically selects your default microphone, speakers, and camera. If you need to check or adjust the configuration, use the Windows 8 Settings charm to open Skype's settings. Choose Options to configure Skype's audio and video settings.

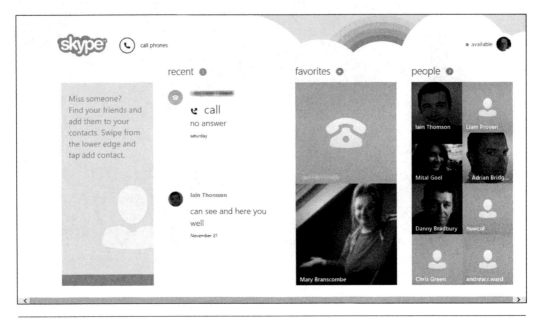

FIGURE 10-1 The new-look Windows Store Skype app shows a list of recent contacts on the right of the screen, along with favorite contacts and recent conversations.

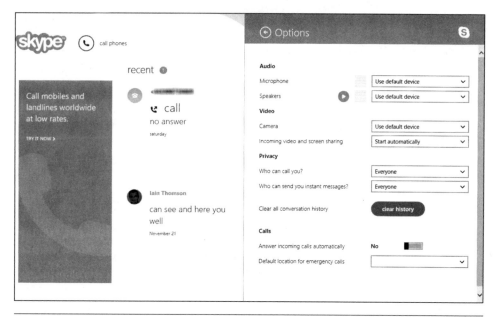

FIGURE 10-2   Test your sound and change settings from the Skype options pane.

You can use the settings pane, shown in Figure 10-2, to switch between devices and test sound levels. Click or tap the Play icon to the right of Speakers to check sound levels. You should hear the Skype ring tone and see a set of sound level bars.

If you want to use a device other than the default device for audio or video, choose the device you prefer to use from the corresponding drop-down list. You can use these settings to switch to audio and video devices connected to USB ports, such as an external microphone or video camera. Skype will offer you a list of currently connected devices, as shown next; just click or tap to select the device you want to use.

If you still can't connect to your speakers, microphone, and/or video camera, you may need to use the Windows troubleshooter to pinpoint the problem. You can keep the Skype app open in a Windows 8 snapped view while you switch to the desktop to access the troubleshooting tools, which you can learn more about in Chapter 19.

The Options pane also lets you control your Privacy settings. As shown in Figure 10-2, you can choose who can call you, the options being either everyone with a Skype account or just your designated friends. Similarly, you can lock down instant messaging to allow just your friends to send instant messages to you. The other Privacy option lets you clear your conversation history.

Under Calls, you can choose whether to answer incoming calls automatically. Unless you don't mind being interrupted by calls regardless of what you are doing or where you are, set this option to No so that you can choose to answer calls manually. You can also set a default location (a country) for any emergency calls you may use Skype to make (though we recommend that you not rely on Skype in an emergency).

Tap or click the Windows 8 Settings charm to open Skype's Profile view (see Figure 10-3). This gives you a basic view of your Skype profile, with a text box in which to enter a mood message (Skype's version of a Facebook status update) and a choice of whether to be available or invisible online. You can also add a picture or update an existing Skype picture. Click or tap the user picture to open a Pictures File Picker. This lets you choose an image from your PC, or any image application on your PC that offers access to its files, including the Windows 8 camera application.

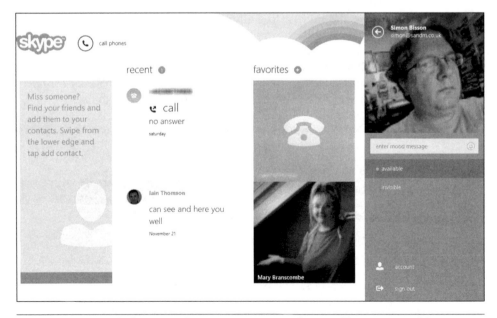

FIGURE 10-3 Click or tap the user picture in the Profile view to add a new image.

Click or tap the Account link to open your Skype account online, where you can add additional services or edit a more detailed profile. This takes you to the Skype web site, where you can add contact details and location. Although doing this is not essential, it's a good idea to have at least some basic contact information, especially if you find you're receiving calls intended for people whose name is the same as or similar to yours.

Add a Contact in Skype

The Windows 8 Skype app automatically adds your Windows Messenger and existing Skype contacts to its People directory. If this is the first time you've used Skype and you don't have any contacts listed, or if you want to call a new contact, you'll need to add to your Skype account the Skype details for the person you want to call. Click or tap the People link in the Skype app to open your personal Skype directory.

To add a new contact, slide from the bottom of the screen or right-click to open the app bar and click or tap the Add Contact button. This opens the Search charm, ready to search the entire Skype network for the contact details that you enter in the search field. Skype returns a list of all the possible matches in the network, as shown in Figure 10-4. If multiple entries are returned, use their location information to help you choose the right one.

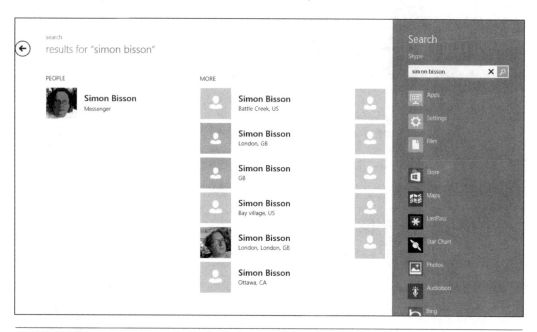

FIGURE 10-4   You'll see a list of all the possible Skype users who match your search terms. Choose the one you want to talk to.

Once you've found the entry for the person who you want to add to your contacts list, you have to request and receive their permission to add them to your contacts list and make Skype calls to them. Click or tap their name to open the contact request form, shown next, enter your request, and click Send. The person then has the option of whether or not to allow you to add them to your contacts list and make Skype calls to them. If they accept your request, you'll see their status as Available, and will be able to call or message them.

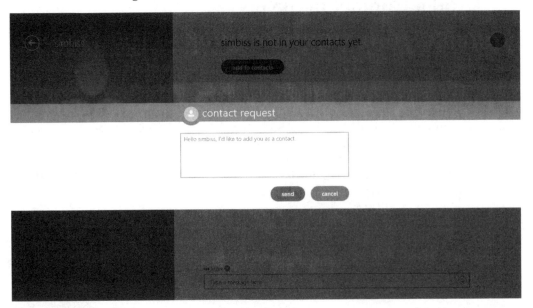

You will then find their contact information in both Skype and in the Windows 8 People app. Contact cards for Skype contacts can be linked to other contact cards in the People app, so you only need to look them up once. Contact card information includes an email address, phone number, full name, and Skype username if there is one. If you call a fellow Skype user using voice or video, the calls to that user are free of charge.

Make a Voice Call

There are three ways to make a voice call using Skype in Windows 8:

- Click or tap on a contact in your Skype contacts list and then click or tap the green phone icon. This starts a free Skype-to-Skype conversation.

Time to say hi! When you start chatting with Mary Branscombe, your messages and call history will appear here.

via Messenger

Type a message here

- If you're trying to call someone who's not in your contacts list, like a business or a toll-free number, click or tap the Call Phones button in the top left of the app, next to the Skype logo. This opens a dialer, shown next, where you can click or tap in a number. You'll need to have a subscription or pay-as-you go call credit to call a landline or a mobile number, unless the call is toll free. Use the Skype website to buy call credit or to set up a subscription.

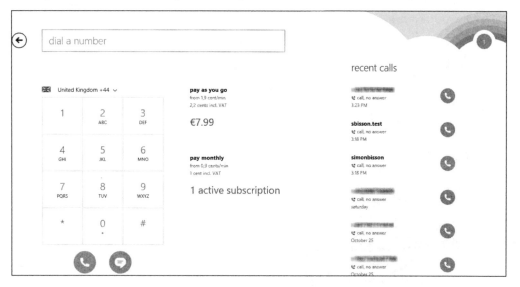

- You can call a contact from the Windows 8 People app. Click or tap on a contact's number to start a call or, if their Skype account has been registered, to make a direct Skype-to-Skype call or send a message. If you have sufficient call credit, you can also use Skype to send SMS messages from your PC.

Make a Video Call

If you have a video camera connected to your system, you can make a video call to any other Skype contact by clicking or tapping on the contact in the Skype contacts list. In the contact information on the left side of the call window, shown next, click or tap the video camera button. The video call window opens and starts to make the call, and if the other person also has a video camera connected, you can see each other talking. If they don't have a camera they'll still be able to see you, and you'll be able to hear them—just like a normal Skype call. Make sure that you have a microphone, such as one connected to your video camera, ready to go before you start your call. Skype adds a video call option to the Windows 8 People app, where you can click or tap to start a Skype video conference.

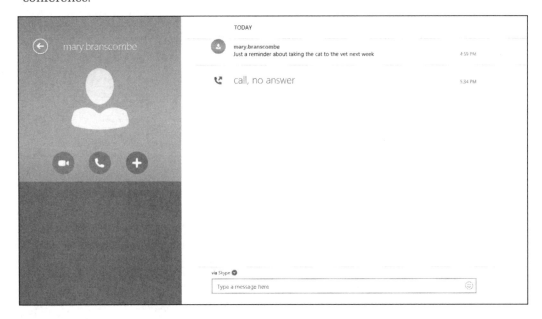

Manage Contacts and Favorites

Skype's People view complements the Windows 8 People app, showing only your Skype contacts. Click or tap People in Skype to open your contacts list (see Figure 10-5). Click All or Available to switch between seeing all contacts and seeing only those who have set their Skype status to Available. You'll see that the Available link also indicates how many contacts can be called at the moment. You can also use Semantic Zoom by pinching the page to quickly jump to a section of your contacts list if you have a lot of Skype contacts.

Add a New Contact to Skype

You can add a new contact to Skype by opening the app bar and clicking or tapping Add Contact to search online for Skype users, who will need to approve your contact request. Alternatively, click or tap Save Number to add a telephone number to your Skype directory. Give the contact a name, and choose from the drop-down list whether you're adding a home, mobile, office, or other number. You can also pick a dialing code for the number from a large list of countries, each displayed with its own flag. Click or tap the flag to open the list of countries (see Figure 10-6).

Any Skype contact can be made a favorite and added to the main screen of the Skype app. Open a contact card in the Skype People directory. Swipe up from the bottom of the screen or right click to open the app bar, and then click or tap the

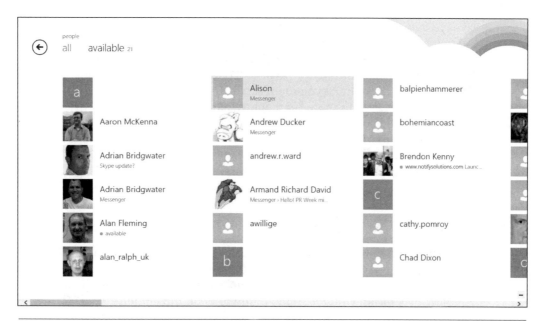

FIGURE 10-5 Skype's People view shows all your Skype contacts. To see only the contacts you can call now, click or tap Available.

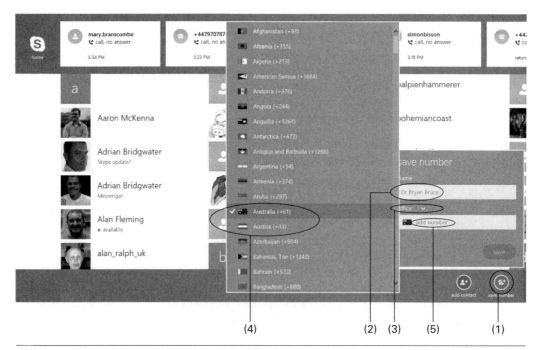

(4)   (2) (3)   (5)   (1)

FIGURE 10-6 (1) Save number, (2) Add contact name, (3) Choose number type, (4) Choose country, (5) Add number.

Favorite button to add a new favorite. The Favorite button will be highlighted in white, and you will find a tile for your contact added to Skype's initial view. You can remove a contact as a Skype favorite by clicking or tapping the tile to open the contact. Open the app bar and click or tap the Favorite icon to remove the highlight. The contact's tile is removed from the Skype main screen.

If you use Skype on more than one Windows 8 PC, you'll find that favorites are not synchronized between PCs. You'll need to add them to each copy of Skype you have. That means you can have one set of favorites on your work PC and a different set of favorites on your home PC, which may be helpful if you need to keep your shortcuts separate for calls to business contacts and calls to friends.

Edit Skype Settings

If your microphone, speakers, and/or video camera weren't working when you set up Skype, or if you need to make changes to one or more audio or video settings (like changing the microphone), click or tap the Settings charm within the Skype window and then click or tap Options in the menu to open the Options pane.

Although the Skype for Windows 8's settings options are sparse compared to those for the desktop version, you'll find everything you need to get started in the Options pane, except the capability to test the microphone settings, which you can do either by installing the desktop version of Skype alongside the Windows Store version, as described later in the chapter, or by using the Windows sound tools, as described in this section.

Change and Test Microphone Settings from Windows

Switch to the Windows desktop and right-click the speaker icon in the notification area. Choose Recording Devices to test the microphone settings. The Recording tab of the Sound dialog box shows you all the available recording devices built into or attached to your PC, as shown next. Select the device you plan to use with Skype. Right-click and choose Set as Default Communications Device to make the device your default recording and communication device.

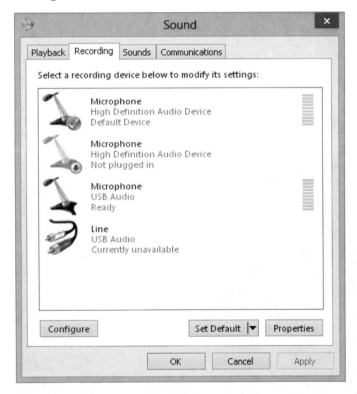

You can start talking into the microphone to see if Skype can hear you. If so, then you'll see green bars in the volume bar. The more green bars you see in the volume bar, the louder the signal the microphone registers.

In the Skype Options pane, use the drop-down list to manually select the microphone you want to use.

Change and Test Speakers and Change Speaker Volume

In the Audio section of the Skype Options pane, click or tap the blue Play button to the right of the speaker name to hear the default Skype ringtone. As the ringtone plays, you can see the volume level highlighted in green, showing Skype is playing the ringtone. You can't adjust the system volume without closing the Options pane, so use this as a diagnostic tool to check that you've correctly set the volume before you make a call.

Click or tap the Speakers drop-down box to select a different set of speakers from the drop-down list. You can then test the speakers by clicking or tapping the green Play button and listening to the ringtone again so you can confirm that the speakers work properly.

Change Video Settings

In the Options pane in Skype, use the Video settings section to choose which camera you want to use for video calls. Unlike the desktop version of Skype, there's no preview view, so if you want to see what you will look like to your contacts, open the Windows 8 Camera app to test your camera settings (see Figure 10-7).

The default setting for Incoming Video and Screen Sharing is Start Automatically, meaning you receive incoming video and shared screens regardless of what you're

FIGURE 10-7 Use the Windows 8 Camera app to test camera settings before making a video call.

currently doing on your computer. This can be awkward, especially if you receive a video call in the middle of a game or while you're working. We recommend switching this option to Ask, which will pop up an alert when you receive a call, giving you the option to accept or decline the call.

How to...   # Use the Desktop Version of Skype

While the Windows 8 version of Skype is a great tool for quickly chatting to friends and for video conferencing, sometimes you will want to use the desktop version of Skype, especially if you want to use Skype add-ins. The Windows Store app security model doesn't let apps use add-ins, so everything needs to be built into the app. That means Skype add-ins won't run in the Windows 8 version of Skype.

Happily, the two versions of Skype will run concurrently on the same PC (though you won't get notifications or Lock screen alerts with the desktop version). That means you can download and install the desktop version of Skype alongside the Windows Store app, and simply switch to the Windows desktop to use Skype add-ins when you want to record a call or play games, for example. Install add-ins from Skype's online store.

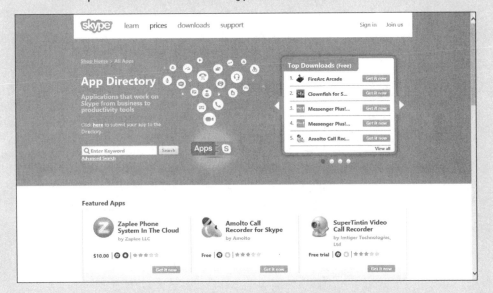

As Skype contacts are stored in the cloud by the Skype service, any changes you make to one contacts list are reflected in the other, so any friends you add to the Windows 8 version of Skype can be called from the desktop, and vice versa.

11

Access Online Social Networks

HOW TO...

- Connect to Facebook and Twitter
- Use the People app to work with social networks
- Pin tiles for your closest friends to the Start screen
- Talk to friends with Facebook and text messages
- Share to social networks from the Share charm
- Find social apps in the Windows Store

With Windows 8, social networks like Facebook and Twitter aren't just websites you visit to catch up with friends. You can put tiles for your friends and family right on your Start screen and use the contact details they share in social networks to send messages to them.

Windows 8 has been designed to work with popular social networks (and with services like Skype that have their own address book). You'll see friends from your social networks in the Mail, Calendar, and Messaging apps and even in the Photos app, but the place to organize your contacts is the People app. In this chapter we'll show you how to see updates from your social networks, send messages to online friends, and combine address books from different social networking sites and services using these apps.

Integrating social networks into Windows 8 relies on using your Microsoft account and Microsoft's Live.com service to link your PC to services like Facebook, Flickr, and Twitter. You'll need a Microsoft account to take advantage of these features; the easiest way to do that is by signing in to Windows with your Microsoft account.

 If you've used Microsoft's Live service (or Windows Phone) in the past, you may have already connected social networks to your Microsoft account. That means Windows 8 will be connected to your social networks as soon as you log in for the first time.

Add Your Social Network Accounts to the People App

Microsoft ships several apps as standard with Windows 8, and the People app is one of the most important. It's not only a contact list, it's also where you can post messages to social networks, as well as see your friends' updates and messages. Because the People app uses the social connections in your Microsoft account, you must log in to your Microsoft account first to use the People app.

If you're using a Microsoft account to log into Windows 8, you'll automatically be signed into the People app. If you aren't using a Microsoft account to sign into Windows and you haven't already added your Microsoft account to the Mail app, Calendar app, or Messaging app, you'll see the message in Figure 11-1 the first time you open the People app. Fill in your account details or sign up for a new Microsoft account.

Once you've added your Microsoft account to the People app, Windows 8 will start to synchronize information from your social networks into both the People app and other apps like Calendar and Photos. You'll start to see notifications for tweets and Facebook messages on the People live tile on the Start screen, as well as Facebook birthdays in the Calendar app.

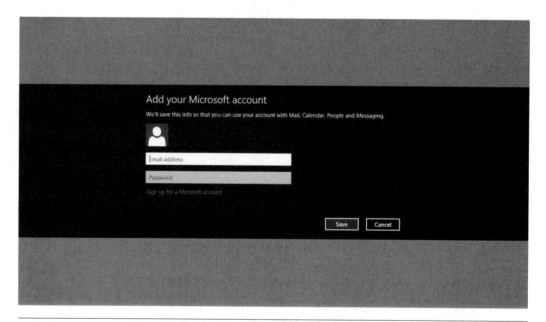

FIGURE 11-1   You need to sign in with a Microsoft account to use the People app.

You'll get a calendar feed of Facebook birthdays for your friends. Unlike Windows Phone, you won't see Facebook events in the Calendar app, so you will need to make your own calendar entries for each Facebook event you're attending.

The live tiles for the People, Mail, and Calendar apps are a quick way to see messages you've been sent, or recent updates from friends. The tiles update regularly, and if you pin tiles for close friends and family to the Start screen, as described later in the chapter, you can see their news at a glance. However, it's important to remember that a notification on a live tile isn't a link to the message or update you see on the tile. Clicking it will only open the app; it won't take you directly to the email or Facebook message that caught your attention.

Connect a Microsoft Account to Your Social Networks

You can tell Windows about accounts you have for specific services like Twitter and Facebook when you set up accounts in the People app (open the Settings charm, choose Accounts, click or tap Add an Account, and then choose the type of account you want to connect). But you can connect to many more social networks if you configure your account on the Microsoft account website as well.

To connect a social network to your Microsoft account, you'll need to log into http://profile.live.com/. This is where you manage your account, and where you'll control the information shared between Windows 8 and your social networks. Under your account picture you'll find two links that allow you to connect and manage networks. Click or tap Connect to add a new network; click or tap Manage to edit existing connections, which is discussed a bit later.

When you click or tap Connect, you can link your Microsoft account to the social network accounts you want to use with Windows. You'll need to authenticate with each service, choose the permissions you want to give to Microsoft's services, and choose what you want to share with the service you're using. You only need to do this once, because after you've connected services, they'll remain in sync. Connecting services to a Microsoft account also means that you can access them from other applications and services, including Outlook.com and Office 2013.

Currently, four social networks are available through the People app: Facebook, LinkedIn, Twitter, and Flickr. You can add your LinkedIn address book to the People app, and you can see and send status updates on Facebook and Twitter—directly or through the Share charm.

 If you have a Flickr account, you can use it to view your online photo gallery in the Photos app.

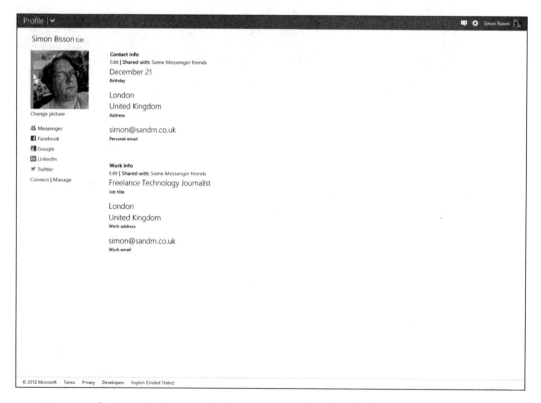

You can change which permissions a service has by clicking Manage. This takes you to a page that shows connected services. Click or tap the Edit button under each service to change permissions—or to remove that service completely. For example, if you want to post updates to Facebook but not use Facebook Chat, you can choose the appropriate check boxes. Once you're done setting permissions, click or tap Save to return to the Manage Your Accounts page of your profile, or click or tap Cancel if you don't want to make any changes after all.

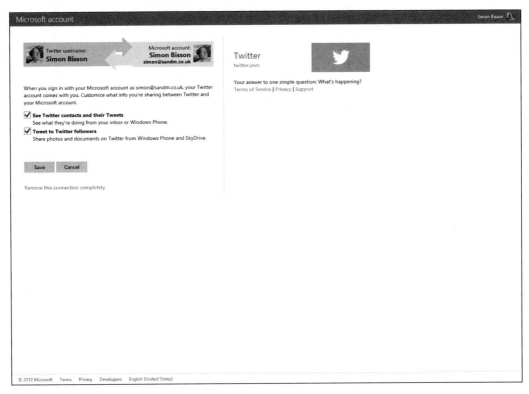

Connecting your social networks to a Microsoft account simplifies moving your settings from one Windows 8 computer to another, and to Windows Phone devices or Windows RT tablets, as you only need to do it once. Simply log in to Windows with your Microsoft account and you're automatically connected to your social networks.

Because it's your Microsoft account rather than your computer that handles the communications with social networks, if you read a message on one Windows 8 PC, it's marked as read on all your other PCs and devices. This makes it a lot easier to keep on top of your notifications—and to avoid re-reading messages again and again.

Manage Your Address Book in the People App

When you open the People app, you see three sections: one for your social connections, one for your favorite contacts, and one that lists all the people in your various address books. Clicking or tapping any contact opens their Contact card, an example of which is shown in Figure 11-2.

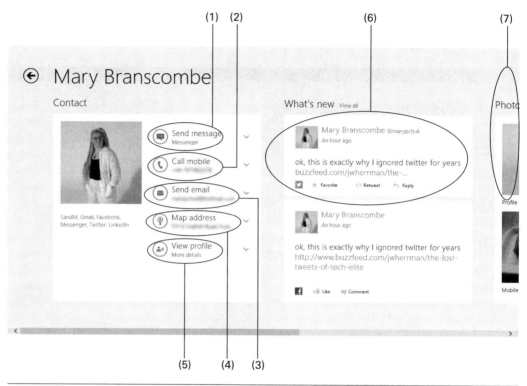

FIGURE 11-2 Typical People Contact card. (1) Send instant and text via Messenger or Skype, (2) Call via Skype, (3) Send email, (4) Show address on a map, (5) See a full profile, (6) Status updates, (7) Recent photos.

Which options you see in a Contact card vary depending on which social networks you've added to your Microsoft account and which other apps you have installed. By default you can send IM messages and reply to their recent Facebook or Twitter updates, as well as seeing their Facebook photos. If you have the Windows Store Skype app installed you can use a friend's Contact card to phone them or send text messages via Skype. (See Chapter 10 to learn how to set up the Skype app.) Contact cards are a one-stop shop for keeping up to date with friends—and for keeping them up to date on your life.

Open the app bar for a Contact card by right-clicking anywhere on screen or by swiping over the top or bottom edge of a touchscreen. The app bar gives you options to link different profiles for the same person into a single Contact card, add the contact to your list of favorites, pin a tile for the contact to the Start screen, edit the contact's details, and delete the contact (see Figure 11-3).

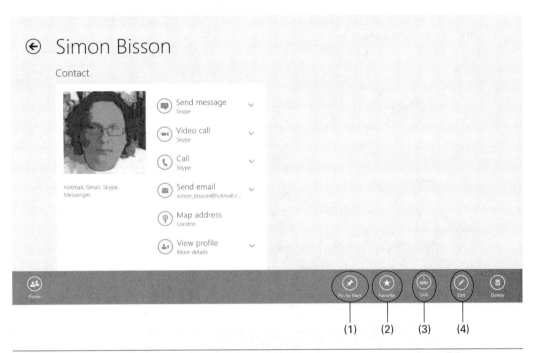

FIGURE 11-3   (1) Pin a live tile for this person to the Start screen. (2) Add to favorites. (3) Link cards. (4) Edit contact details.

 Make close friends favorites in the People app; that puts a tile for them next to your Me tile, so you can quickly stay in touch with them, whether that's sending email, writing messages, or making calls using Skype.

Link Multiple Contacts for the Same Person

You'll probably find that you have the same friend as a contact in your email address book, as a contact on social networks (many people use both Facebook and Twitter), and as a contact in your Skype address book. Instead of having a separate Contact card for that friend on every service (that's connected to your Microsoft account), you can link their various profiles together so that you see in a single Contact card all the ways you can get in touch with them.

Open the Contact card that you want to link the other cards to. Open the app bar and choose Link. This opens a window showing any profiles that are already linked for this person in the Linked Profiles list, and gives you suggestions for profiles that you may want to link to the Contact card in the Suggestions list. Click or tap a profile in the Suggestions list to move it to the Linked Profiles list. You can remove a previously linked profile from the Linked Profiles list by clicking or tapping it, which moves it to the Suggestions list.

When you're done editing links, click or tap Save to return to the Contact card.

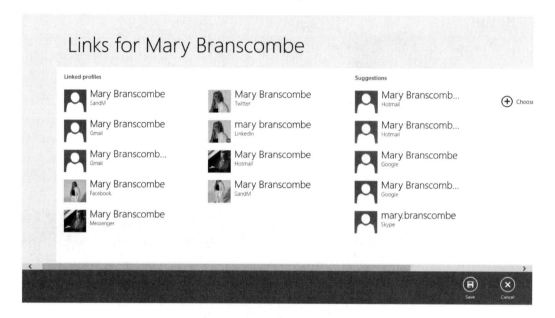

Give Friends Their Own Live Tiles

If you pin a contact to the Start screen, you'll see a live tile for that person showing recent messages they've posted, as well as their photograph. Use live tiles to see the latest news from friends and family you want to stay in touch with. You'll need to pin a live tile for each contact separately on each PC or tablet you use, as live tiles are not synced between computers via your Microsoft account.

Open the app bar and choose Pin to Start. You can type in a different name for the tile in the window that pops up, as shown in Figure 11-4. Click or tap Pin to Start when you're happy with the name.

Edit Contact Information

Some of the information for the people in your address book will come directly from the details they put on services like Skype and Facebook but you can add more information as well. And when it's a contact in your own address book, you can edit all the details for them. Click or tap on the person whose information you want to edit then right-click anywhere on screen or swipe across the top or bottom of the screen to open the app bar and click or tap the Edit icon.

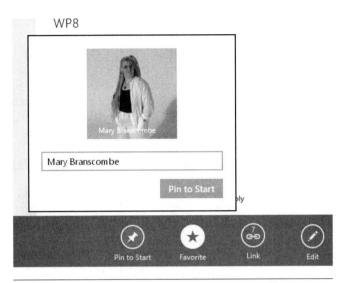

FIGURE 11-4   You can set a custom name for someone's live tile, like Mom or Dad.

The Edit Contact Info screen appears so you can make changes to your contact's information. You can make changes to the contact's first and last name, company name, email address, and mobile phone number. You can also click or tap the plus-sign icons on the screen to add name, email, phone, address, and other information such as a website address.

If you have more than one account for the same person, such as a Microsoft account and a Facebook account, when you select the Edit icon on the app bar you can choose which account you want to edit from the pop-up menu that appears.

Did You Know?

You Can Delete Accounts

You can delete any account you've added to the People app except for your Microsoft account. If you want to delete one or more accounts, click or tap one of the account icons in the upper right corner of the main People view. In the Accounts area, click or tap the account you want to delete. The Accounts area contains information about your selected account, and some accounts (like Google) include a Remove Account button at the bottom of the area so you can delete the account. Other accounts, like Facebook, require you to manage the accounts in your Windows Live account from within Internet Explorer.

See Recent News in a Contact Card

If you're following a contact on Twitter or Facebook, you'll see their last two status updates on their Contact card. Click or tap View All to see their recent updates. You can retweet, favorite, or reply to Tweets, and you can like or comment on Facebook statuses. The People app automatically shows pictures that people put in their updates, and if you click or tap on a status, you'll be able to see if it's been retweeted (and by whom) as well as what other people you follow have said in reply.

The detail view for a message is an important tool, as it also helps you navigate through a conversation. We'll look at this in more detail later in this chapter.

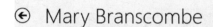

Choose How You See Contacts

If you have a lot of contacts, locating a particular contact by scrolling sideways through a long list of names can take time. To speed things up, use Windows 8's Semantic Zoom to minimize the People list, as shown next, and then click or tap on a letter of the alphabet to jump straight to the contacts whose names begin with that letter. To use Semantic Zoom, pinch your fingers together on a touchscreen or press CTRL and the hyphen key on your keyboard.

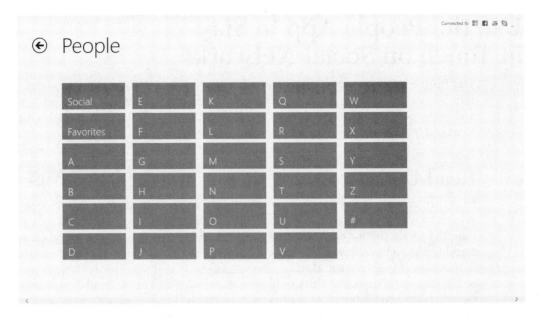

You can also choose how to organize the list of names. Open the Settings charm and choose Options to open the Options pane (see Figure 11-5). Change the slider from No to Yes to sort by surname rather than first name. You can also show only contacts from specific social networks to ensure you don't see too many duplicates. Hidden contacts are still stored on your PC and show up in search results.

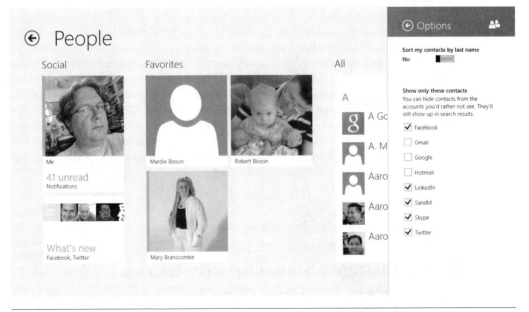

FIGURE 11-5 Choose the accounts you want to show as contacts in People.

Use the People App to Stay in Touch on Social Networks

The People app lets you see what your friends are up to online, read messages they've sent you and post your own updates on social networks. You can also send messages and make Skype calls to the friends you have in your various address books directly from the People app.

Read Updates from Friends on Social Networks

In the main view of the People app (previously shown in Figure 11-2), click or tap the What's New link to see status updates from all your contacts. This opens a new view that includes a tile for each message, with the newest messages displayed on screen; scroll to the right (or swipe left on a touchscreen) to view older messages Use your mouse or a finger to scroll through the messages. If you want more detail, you can tap or click to open the same detail view as from a Contact card. Twitter *hashtags* (words preceded with #) and usernames are live links and launch the Twitter website in the Windows 8 version of Internet Explorer. Web links are also active, though Windows 8 doesn't automatically expand shortened links, so you can't see in advance which website the link opens.

Clicking or tapping a username opens the person's Contact card, so you can continue the conversation via email or instant message, or even initiate a voice call. If someone has posted a picture, it shows in a larger tile, and you can click or tap it to open it in a picture viewer. You'll need to open the message on the Twitter or Facebook website if you want to save a copy of any images though.

Click or tap Reply to reply to a Twitter or Facebook message. You can only reply automatically to the person who sent the message, so if you want to include other users in your reply message, you'll need to type their usernames manually (you can't cut and paste from a message to add them). Clicking or tapping the Retweet button will just retweet a message; you can't use it to add your own comments to a quote.

Open the app bar and click or tap Filter to filter the view to see only Twitter or Facebook conversations, as shown next. This can be useful if you're trying to follow a conversation on one social network and don't want to be distracted by other discussions. You'll also need to refresh the What's New view to see new messages (see Figure 11-6), as People doesn't stream a live feed of updates, unlike some third-party Twitter apps; click or tap the Refresh button on the app bar. Clicking or tapping the New Post button in the app bar takes you to your page in the People app, where you can send messages to Facebook or Twitter.

Read Messages Sent Directly to You

Under your tile in the Social section of People (previously shown in Figure 11-3), you'll see a notification link, either the number of unread notifications or

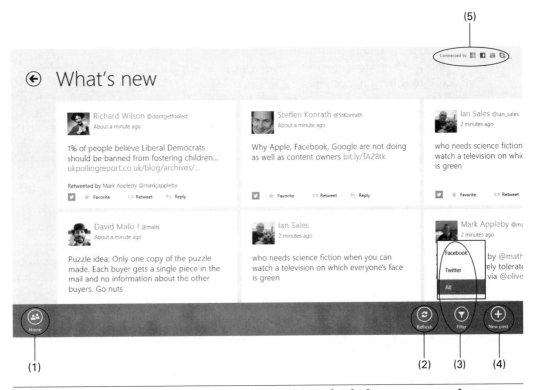

FIGURE 11-6   (1) Click or tap to jump home. (2) Refresh the view to see the latest updates. (3) Filter to see only Facebook or Twitter. (4) Post an update. (5) Connected networks.

a View link. Tap or click this to open the Notifications view, which shows you all the posts on Twitter that mention your name, along with Facebook replies (as well as status messages from contacts that you've marked as a close friend on Facebook). You can't change the size of the font used for messages, so you'll typically see a maximum of 21 messages on screen.

 One downside of using People is that you can't see, send, or reply to Twitter direct messages. If you want to do so, you'll need to download a third-party app from the Windows Store or use the Twitter website. You will see direct messages in your email inbox if you've subscribed to notifications on the Twitter website.

You don't see instant messages in the People app, even if they're from Facebook or Skype; if you miss the onscreen notification for a new message, the live tiles for the Skype and Messaging apps will show you how many messages are waiting for you on each service. Similarly, the People app only displays Facebook status updates for friends. If you want to see content from Facebook groups or pages, or play Facebook games, you'll need to open Facebook in Internet Explorer.

Notifications are shown in chronological order, so scroll to the right or swipe left to see older messages. Tapping or clicking on any message opens a detail view where you can see the comments left on a Facebook post or the details of a Twitter message. If you want to follow a Twitter conversation, click or tap the In Reply To link under the message. This shows other replies to the original message, as well as the thread of your conversation. If you want to see more, click or tap the View on Twitter or View on Facebook button in the app bar.

You don't need to keep tapping or clicking the back button to get back to the Notifications view. Use the Home button in the app bar to jump back to the top of the People app at any time.

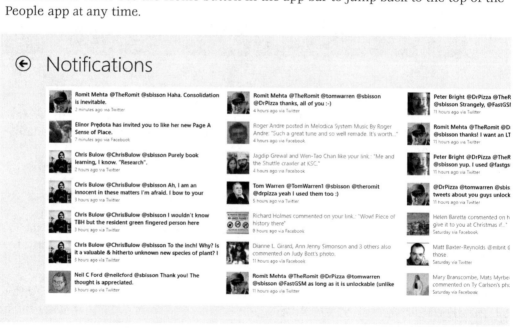

Post an Update to Facebook or Twitter

Tap or click on your picture to open the Me view. This gives you quick access to your profile, your Microsoft account, and your recent posts, as well as a view of your last status update. To post a new update, click or tap in the empty text box and start typing. A character counter keeps you from exceeding the 140-character limit on Twitter. Tap or click the drop-down arrow above the comment box to switch between posting to Twitter and posting to Facebook.

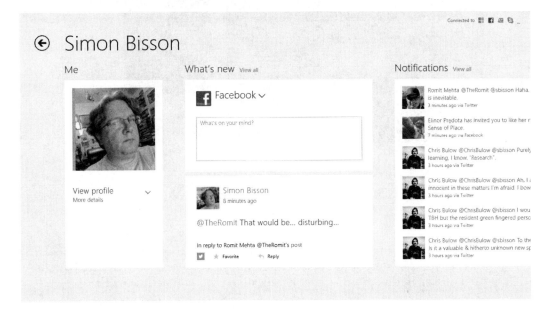

You can't use this tool to upload pictures, as there's no way to attach images to a post. You can cut and paste links from other apps, but in most cases it's easier to use the Share charm in the other app and choose the People app to share to.

If you scroll right or swipe left in the Me view, you'll see your Facebook photo galleries and your most recent notifications. Click or tap on a gallery to see individual images, or scroll to quickly view all the images (see Figure 11-7).

Send Messages and Make Skype Calls from the People App

You can send messages to your friends from their Contact card by clicking or tapping the Send Message button. The button lists the default service used to contact them (usually Facebook), but you can use the drop-down list at the side of the button to

FIGURE 11-7   See your uploaded photographs in a Facebook gallery.

choose a different service with which to get in touch. If they're a contact of yours on Skype, you can start Skype and send them a text message from here. Use the Video Call or Call button to initiate a Skype call to your contact instead.

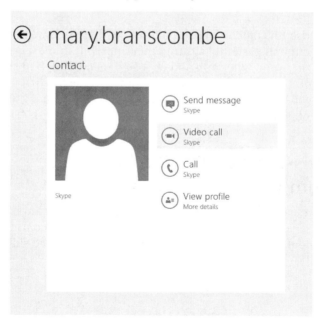

The telephone numbers that you see in a contact card come from all the profiles you have linked for this contact; you might see a cell-phone number that comes from their Facebook account, but when you choose it, the Skype app will open so you can send a message or make a voice call.

When you choose Facebook as the service through which you want to send a message, the Messaging app opens; refer to Chapter 7 for tips on how to talk to your friends with instant messages.

Share to Social Networks from the Share Charm

Windows 8's Share charm simplifies sharing links and content with friends. You're not limited to using email, and if you choose the People app from the Share charm, you can post a message to either Facebook or Twitter.

Click or tap the Share charm in any Windows Store app. If the app supports sharing, you'll see a list of other apps you can send content to in the Share pane: choose the People app. This opens a view with a URL for the content you want to share (or in the case of a video or music link, a link to the Xbox store, from which it can be streamed or downloaded). A drop-down arrow lets you choose between using your Twitter account or your Facebook account, as shown in Figure 11-8. You can then

FIGURE 11-8   Choose to share a link to either Facebook or Twitter from the Share charm and the People app.

type a message to go with the link. Click or tap the Send icon to send the message. If you want to share with more than one social network (for example, to both Twitter and Facebook), you'll need to share the content a second time for the second network.

 Some apps will share only content that's been licensed for sharing by the content provider. For example, you won't be able to share every article in Bing News via social networks. Unfortunately, the only way to find out if you can share an article is to try.

Did You Know?

Share Favorites Speed Up Posting to Social Networks

The services and apps you've shared to most recently appear at the top of the Share pane. If you've already shared something to Facebook or Twitter via the People app, you'll see two separate favorites, Post to Facebook and Post to Twitter, which makes it easier to quickly send a link to your social networks. If you want to post to both networks, you'll need to copy the message before you post it to one service, and then paste it into the message box for the next service after you've posted it to the first service.

Use Windows Store Apps for More Social Networks

Windows 8's built-in social networking tools handle many of the basic features you're likely to need. However, if you need or want additional tools, there's a whole Social section in the Windows Store with plenty of tools for all the social networks we've discussed—and more. In addition to tools for Twitter and Facebook clients, you'll find tools for working with Instagram, Pinterest, Reddit, Foursquare, Tumblr, and App.net, as well as blogging tools and messaging clients. There are official apps for AudioBoo, StumbleUpon, WordPress, and ICQ, and an official Twitter app is due in 2013.

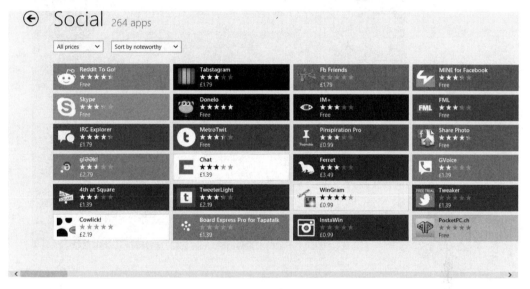

Many of the tools are free, and others have trial versions, so you can find the tool that fits the way you work without spending money up front. Some tools integrate with the Lock screen so that you can see how many messages you've missed while you've been away from your computer; others work well in the Windows 8 snap view (introduced in Chapter 2), so you can keep in touch with your social streams while working. There are also more specialized tools that track specific hashtags that display shared images, for example, or that make it easier to find new people to follow online.

Windows Store apps can take advantage of Windows 8 features, like Lock screen notifications and support for the Share charm, so if you use a social network frequently, a Windows Store app gives you more flexibility. However, if you can't find an app for your social network of choice, you can just open it in Internet Explorer as usual. You can pin links to sites like Twitter to the Start screen, as shown next, giving you quick access to your favorite sites and services. Some sites even use the notification features in Internet Explorer 10 and Windows 8 to show alerts or the number of messages waiting for you on the Start screen tile.

See Chapter 16 for information about the Windows Store.

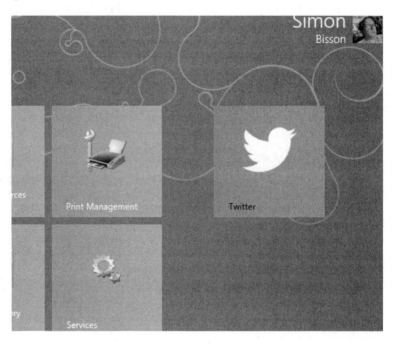

12

Find and Play Music and Other Audio Files

Windows 8 doesn't just come with software to play the music you already have (the familiar Windows Media Player on the desktop and the new finger-friendly Windows Store Music app). You can also stream millions of songs and entire albums free in the Music app using the advertising-supported Xbox Music service, including custom playlists based on your favorite tracks so you don't even need to decide what to listen to next.

As in previous Windows versions, you can still copy music from your own CDs onto your computer by *ripping* them in Windows Media Player and *burn* your own CDs with music you already have on your PC, but now, new in Windows 8, you can buy music online to add to your music library from inside the Music app or subscribe to the Xbox Music service so you can take those free streaming music tracks with you to listen to when you're not online. In this chapter we'll show you how to organize and enjoy the music you already have, and how to get more tracks to listen to.

Play Your Music in the Music App

The tile for the Music app is pinned to the Start screen by default; if you've unpinned it, you can open the Music app from the All Apps screen.

 The Music app in Windows 8 is evolving and adding new features; it's already been updated several times since Windows 8 was released, so you may find more features or see a slightly different interface from the one we show in this chapter. As with the other Xbox apps in Windows 8, it will tell you if there's an update available.

When the Music app opens (see Figure 12-1), it shows the Now Playing section, where you can see the current track that's playing (or paused). If you haven't yet played any music, you'll see tips for using Xbox Music instead of the track details and artwork. If music is currently playing, you can click or tap the Now Playing heading or the large Now Playing tile to see the current list of songs in detail. You can also pick an artist to play, make a new *Smart DJ* playlist of music that's similar to an artist you like, open a playlist you've made in the past, or see music from three featured artists.

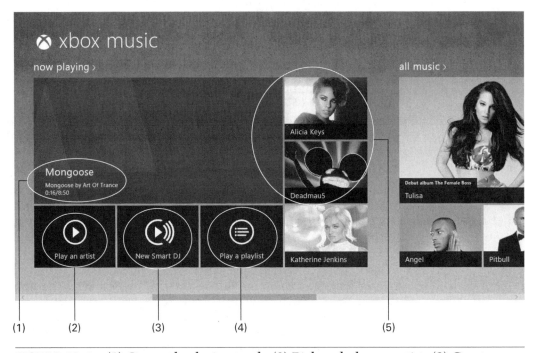

FIGURE 12-1 (1) Currently playing track, (2) Pick and play an artist, (3) Create a new Smart DJ playlist, (4) Play a playlist you created earlier, (5) Currently featured artists on the Xbox Music service

Did You Know?

You Can Stream Music Free from Xbox Music

Windows 8 gives you free streaming from the Xbox Music catalog, which includes millions of tracks. You can also buy individual tracks or entire albums from Xbox Music if you want to be able to listen to them when you're not online, or copy them to other devices to listen to away from your computer. And if you rip songs from your audio CDs onto your PC (we'll show you how to do that later in the chapter), not only can you add them to the same playlists as tracks you stream from Xbox Music but Microsoft also has a music matching service which will add those songs to your Xbox Music account. That means you can listen to them on other devices that you use Xbox Music with, like your phone or your PC at work.

Scroll to the right or swipe to the left to see more music from Xbox Music. Choose one of the artist tiles or click or tap All Music to explore the full catalog. The top music section shows popular albums; click or tap this heading to explore a long list of what other listeners are enjoying. You can also use the Search charm to search Xbox Music. The search results also include tracks from your local music library; click or tap All Music and choose My Music to see only the songs in your local music library that match the search.

Right-click or swipe across the top or bottom of the screen at any point to open the app bar with playback controls. Click or tap Open File to choose a song that isn't in your library using the File Picker. Depending on where you are in the Music app, you might see other controls, such as an option to add the current track to a playlist.

You can also get to songs in your own Music library by scrolling to the left or swiping to the right to get to the My Music section. If you haven't added any tracks to your library, you'll see a list of suggestions for getting music by adding folders to your Music library or opening individual music tracks to play.

 If you want the Music app to show you your own music as soon as it opens, open the Settings charm and choose Preferences. Under Startup View, change the When the App Opens, Show My Music setting from Off to On.

If you have music in your library and you're signed in with a Microsoft account, you'll see tiles for albums, playlists, and Smart DJ lists you've listened to recently. Click or tap the My Music heading to explore your whole music library, or click or tap the Play All Music tile to put all your tracks into the current song list (see Figure 12-2).

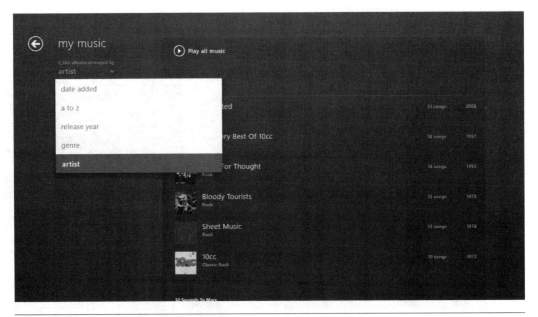

FIGURE 12-2 Sort your music collection by album, artist, or song so you can find the music you want to listen to when you want to hear it.

Remember, you can also use the Search charm to find tracks, albums, artists, and playlists in your own music library.

Select Songs and Albums to Play

When you select an album or artist (from a tile on the main screen or when you're browsing music in the Xbox Music catalog or your own music library), a window pops up with a list of the individual tracks.

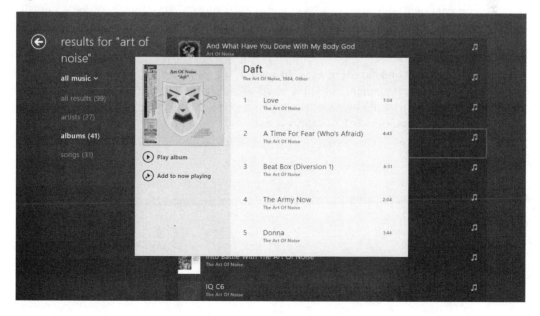

If you want to play the whole album (or everything by that artist), choose Play Album or Add to Now Playing. If you're browsing music from Xbox Music, you can also choose Explore Artist to read more about the artist and their music and see all their albums in Xbox Music. Choose Play Smart DJ at the top of the artist bio to create a playlist of similar music.

To select individual songs, right-click or press and hold on a single track to open the app bar, shown next, where you can play the song straightaway, add it to the Now Playing list, add it to your most recent playlist, or choose another playlist to add it to; you can also see properties like length and genre, delete the track from your library, play the track on your Xbox instead of on your PC, or download or buy the track if the song you're streaming is from the Xbox Music library.

 Many Windows Store apps, like Music, are designed for new widescreen PCs. That means the number of icons you'll see in the app bar will depend on your screen resolution. If there's not enough space on your screen, you'll see a More button that you can click or tap to see the options that don't fit on screen.

 If you're browsing through your music library or the Xbox Music catalog and you want to play a whole album or everything by an artist straightaway, you can right-click or press and hold on the album or artist to open the app bar where you can play it immediately or add to a playlist to listen to later.

See What You're Listening To

You don't have to go back to the Now Playing section of the main screen to see more information about what you're listening to. Click or tap the thumbnail for the current track on the app bar to see a full-screen view with lots of details (see Figure 12-3).

If the music is from Xbox Music, you'll see a biography for the artist on the right side of the screen, and you can scroll or swipe across to see their other albums; click or tap the icon that looks like four arrows to hide these and leave more room for the album artwork or visualization. If the music is from your own collection, you'll see details like the album title and year of release instead. You can switch between the song list and the current track, where you can pause the playback or change to the previous or next track; if you don't see the playback controls in the window, tap on the screen or move your mouse.

There are other controls that will appear here, although they alternate with the album art so that they're not displayed on the screen all the time. When you're playing music from Xbox Music, you'll see an Xbox icon that you can click or tap to open the Xbox SmartGlass app and play the track on your Xbox. (We'll explain more about how this works later in the chapter, but you can also use the Devices charm instead of waiting to see the icon appear.) The other control that appears lets you tap or click Play Top Songs to get a selection of tracks from the same artist. Open the app bar to see controls to add the current track to a playlist or to turn on shuffle or repeat.

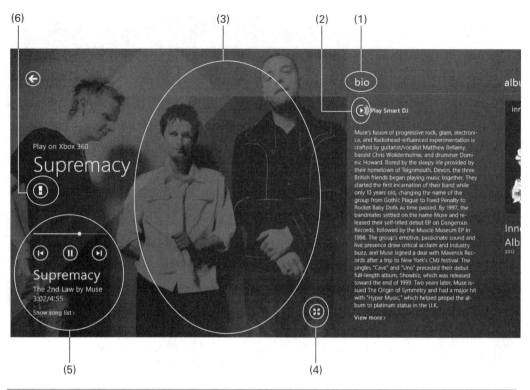

FIGURE 12-3 (1) Artist biography, (2) Create a Smart DJ playlist based on the current artist, (3) Xbox Music visualizations use photos of the artist, (4) Switch to a full-screen view, (5) Onscreen controls, (6) Click or tap to play through an Xbox 360.

Set the Mood with Playlists

Instead of picking individual tracks and albums to listen to, or sticking with one artist, you can save lists of songs as playlists that you can play again later. You can create playlists manually in the Music app, import playlists you've made in Windows Media Player, or ask Xbox Music to create a Smart DJ list with music similar to an artist or track you like.

If you play a song and decide you like it enough to listen to it often, you can add it to a playlist by opening the app bar, clicking or tapping Add to Playlist, and picking which playlist to add it to. If you want to add it to the playlist you've listened to most recently, there's an icon for that on the app bar as well (see Figure 12-4).

FIGURE 12-4   Use the app bar to add songs to your own playlists.

You can make a new playlist by choosing Create New Playlist from the Add to Playlist menu on the app bar, or by using the Create New Playlist button at the top of the Playlists section in My Music and typing in a name for the playlist.

 You can rename and delete playlists in the Playlists section of My Music by opening the app bar.

If you don't have a playlist selected when you open the app bar in the Playlists section of My Music, you'll see the Import Playlists button. This imports any playlists in your Music library that you made with applications like Windows Media Player. It will also import the automatically generated playlists we'll show you how to make in Media Player later in the chapter, but they will not contain any songs.

If you're in the mood for a particular style of music, Smart DJ is a fast way to get a playlist and a fun way to find new artists you might like. You can make a Smart DJ list for almost any artist in Xbox Music. Open the Now Playing screen by clicking or tapping the current track in the app bar; for most artists, there's a Play Smart DJ button at the top of the biography. When you choose a featured artist from the Now Playing section on the main screen of the Music app, a Play Smart DJ button appears in the artist window that pops up. You can also click or tap the New Smart DJ tile in the Now section and search for a specific artist.

 The Smart DJ section of My Music shows Smart DJ lists you've previously made. You can remove any list you don't enjoy from the app bar.

Play Music in the Background

When you're playing songs in the Music app, they carry on playing when you switch to other apps or even to the desktop. You can change the volume from the Settings charm even when you're using Windows Store apps, and when you're on the desktop, you can also use the volume icon in the notification area of the taskbar.

If you have hardware volume controls on your PC or your keyboard, you can use those to control the Music app without switching back to it. Press one of the volume keys to open the player controls in the top left corner of the screen (as well as changing the volume); you can pause the music, go back to the previous track or on to the next track, or click or tap the album art to switch back to the Music app.

Stream and Buy Music in the Music App

As long as you're signed in with a Microsoft account, you can *stream* music from Xbox Music free, which means that as long as you're online, you can play most of the music in the catalog without paying anything. For the first six months, you can stream as much music as you want; after that you can stream for up to ten hours a month. If you want to stream for longer, or want to be able to download tracks to your PC so you can listen to them offline, you'll need to subscribe to an Xbox Music Pass (sign up at www .xbox.com/en-US/music/music-pass, shown next). The Xbox Music Pass also stops the occasional advertisements that you may hear when using the free streaming service.

 If you don't log in to Windows with a Microsoft account, you'll need to sign in to your Microsoft account in the Music app by clicking or tapping Sign In in the top right corner, so you can use Xbox Music. Even if you've signed in to other apps like Mail with your Microsoft account, unless you use it to sign in to Windows you'll need to sign in separately to Music (which means you can use a different Microsoft account for Mail and Music, for example, if you have an Xbox Live Gold account that's different from your Hotmail account). The first time you try to stream music from Xbox Live, the Music app will prompt you to sign in with your Microsoft account. You can still play the music tracks you already have without signing in.

When you choose an artist or album that's on Xbox Music in My Music or the All Music catalog, you'll see an icon on each track in the window that tells you whether that track is Streaming Only (so you can listen to it only when you're online), Downloaded (so you can listen to it offline), or Matched (a song you already own on this PC and you can stream it from Xbox Music on your other devices). If you want to be able to listen to a Streaming Only track when you're offline, right-click or press and hold on the track, select More in the app bar, and choose Download (if you have an Xbox Music Pass) or Buy Song.

Streaming Only track

You can also buy entire albums by clicking or tapping the Buy Album button on the left side of the window. When you select a Buy button, Xbox Music will ask you for your password. If this is the first time you've bought music from Xbox Music, the Music app will ask whether you want to always enter your password before making purchases (you can change this later by opening the Settings charm and choosing Preferences). If you haven't already linked a credit card to your Xbox Live account, choose Next to go to the Xbox Music website, click or tap Change Payment Options, and then select Add a New Credit Card.

Once you've added a credit card, open the Settings charm and choose Account to see details about your Xbox Live membership, your Xbox Music Pass, your payment options, and your billing history. You can also see which other devices are connected to the same Xbox Music account by clicking or tapping Manage Music Devices.

How to...   **Play Podcasts in Windows 8**

If you like to listen to *podcasts*—Internet radio shows from amateur and professional broadcasters that you can download free—you can play them in either Windows Media Player or the Music app by adding the folder you download them into to your Music library. If you're looking for an app for downloading and playing podcasts as well as managing subscriptions to your favorite shows so you don't miss an episode, try the free SlapDash Podcasts app, which you can get from the Windows Store. See Chapter 16 for instructions on getting apps from the Windows Store.

Tip   When you buy a song, it's downloaded to your PC. You'll also be able to stream it from Xbox Music on other PCs, and on other devices like your smartphone.

If an album or track isn't available for streaming, click or tap Preview to hear a short section of the song to decide if you want to buy it.

Play, Organize, and Rip Music in Windows Media Player

The Music app is designed for exploring and playing your music. If you want to organize your music or have more control over how you play it, or if you want to transfer music to and from your PC, you can do that in the Windows Media Player desktop program.

You can find Windows Media Player in the All Apps screen under Windows Accessories; if you plan to use it frequently, remember you can pin any desktop program to the desktop taskbar (see Chapter 2).

The first time you run Windows Media Player, you need to choose some settings in the Welcome to Windows Media Player screen. Click or tap Recommended Settings to make Windows Media Player your default media software and allow it to download album art for your music files, then choose Finish. Click or tap Custom Settings if you want to change any of these options, and then click or tap Next to make your choices; for example, you could make Windows Media Player the default player for just certain types of audio or video files. (You can also change these settings later in the Default Programs section of the Control Panel.)

Windows Media Player opens in the Library view, where you see your playlists along with all the songs and albums in your Music library in the navigation pane. You also see your Videos and Pictures libraries. These are the same libraries that you see in File Explorer, so if you've added folders to the Music library in Explorer, you can easily play the songs in them with Windows Media Player. If you want to add a folder from inside Windows Media Player, click or tap the Organize drop-down menu on the toolbar and choose Manage Libraries.

 If you add a folder on another PC in your homegroup to your Music library in File Explorer, the songs and albums there will show up in the Music section of the Windows Media Player library alongside the audio files you keep on your own PC.

If you have a disc in your CD or DVD player or a removable drive plugged into your PC, you'll see that in the Library view as well, even if there aren't any media files on it. That's to make it easy to copy media to your other drives. The bottom half of the navigation pane shows other media libraries that you can use, like music libraries shared by other people in your homegroup.

How to... Play a CD in Windows Media Player

You can't play CDs in the Music app, even by choosing Open File from the app bar and opening the CD drive in the File Picker. But you can set Windows Media Player to automatically start playing audio CDs you insert into your computer's optical drive. The first time you put a music CD into your PC, you'll see a notification asking you to choose what you want Windows to do with audio CDs, as shown next. Click or tap Play Audio CD (if you have other music software, you'll see it listed here as well). You can always play an audio CD by selecting it in the Media Player library as well.

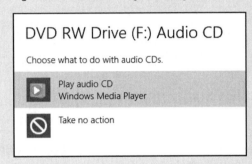

All of the media libraries you can play content from in Windows Media Player are organized into Music, Videos, and Pictures sections; you may also have a Recorded TV section where you can find shows you've recorded with Windows Media Center. The items under Videos and Pictures are listed in date order, whereas the Music sections are organized into Artist, Album, and Genre.

In the Album category, every album title is listed alphabetically. You can click or tap a column heading at the top of the details pane to group the albums alphabetically by artist, by genre, by year of release, by the rating you've given them, or by the length of each album. If you switch to the Artist category or Genre category, the albums are grouped alphabetically by the artist who released the album or by the style of music, respectively.

You can also search your music library by typing an artist name, song title, or album title in the search box at the top.

 Tip If you want to change advanced settings in Windows Media Player, right-click or tap and hold on the menu bar (or press the ALT key on your keyboard) and choose Show menu bar. In the more comprehensive pop-up menu that opens, choose the Tools menu to see the settings you can change.

Listen in Windows Media Player

When you find a song or album you want to listen to, double-click it or tap it twice to start playing it; this replaces any tracks you already have queued up. You can also drag tracks, albums, or artists into the Play pane on the right side of the window to add them to the list of tracks you're listening to. The track that's currently playing appears as a thumbnail in the corner of the toolbar of player controls, shown next; it's also color-coded in blue in the Play pane.

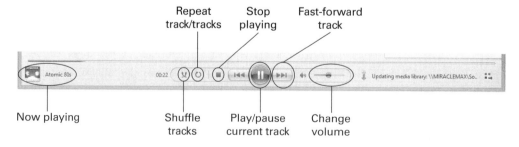

For a simpler interface, switch to Now Playing mode, shown next, by clicking or tapping the icon in the bottom right corner (this is the interface you'll see when you play a video). The player controls at the bottom of the window are the same as in the Library view but they fade away if you don't move your mouse or tap the screen for a few seconds (and they come back when you do). Click or tap the Switch to Library button in the top right corner to get the Library view back.

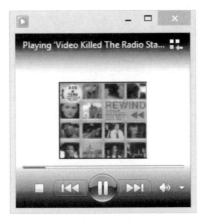

If you make the Windows Media Player window smaller, the controls shrink to fit so you can tuck the window away in the corner of the screen and still be in control. Alternatively, hover over the Windows Media Player icon in the taskbar while you have media playing and the thumbnail preview will include controls for pausing the music or moving to the previous or next track.

Manage Playlists in Windows Media Player

If you want to save the current list of songs to listen to another time, click or tap the Save List button at the top of the Play pane and type a name for it. You can also create a playlist from scratch by clicking or tapping the Create Playlist drop-down menu on the toolbar. If you choose Create Playlist from this menu Windows Media Player creates a blank playlist in the Playlists section of the navigation pane; again, you can type in a name. Drag songs from your media library onto the name of the playlist to add them.

The other option on the Create Playlist menu is Create Auto Playlist; this lets you build a playlist out of building blocks like music you've ripped in the last month, songs you play more in the evenings, all the tracks you have that were released in a particular year, or even music composed or conducted by the same artist. You can limit the length of the playlist by time or size, so you could make a playlist of all your new music that's the right size to fit on your phone or portable music player, ready to sync across, or that's the right length to burn onto a single audio CD.

In the New Auto Playlist dialog box, shown next, click or tap Click Here to Add Criteria. To see new music, select Date Added for the criteria; choose one of the Play

Count options for music you listen to a lot. Choose More to see filters, like music you listen to at specific times of day.

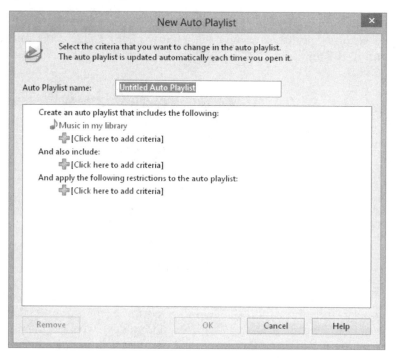

Now click or tap the underlined words in the filter; for Date Added, you can choose Is Before or Is After and then choose from a list of time periods that includes the last seven days, the last month, and the last six months.

If you want a playlist that has all the tracks by your favorite artist, right-click or press and hold on the name of the artist in the details pane and chose Save as Auto Playlist. If you download or rip new music by that artist, it will show up on the auto playlist automatically. If you want to make a playlist that includes only collaborations by your two favorite artists, make a new auto playlist and add both their names as criteria; the playlist will only show tracks they're both credited on.

Delete a Song

If you have music you don't listen to any more, you can remove it from your library or delete the file from your computer. In Windows Media Player, right-click or tap and hold on a song or album and choose Delete in the menu. In the dialog box that appears, choose Delete from Library Only if you want to keep the original file but not show it in the library. Choose Delete from Library and My Computer to delete the original file as well.

Right-click or tap and hold on a playlist in the navigation pane if you want to rename or delete it. When you remove a playlist, make sure you choose Delete from Library Only unless you want to delete the music tracks that are in it completely.

 If you delete a song from the Music app, that deletes it completely; click or tap on the track in My Music and then open the app bar. Click or tap the More button and choose Delete. You can't get the file back unless you restore it from the Recycle Bin or your File History.

Rip Your CDs in Windows Media Player

Use Windows Media Player to copy tracks from an audio CD to your computer and convert them to the right format to play in the Music app or Windows Media Player. Insert the audio CD you want to rip into your optical drive and select it in the navigation pane in Windows Media Player, as in Figure 12-5.

By default, all the tracks on the CD are selected, so they'll all be ripped to your computer when you click or tap Rip CD in the toolbar. If you don't want to rip every track, clear the check boxes for the tracks you don't want to rip before you choose Rip CD.

If this is the first time you've ripped a CD, you'll see the Rip Options dialog box, where you can choose whether you want to add copy protection to the files you rip so

FIGURE 12-5 Windows Media Player looks up the audio CD in your CD drive and shows you the track listing.

you can only play them on your own computer. Choose Do Not Add Copy Protection to Your Music if you want the tracks to play on a wider range of devices. You also have to select the check box to declare that you understand that music on CDs is protected by copyright (you're allowed to make a digital copy for your own use, but not to give a copy of the file to a friend, for example). If you use peer-to-peer software, make sure that your music collection isn't included in files to be shared.

Windows Media Player shows a progress bar for each track you're ripping, so you can see how long it will take.

Windows Media Player will save the ripped audio files in the default folder of your music library, so they will show up in the Music app automatically. If you want to change where CDs are ripped to, choose More Options from the Rip Settings drop-down menu and click or tap the Change button to pick a different folder.

 You can burn CDs and DVDs of photos or videos from Windows Media Player as well. We'll look at how to do that in Chapters 13 and 14.

You Can Change the Format of the Tracks

Click or tap Rip Settings if you want to change the format tracks are ripped in or the audio quality. Choose to use MP3 if you want to play the files on the widest range of devices. Lossless file formats like Windows Media Audio Lossless take up more disk space; they produce higher-quality files, but you may not hear the difference on your PC speakers. Audio quality is measured in *bitrate*—how many of the bits that make up a second of the original music track will be copied into the new compressed file. The default bitrate of 128 Kbps gives you the same level of audio quality as music you hear on the radio; if you choose 160 Kbps, you're getting audio quality closer to what you hear on a CD, but the higher the bitrate you rip at, the larger the files you create will be.

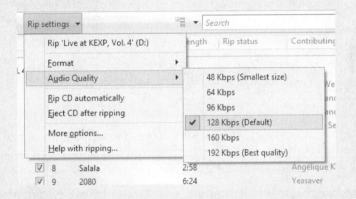

Take Your Music with You

You don't always want to sit down in front of your computer to listen to music. You might have much better speakers on your hi-fi system or your television. The Play To features in Windows Media Player and the Music app let you play the music you're listening to on your PC on another device that's on your network; that could be another PC in your homegroup, an Xbox gaming console connected to your TV, a digital media adapter plugged into your hi-fi system, or a connected television set.

> **Tip** To stream media to an Xbox console, it needs to be an Xbox 360 with the Fall 2012 dashboard update. It also needs to be connected to your home network.

For Play To media streaming to work, you have to enable sharing on your network; we covered how to do this in Chapter 5. You also need to add the devices you want to stream music to in the Devices section of PC Settings (unless you're streaming to another PC), as covered in Chapter 7.

If you want to send music to an Xbox, install the Xbox SmartGlass app from the Windows Store (see Chapter 16 for instructions).

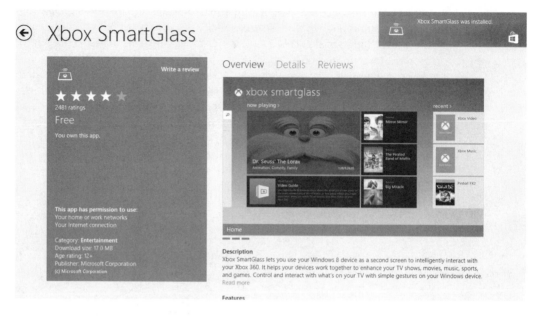

Sign in to SmartGlass with the same account you're signed in to your Xbox with. Turn on SmartGlass on your Xbox; from Xbox Home, select Settings | System | Console Settings | Remote Devices. Under Xbox SmartGlass Apps, select On.

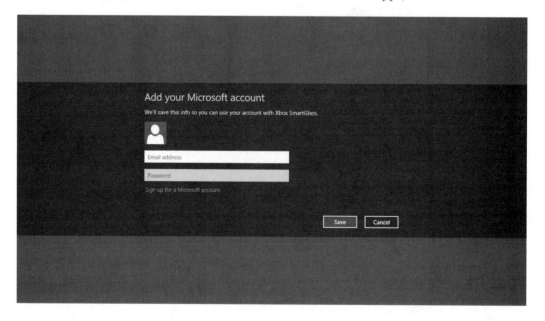

Smart glass will then connect to your Xbox.

You'll see a list of available and currently running apps. Click an app to launch on the Xbox and to control it from your PC.

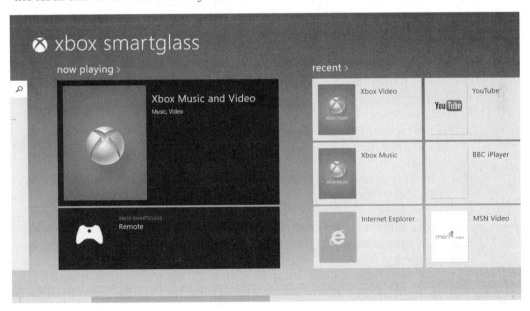

Finally, click or tap the Stream drop-down menu in Windows Media Player and choose Turn on Media Streaming with HomeGroup to open the Media Streaming Options section of the Network and Sharing Center to choose which other devices on

Did You Know?

Not All Streaming Devices Work with Windows 8

New digital media streaming devices that are designed to work with Windows 8 have to meet certain requirements (supporting the latest video file formats, receiving video over a wireless connection without the playback stuttering, connecting directly over Wi-Fi so setup is easier, and going into standby to save power but waking up when you send media to the device). When you connect one of these devices to your Windows 8 PC, it will be labeled Windows Certified in the Devices section of PC Settings. Older streaming devices will have a Not Windows Certified label, which means you can't send media to them from Windows Store apps that play videos, music, or photos. However, you can still stream media to them using the Play To menu that's on the Music Tools, Picture Tools, and Video Tools tabs in File Explorer.

your network you want to stream media files to. (Once you turn on streaming, the More Streaming Options command appears at the bottom of the Stream menu so you can go back and add or remove devices later.)

If you're streaming to another PC, open Windows Media Player on the other PC and choose Stream | Turn on Media Streaming with HomeGroup and select the computers you want to stream to and from. If there isn't already a check mark next to Allow Remote Control of My Player in the Stream menu, select this and click or tap Allow Remote Control on This Network.

In Windows Media Player, you can use the Play To icon at the top of the Play pane to choose another device to hear your music on. You have to be playing music already for the Play To menu to be active; the Play button on the icon changes from gray to green, and you can click or tap it to see the Play To menu with a list of available devices (which will include your Xbox if it's turned on).

In File Explorer, you'll find Play To in the Play tab of the ribbon (which only appears when you're in a folder that contains media files); select the files you want to play and click or tap Play To to see the same list of available devices.

In the Music app, open the Devices charm to see a list of devices you can stream to; you can't stream music from Xbox Music to anything except an Xbox (because of the license agreement with the record labels). We'll cover using SmartGlass to watch videos on your Xbox 360 in Chapter 14, and we'll look at how you can use your PC as an Xbox remote in Chapter 17.

Burn Music to a CD

You can burn your music onto an audio CD (as long as it's not protected; some music that you download from online music services is protected by a *Digital Rights Management* license that limits what you can do with it). Right-click or press and hold on a track in the details pane, choose Properties, and then look in the Media Usage Rights tab to see what you're allowed to do with it. If you add to the list of files a protected file that you're not allowed to burn, Windows Media Player will show you a warning icon and the file won't be burned.

Put a blank CD into your optical drive, then click or tap the Burn tab to open the Burn pane, shown in Figure 12-6. You can drag songs, albums, or playlists into the Burn List to add them to your CD.

After you drag the songs into the Burn List, click or tap Start Burn at the top of the Burn pane.

How to... Choose the CD Type

Click or tap the Burn Options button at the top of the Burn pane if you want to choose what kind of disc to burn your files on.

	Choose if...	Capacity	Use For
Audio CD	You want to make a custom music CD that will play in your car, your hi-fi system, or any PC with a CD drive.	80 minutes maximum	Music files only
Data CD	You want to back up your music files, or your device can play digital music files like WMA or MP3.	700 megabytes (MB), or about 8 hours of music	Music, pictures, and videos
Data DVD	You have too many files to fit onto a data CD.	4.7 gigabytes (GB), or about 54 hours of music	Music, pictures, and videos

FIGURE 12-6 After you drag the song to the Burn List, you'll see the song title and play time.

Sync Music to Other Devices

If you'd like to copy audio tracks onto your phone to listen to, or even onto a removable drive (more and more cars now have a USB port so you can plug in a drive of audio tracks you can play on your car stereo, for example), you can do that in Windows Media Player as well, using the tools in the Sync pane. You can find detailed instructions in Chapter 4.

13

View and Manage Photos

HOW TO...

- View photos
- See photos from Facebook, Flickr, and SkyDrive
- Watch slideshows of your photos
- Crop and rotate photos
- Delete and rename photos
- Use your favorite photo as your Windows Lock screen
- Set the background photo in the Photos app
- Import pictures from a digital camera or removable drive
- Send photos by email
- Share photos on SkyDrive, Facebook, and Twitter
- Burn photos to a DVD

Now that digital cameras are so popular and the quality of smartphone cameras is so good, you probably have hundreds of photos on your computer, with more stored online in services like Facebook, Flickr, and SkyDrive. The new Photos app in Windows 8 is an easy way to see all your photos in the same way, whether they're on the computer you're using, on another PC you use, or online. You can also import images from your digital camera, print your photos, upload pictures to SkyDrive, and share photos with your friends on social networks directly from the Photos app.

View Your Pictures in the Photos App

Open the Photos app from the Photos tile on the Start screen. Depending on which online services you use, and which you have linked to your Microsoft account, you'll see different tiles displayed in the Photos (see Figure 13-1). (Refer to Chapter 11 to learn about linking different online services to your Microsoft account.)

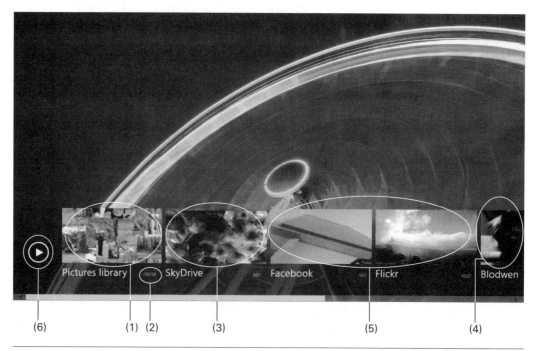

FIGURE 13-1 (1) your Pictures library, (2) number of images in your Pictures library, (3) photos in your SkyDrive account, (4) photos stored on other PCs that you use the SkyDrive desktop app with, (5) photos from online services including Facebook and Flickr, and (6) see your images displayed in an animated collage.

If you haven't set up your Pictures library or signed in (to Windows or the Photos app itself) with a Microsoft account, you won't see any images in the tiles; instead, every tile will have a hint like "Add some photos," "Add a device to see photos," or "See yours here." Click or tap the Pictures library tile to see how to set up your library (we'll cover that later in this chapter) or choose one of the online services to add your Microsoft account.

If there are tiles for services you don't use, click or tap the Hide button on the tile to remove it from the Photos app. You can also remove tiles or get them back by opening the Settings charm and choosing Options; clear the check box next to any services linked to your Microsoft account that you don't want to see in the Photos app.

See Facebook, SkyDrive, and Flickr Photos in the Photos App

Once you've signed in, the Photos app uses your Microsoft account to connect the social networking sites on which you have photos and display tiles for them. You probably already have Facebook and/or Twitter linked to your Microsoft account, but another of the social networks Microsoft supports in Windows 8 is the Flickr photo-sharing servicer run by Yahoo.

Images that you store on SkyDrive will appear in the Photos app automatically when you connect your Microsoft account. The connection to SkyDrive also lets you see images that are stored on any other computers on which you've installed the SkyDrive desktop program. That's different from the Windows Store SkyDrive app that comes with Windows 8; you can download the program from https://apps.live.com/skydrive and use it not just to see the files you have stored in your SkyDrive account but also to sync them to your PC so you have copies even when you're not online.

You can connect remotely from the SkyDrive website to any PCs that you're running the SkyDrive desktop program on, as long as those PCs are turned on. For example, if you're out of the office and need to retrieve a file on your PC at work, as long as your

How to...   Add Your Flickr Account to the Photos App

You can see photos you've uploaded to Flickr in the Photos app by connecting your Microsoft account to your Flickr account. If you haven't already done that, the Photos app will ask you if you want to connect to your Microsoft account when you first sign in to Photos with your Microsoft account. Click or tap Connect if you want to see your Flickr images in Photos, and then sign in to your Yahoo! account and choose Save. (Click or tap Cancel if you don't want to connect your Flickr account.)

Once you've done this, the Photos app starts downloading your Flickr photos. If you have a lot of photos online already, the download can take

(Continued)

some time—and because Photos is a Windows Store app, you need to keep it open for the photos to download. Once the initial synchronization is complete, new photos will download as they're added to the website.

Flickr images aren't downloaded at their highest resolution. To see the original image, open the app bar and tap View on Flickr to open the website and see the picture (and comments people have left about it).

You can't upload photos from your PC to Flickr using the Photos app. If you want to upload images, you'll need to use the Flickr web uploader or a third-party Flickr app from the Photo section of the Windows Store.

work PC is turned, you can download a copy by connecting from the SkyDrive website. That same connection lets you browse images in the Pictures libraries on those PCs from the Photos app, as long as the PCs are on.

Once you have all your online services connected, there may be more tiles than you can see on screen at once; scroll or swipe across the screen to see more of them (see Figure 13-2).

FIGURE 13-2   Some tiles, such as the Flickr and Facebook tiles, are live tiles, so you'll see different photos appear.

Browse Your Photos

You can open one of the tiles to explore your photos, or click or tap the Play button on the left to start a slideshow that looks like an animated photo album or collage. The slideshow picks a theme—such as photos you took at the same time, or photos from the same place, or a random set of images—and arranges a selection of images on screen. Every few seconds, one of the photos fades out to be replaced by a new image, so you can sit and watch your photos go by. When you're done viewing the slideshow, click or tap on the screen and select the back arrow button that appears in the upper left corner of the screen.

To see the photos on your computer, click or tap the Pictures Library tile; as shown in the following example, you'll see all the folders in your Pictures library (and any images that are in the top-level folders you've put in your library). When you open a tile for one of your online photo services, you'll see the folders or albums you've used to organize your photos there.

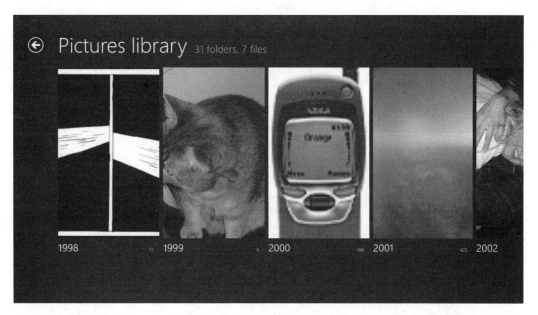

You can see at the top of the screen how many folders and files are in the library. Scroll right to see more images, or click or tap on a folder to open it. If there are a lot of folders and pictures to navigate at the current level, turn on Semantic Zoom by pinching with your fingers or pressing CTRL and the – key; this makes the tiles for the folders and images smaller, so you can see more of them on screen.

You can also switch to looking at your pictures in date order; right-click or swipe up from the bottom of the screen to open the app bar, and choose Browse by Date (or Browse by Folder to go back to the usual view). Again, you can use Semantic Zoom to fit more tiles on screen at once.

How to... Go Back to the Previous Folder

If you want to go back to the previous folder, just click or tap the left-arrow button in the upper left corner of the screen. If you're in the highest-level folder, such as the Pictures library, then you'll return to the Photos app home screen.

Click or tap on a photo to open it full screen. If you have a touchscreen, you can use your fingers to zoom in or zoom out on the image to see it in more or less detail, respectively, or you can swipe left to move back to the previous photo or swipe right to move on to the next. If you have a mouse, move it and arrows will appear on the left and right sides of the screen so you can navigate: click the plus- and minus-sign buttons in the bottom right corner to zoom in and out.

If you see an arrow only on one side of the screen, you've reached the beginning or end of the folder.

Tip   It's not immediately obvious how to get back to the Photos app when you're finished viewing a photo. Click or tap on the image and a small arrow button will appear in the upper left corner of the screen. Click or tap this button to go back to the folder your pictures are in.

View a Selection of Photos in a Slideshow

You can start a full-screen slideshow of your photos at any point by clicking or tapping the Slide Show button in the app bar. If you're looking at a photo, the slideshow will move on to the next image in the folder after a few seconds. If you choose Slide Show when you're in a folder, the slideshow starts with the first picture (see Figure 13-3). When the slideshow reaches the last photo in the folder, it will loop back to the first photo and start playing again.

You can pause the slideshow at any time by zooming in (to see more details in the current image), zooming out (to see more photos in the folder), opening the Share charm to share the current image, or opening the app bar to edit your photo.

Edit Pictures in the Photos App

The Photos app doesn't have the same powerful image editing tools offered in a desktop image editing program like Photoshop Essentials or Windows Live Photo Gallery, but it does enable you to trim out unwanted areas in your photos or rotate images that are the wrong way round.

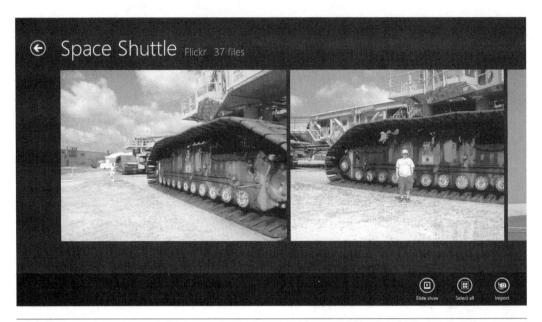

FIGURE 13-3   Start a slideshow of all photos in your folder by clicking or tapping the Slide Show icon in the app bar.

In the Photos app, you can edit only photos that are in your Pictures library. If you're looking at a photo from SkyDrive, Flickr, or Facebook and you want to edit it, click or tap the View On icon on the app bar to open the image in the corresponding website, where you may be able to edit (or rename) it.

Right-click or swipe over the top or bottom edge of your touchscreen to open the app bar. If you want to make your photo smaller, click or tap the Crop button and then drag the round handles in the corners of the selection that appears on your photo to choose which areas to cut off. If you want to make the result the right size and shape to use for the Lock screen in Windows 8 or as a desktop background, or to keep the original ratio of your photo, click or tap the Aspect Ratio button in the app bar and choose the ratio you want from the menu (see Figure 13-4).

When you're happy with the new shape and size of your photo, click or tap Apply in the app bar. If you like the effect, choose Save Copy to keep it. The cropped photo is saved in the same folder as the original photo, with the same name but with (2) at the end to show it's a different version. Your original image will still be in the same folder; if you don't want it any more, you can delete it.

FIGURE 13-4   Use the Aspect Ratio menu to make your photo the right size and shape to use in a specific place in Windows 8.

If your photo is the wrong way up, click or tap the Rotate button; the image will rotate 90 degrees to the right. Keep using the Rotate button until the image is correct. You don't have to do anything to save the rotation; the Photos app applies it immediately.

Use Your Photos in Windows

The background of the Photos app is a striking image of a Ferris wheel at night, but you might prefer to see one of your own images there instead. You can also set a single image to use as the Start screen tile for the Photos app instead of rotating through random images (which sometimes puts your worst photos on the Start screen).

When you find a photo you'd like to use instead of the default Ferris wheel, open it in the Photos app, right-click or swipe up from the bottom of the screen to open the app bar, and click or tap the Set As icon. In the Set As menu, shown in Figure 13-5, choose App Background to use the photo as the background of the home screen of the Photos app (see Figure 13-6). Choose App Tile to use the photo as the Start screen tile for the Photos app. If you want to use the photo as the image that appears when you first turn on your PC (or when you wake it up after you've been away from your computer for a while), choose Lock Screen.

 Use the Aspect Ratio menu on the app bar first to make your photo the right size and shape so it fits perfectly.

How to... **Delete Images in the Photos App**

There are two ways to delete images in the Photos app:

- To delete the photo you're looking at, right-click or swipe up from the bottom of the screen to open the app bar, and then click or tap the Delete icon.
- In the folder list, right-click or swipe up to select one or more photos you want to delete, and then click or tap the Delete icon in the app bar. You can use Semantic Zoom to work with several images at once.

After you click or tap the Delete icon, a pop-up window appears to tell you how many images you're deleting (in case you've selected more images than you intended to; check that you're not deleting more photos than you planned to). Click or tap the Delete button to delete the photo or photos.

From within the Photos app, you can't delete photos that are stored online in SkyDrive, Facebook, or Flicker, or photos that are on other PCs you can reach through SkyDrive. You can't rename files in the Photos app, either; you need to do that in File Explorer on the desktop.

FIGURE 13-5   Choose where in Windows you want to use your photo: as the Lock screen photo or as an image for the Photos app itself.

FIGURE 13-6   Use one of your own images as the background for the Photos app.

Add Pictures to the Photos App

The images you see in the Photos app come from your Pictures library and the online services linked to your Microsoft account. Use File Explorer to choose which folders are included in the Pictures library. In the navigation pane of File Explorer, click or tap the Pictures library and open the Library Tools Manage tab that appears in the ribbon. Select Manage Library.

In the Picture Library Locations dialog box, shown in Figure 13-7, click or tap the Add button to choose new folders you want to include in the library.

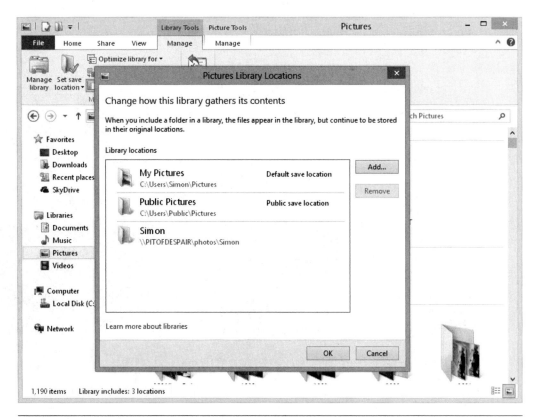

FIGURE 13-7 Add a new photos folder to the list of Pictures library locations by clicking or tapping the Add button.

If there are any folders in the Pictures library you don't use, like the Public Pictures folder, click or tap on the folder name and then choose Remove.

One of the folders in the Pictures library will be marked as the Default Save Location. This is where Windows puts images that you save into the Pictures library without specifying a folder. If you want to use a different folder, add it to the Pictures library, right-click or tap and hold on the folder name, and then choose Set as Default Save Location.

 If you create a new default folder, the next time you open (or switch to) the Photos app, you'll see the photos in that new default folder in the app home screen.

Import Images in the Photos App

When you insert the memory card from your digital camera into your PC for the first time, Windows 8 will display a notification in the top right corner of the screen asking you to choose what happens when you plug in a memory card. If you choose Import Photos and Videos (Photos), the Photos app will open and show you the images on the card.

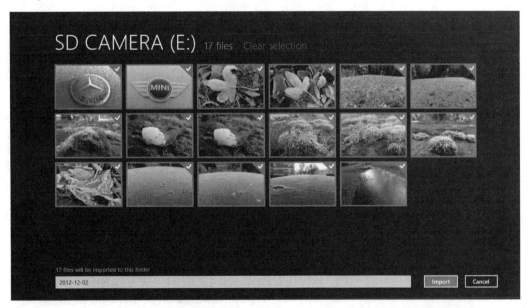

All the pictures are selected by default (indicated by a check mark in the upper right corner of each thumbnail); if you want to import all of them, type a name for the folder (unless you want to keep the automatic name, which is the date the photos were taken) and click or tap Import. That creates a new folder in the default save location for your Pictures library (which the previous section showed you how to change) and imports the photos.

 If you don't want to import all of the images on the storage card, click or tap Clear Selection at the top of the screen to clear all the check marks, right-click or swipe up on the individual pictures you want to import, and then click or tap Import.

If you don't have Photos set up to import pictures from your camera card automatically, or if you want to copy images from a removable drive like a USB stick, open the app bar and click or tap Import. Click or tap the drive on which your images are stored in the Choose a Device to Import From window that pops up, and you'll see the same interface for selecting and importing your images.

Share Your Photos

You can also use the Photos app to share images with your friends. The way this works depends on how you want to share them and where the photos are stored. Start by opening the photo you want to share. To share multiple images, right-click or swipe up on the images you want to share in the folder view. You can navigate to another folder to select more files without losing the ones you've already picked; the app bar will show you how many images you have selected already.

Open the Share charm and choose an app to send the photo(s) to.

 The Share charm may also show Windows Store apps you have installed that you can use to edit your images. If you choose one of those apps, your photo will open in that app, ready to edit.

Share Photos with Mail and SkyDrive

If you're sharing a photo that's on your PC (or on one of the other PCs you can see photos from through SkyDrive) or any of the online services you can see in the Photos app, you can send it as an email attachment by choosing Mail from the Share charm.

Type the email address in the To box, or type the name of a contact from the People app, and add a title and message. You see a thumbnail of the image in the mail message while you're writing, but it will arrive as a full-size image in an attachment.

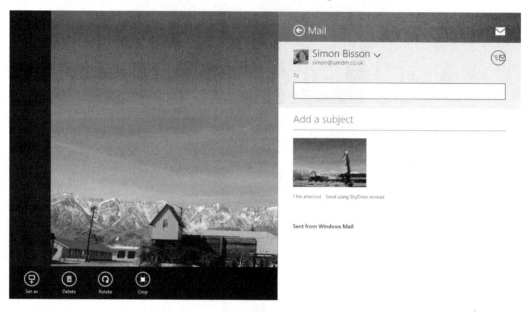

If you have a high resolution digital camera, your photos will be large files. Many email services have a limit on the size of email attachments they will send (or accept). Especially if you want to send multiple images, your email may be blocked by the mail service of the person you're sending it to. To avoid this, send it via SkyDrive. Click or tap the Send Using SkyDrive Instead link below the photos in your email message. Now when you click or tap the Send button at the top of the message, instead of attaching the images to your email message, Windows uploads them to SkyDrive and puts them into a new folder (named New Folder, although you can change that on the SkyDrive website later).

 If you change your mind about using SkyDrive while you're writing your message, click or tap Send Using Basic Attachments Instead.

When the email message arrives, it has thumbnails of all the images you've sent to SkyDrive, with a link to open the folder on SkyDrive, where the recipient can view and download one or all of the images (which is handy if you're sending a selection of images to someone who's going to choose one to use and doesn't need all of them). There's also a Save All link that opens the SkyDrive folder in the browser and packages the images into a single Zip file; choose Open to view the file in Explorer or choose Save to save the Zipfile.

If you prefer to upload your images to SkyDrive and share them using the tools on the SkyDrive website, choose the SkyDrive app from the Share charm instead. That way, you can choose where to put the image files from the list of folders that appears in the Share charm.

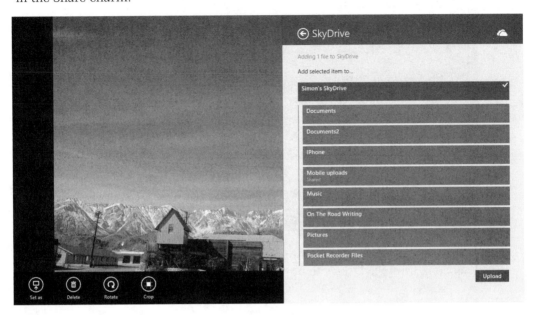

Share Photos to Facebook and Twitter

Sharing a picture via social networks isn't quite as easy as using email, unless the image is already on SkyDrive. If it is, you can select it in the Photos app and choose the People app from the Share charm to post it to Facebook or Twitter.

If the photo is not on SkyDrive, you have to upload the image to your SkyDrive first—even if it's already on Flickr or Facebook. You can use the Share charm to upload the picture to SkyDrive from Photos, and pick which folder to put your image in. Once the picture is in SkyDrive, open the Photos app to the SkyDrive folder where you saved your image and open or select it.

To send a picture to Facebook, pick the picture from the SkyDrive gallery, open the Share charm, and pick the People app. Use the drop-down menu to choose Facebook if it's not already selected, and then add a message. If you want to post a link to Twitter, choose Twitter from the drop-down menu instead. The picture remains on SkyDrive, and your post includes a link to the image.

If you've used the People app to share to Facebook or Twitter before, you can pick Facebook or Twitter from the list of favorites at the top of the Share charm (see Figure 13-8).

FIGURE 13-8 In the Photos app, use the Share charm to upload a photo to Facebook from SkyDrive, along with a comment.

How to... **Share Photos Directly to Twitter**

If you have installed a specific Twitter app from the Windows Store that uses photo sharing services that work with Twitter (and you already have photo sharing configured in the app), you can send a photo directly to Twitter wherever it's stored, by choosing your Twitter app in the Share charm.

Save Your Photos on a CD or DVD

If you want to share photos with friends and family, online services are a great way to do that. But sometimes you may need to send images to a family member who isn't online, or you may want to commemorate a special occasion like a wedding by creating a souvenir CD or DVD of photos. If you burn your photos onto a CD or DVD, that disc can also be played back in most DVD players. Saving your photos to CD or DVD is also a cost-effective option for backing them up if you have a lot of photos on your computer.

Burning photos onto a CD or DVD from Windows Media Player is very similar to creating an audio CD, as described in Chapter 12. Open Windows Media Player and select the Pictures section of your library, as shown next. The images are arranged in date order rather than in the folders they're saved in; you can click or tap a column heading to arrange the photos by tags or ratings (if you've already added those to your images), or you can use the search box to look for specific filenames. Select and drag the photos you want to copy into the Burn List. When you have all the photos you want to put on the disc in the Burn List, click or tap the Start Burn button at the top of the Burn pane.

If you add to the Burn List more photo files than will fit onto the CD or DVD you're copying to, Windows Media Player automatically splits the burn list between two or more discs. The list shows you which files will be burned to which disc. When the first disc is full, Windows Media Player will prompt you to insert a new CD or DVD so it can finish burning the files.

 You can also burn images to an optical disc directly from File Explorer. You'll find step-by-step instructions for copying files onto a CD or DVD in Chapter 4.

14

Watch and Organize Videos

HOW TO...

- Find and watch videos in the Video app
- Rent and buy videos from the Xbox video store
- Set up your Xbox LIVE account
- Manage your Videos library
- Watch videos in Windows Media Player
- Stream videos to your Xbox from the Videos app, Windows Media Player, and Internet Explorer
- Add Windows Media Center to Windows 8
- Share links to online videos

Like the Windows 8 music software covered in Chapter 12, the video applications in Windows 8 let you play the videos you already have and find more to watch in the Xbox video store. You can play your videos in the new Windows 8 Video app with a full-screen interface that lets you concentrate on what you're watching, or you can play them in Windows Media Player on the desktop, next to the other programs you're working with. If you have a PC with an extra-large screen and a TV tuner, or a PC connected to your TV, you can also use Windows Media Center to record TV shows and enjoy them on your own schedule. And if you have an Xbox, you can stream videos to watch them on the big screen, even when you're browsing the Web.

Find and Watch Videos in the Video App

The new Windows 8 Video app, shown next, is pinned to your Start screen by default; if you've unpinned it, you can open it from the All Apps screen.

When you open the Video app, it shows you the latest movies and television shows in the Spotlight section. Scroll right or swipe to the left to see the movies and television store; in each section you can click or tap on the heading to see more titles (new releases, featured and top-selling videos, and titles organized by the genre, studio, or television network they come from). You can also search both the Xbox video store and your own files from the Search charm, as shown here.

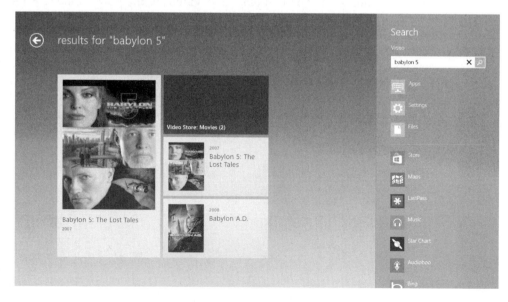

Click or tap a title to see more details and options to buy or rent the video so you can watch it straightaway. (Click or tap anywhere outside the detail window to close it.)

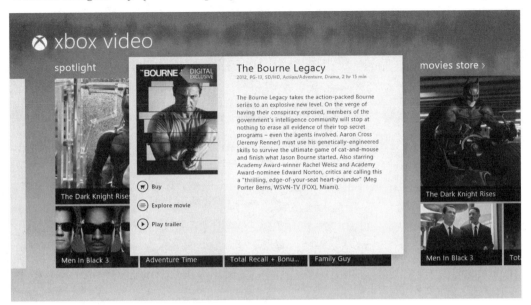

Click or tap Explore Movie to see the same information full screen, with a list of related titles you might also enjoy. If there's a trailer, click or tap Play Trailer to see it in the same full-screen view. (Click or tap on the screen while the trailer is playing to see the playback tools that are introduced later in this chapter.)

Scroll to the left or swipe right to see your own videos in the My Videos section. As with the other media apps in Windows 8, the content you see here comes from your Windows 8 libraries; here it's from the Videos library.

 You can set the Video app to open directly to your video library. Open the Settings charm and choose Preferences. Under Startup View, change the Open My Videos when I Start the App setting from Off to On.

Set Up Your Xbox LIVE Account

Although you can browse the Xbox video store and watch trailers without needing to sign in, if you want to watch any of the videos (even the free ones like the TV pilots and sample episodes), you'll need to sign in with a Microsoft account and choose how to pay for content.

If you sign in to Windows with a Microsoft account, the Video app will use that account. Otherwise, click or tap the Sign In button in the top right corner of the screen and fill in the username and password for your Microsoft account (or sign up for a new one).

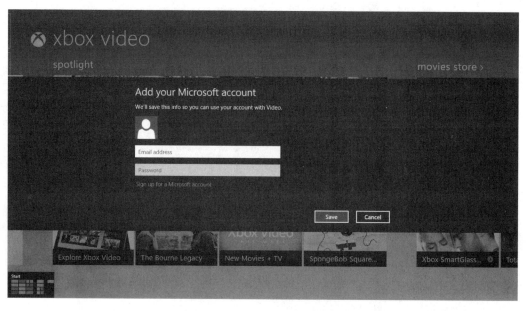

If you haven't used any Xbox services before, you'll need to set up your Xbox profile in the browser window that opens; click or tap I Accept to confirm that you agree with the terms and conditions.

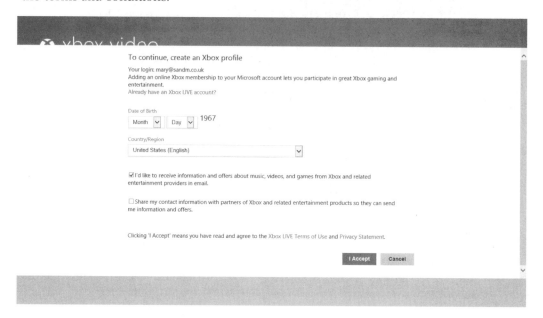

You can see more details about your account and set up your payment options by opening the Settings charm and choosing Account, as shown in Figure 14-1. You can

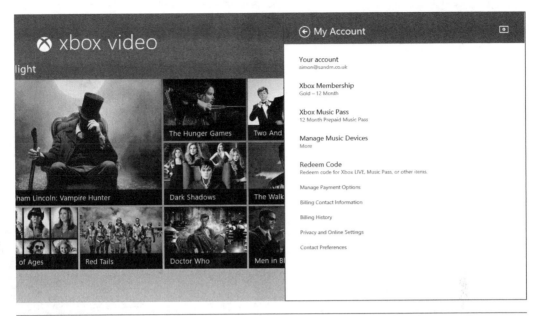

FIGURE 14-1   Manage your Xbox account: upgrade your membership, get features, and redeem codes.

also change the account you use for the Video app; click or tap Sign Out in the top right corner and then choose Sign In to enter a new Microsoft account.

By default, the Videos app will ask you to enter your password again any time you change your account settings or buy content. That way, if you let your children use your computer to watch videos you already own, they can't buy anything without your permission. You'll be asked to confirm this setting the first time you make a change to your settings or buy a video. If you want to change the setting later, open the Settings charm, choose Preferences, and then move the slider under "Ask me to sign in before completing purchases or managing my account" from On to Off.

 Tip   Every Microsoft account includes a free Xbox LIVE Silver membership. You can click or tap Xbox Membership under My Account to buy an Xbox LIVE Gold membership if you'd rather do that here than on your Xbox console. Prices range from $9.99 for one month to $99.99 per year for the Gold Family account.

To fill in your credit card details so that you can rent and buy movies, click or tap Manage Payment Options; this opens Internet Explorer and takes you to the Xbox LIVE site. To protect your credit card details, Microsoft requires you to sign in again, and if you protected your account with a phone number or alternate email address when you made your computer a Trusted PC (refer to Chapter 4 for details), you'll also need to type in a security code that Microsoft sends to you before you can log in. If this doesn't arrive quickly, click or tap I Didn't Get the Code to request a new one.

You can pay for videos by credit card or through your PayPal account; select the button for the payment method you want to use and type in the details.

If you have a gift card or a promotional code to enter, click or tap Redeem Code in the My Account pane and fill it in on the Xbox LIVE site.

Rent or Buy a Video from the Xbox Video Store

When you click or tap the title of a video to see more details, the Buy button shows you the lowest price for the title; click or tap that to see different prices in Viewing Options. The cheapest option is to buy the right to download and stream a standard-definition copy, but you can choose to pay extra to see the video in HD.

For a TV series, you'll need to click or tap View Seasons; choose a specific season from the list in the full-screen view, and the Buy Season button in the details view shows the price to buy the whole season. If the show is in the middle of a season, the button will say Buy Season Pass. Click or tap an episode from the list to see the Buy Episode price, as well as a synopsis of the episode.

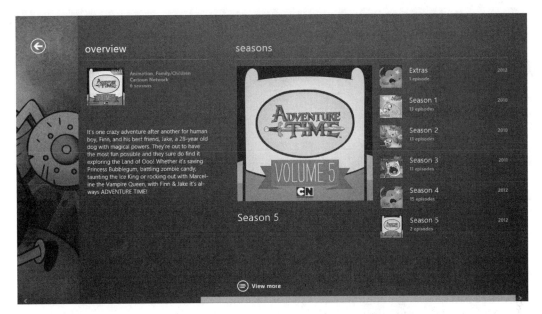

If you don't expect to watch a video more than once, you may be able to rent it. When you rent a video, you have 14 days to watch it; once you start watching the video, you can pause it and come back to it or play it as many times as you want within 24 hours. After that, you will have to pay to see it again.

Play Videos You've Bought in the Xbox Music Store

Once you've bought a video, you will see it in My Videos along with your local video files. If you want display your videos alphabetically instead of seeing the most recently added videos at the top of the list, click or tap the Date Added drop-down menu, as shown next, and choose a to z. You can also filter which videos are listed by clicking or tapping either the Movies header to see only films (which includes documentaries and one-off shows) or the TV header to see only episodes from TV shows. These lists only show movies and TV shows you've bought or rented from the Xbox video store; to see your own files, look under Other (the default All view shows both).

Click or tap the title of the video you just bought or rented from the Xbox video store. In the detail view, you can click or tap Play to watch it straightaway by streaming it from the store, or you can choose Download to save a copy on your PC (if you've already downloaded the file, the Download button and the reminder that the video will stream disappear). Click or tap View Seasons to go back to the Xbox video store if you want to get more episodes of a TV series you're enjoying (for a movie, you'll see the Explore Movie button instead).

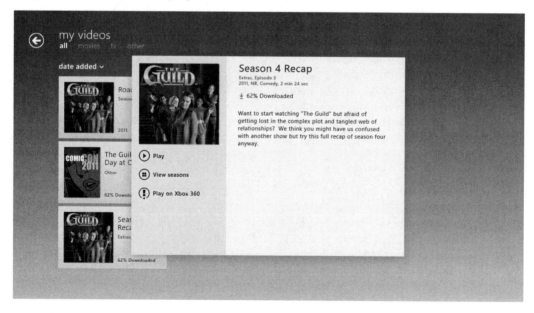

You may also see the option to Play on Xbox 360; we'll cover how that works later in the chapter.

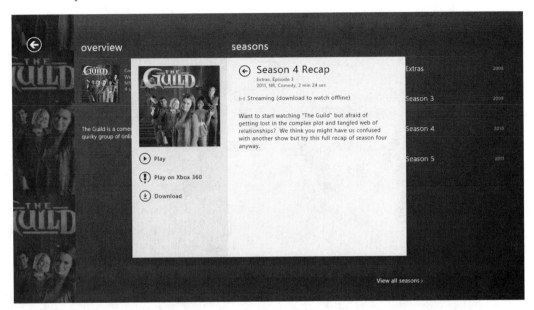

 Right-click the title of a video in the My Videos screen or swipe up over it with your finger to select it and open the app bar, which offers options to download or delete the file as well as playback controls for any video you're already playing. Tap the thumbnail of the current video to switch to watching it.

When your video starts playing, you'll see the playback controls briefly; if you don't move your mouse or tap the screen, they'll fade away while your video plays. Click or tap on the screen to open the controls again. The Back button takes you back to My Videos so you can choose something else to watch. Click Pause/Play to pause your video or start playing it again. Click or tap Now Playing to see a reminder of which video you're watching. The Timeline shows how far through the video you are and how long it lasts. Click or tap the round playback handle and drag it right to skip forward through the video or left to skip back through the video. Click or tap More

Info to open the synopsis for your movie, or to open the full-screen view of a TV series, where you can buy more episodes.

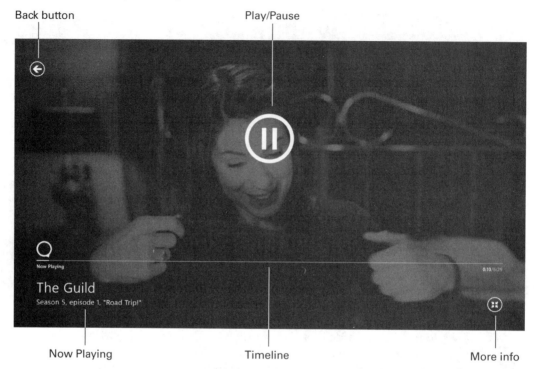

Back button   Play/Pause

Now Playing   Timeline   More info

Right-click or slide your finger over the top or bottom edge of a touchscreen to open the app bar with more controls; you can pause the video, skip back or ahead 15 seconds, turn on repeat stream the video to your Xbox, or open a video file from the File Picker (look under Playback Options if your screen isn't wide enough for all the icons).

Open Your Own Video Files

The My Videos section of the Video app shows the video files in your Videos folder as well as the titles you've bought or rented from the Xbox video store; click or tap the Other heading to see only your own video files.

If you haven't included any folders in your Videos library yet (and you don't have any videos in the default folder), the My Videos section shows you instructions for adding files to your video library, and a button to open a video to watch using the File Picker. (See Chapter 2 if you need a refresher on navigating in the File Picker.)

Unless you have a title from the Xbox video store selected, you can open one of your own files at any point; right-click or swipe over the top or bottom edge of your touchscreen to open the app bar, and choose Open File. This shows you the File Picker, where you can see the folder structure you've used to organize your videos. Although this is the way to open files that aren't already in your video library, that's where the File Picker starts (click or tap Go Up or Files to move to other folders and drives or to see your homegroup network). If you have a lot of videos in your library, navigating to the right folder may be easier than scrolling through a screen of tiles. Select the file you want and click or tap Open to play it.

You can also search using the Search charm; the results include your own files, listed before matches in the Xbox video store.

Manage Your Videos Library

You can't add folders to or remove them from your Videos library in the Video app; you do that in File Explorer.

In the Navigation pane of File Explorer, click or tap the Videos library and open the Library Tools Manage tab that appears in the ribbon. Select Manage Library to open the Videos Library Locations dialog box, shown in Figure 14-2. Click or tap the Add button to choose new folders you want to include in the library (without moving the files). If there are any folders in the Videos library that you don't use, like the Public Videos folder that's shared with other users on your computer, click or tap on the folder name and then choose Remove.

One of the folders in the Videos library will be marked as the Default Save Location. This is where the Videos app saves videos you download from the Xbox video store (organized into Movies and TV folders). If you want to use a different folder for this, add it to the Videos library, right-click or tap and hold on the folder name, and choose Set as Default Save Location.

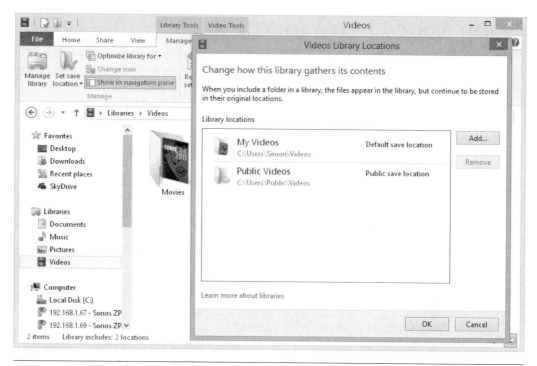

FIGURE 14-2 Add a new folder to the Videos library by clicking or tapping the Add button.

Watch Videos in Windows Media Player

If you haven't already pinned Windows Media Player to your taskbar (see Chapter 2), you can open it from the All Apps screen under Windows Accessories, or you can use File Explorer to find the video you want to watch and use the Open With menu on the Home tab of the ribbon to open it in Windows Media Player. We explained the Windows Media Player interface in Chapter 12, so you may want to read through the details in that chapter first if you haven't already done so.

To browse video titles, click or tap Videos in your media library (or a media library shared from another computer in your homegroup) in the Navigation pane, as shown in Figure 14-3. You see all the videos in your Videos library as tiles; use the column headings at the top of the window to change how the list of videos is sorted, or type a word in the search box to find matching titles. Double-click or tap quickly twice on a video file to start playing it, or select the video file and click or tap the Play button in the player controls at the bottom of the window. If you want to queue up several videos to watch one after another, drag them into the Play pane on the right and then click or tap the Play button.

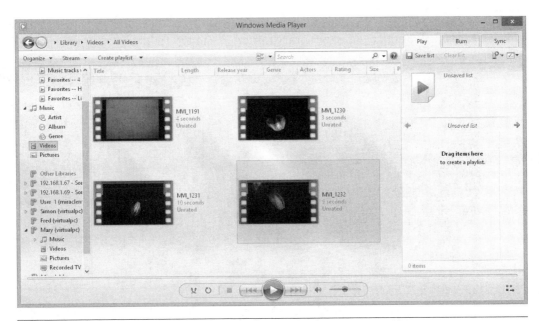

FIGURE 14-3   Browse your Videos library in Windows Media Player.

To play a video file that isn't in your Videos library, you can open it from the File menu; right-click or press and hold on the toolbar or press the ALT key on your keyboard and choose Show Menu Bar to open the menu bar for Windows Media Player. Alternatively, you can navigate to the file in File Explorer and use the Open button in the ribbon to open the file in Windows Media Player.

 Unlike previous versions of Windows, you can't watch a DVD movie in Windows Media Player in Windows 8, but if your PC has a DVD drive (or you've installed a DVD drive yourself), it should have software that lets you play DVD movies. If you install Windows Media Center, as described later in the chapter, that can also play DVD video.

When you play a video, the Windows Media Player window changes to the Now Playing view and automatically resizes to the right size and shape for the video; you can resize the window like any other, but if you want to play the video full screen, click or tap the Full Screen button in the bottom right corner. Use the playback controls at the bottom of the screen to pause or stop the video, go back to the last file you watched or forward the next one that's queued up, change the volume, or mute the video. The timeline shows you how much of the video you've watched; click or tap on it to jump to a different part of the video. If you want to go back to the Library view, click or tap the Go to Library button in the top right corner of the window.

 Although you can burn video files to a CD or DVD using Windows Media Player by choosing a Data CD or DVD as the disc type at the top of the Burn List, or directly in File Explorer, that's only useful for backing up your files. It doesn't create a movie DVD that you can use in a DVD player to watch your videos. Refer to the instructions in Chapter 12 for burning discs from Windows Media Player or refer to Chapter 4 to learn how to burn a disc from File Explorer.

Stream Videos to Your Xbox 360

If you're watching a video on your PC and you'd rather see it on a bigger screen, you can watch it on your TV if you have an Xbox 360 connected to your TV; you can stream many videos to it from the Videos app, from the Windows 8 version of Internet Explorer, from File Explorer, or from Windows Media Player.

To stream media to an Xbox console, it must be an Xbox 360 with the Fall 2012 dashboard update; it also needs to be connected to your home network. Refer to the instructions in Chapter 12 for setting up the Xbox SmartGlass application, enabling homegroup media streaming, and turning on Play To.

How to...   ## Troubleshoot Streaming to Xbox

If you don't see your Xbox listed as a device that you can play videos to, make sure it's turned on and open to the dashboard (rather than running an application or playing a game), and that you're logged in with the same Microsoft account in both places. Then, look in the Devices section of PC Settings to make sure it's listed as online. (If your Xbox is listed as offline in the Devices section even when it's online, click or tap to select it in the Devices list, click or tap the – button to remove it, and then click or tap Add a Device to add it again.) The file format of the video also has to be one that the Xbox can play.

Stream Videos from Windows Media Player

In Windows Media Player, drag the video you want to watch to the Play list; if you're already playing a video, you need to click or tap the Go to Library button in the top right corner of the window to go back to the Library view. If there are devices available that you can stream the video to, you'll see the Play To icon with a small, green play button on at the top of the Play pane. Click or tap this to open the Play To menu, and choose Xbox 360. This opens the Play To window, where you can see the list of videos you have queued up. Select the first one you want to watch, and then click or tap the Play button. You can control the playback from the Play To window on your PC or with your usual Xbox controller or remote control.

Stream Videos from File Explorer

In File Explorer, select one or more video files, click or tap the Play To icon in the Play tab of the ribbon (which only appears when you're in a folder that contains media files), and select Xbox 360 from the drop-down menu. As in Windows Media Player, you'll see the Play To menu with your play list and the playback controls.

Stream Videos from the Video App

In the Video app, the controls differ slightly depending on where the video you want to stream comes from. When you click or tap a video title in the Xbox video store to see the details, you can click or tap Play on Xbox 360. If you're already watching a video that comes from the Xbox video store, right-click or swipe up to open the app bar and choose Play on Xbox 360.

This opens Xbox SmartGlass, and if the SmartGlass Video Guide has information about the movie or TV show you're watching, you can see it on your PC screen while your video plays on the Xbox. Open the app bar, as shown next, to control the video from your PC with the Play/Pause, Previous, and Next buttons. If you tap on the timeline in the app bar, you'll see the usual full-screen playback controls for the Videos app, enabling you to drag the handle to change which part of the video you're watching.

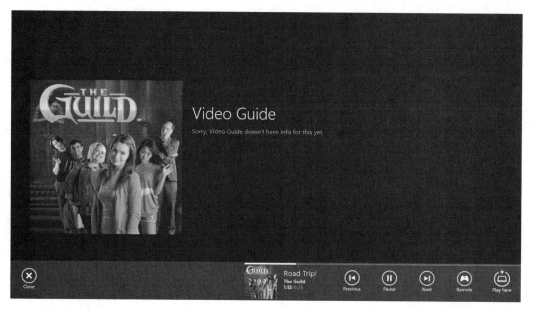

If you prefer to control the video using the onscreen controls on the Xbox, open the app bar and click or tap the Remote button to get a touchscreen version of the Xbox gaming controller, complete with the A, B, X, and Y buttons. You can also click or tap Play Here if you want to switch back to watching the video on your own screen.

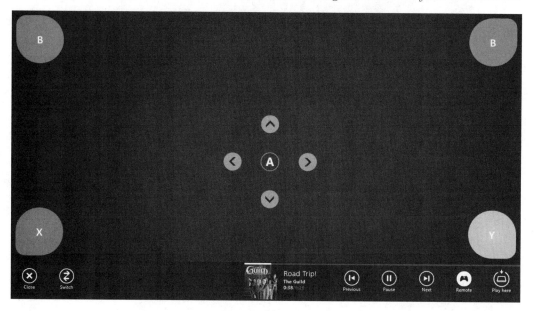

When you're playing your own video files, you can stream them to Xbox 360 or to any other video streaming devices on your home network, like a digital media adapter connected to your TV (if it's Windows 8 certified), so the options on the app bar are different. (You can't stream video from the Xbox video store to anything except an Xbox 360 because of the license agreement with movie studios and television networks.) Open the app bar and choose Play To; the Play To pane opens at the side of the screen with a list of the devices you can stream to, which will include your Xbox 360. You can also open the Devices charm to see a list of devices you can stream to.

The video starts playing on your Xbox, but the usual full-screen playback controls stay open on your PC so you can control playback.

Stream Videos from Internet Explorer

When you're looking at websites in the Windows 8 version of Internet Explorer, you can stream some of the videos you see on web pages to your Xbox.

 The only videos you can stream from Internet Explorer are those in HTML5 format. It's not often clear which format the videos on web pages are in, so the best way to find out if a video will stream to your Xbox is to try it. You can set YouTube to show you HTML5 videos when they're available, although this is an experimental service and you'll have to be signed in to YouTube to get HTML5 versions. Visit www.youtube.com/html5 and click or tap Join the HTML5 Trial.

Start playing a video in Internet Explorer by clicking or tapping the play control on the web page; it doesn't matter whether it's in a window or playing full screen. Open the Devices charm and choose Xbox 360, as shown next. You'll see the message Media from Internet Explorer on the Xbox screen, and your video should start playing automatically. If you don't see Xbox 360 listed in the Devices charm but you can see it

---

How to... ## Share Videos with Your Friends

If you're enjoying a video, use the Share charm to tell your friends about it. You can't share when you're actually watching a TV show or a movie, but you can share links to titles in the Xbox video store. Click or tap on the title to open the details window, and then open the Share charm and choose either Mail to send an email or People to post a message to Facebook or Twitter; if you choose Mail, the message includes a thumbnail of the video cover image. The link you send opens details of the video on the Xbox website, where your friends can buy or rent the video.

on the Play To menu in Windows Media Player or File Explorer, then the video isn't in the right format and you can't stream it to your Xbox.

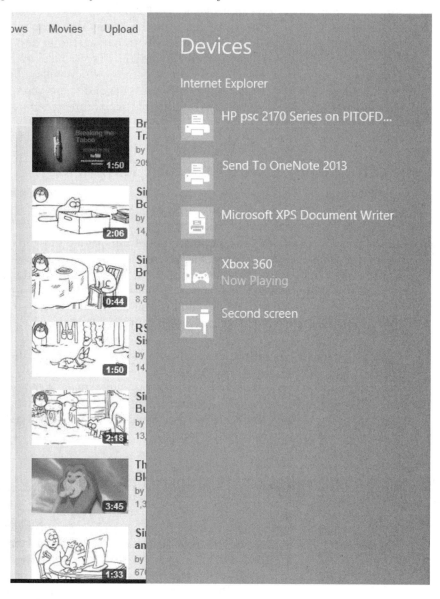

Add Windows Media Center to Windows 8

You may have used Windows Media Center in previous versions of Windows to record TV or to organize and play music and video files and look at photos in an interface that's designed for a TV screen and is easy to drive with a remote control. Windows Media Center isn't installed by default in any edition of Windows 8, but if you have Windows 8 Pro, you can add it to your system; if you only have Windows 8, you can upgrade to Windows 8 Pro and get Windows Media Center as well by buying Windows 8 Pro Pack. You can order both upgrades at http://windows.microsoft.com/en-US/ windows-8/feature-packs.

Once you receive the license key for your upgrade, open the Control Panel and enter **add features** in the Search box. Choose Add Features to Windows 8 from the search results and click or tap I Already Have a Product Key. (You can also choose I Want to Buy a Product Key to go to the Microsoft Store and pay for the upgrade.) Enter your product key and choose Next.

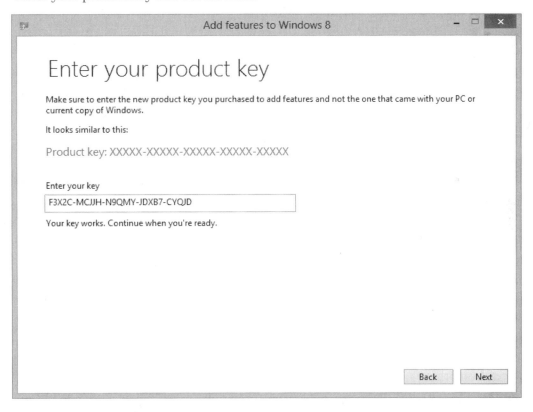

On the Ready to Add New Features screen, select the check box to accept the license terms and then click or tap Add Features.

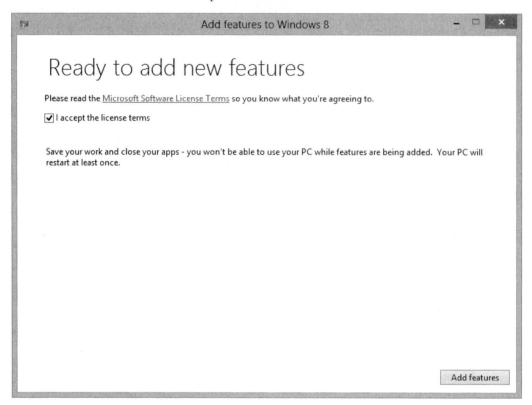

Windows displays the following Adding Features screen as it downloads the feature pack. After downloading the feature pack, Windows automatically restarts to upgrade your system.

Adding features

This might take a while depending on your PC and whether it needs any updates. Your PC will restart at least once.

When Windows restarts, Windows Media Center will be installed. You can open it from the All Apps screen. The first time you open Media Center, it displays a setup page; click or tap Continue and then choose Express unless you need to use Custom setup to configure hardware like a TV tuner.

Media Center uses your Music, Videos, and Pictures folders to find media files; make sure you include any folders with content you want to play in those libraries, so you can see it in Media Center.

15

Read, Navigate, and Connect

HOW TO...

- Open PDF documents in Reader
- Find information in a PDF document
- Search the Web with Bing
- View maps and get directions in Bing Maps
- Stay up to date with news, sports, finance, and travel information

Windows 8 comes with several other Windows Store apps installed that can help make your life easier—and keep you amused and informed:

- You can search with the Windows 8 Bing app and preview results on tiles in a finger-friendly interface.
- The built-in Maps app shows you where you are and what's around you (handy if you take your Windows 8 tablet out and about), but you can also use it to get travel directions and traffic information before you leave.
- You can read top news and sports stories, see the latest results for financial markets, and read about travel destinations (and then check flights and book hotels).
- If you ever need to access files on your home PC when you're away from home (for example, from work or while on vacation), you can use SkyDrive to access your files.

Live tiles from these apps keep you up to date right from the Start screen.

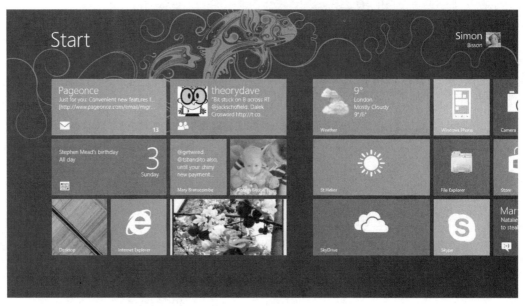

View PDF Documents in Reader

Adobe's Portable Document Format (PDF) is very common; brochures, manuals for appliances, transit maps, and even online bank statements are often in PDF format. You can install the free Adobe Reader program to open PDF files on the desktop, but Windows 8 comes with its own Reader app that can open both PDF documents and Microsoft's own XPS format, which is what you get if you save a printout instead of sending it to the printer—handy for keeping receipts and other important information.

Open a PDF Document in Reader

The Reader app isn't pinned to the Start screen by default; you'll find it on the All Apps screen. You can also open a PDF or XPS document straight into Reader by using the Open menu on the ribbon in File Explorer. If you haven't installed any other applications that can open PDF files, Reader will be the default program for this type of file, and you can just double-click or double-tap on a file to open it in Reader.

When you open the Reader app itself, rather than opening a PDF document, you'll see a list of any PDF files that you've opened recently along with a Browse tile, as shown next. To open a specific file, click or tap the Browse tile. This opens the File Picker in the Documents library; click or tap to open folders, scroll or swipe across the screen to see any files in the top level of the library, or select Files at the top of the screen to look at files elsewhere on your computer, on your network, or even in SkyDrive. If you need a reminder of how to navigate in the File Picker, look back at Chapter 2. Click or tap the file you want to open and then choose Open.

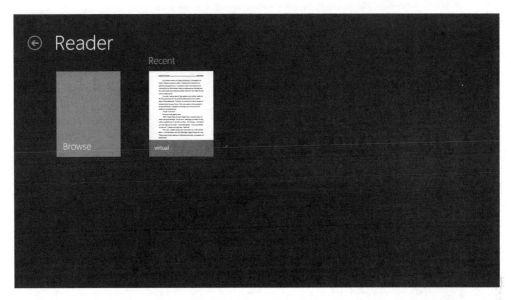

When you first open a document, Reader zooms the document so that it's as wide as the screen and you can scroll down and see the next page; that's called Continuous View. The number of pages in the document is briefly displayed in the top left corner, and you'll see plus- and minus-sign icons in the bottom right corner for zooming in and out of the document; if you have a touchscreen, you can also zoom by pinching or spreading your fingers on screen. If you zoom all the way out, Reader displays your document as individual pages, which is helpful if you want to quickly scroll or swipe through the document to see what's in it or find a particular page.

If your PC has a mouse or a trackpad, you'll also see a scroll bar at the side of the screen. If you don't move your mouse for a few seconds, these controls fade away so that you can see more of the page.

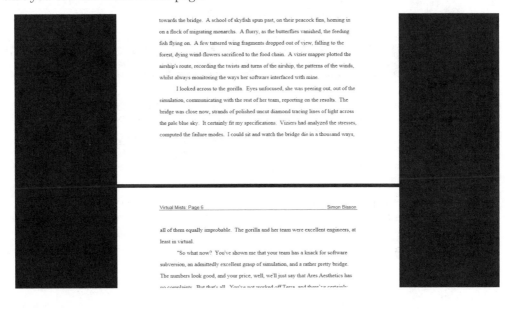

Some PDF documents are protected so that you can't change or even print them, to protect confidential information. You see what you're allowed to do with a PDF, as well as details like the name of the file, when it was last saved and how many pages are in it by opening the app bar and choosing More, then clicking or tapping Info.

If you prefer to click on either side of the screen or to swipe sideways to move through the pages of the document (instead of scrolling or swiping down), open the app bar and click or tap One Page. Choose Two Pages to see two pages on screen at once; again, you can click the navigation buttons at the sides of the screen or swipe sideways to move through the document.

If you're reading a PDF that starts with a cover page, like a printed book, and you want to see the same layout as you would on paper (with even-numbered pages on the left and odd-numbered pages on the right), click or tap the Cover Page command that appears on the app bar when you're in two-page view. This adds a blank page in front of the cover page to make the layout work.

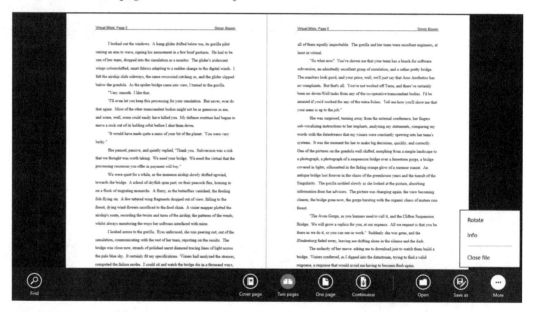

 If your PDF file is the wrong way up (which usually means someone scanned a document and forgot to rotate the pages), open the app bar and click or tap the More icon and choose Rotate. This rotates your page 90 degrees to the left; if you need to rotate it more, choose Rotate to move it another 90 degrees. This rotates all the pages in your document.

If you want to mark useful sentences in the PDF so you can find them again quickly or add a comment, first select the words with your mouse or with your finger (tap on one word and drag the handles to select the text you want). Next, right-click or press and hold on the words you selected; you can then choose Highlight or Add a Note.

Find Information Inside a PDF Document

To search inside your document, press CTRL-F on your keyboard or click or tap Find on the app bar. Type the text you're looking for and then press ENTER, or click or tap the Search button. Reader jumps to the first page that has a match for your search term and highlights the match. Click or tap the Next button to see subsequent matches (you can click or tap the Previous button to move back through matches), or click or tap Results to see a list of matches that you can scroll or swipe through. Click or tap one of the results to open that page.

Save the Document

You can't make any changes to PDF documents apart from rotating them, but you can save a copy of the document in another folder. This is useful if you opened a PDF document directly from a website and you want to keep a copy on your PC to look at later. Open the app bar and choose Save As.

Open Another Document

You can have only one document open at a time in the Reader app. If you want to look at a different document, open the app bar, click or tap the Open icon, and find the document in the File Picker.

Search with Bing

Although you can search the Web from Internet Explorer, either in the browser or directly from the Search charm, Windows 8 also comes with a dedicated Bing app that you can use to get search results in a finger-friendly tile interface, and see the latest topics other people are searching for.

The Bing app is pinned to the Start screen by default. Before you run it for the first time, the tile shows one of the daily Bing backgrounds; once you start using it, it becomes a live tile that shows the latest Bing daily image and currently popular search terms, so you can glance at it and see trending topics.

When you open the Bing app, you see today's daily Bing image with highlighted squares you can click to find out more about the subject of the picture (see Figure 15-1). Click or tap one of these to read a clue about the image in the form of a question; follow the link in the clue to see search results that answer the question. Click or tap the 'i' icon in the bottom left corner to find out what the picture shows. Topics other people are searching for are shown at the bottom of the screen; click or tap one of those links to search for the same thing, or click or tap the More arrow for an overview of trending stories.

If you type your own search term into the search box at the top of the screen, Bing will suggest words you might want to include in your search, including

FIGURE 15-1 (1) Search box, (2) Link your social network accounts to Bing, (3) Go back to previous results, (4) Popular searches, (5) List of currently trending searches, (6) Get details of today's Bing image, (7) See the list of trending searches, (8) Receive a clue about the image, and link to related searches

corrections for possible spelling mistakes. Click or tap one of the suggestions to run that search, or finish typing in your own search term and press ENTER (or click or tap on the magnifying glass icon).

Search results include images and videos, plus suggestions for related searches (see Figure 15-2). If you search for a place, you might also see maps and business listings. Sometimes you'll see ads as well; the tiles for these are color-coded green and are marked as ads so you don't open them by mistake.

If you only want to see images, click or tap the IMAGES link at the top of the screen. Swipe or scroll to the right of the screen to keep loading more results. Click or tap the tile for an image to preview it in the Bing app. When you click or tap one of the tiles in the web results, the corresponding web page opens in Internet Explorer so that you can read the full web page.

If you want the searches you make in the Bing app (and the websites you open from the list of results) to appear in your main Bing search history (and be synced to other PCs on which you sign in to Windows 8 with the same Microsoft account), open the Settings charm and choose Accounts to sign in with your Microsoft account.

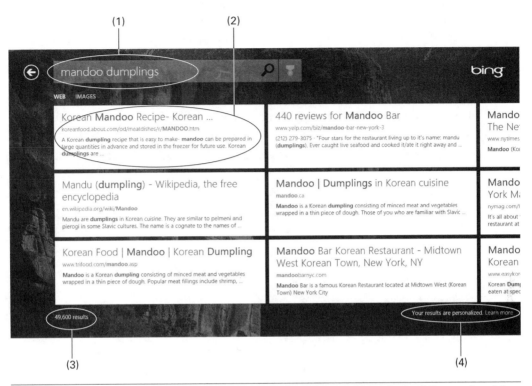

FIGURE 15-2   (1) Search terms, (2) Results tile, (3) Number of possible results, (4) Find out how Bing personalized your search.

If you sign in with your Facebook account as well, Bing will use information from your friends on Facebook as one of the ways it ranks results.

 By default, Bing filters out any search results with adult images, but your results might include words considered inappropriate for children. To remove search results that include any such words, open the Settings charm, choose SafeSearch, and set the SafeSearch filter to Strict.

Find Places and Routes in the Maps App

If you want to get directions or track down an address or local business, try the Maps app that comes with Windows 8.

The Maps app is pinned to the Start screen by default; if you've unpinned it, you can open it from the All Apps screen. The first time you open the Maps app, it asks for permission to use your location. Click or tap Allow to let it pinpoint where you are based on the details of your network connection. It'll then show you a map of your current location. Click or tap the diamond that shows your exact location to see the address and check how accurate it is.

You can swipe or scroll around the map to see other places, and zoom in to see more details about the current location or zoom out to see more places on the map. If you have a touchscreen, you can pinch with your fingers to zoom in and out; if you have a mouse, you'll see zoom buttons you can click when you move your mouse around. You can also double-click or double-tap on the map to zoom in.

Use the Map Style icon on the app bar to switch between Road View, which shows a stylized map, and Aerial View, which shows satellite images. Zoom in to street level in Road View and you'll see transit locations, the directions of one-way streets, the names of businesses, and 3D models of some buildings. If you continue to zoom in when in Aerial View, at a certain point the map switches to a 3D view, still with aerial photographs, so you can see the details of buildings and other features. For many areas, you can click or tap the compass icon on the right side of the screen to switch the angle that you're looking at the map from, so you can see the side or back of a building. If you have a touchscreen, you can rotate the view by pressing two fingers on the screen and rotating them around.

Open the app bar and choose Show Traffic to see a color-coded overlay of current traffic speeds, as shown next; as you zoom in, you'll see traffic details for more streets.

Click or tap the My Location icon in the app bar to center the map on your current location if you've moved it off screen while exploring.

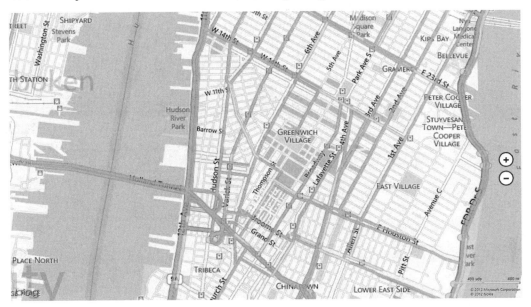

Use the Search charm to find a specific address or local businesses. You'll see a numbered list of matching businesses across the top of the screen and numbered locations on the map. Click or tap a business name to see it highlighted on the map, or click or tap a location on the map to see the business highlighted in the top of the screen. Click or tap the label that appears when you select a business to see more details (like the street address and a link to the website) and get directions.

If what you're looking for matches an address or district as well as a business name, you'll see the same kind of label on the map.

If you get too many results or you can't find what you're looking for, open the app bar and choose Refine to get a search pane in which you can type the business name and address separately.

Click or tap the Directions button on an address or choose the Directions icon from the app bar to search for a route from one place to another.

If you want to mark a point on the map, open the app bar and drag the Add a Pin icon onto the map; you'll see an orange dot where you drop it. Click or tap the orange dot and choose Directions to open the Directions pane with the address of the pin as your destination.

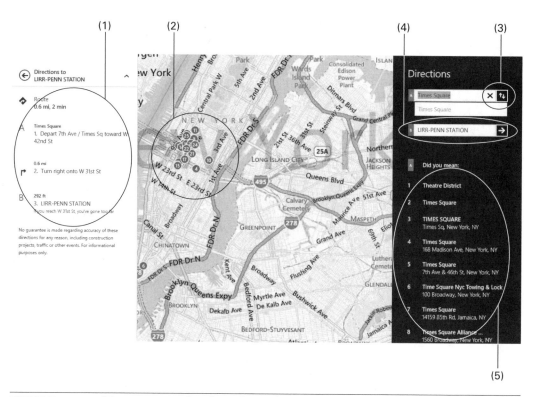

FIGURE 15-3 (1) Directions for the selected route, (2) Map showing search results for route start, (3) Switch start and end of route, (4) End of route, (5) Possible results for an address search

If you have an address selected or you've put a pin in the map, you'll see that as the destination in the Directions pane, and Bing assumes that you want to get directions to that destination from your current location. If that's correct, press ENTER on your keyboard or click or tap the Get Directions arrow next to the destination. Otherwise, you can type in a different address to navigate to or from (see Figure 15-3).

The suggested route appears as a blue line on the map, with numbers for each of the turns. Click or tap on the Directions To box that appears on screen to see detailed instructions, with the total distance and estimated driving time.

You can scroll or swipe through the directions, click or tap on individual steps on the route to zoom in to that turn on the map, or click or tap the numbered turns on the map to see the corresponding instructions.

Stay Up to Date with Bing Apps

Windows 8 comes with five other Bing apps that you'll find pinned to the Start screen, with live tiles that give you a peek at the latest news: Weather, News, Finance, Sports, and Travel. (As always, if you've unpinned any of these tiles, you can open the app from the All Apps screen.) Use these apps to search for specific information or to browse what's going on in the world. With the News, Sports, and Finances apps, you can swipe or scroll sideways to read headlines and articles.

Check the Forecast with the Weather App

When you first open the Weather app, it asks for your location; type in the name of your town or city, or click or tap the location icon to have the app find your location automatically. This becomes your Home location, and you'll see the weather forecast for it on the Weather live tile on the Start screen. Right-click or swipe over the top or bottom edge of your touchscreen to open the app bar. Choose Places and click or tap the + button on the blank tile to add a new location, or choose World Weather to see a map with temperatures around the world. Double-click or tap twice to zoom in on a country or pick a specific town from the map.

If you're looking at the weather for a location other than your Home location and you want to keep track of that location (if you are preparing for a vacation, for example), open the app bar and pin that location to the Start screen as another live tile (or choose Set as Default to make it your new Home location).

Each weather forecast gives you predictions for the next five days, as shown next; use the arrows at the side and bottom of the forecast to see another five days of predictions or extra details like the humidity, along with forecasts from other weather services, for comparison. Scroll to the right or swipe left to see hourly forecasts, maps of temperature, rainfall, and cloud cover plus historical weather patterns.

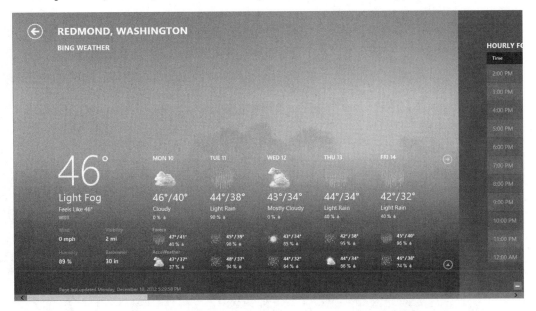

Stay Informed with the News App

The News app has national, world, technology, entertainment, politics, sports, and health sections. Use the Search charm to look for stories on specific topics. Open the app bar and pick Sources if you prefer to read stories from specific publications, with choices ranging from ABC News and Associated Press to the *Washington Post* and *USA Today*. To create a custom news feed on a topic that you follow, choose My News from the app bar and then choose Add a Section. Open a section and use the app bar to pin it to the Start menu to see the latest headlines.

If you want to see a different selection of publications and sources, open the Settings charm and choose Options. Click or tap the Change App Language and Content To drop-down menu and choose where your news comes from and/or which language it's in.

Follow Your Favorite Teams with the Sports App

You can browse top sports news stories in the Sport app or open the app bar to see headlines, schedules, results, rosters, and top players and teams for specific sports like golf and tennis and leagues like the National Football League, National Basketball Association, National Hockey League, Major League Baseball, and Formula One. Choose Favorite Teams from the app bar to drill down to the same details for a specific team; again, you can pin a live tile to the Start screen to see headlines and results for that team.

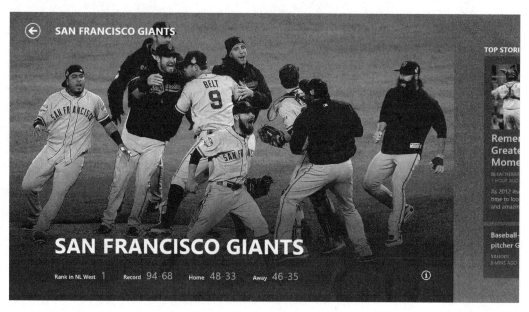

Track Markets with the Finance App

In the Finance app, you can read financial news stories, see figures for rates, currencies, and world markets, and maintain a watch list of stocks. Add the stocks you follow by choosing Watchlist from the app bar and clicking or tapping the plus icon, then entering a company name or stock ticker; pick the correct stock from the list of results then click or tap Add in the app bar. You can also search for a stock directly from the Search charm, but you still need to choose Add on the app bar to put it on your watchlist after you open it. If you follow the market of a specific country or you want to get news in a different language, open the Settings charm, choose Options, and then select a different country or language from the Change App Language and Content To drop-down menu.

Plan a Vacation with the Travel App

The Travel app has articles about more than 2,000 holiday destinations. Pick a featured town or city to read a guide from *Frommers*, see weather and currency information, look at photos, maps, and 360-degree panoramas, or get details about attractions, hotels, and restaurants, complete with phone numbers, hours of operation, and websites. Use the Search charm to find details about a specific place (if the Travel app doesn't cover it, you won't see any results in the Search pane but you can always choose Bing from the list of other apps to look for information on the web).

You can also use the Travel app to search for hotels and flights (using Kayak's booking service). Open the app bar and choose Flights or Hotels. Fill in the name of the city where you want to go and the dates when you want to travel. As shown next, you can sort or filter the list of flights by price, number of stops, airline, or departure time to find the flight that suits you best. Sort or filter your hotel search by price or class of hotel, or see only hotels that have the facilities you want (like a fitness room or swimming pool).

You can Access Your PC Remotely Through SkyDrive

If you're running the SkyDrive program on your desktop to sync files between your PC and your SkyDrive account automatically, as described in Chapter 4, you can use the SkyDrive website to remotely access files on any computer that you're running the SkyDrive desktop software on, as long as it's turned on. This is how the Photos app shows you pictures from your other SkyDrive PCs.

First, install the SkyDrive desktop software on the computer you want to fetch files from; you can download it from https://apps.live.com/skydrive. When it's running, right-click or press and hold the SkyDrive icon in the notification area of the taskbar and choose Settings; on the Settings tab, select the check box for Fetch Your Files from Anywhere. Now open the SkyDrive website at https://skydrive.live.com/ (you can't do this from the Windows Store SkyDrive app on your PC, just the website). In the navigation pane on the left, you'll see the heading PCs, with a list of the computers that SkyDrive knows about. Click or tap the name of the computer you want to reach, and you'll see the folders and files listed in the SkyDrive website so that you can open or copy the file you need.

16

Get More Apps and Games for Windows 8

HOW TO...

- Explore the Windows Store
- Search for apps and read reviews
- Download and install apps
- Find apps you've downloaded
- Set up a different Microsoft account
- Enter your payment information
- Use Family Safety to control which apps children can install
- Block PCs you don't use any more
- Find Xbox games for Windows 8
- See your Xbox friends and messages in Windows 8
- Control your Xbox 360 with Xbox SmartGlass

The Windows Store apps we've looked at in previous chapters are automatically installed with Windows 8, but there are many more apps for Windows 8 that you can get from the Windows Store.

If you're familiar with the Apple App Store or Google Play, the Windows Store is a similar marketplace. You can explore it using the Windows Store app that comes with Windows 8. In this chapter we'll explain how the Windows Store is organized, how to search for apps and install them, and how to set up a way to pay for apps. You can run Windows Store apps on up to five different PCs, so we'll show you how to use your Microsoft account to share your apps with other members of your family.

The Windows Store is the only way you can get Windows Store apps. That doesn't mean you can't purchase desktop programs online (and of course you can still buy boxed software at your favorite physical store). In fact, you will also find some desktop programs in the Windows Store itself. You don't buy them through the Store itself; instead, the link on the details page for the program takes you to the online site of the software company that makes the program, where you buy from that company directly.

You can find plenty of games in the Windows Store, but you can also find games from Microsoft (including free Windows 8 versions of familiar Windows games like Solitaire and Minesweeper) in the Games app, where you can also stay up to date with your Xbox LIVE friends and see scores and achievements for games you play on Xbox 360 and Windows Phone.

Explore the Windows Store

The easiest way to use the Windows Store is through the Windows 8 app, which you open by clicking or tapping its tile on the Start screen. If you've unpinned it, you can find the Windows Store app on the All Apps screen.

When you open the Store, the first section you see is Spotlight, with a selection of new and popular apps, plus tiles to see the top free apps and the hundred or so most recent new apps across all categories.

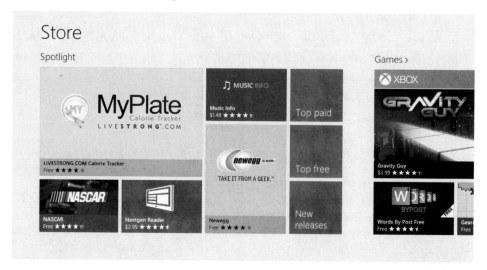

Swipe or scroll through the app to see the various categories in which the apps in the Windows Store are organized: Games, Social, Entertainment, Photo, Music & Video, Sport, Books & Reference, News & Weather, Health & Fitness, Food & Dining, Lifestyle, Shopping, Travel, Finance, Productivity, Tools, Security, Business, Education, and Government. Plus there may be a category of apps specially selected by the maker of your PC. For each category, you'll see larger tiles for a selection of recent and popular apps, plus the Top Free and New Releases tiles for that category. Click or tap the category heading to see all the apps, with tiles that show the title, rating, and price. If there are a lot of apps in a category, click or tap the All Subcategories drop-down menu; for example, in the Games category, you can choose from 15 genres ranging from Action to Card to Kids to Puzzle to Strategy.

You can filter apps so that you see only free apps or apps that are either free or have a free trial; or you can choose to view only paid apps if you prefer. Click or tap the All Prices drop-down menu to choose.

By default, the apps in a category are sorted according to how interesting the Microsoft team running the Windows Store thinks they will be to users. To arrange the apps by newest, highest rated, or highest or lowest price instead, click or tap the drop-down menu that initially lists Sort by Noteworthy and pick a different order.

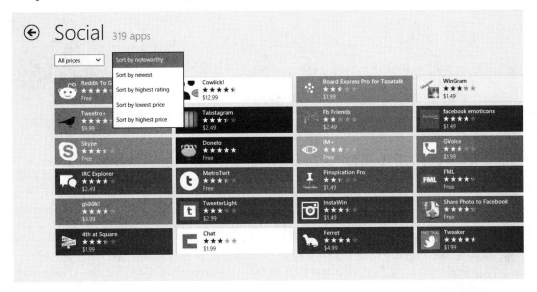

If you're looking for something specific, open the Search charm and type in either an app name or what you want it to do (see Figure 16-1). The tiles in the list of results show the category of the app as well as the title, price, and rating. Tiles for desktop programs are clearly labeled.

 When you look at apps in a category or a search, the tiles don't show whether you already have the app installed; you have to open the app details to find out.

You can filter the results by category and price, and change the way they're sorted. The default is to put the best matches at the start of the list (Sort by Relevance). If you want to see the most recent or highest-rated apps first, even if they're not as good a match, or sort by price, click or tap the drop-down menu that initially lists Sort by Relevance and make your selection.

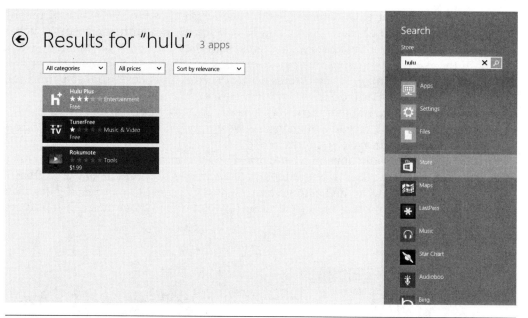

FIGURE 16-1 Use the Search charm to find the app you want.

Improve Your Search Results

Some apps in the Windows Store are available only in languages other than English. If you don't want to see those listed, you can tell the Windows Store to prioritize apps in your chosen language. Open the Settings charm and choose Preferences. Drag the slider under "Make it easier to find apps in my preferred languages" from No to Yes. You can also use this if you want to see apps in the default language you use in Windows listed first—even if that isn't the primary language for the Windows Store in your region.

You can also ask the Windows Store to prioritize apps that the developer says have accessibility features, which may make them easier to use if you have a disability. Drag the slider under "Make it easier to find apps that include accessibility features" from No to Yes, and the Windows Store will place apps at the top of the category lists that claim to have accessibility features.

Use Family Safety to Make the Windows Store Child Safe

Use the Family Safety controls in Windows 8 to control which apps are visible in the Store when your children sign in with their own accounts. You can limit which games and apps they see by the age ratings or by the content ratings, or you can allow and block specific apps. Refer to Chapter 3 to learn how to create accounts for your children and set up general Family Safety settings for them.

Open the Control Panel and select User Accounts and Family Safety, then tap or click Family Safety and choose the account of the child you want to set limits for. This opens the User Settings page, where you can make sure Family Safety is set to On, Enforce Current Settings. Under Windows Settings, click or tap Windows Store and Game Restrictions and select Only Use Games and Windows Store Apps I Allow. Once you select this radio button, you can fine tune the settings:

- To use the ratings on apps and games in the Windows Store to control what's available, click or tap Set Game and Windows Store Ratings and choose Block Games with No Ratings. Choose the ratings level you want to allow your child to see.
- If you want to block or allow games that are already installed, click or tap Allow or Block Specific Games. You'll see a list of all the games installed on the child's account. For each game, you can choose Always Allow, Always Block, or leave it on the User Rating Setting so the ratings level controls which games are available.

If you want to block specific apps and desktop programs as well, return to the User Settings page and click or tap App Restrictions under Windows Settings. Change the setting at the top to Only Use the Apps I Allow. Select the check boxes next to the apps they're allowed to run.

You may not want to change these settings on your child's computer directly, especially if you have several children with their own PCs. You can change the same

settings remotely by visiting the Family Safety website at https://familysafety
.microsoft.com/safety/; there's also a link to the website on the front page of the
Family Safety control panel.

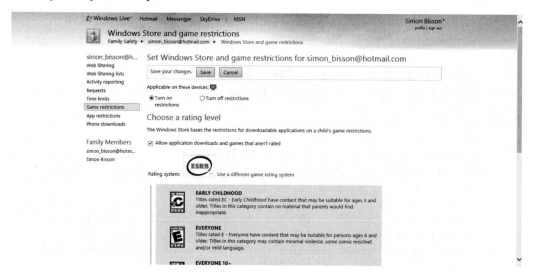

Enter Your Credit Card Details

You don't have to log in with a Microsoft account to browse the Windows Store, but
you will need to add your Microsoft account details to download any apps. The first
time you click or tap the Install button for a Windows Store app, if you aren't signed
in to Windows with a Microsoft account, you'll be asked for your Microsoft account
details. You can also open the Settings charm and click or tap Your Account to add
your account. If you sign in to Windows with one Microsoft account but you want to
use a different Microsoft account to download apps from the Store (perhaps a shared
family account so you can share the apps you buy, because they can be installed on
up to five machines), choose Your Account and click or tap Sign Out to set up the
Store with a different account.

Once you've added your account, open the Settings charm again and choose Your
Account. Under Payment and Billing Info, click or tap Add Payment Method; this
opens the Payment and Billing screen, shown next, where you can add a credit card
or set up your PayPal account. If you choose PayPal, when you click or tap the Submit
button, the Store will ask you to confirm that you want to open the PayPal website
so you can link your account to the Windows Store. If you add a credit card to your

Windows Store account, Microsoft will authorize it by making a small, temporary charge and then refunding it; setting up your credit card details won't cost you anything until you start buying apps.

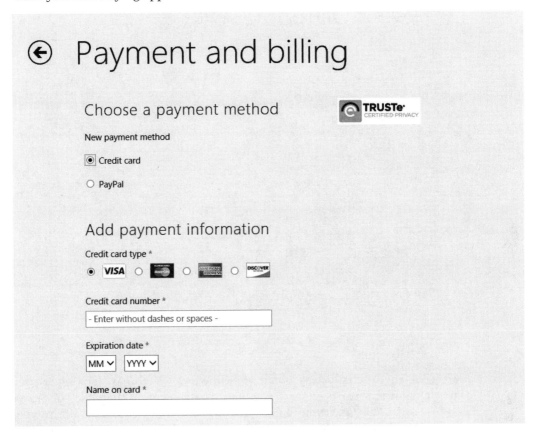

The credit card you use in the Windows Store needs to be from the same country or region as the Home location you've set for your PC. For example, if you're buying an app from the Windows Store on a PC with a Home location of the United States, you need to use a credit card from a U.S. bank.

To make sure you don't accidentally buy an app by clicking or tapping in the wrong place on screen (and to stop your children from buying apps if you let them use your PC), the Store will ask you to type in your Microsoft account password every time you buy an app. If you don't want to keep that protection, change the slider under

"Always ask for your password when buying an app" from Yes to No; you'll have to type in your Microsoft account password to confirm the change.

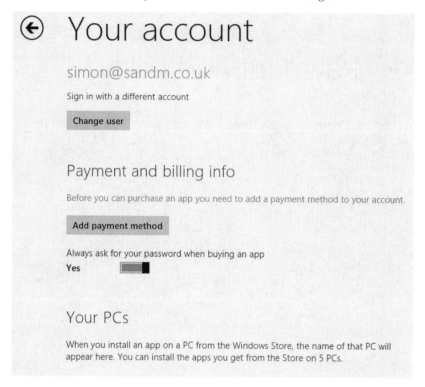

You can check what you've bought in the Windows Store by looking at your billing history. Open the Settings charm and choose Your Account, then click or tap View Billing History. This takes you to the Windows Store billing website, where you'll need to sign in with your Microsoft account.

Download and Install Apps

Click or tap the tile of an app to learn more about it (see Figure 16-2):

- **Rating** You see not only the star rating for the app but also how many people have rated the app, so you can gauge how much to trust the score.
- **Install** If you have to pay for the app, this button is labeled Buy; if there's a trial period available, it's labeled Try. If you already have this app installed on any of the PCs where you buy apps with this Microsoft account, the label changes to You Own This App.
- **Permission** Some apps want to use your location or camera. You get a chance to allow or block this when you first run the app, but often apps won't work without these permissions.

Rating

Details Reviews

Screenshots

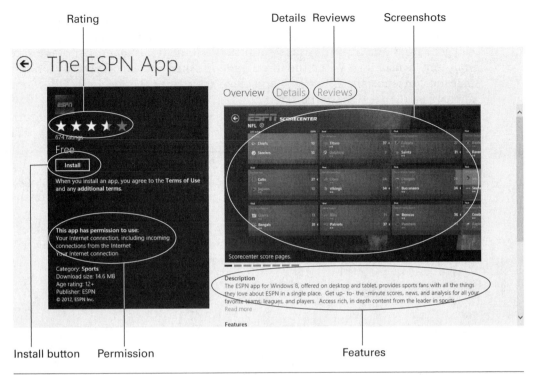

Install button   Permission

Features

FIGURE 16-2 Use the description and rating to help you decide if a Windows Store app is right for you.

- **Reviews**   Read what other users have said about the app as well as their ratings.
- **Features**   Scroll down to see more information.
- **Details**   Support information, including whether the app runs on Windows 8 and Windows RT.
- **Screenshots**   You can check out what the app looks like before you decide whether to install it.

Scroll or swipe down to read the description of the app; click or tap Read More to show any hidden text, then click or tap Hide Less to collapse it again. At the bottom of the page, you'll see links to open the app developer's website in Internet Explorer to learn more.

 If you see an app you don't think should be in the Windows Store, click or tap Report This App for Violating the Store's Terms of Use. Click or tap the Reason drop-down menu to choose what you think is improper about the app, then type a brief explanation of why you're reporting the app. Click or tap Submit to send it. You can also report reviews that you think are offensive or are thinly disguised advertising, and you can mark the ones you find useful to help other users out.

Click or tap the Install button to download and install a free app, or the Try button to install a trial version of a paid app. The app page will close and take you back to the category page. You'll see message notification in the top right corner of the screen that your app is installing. When the installation finishes, this is followed by a notification that the app is installed. On the Start screen the tile for the newly installed app appears on the far right of the screen.

To buy a paid app, click or tap the Buy button, then click or tap the Confirm button that replaces it (or the Cancel button if you've changed your mind). When you click or tap Confirm, you'll be prompted to enter your Microsoft account password (unless you've already turned this confirmation off, as described in the previous section). After you type your password and click or tap OK, the Store processes the payment and starts the download, at which point you don't have another chance to cancel.

If the software you're looking at in the Windows Store is actually a desktop program, the button is labeled Get App from Publisher with a link to open the publisher's website (see Figure 16-3) in Internet Explorer.

FIGURE 16-3 Find desktop applications in the Windows Store and then download them from the Web.

The Windows Store Tells You When to Update Your Apps

Windows Update checks the Windows Store for updates to the apps you have installed when it's looking for updates to Windows. The Windows Store live tile shows how many updates are waiting for you, and you'll also see a message in the top right corner of the app. If you think there are updates you're not seeing, open the Settings charm, choose App Updates, and then click or tap Check for Updates.

Find Your Downloaded Apps

When you buy an app in the Windows Store, you can install it on up to five different computers. If you can't find an app you thought you installed, or if you're looking for an app that you uninstalled and now want back, check the list on the Your Apps screen, shown in Figure 16-4, which you can open from the Windows Store app bar. This appears at the top of the screen, but you open it like any other app bar, by right-clicking anywhere on any screen within the Store app or by swiping down from the top or up from the bottom edge on a touchscreen.

By default, the Your Apps screen displays all the apps that you have downloaded at some point but that are *not* installed on your computer (so you can add them quickly),

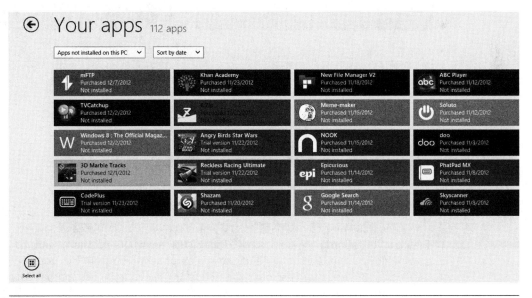

FIGURE 16-4   The apps you've previously downloaded appear in the Your Apps list. You can select them all by clicking or tapping the Select All icon.

sorted by date, with the most recent purchases appearing at the top of the list. If you want to install an app and you know which other PC you've installed it on, click or tap Apps Not Installed on This PC and choose the computer with the app you want so you can find it quickly. You can also choose All Apps to see everything you've installed on any computer.

The list of apps is sorted by date, with the most recently installed apps at the top; click or tap the drop-down menu showing Sort by Date if you want to change to an alphabetical list (choose Sort by Name).

Click or tap Select All if you want to install all the apps from another PC on your computer, or click or tap individual apps to select them (a check mark appears in the upper right corner of the app's tile, as shown next). If you select a single app, you can click or tap View Details to see its Store page. Click or tap the Install button to install your selection of apps.

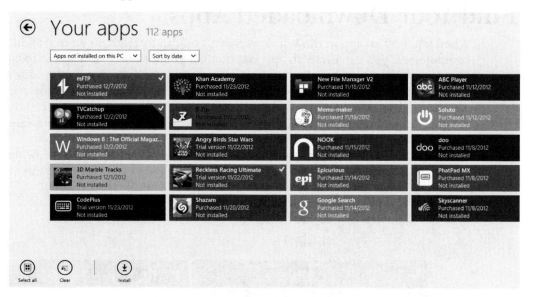

<table>
<tr><td></td><td>**Go Back to the Home Screen from Any Category Screen**</td></tr>
</table>

How to... Go Back to the Home Screen from Any Category Screen

If you're in a category or subcategory screen or looking at the details of an app and you want to get back to the home screen, you don't have to keep clicking or tapping the Back arrow. Right-click anywhere on the screen, or swipe down from the top edge of the screen or swipe up from the bottom edge if you have a touchscreen, then click or tap Home in the app bar to return to the home screen.

Remove a PC from Your Account

If you have a PC where you don't want to use apps from your Microsoft account any more, for example because you have reached the limit of five computers on which you can run apps installed through the same Microsoft account, you can remove it from your account directly from the Windows Store app. Open the Settings charm and choose Your Account. Swipe or scroll down to the Your PCs section at the bottom of the screen, where you will see all the PCs you've installed Windows Store apps on. Click or tap the Remove button under the name of the PC you're no longer using and then click or tap Confirm.

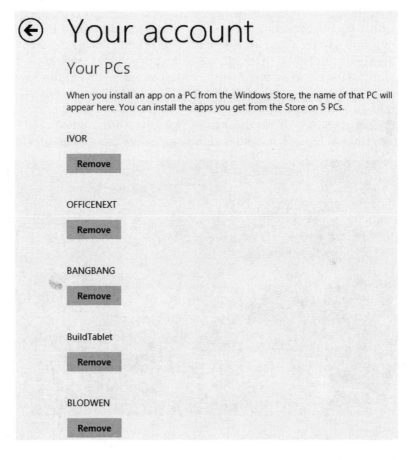

If you like an app, use the Share charm to mention it on a social network or to email the details to a friend. The message will include a link to see the details of the app on a web page, with a button they can click to open the app in the Windows Store where they can download it themselves.

Download Games for Windows 8

The usual Windows games like Solitaire, Minesweeper, FreeCell, and Spider aren't included with Windows 8, but you can download free Windows 8 versions of them from the Windows Store. You can also get more games for Windows 8 and for the Xbox 360 from the Games app, where you can also see your friends from Xbox LIVE as well as your scores and achievements in Xbox games you play on your PC, your Xbox, or a Windows Phone.

The tile for the Games app is pinned to the Start screen by default; if you've unpinned it, you can open it from the All Apps screen. Although you can browse without it, to download any games or see your Xbox LIVE profile, you'll need to sign in with a Microsoft account; if you log in to Windows with a Microsoft account, the Games app will pick that up automatically. If not, click or tap Sign In at the top right of the screen and enter your username and password (or create a new Microsoft account). Like the Windows Store, the Games app opens in the Spotlight section, as shown next, displaying tiles for the latest Xbox Studio games you can play on Windows. The Games app doesn't show all the games you can get for Windows 8 in the Windows Store; it showcases titles from the Xbox Studio brand (which includes games from Microsoft and other game publishers that integrate with Xbox LIVE).

Scroll right or swipe to the left to see more Xbox Studio games for Windows 8 in the Windows games store as well as the Xbox 360 games store, where you can buy and launch games to play on your Xbox. Click or tap the Windows Games Store heading or Xbox Games Store heading to explore the different categories and genres of games,

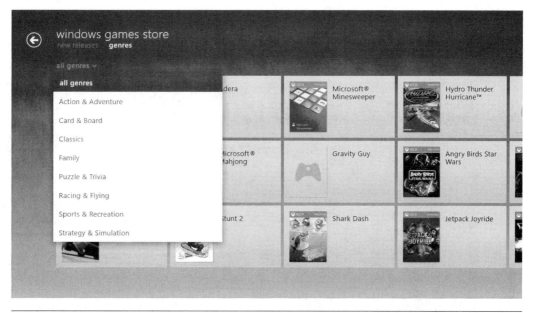

FIGURE 16-5   Click or tap All Genres to view a list of game genres you can choose from in the drop-down menu.

as shown in Figure 16-5 (and, as always, you can search for specific games from the Search charm). Click or tap a game to learn more about it.

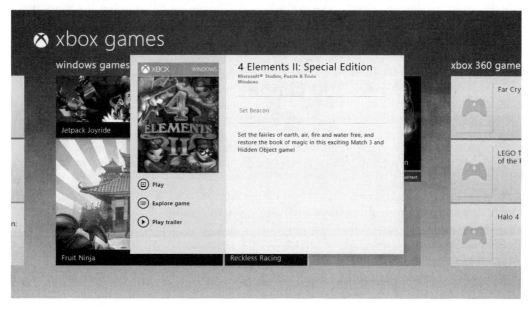

Some games have trailers you can watch to see the gameplay. Click or tap Explore Game to see a full-page view with a description of the game, extras you can buy, and achievements you can unlock. If you've already played the game, you'll see your progress here.

Click or tap Play on the details pane of a Windows game to begin playing it. If you don't already have the game, you'll be prompted to get it from the Windows Store (which is like installing any other app from the Store; you pay for it using the account you've already set up for the Windows Store). If you do have a game installed, you can launch it directly from here.

Buy an Xbox 360 Game

For Xbox 360 games that you can buy online (titles in the Games on Demand section of the Xbox 360 Games Store), you can click or tap Buy Game for Xbox 360. If you already own the game, click or tap Play on Xbox 360 to open the SmartGlass app so you can control your Xbox from your PC; we'll explain how that works later in this chapter.

Click or tap Set Beacon to add a message to your Xbox LIVE profile telling your friends you're looking for someone to play this game with (you can change the message of the beacon). If one of your Xbox LIVE friends has already set a beacon for a game, you'll see that on the tile for the game and you'll see their avatar when you look at the game details.

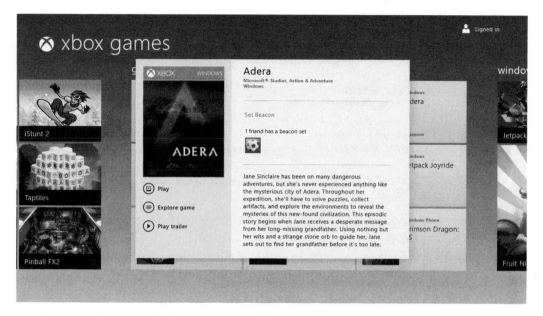

You can also see which games your Xbox LIVE friends have played recently—and whether they're currently online, so you can challenge them to play against you. Click or tap their avatar to jump straight to their profile.

If you've already entered details of your credit card in the Microsoft account you use with the Windows Store, you don't need to fill in payment information again to buy Xbox games. If you haven't entered your credit card details, open the Settings charm and choose Account (see Figure 16-6), then choose Manage Payment Options (or click or tap to buy a game and then give your credit card information when prompted).

As with the Windows Store, the Games app will ask for your password every time you buy a game, and the first time you buy a game you are given the option to turn off that confirmation. If you share your PC with other people, you'll probably want to keep this extra security feature turned on to make sure no one can run up charges on your credit card. You can do the same for Xbox 360 games, as in Figure 16-7.

Make sure to check details like the game title, the rating, the price, any restrictions on how you can play the game, and the Xbox LIVE account you'll be using to pay for it in the Confirm Purchase screen, as you can't cancel the purchase or get a refund once you click or tap Confirm Purchase. The Confirm Purchase screen shows. If you want to add a new credit card (or if you haven't filled in your credit card details yet), click or tap Change Payment Options.

Choose Confirm to buy the game; once your payment has been processed you'll get a message telling you the game is in your Xbox download queue and explaining how to find the game on your Xbox console.

See Your Games, Friends, and Achievements

The Games app also organizes the Xbox Studio games that you already have on your PC, on your Xbox 360 or Windows Phone (if you have one). To see games you've

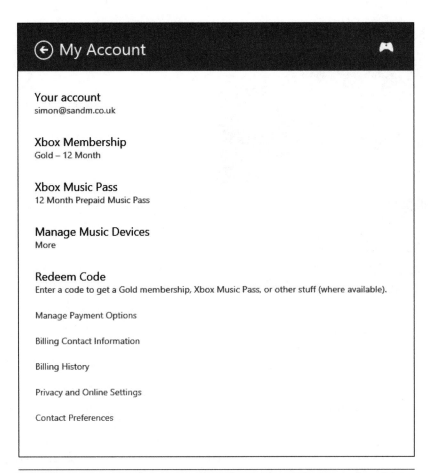

FIGURE 16-6 Change your user information, Xbox membership, payment method, online settings, and contact preferences in the My Account area.

played recently, scroll right or swipe left from the Spotlight section to see the Game Activity section, between the Spotlight and Windows Games Store sections. Click or tap one of your games and choose either Play to open it (or Play on Xbox 360 if it's an Xbox 360 game) or Explore Game to see your achievements, as shown in Figure 16-8. If a friend has set a beacon to leave a message about a particular title, you'll see that in the Game Activity section.

Scroll left or swipe right left in the Games app to see your Xbox profile and friends, complete with avatars if you've already set them up. If you're new to Xbox LIVE, you can click or tap Edit Profile to fill in your name, a short motto, where you live, and more information you want to share in your bio. Remember, all this information is displayed to the public; it will help friends and other Xbox gamers connect with you online. Click or tap Share Profile to open the Share charm and send a link to your profile using Mail, the People app, or any of your other social network apps.

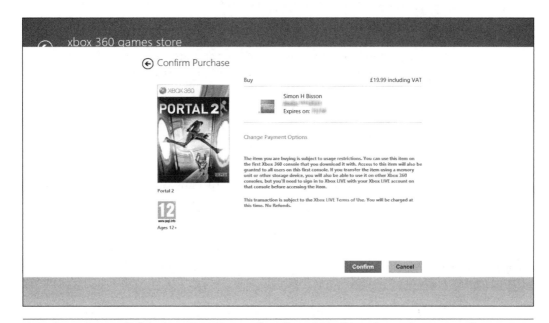

FIGURE 16-7 Click or tap Buy Game for Xbox 360 if you haven't previously purchased the game, so you can play it on your Xbox. You'll confirm purchase on the next screen.

FIGURE 16-8 In the game information screen, scroll to the right to view the Achievements section and see the achievements you can win.

Click or tap Customize Avatar to make your 3D avatar look more like you. Under My Style, you can choose clothes, hats, glasses, and other accessories and change everything from your avatar's height and hair style to the shape of your ears and chin.

You can also see your achievements in all your Xbox Studio games by clicking or tapping View Achievements (rather than tapping Explore Game for each title) as shown in Figure 16-9. By default, your achievements are organized by each game you've played, but you can see them by date if you want to browse through your gaming history. If you're particularly proud of an achievement, click or tap to select it and then share it from the Share charm.

Xbox LIVE enables you to connect to friends and rivals that you want to compete with in multiplayer games. You can click or tap View Game Alerts to see messages from your friends on the Xbox LIVE network (including potential new friends who want to add you to their friends list), or you can look in the Friends section to see their profiles, complete with avatars.

 Open a profile and click or tap Compare Games to see which titles you both have that you could play together.

Open the Friends section by clicking or tapping the heading, and then click or tap the green plus-sign button to type in the *gamertag* or Xbox LIVE user ID for a new friend (see Figure 16-10).

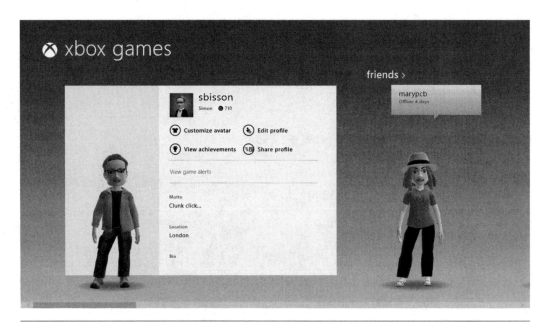

FIGURE 16-9 See how well you're doing in different games you've played by tapping View Achievements.

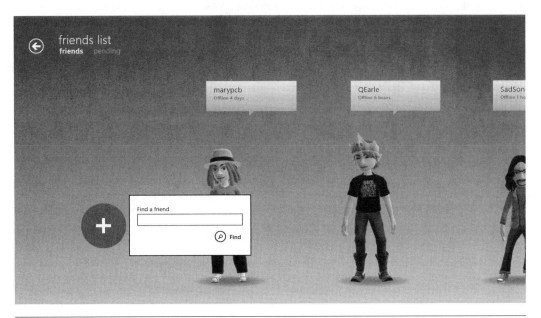

FIGURE 16-10   Type a gamertag in the Find a Friend box.

After you enter their username, click or tap the Find button. Make sure the profile is that of the person you're looking for, and then click or tap the Add Friend button in their profile to add them to your network. Until they approve your request, you'll see them in the Pending section of your friends list.

Control Your Xbox 360 with SmartGlass

The Games app lets you not only find and launch Xbox Studio games on your Xbox, but also control games and other features on your Xbox from a Windows 8 PC or tablet with the Xbox SmartGlass app.

We mentioned the Xbox SmartGlass app in Chapters 12 and 14 as a way to stream music and videos to an Xbox 360. SmartGlass also turns your Windows 8 PC into a controller for your Xbox. If you have a touchscreen PC, you can tap and swipe to control games as well as the browser and other apps. There are also SmartGlass companion apps that connect to your Xbox game and give you related information, like a map of where you are in the game.

Follow the instructions in the "Take Your Music with You" section of Chapter 12 to install and set up the Xbox SmartGlass app. When you choose Play on Xbox 360 for a game you own, the SmartGlass app opens automatically, contacts your Xbox, starts the game, and opens the Xbox remote. This is a virtual Xbox controller, with all the main buttons and a swipe controller that replaces the joystick. Use the Switch button to swap between control modes. Different options are available in different Xbox applications, including a keyboard and a browser control. You also get media controls for video and music.

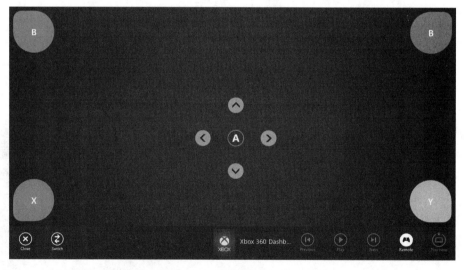

You can also open the SmartGlass app directly. SmartGlass connects to your Xbox and shows you what's open on the Xbox in the Now Playing screen (if you're not connected, you'll see Last Played instead). Scroll or swipe left to the Bing section to search for movies, games, and music you can play on your Xbox. You can restart games you've played before from the Recent section of SmartGlass by clicking or tapping the game tile and choosing Play on Xbox 360. Or, you can click or tap the Remote tile to open the SmartGlass Xbox remote if you want to control an Xbox app you can't launch from SmartGlass, like the Xbox browser or the YouTube player.

If your PC screen is wide enough, you can snap SmartGlass to the side of another Windows Store app or even the desktop, so you can carry on browsing or working on your PC and have your Xbox controls handy.

17

Keep Windows 8 Tuned Up

HOW TO...

- Keep your PC secure and up to date
- Monitor Windows with Action Center
- Scan for malware with Windows Defender
- Use built-in disk and performance utilities
- Uninstall software you don't use and Windows features you don't need
- Remove old files to make more space on your disk drive
- Combine multiple drives into a Storage space
- Set the right resolution for your screen
- Tweak color and font settings to look better on screen
- Set power options so you don't waste precious battery life
- Put the Hibernation option back on the menu
- Make Windows more accessible

With previous versions of Windows, you might have found that your system slowed down after you'd been using it for a while, caused by applications starting automatically, running in the background, or otherwise using up more resources than you expected. Windows 8 is designed not to slow down in this way. If it does, it has new tools that help you to find and remove any programs that are reducing performance or, in the worst case, to reset Windows to the way it was when you first installed it.

In this chapter we'll explain when you should consider using these various tools and options to keep your system in tune, and show you some advanced settings that can help you to sort out configuration problems. We'll also show you how to use the built-in utilities that protect you from viruses and malware. Plus, we'll cover some extra ways to customize Windows, such as tweaking display settings, optimizing your power settings for notebooks and tablets so you can choose between performance and battery life, and turning on accessibility options.

Drivers Control Your Hardware

This chapter refers several times to drivers. A *driver* is a small piece of software that tells Windows how to operate a hardware device or peripheral. For example, a software driver for a printer tells Windows how to send commands to the printer so any software, such as Microsoft Word, can print a document so it appears on the page as it does on the screen. A new version of a driver might be more efficient, fix a bug, or even give you new features.

Keep Windows 8 Running Smoothly

Once a day, Windows 8 runs its own series of checks and maintenance tasks to keep your system up to date and working well. If it identifies any problems you need to deal with, you'll get a message from the Action Center tool in Windows. For example, if there are programs that start up automatically when you open the desktop, Action Center will warn you if these make your PC slower, as shown next. If you've had a problem with a program that crashed, or a fault caused by a driver for your PC hardware, Action Center might show details of an update you can install so that the problem doesn't happen again.

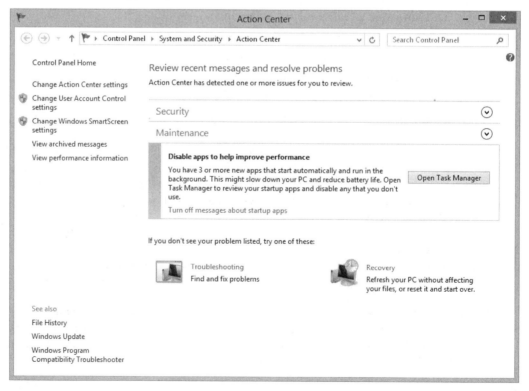

Messages from Action Center appear next to your taskbar on the desktop. If you miss them, the Action Center icon (which looks like a flag) will appear in the notification area of the taskbar.

The following are maintenance tasks you will want to do yourself, some regularly and some when you run low on disk space:

- Look in Action Center at least once a week in case you've missed a notification on the taskbar.
- Check for app updates in the Windows Store as well as for other software you have installed. The Start screen tile for the Windows Store will show the number of updates that are available for your apps.
- If you don't have automatic updating turned on, check Windows Update at least once a week.
- Check that the drive you use for File History is connected and working.

File History makes it easy to protect your documents, photos, music, and video files, so make sure you set it up (using the instructions in Chapter 4) before you lose anything important. Remember, even if you're careful, all hardware fails eventually; a drive might develop a fault or your computer might be affected by a power surge. If you want to keep a full backup of your PC and not just your documents, put that backup on external media such as a DVD or an external drive and update it regularly. After you save your backup, store the external media in a safe place such as a fire-resistant, waterproof safe, or even outside your home (for example, take it to the office or swap backup drives with a friend).

- Check your computer for *malware* like viruses and *spyware*. Malware is software that is designed to damage or destroy data, apps, and even Windows itself or allow an attacker to use your system remotely. Some malware can copy itself onto other PCs, spreading through email or by infecting USB drives; other malware tricks you into downloading or spreading it yourself. *Spyware* is malicious software that collects information about you and your computer activity without your knowledge. Windows Defender checks your system for all kinds of malware regularly, but it's a good idea to run a full scan at least every month (or any time you think your computer is behaving oddly).
- If you start to run out of storage space, you can clean up your disk drive to remove any files or settings that you no longer use and thus are taking up valuable space on the drive unnecessarily. Or you can combine two drives into a single storage space. You can also optimize the way files are stored on a disk.

In general, it's better to leave Windows 8 to do maintenance automatically. Don't run third-party registry cleaners or fix-it utilities that claim to improve performance. You don't need them, and they can do more harm than good. In particular, don't use system tools designed for previous versions of Windows. They may not work at all, and if they do, they won't work well and may actually cause problems.

We'll cover how to handle all the preceding tasks in this chapter, starting with the most important ones.

Keep Your PC Up to Date

If you accepted the Express Settings defaults when you set up Windows 8, Windows will keep itself up to date with security improvements and new drivers. It will even update the version of Flash that's built into Internet Explorer, but you should make sure your other programs and tools are up to date to avoid problems. There are several ways to get updates:

- By default, Windows 8 automatically downloads and installs important updates, once a month (or more often if the update is for a major security problem). Windows Update checks for new updates once a day.
- You can manually check Windows Update for optional updates that you might want to install, including updates for any Microsoft desktop programs that you have installed.
- The Windows Store checks for apps you have installed on your system, including those that came preinstalled with Windows. If you see a number on the Windows Store live tile on the Start screen, that's how many of your Windows Store apps have updates you can install.
- Many software companies offer (and tell you about) updates for their programs. You can visit the website of each software vendor to check for available updates. Some programs will notify you about updates. For example, the Adobe Application Manager utility will inform you about updates to Adobe Creative Suite, and Adobe Acrobat Reader will pop up a dialog box when there's an update you can install.
- Hardware companies often put updates to their device drivers in Windows Update, but you have to choose to install these. You can also visit the website for your hardware to look for updates.

We'll cover how to do these different kinds of update next.

Update Windows 8

There are two different interfaces for Windows Update, depending on what you need to do.

If you just want to see when updates were last downloaded and see if this means Windows 8 will need to restart (which will happen automatically, by default), or if you want to check for critical new updates yourself, go to the Windows Update section of PC Settings (which you can open from the Settings charm, wherever you are in Windows) and click or tap Check for updates now. You'll always get a warning before Windows restarts, but be prepared to save your work if you want to apply updates straightaway.

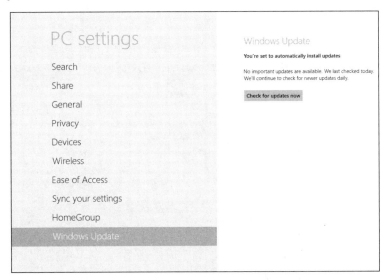

To see more details, use the Windows Update tool in the Control Panel on the desktop (you'll find it in the System and Security section). If an update has already been downloaded but your computer needs to be restarted to install the update, you can tell Windows to do that right away (or you can postpone the restart until a time that's convenient, if the update isn't an important one). Or you can check for all updates, including optional updates like drivers and updates to some Microsoft software, see which updates have already been installed, or change the settings for Windows Update (by choosing Change Settings in the navigation pane, which opens the window shown in Figure 17-1).

Install Updates Immediately

When Windows Update automatically downloads an update to your computer, the update is installed in the background. Some updates need to replace system files, which are in use while you're running Windows, so you need to restart your computer before Windows Update can apply the update. If there are updates downloaded that require a reboot, you are notified in the Windows Update section of PC Settings and in the Windows Update control panel. Once Windows Update has downloaded the monthly release of updates (assuming there's an update that requires your PC to restart so it can install), it schedules a time to automatically reboot your computer. You'll see a message in the lower right corner of the login screen where you enter your password

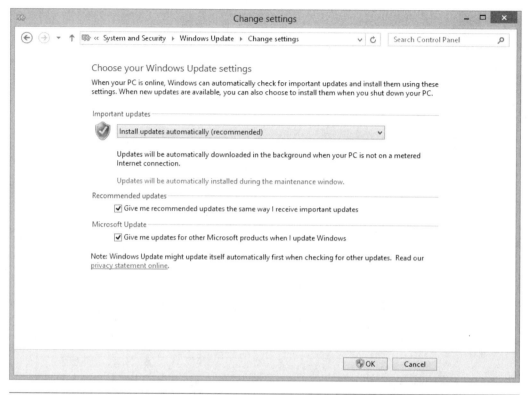

FIGURE 17-1 Choose whether Windows Update downloads and installs recommended updates and updates for Microsoft software.

warning you about this for the three days before the restart. The message tells you how long you have until the system will reboot and finish the installation.

There might be more than one update a month that requires a restart, but Windows Update waits until the monthly update (on the second Tuesday of every month) so you only have to restart once a month. The only exception is for serious security fixes that are so important they're released straightaway, rather than waiting for the monthly release; if they're too important to wait for, so is the restart—so you'll see the restart notification as soon as they download.

When the time comes to reboot, Windows displays a full-screen notification before it restarts and gives you the chance to postpone the restart, but if you're away from your computer at the time, you won't be able to close your programs and save your files. To avoid losing data in that situation, if you have applications open in the background or files that haven't yet been saved, Windows Update won't restart if your PC is on but you're not actively using it at the scheduled time (or if you're playing a game or giving a presentation in full-screen mode, which means it can't display the notification). Instead, it waits until the next time you log in to Windows. When you do so, you'll see a message that the PC is going to restart, and you'll get 15 minutes to close applications and save files, but you can't postpone the restart any further.

Because you can no longer postpone restarts indefinitely, you may prefer to finish installing the updates before Windows restarts automatically, at a time that's convenient to you. If you're logging in to Windows, you can click or tap the notification on the login screen to install and restart straightaway, or use the Power icon; the usual entries you see on the menu when you click or tap the Power icon change to include Update and Restart and Update and Shutdown.

If you've already logged in to Windows, open the Control Panel, choose System and Security, and then choose Windows Update. If there are updates waiting to be installed that require a restart, click or tap the Restart Now button, shown in Figure 17-2. This is also a good time to check for any optional updates that might be useful for you; do this before you choose Restart Now.

Did You Know?   You Should Never Turn Off Your Computer During Installation

As Windows updates your PC, you will see a warning on the installation screen: "Do not turn off your computer." If you become impatient during the installation process and turn off your computer (or you lose power during the process), Windows might be able to roll back the unfinished update and restart without a problem. But if you're unlucky, you might have major problems; if the system files that make up Windows are corrupted, your PC might not be able to start. In the worst case, you might have to reinstall Windows and maybe lose documents you haven't backed up. Don't panic if the power runs out during an update, but don't try to rush Windows Update by hitting the power switch either.

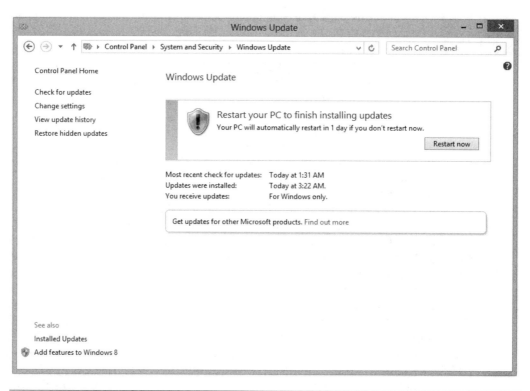

FIGURE 17-2   Click or tap Restart Now to restart and apply updates immediately.

Windows goes through the installation and restart process. When it's done, you can log in to Windows as normal.

 If an update requires Windows to restart to install the update, just downloading the update isn't sufficient to fix any bugs or security holes that the update addresses. Your system is protected by the update only after Windows has restarted.

Check for Updates

If you leave automatic updating turned on, Windows Update will always download and install important updates, and you can set it to treat updates to other Microsoft software in the same way, as shown in Figure 17-1. That still leaves what Microsoft calls optional updates, which include new drivers for your PC hardware, and any updates that mean accepting new terms and conditions. Check to see if there are any optional updates for your system (and recommended updates, if you're not treating those like important updates) by clicking or tapping Check for Updates in the navigation pane on the left side of the Windows Update control panel.

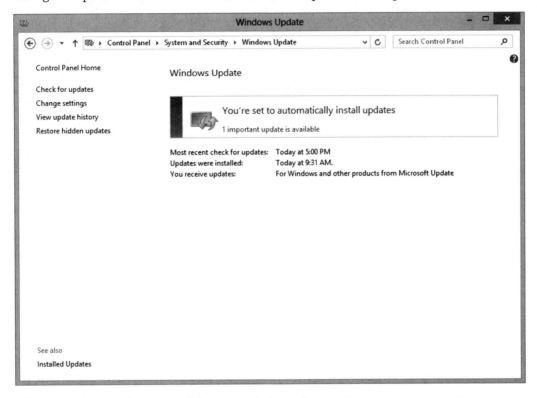

Windows checks to see if there are updates that apply to your system. You can see the settings you've chosen for installing updates as well as the number and type of updates available. If there are no optional updates, you can click or tap Install Updates. If there are optional updates available, click or tap where Windows Update shows the number of updates to see what's available and select the ones you want. (It doesn't matter whether you click the link to optional updates or the link to important updates because they both open the same dialog box.)

The list of updates in the Select Updates to Install screen, shown next, includes both important and optional updates. Important updates are checked by default, and you can select any optional updates you want to install as well. Click or tap the Install button to apply all the selected updates

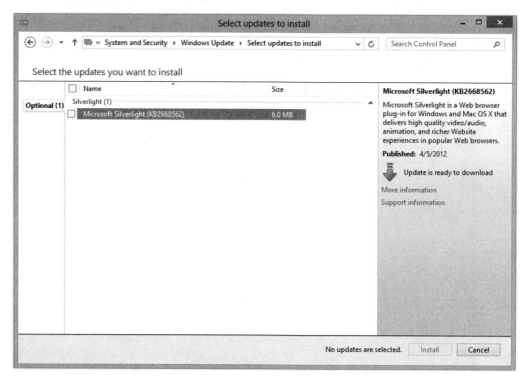

Windows Update shows you a progress bar as it downloads and installs the updates, although you can carry on using your computer for other things if you want. Click or tap the Stop Installation button at any point to stop installation. When installation is complete, you'll see a message confirming that the updates were installed.

 If any of the updates don't install correctly, Windows Update will display a warning, which you can click or tap to view more information so that you can see what the problem may be, fix it (which may mean restarting your PC), and try installing the update again.

Change Windows Update Settings

To make sure your PC is always protected, it's best to leave automatic updating turned on. If you really want to control updates manually, click or tap Change Settings on the left side of the Windows Update control panel. Use the drop-down menu under Important Updates to choose between the four options shown in Figure 17-3:

- **Install updates automatically (recommended)** The default setting gives you the most protection. Windows Update downloads and installs important updates without asking for confirmation.

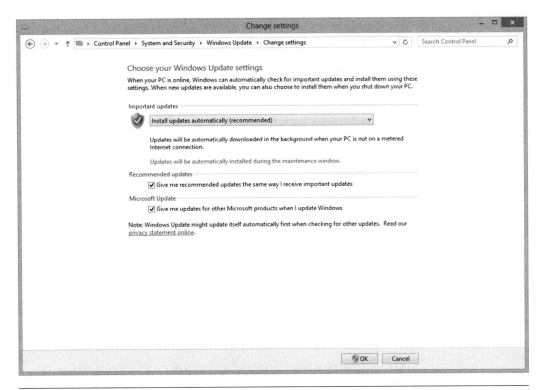

FIGURE 17-3 The default option in the Important Updates list is to install updates automatically.

- **Download updates but let me choose whether to install them** Windows Update downloads updates automatically, but it lets you decide if you want to install them. This option is useful if you want to review updates before you install them.
- **Check for updates but let me choose whether to download and install them** Windows Update notifies you when updates that apply to your system are available, but it lets you decide if you want to download and install them.
- **Never check for updates (not recommended)** This is the most dangerous option because you won't get Windows Defender antivirus updates or any other security fixes unless you manually check for, download and install them.

Some updates aren't security fixes or otherwise critical but are still useful updates, like adding support for new digital camera formats. You can set Windows Update to treat these the same way as important updates. You can also choose to get updates for other Microsoft software, like Microsoft Office, through Windows Update (which will give you automatic security and performance fixes when they're released).

If you change the default of having updates downloaded and installed automatically, you'll see a message on the login screen when there are updates waiting to be downloaded or installed manually. Unlike in Windows 7, Windows Update in Windows 8 does not show a pop-up notification or a notification icon in the taskbar when there are updates waiting to be downloaded or installed. The only place you'll see that notification is on the Windows login screen (or in the Windows Update control panel), so if you do turn off automatic updating, make sure to check for updates regularly.

View Installed Updates

If you want to see which updates you've installed, click or tap View Update History in the navigation pane of the Windows Update control panel. This shows which updates have been downloaded and when, whether they were important, recommended, or optional, and whether the installation succeeded or failed; open an update for more details (see Figure 17-4).

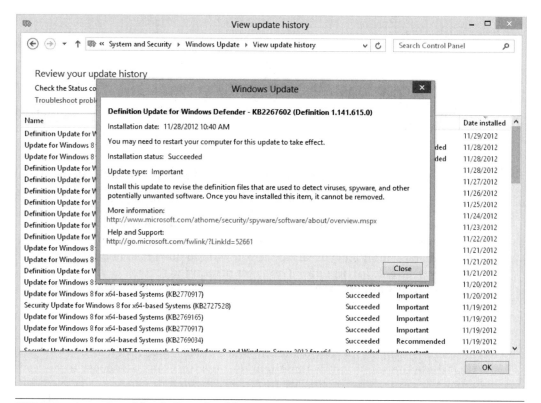

FIGURE 17-4 Double-click or double-tap an update in the list to view more information about it.

Update Apps in the Windows Store

The Windows Store live tile on your Start screen notifies you when new updates are available for any of the Windows Store apps you have installed. When you open the Windows Store app, the Updates link in the upper right corner of the Store home screen shows how many of your apps have updates you can install.

Click or tap Updates to open the App Updates page with a list of which apps have updates. The Store selects all your apps for updating by default—all you have to do is click or tap the Install icon at the bottom of the screen. You can carry on browsing the Store while the updates download.

 Tip   You can also check for app updates using the Settings charm in the Windows Store. Open the Settings charm, click or tap App Updates, and click or tap the Check for Updates button.

 How to...   **Synchronize Your Windows Store App Licenses to Fix Updates**

If you don't think you're getting the latest updates for one or more of your Windows Store apps, it may be that the license information in the Windows Store isn't correct. Open the Settings charm and choose App Updates, then click or tap the Sync Licenses button. After a few seconds, the Store syncs your apps with the licenses and informs you when your app licenses are up to date. Now you can check for updates again.

Find Third-Party Updates

There are several ways to update programs and drivers on your computer that aren't apps installed from the Windows Store:

- **From within the program itself**   For example, if you install another web browser on your computer, that browser will check for updates and notify you when an update is available, or if you use the popular Paint.NET image editing program, it will look for updates every time you run it. You can also manually check for updates within many programs. Look in the help file for your application to find out how often it looks for updates, how it notifies you, and which menu item to use to check for updates yourself.
- **From a separate tool that monitors several programs from the same software developer**   For example, if you install software from Adobe, like Creative Suite, you also get the Adobe Application Manager utility, which checks regularly for updates to your Adobe tools and tells you when there are new updates so you can download and install them.
- **Using the update tools installed by your PC manufacturer**   Many Windows 8 PCs come with either a Windows Store app or a desktop utility that you can use to check for updates that are designed specifically for your computer.
- **From the website of the software developer or hardware supplier**   For example, if you have a Dell or HP PC, you can visit the support section of the Dell or HP website to download new drivers for your hardware or updates to the software that came with your PC. On some support sites, you'll need to know the model number of your computer, but some PC makers have tools on their websites that can identify your PC automatically and show you a list of updates that you can download and install.

 If you've upgraded a PC from a previous version of Windows, the Windows 8 installer will automatically download many of the drivers you need. It's also worth visiting the website of your PC maker to see if there are drivers, tools, utilities, or software updates for your specific computer to use with Windows 8. Do the same for peripherals like printers, scanners, and digital cameras that you use with Windows 8, as you might get extra features with their own drivers.

Check Your PC with Action Center

Windows 8 collects together in Action Center all the messages and warnings about any security or maintenance problems it has detected with your system. Open Action Center from the System and Security section in the Control Panel or by clicking or tapping the Action Center icon (which looks like a flag) in the notification area on the taskbar.

 Important messages in Action Center have a red icon to indicate there's a serious problem, like your antivirus software being out of date. You'll see a red X on the Action Center icon in the notification area if a red message is waiting for you. Suggestions from Action Center (like installing an update for one of your programs or submitting further details about any problems that have occurred in Windows to Microsoft) have a yellow flag and don't change the icon in the notification area.

If Action Center has messages for you, they will appear under the two main headings, Security and Maintenance. Click or tap the arrow next to each heading to expand the section and see the tools and status updates there. Action Center monitors a range of options.

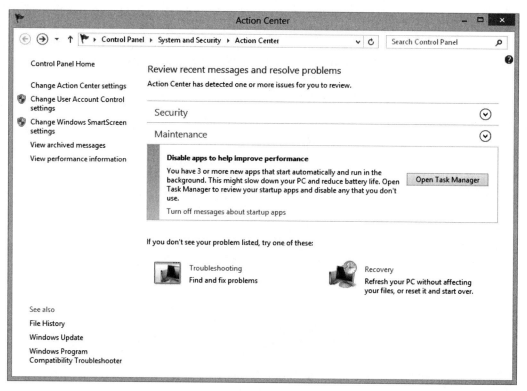

Check Security Settings in Action Center

Action Center is a convenient place to check that all your security options are correct.

- **Network firewall**   See whether Windows Firewall is running.
- **Windows Update**   See whether updates are being automatically downloaded and installed.
- **Virus protection and spyware and unwanted software protection**   See whether Windows Defender (or your other antimalware software) is running.
- **Internet security settings**   Check that you have the most secure options set.
- **User Account Control**   See what UAC is set to warn you about, and change the settings.
- **Windows SmartScreen**   Check that the SmartScreen service is checking that any program files you download or copy onto your PC are legitimate (and not malware that has the same filename), and decide what to do with unrecognized programs.

- **Network Access Protection**   This is a service that businesses can use to check if PCs that connect remotely have up-to-date security protection.
- **Windows activation and Microsoft account**   Ensure your copy of Windows has a legitimate license key and the Microsoft account you log in with is set up correctly.

Check Maintenance Settings in Action Center

Action Center is a convenient place where you can check and change settings for key system tools, and run troubleshooting, maintenance, and recovery tools

- **Check for solutions to problem reports**   If Windows or other Microsoft software you use crashes, Windows Error Reporting automatically sends information about the problem to Microsoft and looks for updates or suggestions that might fix the problem. You'll see any answers to your problem reports in Action Center, but you can also click or tap Check for Solutions to have Windows send its reports and look for answers straightaway. You can also change the settings for how much information Windows can include in the reports without asking for permission each time.
- **Automatic Maintenance**   Once a day, Windows runs a set of housekeeping tasks, which include checking for software updates, scanning your system with Windows Defender, and running system diagnostics. You can run the maintenance checks manually from here or change when they're scheduled to run.
- **HomeGroup**   If your computer is part of a homegroup, you can see if you're logged in correctly or if you need to type in a new password.
- **File History**   Check whether the drive you use for backups is connected, see when files were last backed up, restore files, or change other File History settings.
- **Drive status**   See if all your disk drives are working correctly.
- **Device software**   See if you need to install extra software to make any of your hardware or peripherals work.

You can choose what Action Center warns you about by clicking or tapping Change Action Center settings in the navigation pane on the left and clearing the check boxes for any of the Security and Maintenance messages listed. If you use a different backup tool, for example, you don't need to see messages from Action Center about Windows Backup. Generally, it's a good idea to leave all the messages turned on, because if you tell Action Center not to show you messages for a security or maintenance setting, it also stops checking for those problems.

How to... Change When Windows Does Automatic Maintenance

The default time for Windows 8 to run its daily housekeeping tasks is 3:00 A.M., when you're not likely to be using your computer, but Windows doesn't automatically wake up your PC to run those tasks. If your PC isn't turned on at 3:00 A.M., Windows will run the tasks when your PC is next on but you're not using it. To make sure your system is always protected, you can choose to have Windows 8 do automatic maintenance at a different time, when you know your PC will be on, or you can allow Windows to wake up your PC at 3:00 A.M. (or any time you designate). Click or tap Change Maintenance Settings under Automatic Maintenance in the Action Center Maintenance section and either pick a new time from the drop-down list or select the check box for "Allow scheduled maintenance to wake up my computer at the scheduled time."

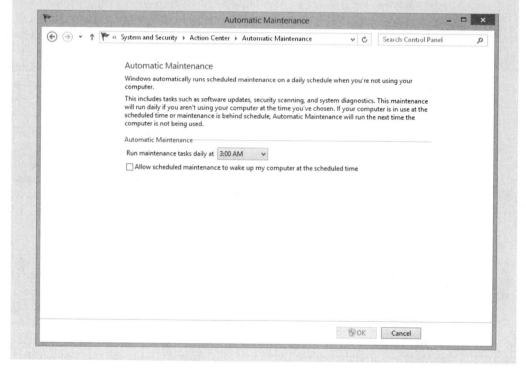

Use Windows Defender to Detect and Remove Malware

There are thousands of different pieces of malware that try to infect your PC. You might get a spam email with a piece of malware as an attachment (or directing you to a website containing malware to attack your browser), or malware can get onto your

You Can Try Other Antimalware Tools

Windows Defender gives you good protection from malware. Like Microsoft Security Essentials, which is the same malware protection engine in a program you can install on other versions of Windows, Windows Defender scores well in tests of antimalware software and doesn't use as many system resources or have as much impact on performance as some other antimalware tools. Best of all, it's built into Windows 8 and is free.

But there are also many other antimalware and antivirus tools on the market, and you may prefer other security software over Windows Defender. Many of these utilities offer trial versions, so you can see if they meet your needs before you decide to buy, and some are free for personal use.

Make sure that you don't have more than one antimalware program installed and running at the same time. Not only will having two security tools running at once make your PC much slower, the two packages may also interfere with each other.

computer when you visit an infected website, or it might come from a removable drive that someone lends you to share a file. Attackers can also try to send malware to your computer remotely. For the first time, Windows 8 includes a free antimalware tool, Windows Defender, which protects you against most of these attacks. Defender runs in the background, and you usually won't need to change the settings from the defaults. But it's a good idea to take a look at the interface so that you know how it's set up. Open the Windows Defender app from the All Apps screen.

Windows Defender is a desktop program, but it also protects your PC when you're using Windows Store apps. You can see on the Home tab whether it's running correctly and when it last scanned your system. By default, Windows Defender checks your computer regularly for malware and other unwanted software, and it regularly updates the list of malware it looks for.

Scan Your Computer

If your PC is doing something strange, or your system is running unusually slowly, use Windows Defender to check for malware, as shown in Figure 17-5. The Scan Option section of the Home tab offers three kinds of scan:

- **Quick scan**   Looks in areas on your disk drives where spyware and other malicious software such as viruses are most likely to be deposited. Defender automatically runs Quick scans in the background on a regular schedule.
- **Full scan**   Checks all your disk drives and all running software for any spyware, viruses, or other malicious software on your computer. Since this search is more thorough than a Quick scan, it takes more time (how long depends on how many drives are in your computer and how much data is on each drive).
- **Custom scan**   Lets you choose a file or folder that you're suspicious of and want to check.

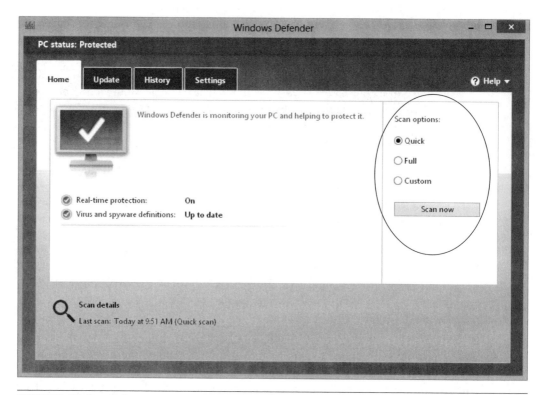

FIGURE 17-5 Select your scan option in the Scan Options list and then click or tap Scan Now to scan your system.

When you click or tap the Scan Now button, Windows Defender scans your system (or the file or folder you designated for a Custom scan). When the scan is complete, Defender will notify you of any issues it has detected and take you through the steps of removing any problem software.

Update Definitions, View Scan History, and Change Settings

You usually won't need to make any changes to the way Windows Defender is set up, but the Update, History, and Settings tabs do have some useful information you may want to check out:

- **Update**   To identify malware, Windows Defender regularly downloads new *definitions*, the latest information about malicious software. Windows Defender uses these definitions when it runs a scan, looking for infected files that match the signatures of all the malware it knows about. You can see when Windows Update last downloaded an update and when those definitions were created. If you're planning to run a scan, you should check for the latest updates first by clicking or tapping the Update button.

- **History**   If Windows Defender finds a file that appears to be infected, you'll see a warning straightaway. You can also go to the History tab to review those warnings and what you instructed Windows Defender to do about each file it found. There are separate lists for Quarantined items (files that Defender blocked but didn't remove from your computer), Allowed items (files that Defender detected but that you confirmed as false positives), and All detected items. Because you might decide to unblock potentially dangerous files from the list, the View Details button is one of the settings protected by User Account Control and you may have to type in an administrator password to see the list of items.
- **Settings**   Although you can turn off real-time (that is, constant) monitoring and protection and exclude specific files and processes from being scanned, that will reduce the level of protection Windows Defender gives you, so it's not a good idea. If you want Windows Defender to scan any removable drives connected to your PC (which means scans take longer), change that setting under Advanced. You may also want to change the setting for MAPS (Microsoft Active Protection System) from the default of Basic Membership to Advanced Membership. Windows Defender reports to Microsoft any malware it finds on your system, which helps improve the definitions that detect malware. If you're happy to send more details about how the malware affected your PC by choosing Advanced membership, that might help protect you and other users from new variants of malware. The more information you send, the more likely it is that Windows Defender will be able to download the right signature to help remove unwanted software it hasn't come across before. Microsoft also shares information with other security software firms, so you're keeping everyone safer.

Make the Most of Your Disk Space

Windows 8 includes several utilities for working with your disk drives:

- Make sure your disk drives are free of problems that could slow down performance.
- Remove programs and features you don't use that take up space on your system or maybe even slow down Windows as it starts up.
- Combine multiple drives into a single storage area.

Optimize Your Disk Drives

Windows has two tools to help you optimize your drives:

- **Disk Cleanup**   Removes temporary files and unwanted system files that aren't being used by Windows
- **Optimize Drives**   Rearranges the files on your drives to make the drives more efficient

You can find both tools on the Manage tab of the File Explorer ribbon when you select a drive in the Computer section. Some types of drive can't be optimized, so you won't see all these tools on the ribbon when you select them.

To show the Disk Cleanup tool in the All Apps screen, change the Show Administrative Tools setting to Yes on the Settings menu in the Start screen. You can also run the Disk Cleanup and Optimize Drives utilities from the System and Security section of the Control Panel under Administrative Tools.

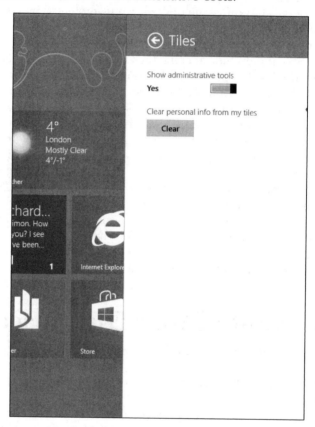

Use Disk Cleanup

As you use Windows, it can accumulate files that are no longer necessary: temporary files that weren't cleaned up by the program that created them, reports about crashes and other problems on your PC, log files from installations, duplicate system files that have been replaced by newer versions, files you've deleted and left in the Recycle Bin, and files left over from previous versions of Windows when you upgraded to Windows 8. If your PC is running low on disk space, use the Disk Cleanup tool to recover the space taken up by these unnecessary files.

When you run Disk Cleanup, it first calculates how much space is taken up on the selected drive by different categories of files that may no longer be needed. After a short while, the Disk Cleanup window appears, showing how much space you can reclaim by deleting files in the different categories, as shown in Figure 17-6.

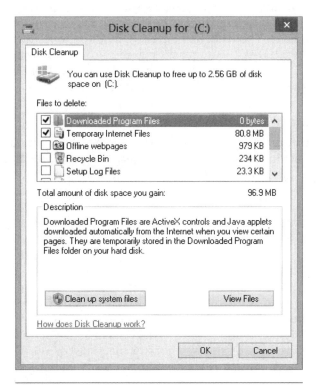

FIGURE 17-6   Select the categories of files
you want to delete to make space on your drive.

Click or tap on each category to see an explanation of what kind of files you'll be
removing if you choose to include that category in the cleanup. For some categories of
files (like the Recycle Bin and Temporary Internet Files), you can click the View Files
button to open File Explorer and see the files. If you prefer, you can then delete some
of the files and not others.

Select the check boxes for the different categories of files you want to delete. As
you select categories, Disk Cleanup shows the total amount of hard drive space you'll
gain below the Files to Delete list.

How to... **Clean Up System Files**

Some files that you can remove with Disk Cleanup are part of Windows:
system files that have been backed up from a previous Windows installation,
Windows Defender files, and Windows upgrade log files. To remove these files,
you have to click or tap the Clean Up System Files button (and you may need
to type in an administrator password). After Disk Cleanup removes these
files, you won't see the Clean Up system files button anymore, because you
have no other system files to delete. You can then clean up other categories
of files or close the Disk Cleanup window.

If you want to delete any system files, do that first, by clicking or tapping Clean Up System Files. Then, click or tap the OK button to remove all the categories of files you've selected. Disk Cleanup asks you to confirm that you want to permanently delete the files. Click or tap the Delete Files button. Disk Cleanup displays a progress bar while the files are being deleted, and then it closes.

Defragment and Optimize Your Drives

The files that make up Windows, your Windows Store apps and desktop programs, and your documents are stored on the disk drives in your PC. A single application or document file isn't necessarily stored all in the same place; it might be split into different places on the drive, either because there wasn't a single space large enough to put it in or because it's actually more efficient to split it up so Windows can load more than one section of the file at once and Windows 8 does that automatically.

As you create, edit, and delete files and install more Windows Store apps and desktop programs, the different pieces of your files can get moved around, and sometimes that can make your drives less efficient. *Defragmenting* a hard drive moves those fragments of files around to create larger areas of empty space. If you have a hard drive in your PC, Windows 8 checks once a week to see if it needs to be defragmented and, if so, defragments it automatically.

Some notebooks and all tablets have a solid-state drive (SSD) instead of a hard drive. SSDs are smaller and much faster than hard drives because, instead of a spinning platter, they store information on the same kind of flash memory that's in a USB memory stick or an SD card in your digital camera. Defragmenting SSDs is a bad thing because it makes them wear out more quickly (and it doesn't speed them up anyway), but you do want to make sure the drive controller knows which blocks of data on the drive are no longer being used and can be reclaimed to use for other files. This is called *trim optimization*.

The Optimize Drives tool, shown in Figure 17-7, can do both defragmentation and trim optimization (and it knows which kind of drive is which). Windows automatically optimizes the drives in your system at regular intervals. If you want to check how often that happens (once a week by default) or optimize a drive straightaway, select the drive in the list in Optimize Drives. This list shows the drive name, the type of media (whether it's a hard disk, SSD, or removable drive), the date and time the drive was last optimized, and the current status.

In the Scheduled Optimization area under the list, you'll see that drives are optimized automatically every week by default. If you want to change the settings,

Did You Know? You Can Optimize Removable Drives

If you have a removable drive such as a USB memory stick or an external hard drive that you plug into a USB port, you may be able to optimize that drive. Click or tap Optimize on the Manage tab of the File Explorer ribbon to find out. If you can't optimize the drive, the Current Status column for the drive will say Optimization Not Available.

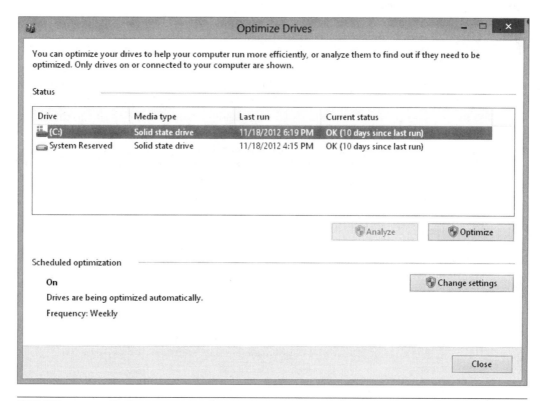

FIGURE 17-7   Before you spend time optimizing, click or tap the Analyze button to see if your drive needs it.

click or tap the Change Settings button. In the Optimization Schedule window that opens, you can change the schedule to daily or monthly.

You can also analyze a drive to see if it needs to be optimized. Select it in the list and then click or tap the Analyze button. After you see the results, you can click or tap Optimize, but this won't improve performance unless the analysis results tell you the drive is fragmented enough to require optimizing.

Set Up Storage Spaces

If you have several different disk drives inside your computer, or even removable drives that are always plugged in, you can combine the drives into one single area, called a *storage pool*, where you can store files without worrying about drive letters or which disk or partition to put a file onto. You can create one or more *storage spaces* using the space in the pool; these are virtual disk drives that appear in File Explorer that you can copy and save files to like any other drive.

You can keep adding more drives to a storage space to make it larger. For example, if you have a lot of digital photos, you can just add another drive to the storage space you keep them on instead of having to split them across two different locations (and having to remember which pictures are where) or buying a new drive that's big enough for all of them and waiting while they copy across.

The drives you use to make a storage pool will be formatted and you'll lose any files that are already stored on them.

If you use two drives to create the storage pool in which you put your storage space(s), you won't lose files even if one of the drives fails. If you use three drives, you can set up the storage space so that it doesn't matter if two of the drives fail (as long as there's enough space on the remaining drive for all your files). The drives don't need to be the same size, from the same manufacturer, or even the same type of drive (but they have to be different physical drives, not partitions on one large drive).

To create a new storage space, open the Storage Spaces tool from the System and Security section of the Control Panel, and click or tap Create a New Pool and Storage Space. If you haven't already created a storage pool, you have to do that first. Select the drives you want to use for the pool.

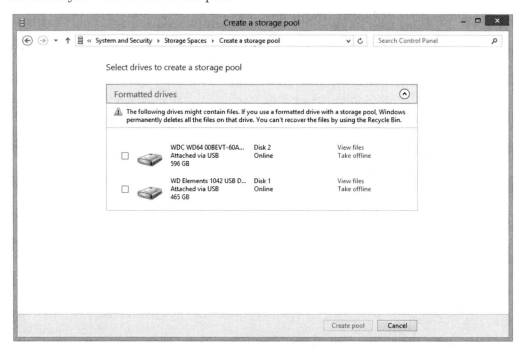

Click or tap Create Pool, choose a name and a drive letter for your first storage space, and then pick the Resiliency type you want to use:

- **None** Windows will store only a single copy of your files. This gives you the full capacity of all the drives in the pool, but if one of your drives fails, you'll lose the data stored on it. Don't use this option unless you back up your storage spaces regularly or you don't mind if you lose the files.
- **Two-way mirror** Windows will store two copies of your data, so if one of your drives ever fails, you won't lose data. This requires at least two drives in the pool.

- **Three-way mirror**   Windows will store three copies of your data, so you won't lose your data even if two drives fail at the same time. This requires at least three drives in the pool.
- **Parity**   If you have at least three drives in a storage pool, you can use more of the space on them by using parity instead of mirroring. Instead of a complete second copy of each file, this option stores extra information about your data so that Windows can recover the files if one of your drives fails. Parity gives you more storage space, but accessing the files (especially saving them) is slower, so it's better for storing large files like video and pictures that you don't change often.

You don't have to add all the drives you plan to use for a storage pool straight away, but you do have to specify how large the pool can be. If you have two 500GB external hard drives, for example, you can still make a 2TB storage pool; when you're close to filling up both drives, Action Center will remind you to add more space, and you then can plug in another hard drive. Tap or click Create Storage Space and you'll see the new space listed in the Storage Pool area along with details of how much of the pool you've used and what drives are in the pool. Once you've created the storage pool and your first space, you can make another space by clicking or tapping the Create a Storage Space link in the Storage Spaces control panel.

Uninstall Programs and Windows Features

It's easy to uninstall Windows Store apps and desktop programs that you no longer need, and you can turn some Windows features on and off as well to save space. The easiest way to remove an app or program is to select the tile for it on the Start screen or the All Apps page, right-click or swipe your finger up on the tile, and then click or tap Uninstall in the app bar.

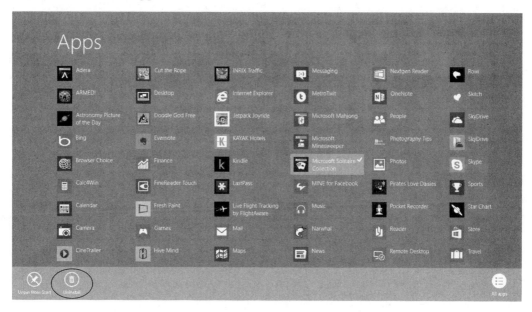

Windows Store apps are uninstalled as soon as you click or tap Uninstall in the dialog box that pops up asking you to confirm that you want to remove the app. For desktop programs, Windows opens the Programs and Features control panel, shown next, and selects the program in the Organize list. Click or tap the button at the top of the list, which might say Uninstall, Uninstall/Change, or Repair.

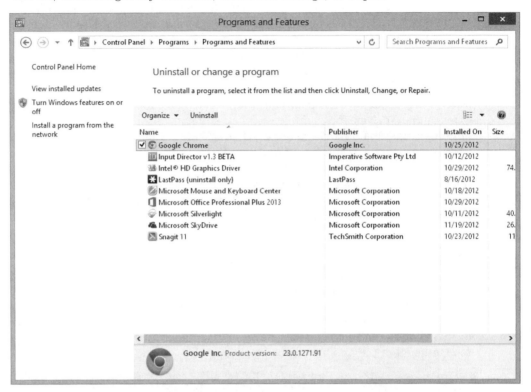

- **Uninstall**   Click or tap this option to uninstall the app or program from your computer. Some uninstallers remove everything associated with the program, but in some cases you may need to manually delete program files and folders left behind.
- **Change**   If you need to change the features that are installed with a program, click or tap the Change option. This opens the same installer you used to put the software on your computer.
- **Repair**   Click or tap this option if the program isn't operating correctly (or at all). Repairing the installation may solve the problem. If not, consider uninstalling the program and reinstalling it.

You can also go straight to the Programs and Features control panel by choosing the Uninstall link under the Programs heading in the Control Panel.

Turn Windows Features On or Off

To choose which Windows features are installed, open the Programs section of the Control Panel and click or tap Turn Windows Features On or Off.

Tip If you already have the Programs and Features control panel open, you can click or tap Turn Windows Features On or Off in the navigation pane on the left.

You have to wait briefly for the list of Windows Features to appear. You can see from the icons which features and options are already installed. Click or tap the different features to see a tip explaining what each feature is for.

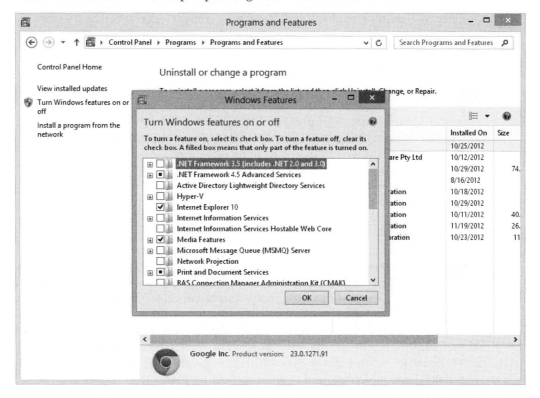

- Features that are completely installed, such as Internet Explorer, have a check mark in the check box by the feature name.
- Features that are not installed have blank check boxes.
- If there are several options for a feature, it has a plus-sign icon to the left of the check box. Click or tap this icon to expand the list. For example, under Print and Document Services, there are five features that you can turn on and off. The Internet Printing Client and Windows Fax and Scan features are on by default.
- If only some of the options for a feature are installed, the check box next to its name is filed in with a small square rather than a check mark.

Select or clear the check boxes for any features you want to turn on or turn off, respectively; click or tap the OK button to make your changes. If Windows can make all the changes straightaway, click or tap the Close button when it finishes. To turn on or off some features, Windows will need to reboot your PC; choose Restart Now if you want to turn on or off the features immediately, or choose Don't Restart if you want to wait until the next time you reboot to turn on or off the feature.

Make Windows 8 More Your Own

Chapter 3 covers the most common ways of customizing Windows 8, like choosing your desktop background. There are many other options you can change. Here we'll show you how to check that your screen is giving you the best image, how to change power options and enable hibernation, and how to turn on the Windows accessibility tools.

Get the Best Display Settings

To make Windows 8 look as good as possible on your hardware, check that you have the right display settings for your screen. Make sure that you're using the resolution your screen was designed for (called the *native* resolution), which is usually the highest resolution it can display.

Right-click or press and hold on a blank area of the desktop and choose Screen Resolution. Click or tap on the Resolution drop-down menu and choose the resolution marked (Recommended); it's usually the highest resolution in the list.

 If you have an older CRT monitor rather than a more recent LCD flat-screen monitor, you need to choose the highest resolution that gives you 32-bit color and a 72-Hz (or higher) refresh rate. If you have a lower refresh rate, you may notice your screen flickering, which can be very tiring to use.

If you find that text and icons on the desktop are too small for you to read comfortably, don't change the resolution to make them bigger; change the display size of text instead. Open the Appearance and Personalization control panel and click or tap Make Text and Other Items Larger or Smaller under the Display heading. Choose one of the sizes listed:

- **Smaller – 100% (default)** This keeps text and other items at the normal size.
- **Medium – 125%** This sets text and other items to 125% of normal size so they're easier to read.
- **Larger – 150%** If your screen resolution is at least 1200 × 900 pixels, you can make text and other items appear at 150% of normal size.

- **Custom sizing options**   If you want to make text larger even if you don't have a high-screen resolution, choose this; you can pick 100%, 125%, 150%, or 200% from the drop-down list, type a percentage into the box, or drag the ruler to pick a size (up to 500%). The line of text and the ruler divisions change to show you how large a line of text will look in the font used by the Windows interface.

Click or tap Apply to save your changes. You will have to sign out of Windows and sign in again to see the new interface size.

Adjust the Colors You See on Your Screen

You can tweak the way colors appear on screen by running the Display Color Calibration tool. Open this tool by clicking or tapping the Calibrate Color link in the navigation pane in the Display control panel.

You have to make most of the changes for color calibration using the controls on your monitor (controls like contrast and gamma correction aren't usually available on notebooks and tablets). The calibration tool is useful because it gives you sample images to try out the settings with and provides suggestions for what to look for as you make your adjustments. There are two settings that will work on notebooks and tablets: gamma and color balance. To adjust the gamma correction, move the slider until the white circles in the middle of the gray dots are less distinct. Adjust the color balance by moving the red, green, and blue sliders until the bars on screen are a neutral gray without hints of other colors, as shown in Figure 17-8.

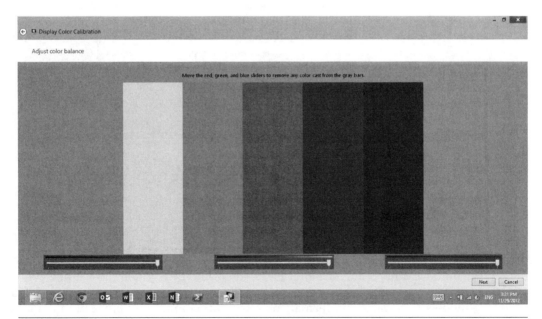

FIGURE 17-8   Change the different color settings until the display looks right to you

How to...

Tune ClearType

Windows includes a technology called ClearType to make text look smoother and clearer on screen so that it's easier and less tiring to read. Because all screens are a little different, you can tweak ClearType to get a better result on your screen using the ClearType Tuner, shown next. There's an option to run this at the end of the Display Color Calibration tool, or you can click or tap Adjust ClearType Text in the navigation pane of the Display control panel.

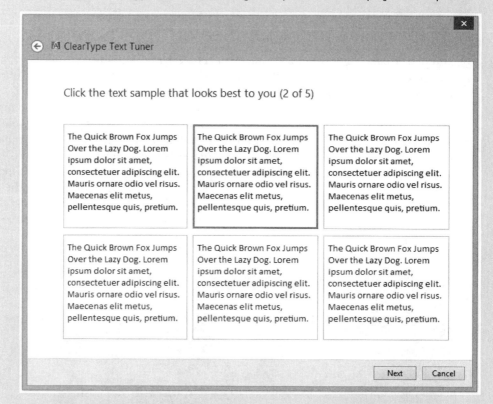

For each of the five sets of samples, tap or click the sample that looks best and is easiest to read, and then click Next. On the last page, click or tap Finish.

Control Power Settings and Screen Brightness

If you have a notebook or tablet PC, some of the time you'll have it plugged in to an electrical outlet, while other times it'll be running on the battery. By default, Windows 8 has faster performance when your computer is plugged in it and it turns off some background activities (like indexing files, so you can find them when you search) when on battery power. You can tune these settings and even create your own power plans to get the performance and battery life you want. You can also change screen brightness.

Click or tap the Power icon in the notification area of the taskbar to choose between the two most recent power plans. Click or tap More Power Options to open the Power Options control panel, shown in Figure 17-9, pick from other power plans.

Choose a Power Plan

The default power plan is Balanced, which means Windows is striking a balance between the performance your PC delivers with its energy consumption. This is the only power plan displayed on some low-power Windows 8 systems (typically tablets with Atom processors, or Windows RT devices) that support a new way of saving power called *Connected Standby*.

This means that as soon as the screen goes dark, the PC acts as if it's turned off. The processor and most of the hardware stop running, to save power (the *standby* part), but the Wi-Fi connection is still active and can receive messages like emails and incoming Skype calls (the *connected* part). As soon as you touch the keyboard or tap

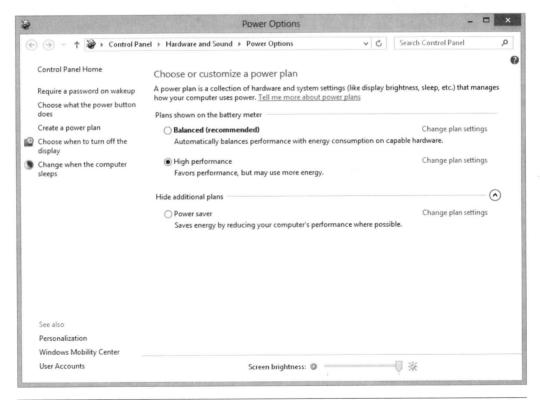

FIGURE 17-9   Choose or customize a power plan in the Power Options control panel.

the power button on a Connected Standby system, it will wake up, with all your apps and documents still open (like pressing the power button on your phone to turn the screen back on).

On both Connected Standby systems and other PCs that come with Windows 8 already installed, the default might be a power plan set up by the PC maker. You can create your own power plans as well, but you'll get the best results from Connected Standby by using the Balanced plan.

One other systems, you can also switch to the Power Saver plan (which gives you slightly lower performance in exchange for longer battery life), the High Performance plan (which trades shorter battery life for higher performance), or any power plans you create yourself. You can change settings for each plan by clicking or tapping Change Plan Settings to the right of each plan name.

Choose When to Have the Display Turn Off

The basic settings let you set how bright the screen is (which has a major effect on battery life) and set how quickly Windows saves power by dimming the screen, turning the screen off, and putting the computer to sleep.

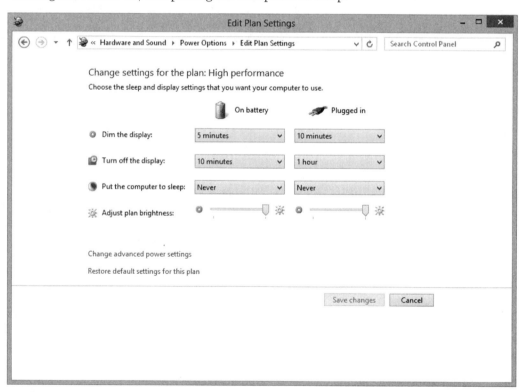

 You can also reach the basic settings for the current power plan by clicking or tapping either Choose When to Turn Off the Display or Change When the Computer Sleeps in the navigation pane on the left side of the Power Options control panel.

To save power, Windows first makes the screen dimmer, then turns the display off when you haven't done anything with your computer for a set time, and finally goes to sleep. Windows is still running when the display is off, even though the screen is dark, and you can turn the display on by tapping a key on the keyboard, moving the mouse, or touching your touchscreen. When the PC goes to sleep, you may need to use the power button to turn it back on.

To change how long Windows waits before dimming or turning off the screen, if you find it turns off too quickly when you're reading the screen but not touching the keyboard or mouse), click or tap the drop-down menu for each setting. You can choose different intervals of time, from Never to 5 hours, and you can have the screen turn off and have the PC go to sleep faster when your PC is running on battery than when it's plugged in.

There are a number of more advanced settings you can change that affect power consumption, like whether your computer can go to sleep while you're sharing media files, the minimum and maximum speeds for your computer's processor, whether the desktop background changes when your PC is not plugged in, and how your graphics adapter and other system hardware behave. Click or tap Change Advanced Power Settings, then choose Change Settings That Are Currently Unavailable to see the full range of options.

Click the plus-sign icons to expand the different options and make changes. The settings you can change are highlighted in blue text; click or tap this text to make changes. You have to change the settings for each plan separately, so use the drop-down menu on the Advanced Settings tab to pick a different plan to change. Click or tap OK to apply your changes.

You can also change at what point you see warnings about your PC running out of battery, and alter what your PC does when the battery level is low or critical. Expand the Battery section and change the settings for the options listed there.

If you change your mind or find that your new settings reduce performance too much or cause other problems, click or tap Restore Plan Defaults to put things back the way they were.

Change Settings for the Power Buttons

There are some power settings that apply to all the power plans. You can change these from the navigation pane in the Power Options control panel by choosing Require a password on wakeup, Choose what the power buttons do or Choose what closing the lid does.

When the System Settings control panel opens, click or tap Change Settings That Are Currently Unavailable.

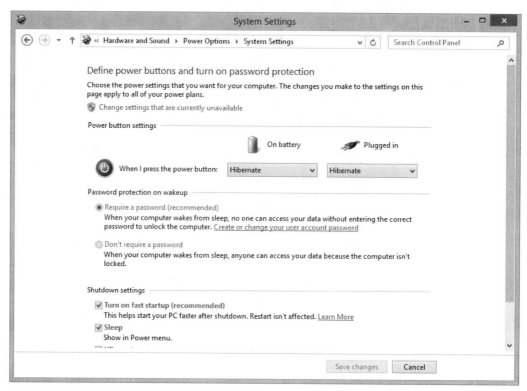

Under Power Buttons and Lid Settings (or Power and Sleep Buttons and Lid Settings, if your PC has a sleep button), shown in Figure 17-10, you can choose what Windows does when you press the power button or sleep button (if your PC has one), and when you close the lid of a notebook. The options for each are Do Nothing, Sleep, Shut Down, and Hibernate (once you've enabled it, as explained later).

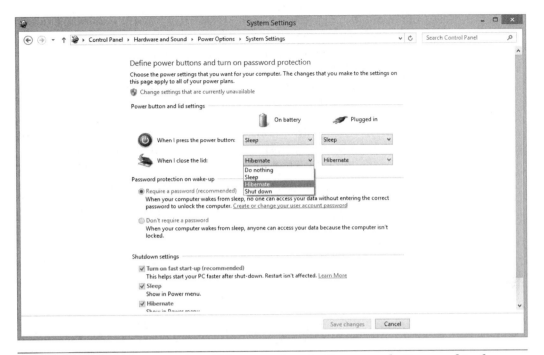

FIGURE 17-10 You can assign different actions to the power buttons and to the notebook lid closing depending on whether your PC is plugged in or using battery power.

 You won't see the settings for the Sleep button if your PC doesn't have one. If you're using a tablet that doesn't have a keyboard attached, you may not see the settings for closing the lid.

Choose What You See on the Power Menu

There are several ways to turn your PC off. To choose which of these you see in the Power menu in the Settings pane, scroll down to the Shutdown Settings area.

Hibernation means your PC is turned off and isn't using any power, but when you press the power button, Windows starts up again exactly where it was before, with your applications and documents open. When you choose Hibernate, Windows saves the state of all your files and open programs into a large file on disk and then turns your PC off. When you turn the computer back on (for example, by pressing the power button), instead of starting from scratch, Windows loads the hibernation file, enabling you to carry on working as if your PC had been on all the time.

Even if you don't hibernate, when you shut down your PC, Windows 8 closes all your files, apps, and programs and saves the state of Windows itself into a similar file, then shuts off your computer. That means Windows 8 starts up more quickly than previous versions of Windows, which didn't save Windows state, but you still have to reopen your apps, programs, and documents. This is the Fast Start-up option you see under Shutdown Settings at the bottom of the System Settings control panel; it's on by default and we don't recommend turning it off.

 If you're shutting down your PC to fix a problem in Windows, chose Restart rather than Shut Down.

If you want to add the Hibernate option to the Power menu, select the Hibernate check box.

Locking your computer when you step away from it protects your information, by requiring a password to get access. If you don't use the Lock or Sleep commands on the Power menu, you can remove them by clearing the check boxes. When you're done, click or tap the Save Changes button.

You won't see the option to enable Hibernate on a PC that has Connected Standby, because Connected Standby uses very little power and gives you more benefits than hibernation (you can make it use even less power by turning off Wi-Fi when you're not using your PC for a while, but then your email won't be waiting for you when you turn the screen back on). You don't have to do anything to enable Connected Standby; if your PC hardware supports it, it will work automatically when your PC goes to sleep.

Create Your Own Power Plan

You can customize all the power plans that are already set up, or you can make your own power plan by clicking or tapping Create a Power Plan in the navigation pane of the Power Options control panel. This opens the Create a Power Plan wizard, as shown in Figure 17-11, where you can pick one of the standard power plan types to customize.

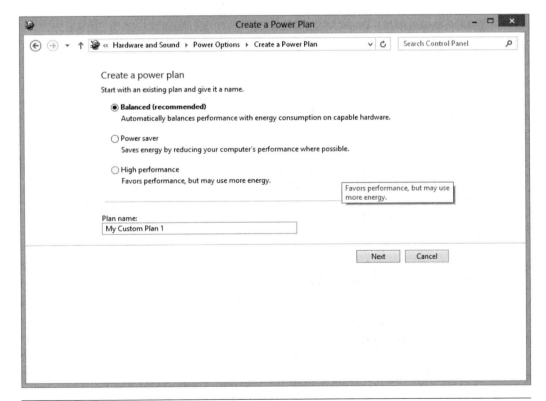

FIGURE 17-11   Each plan contains a brief description of what the plan does.

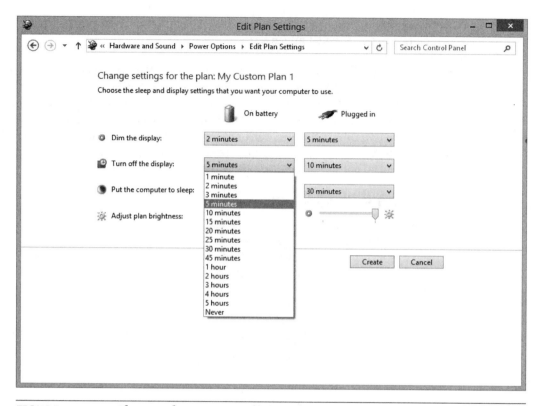

FIGURE 17-12 Choose when to turn off the display when your PC is on battery power and when it is plugged in.

Give your plan a name and then click or tap Next. On the Edit Plan Savings page, shown in Figure 17-12, choose the times for the basic settings (explained previously in the "Choose When to Have the Display Turn Off After Inactivity" section). Click or tap Create to see your plan in the Power Options control panel, where you can change the advanced power options (as also explained previously).

Make Windows More Accessible

If you find it hard to read a standard Windows screen, Windows has built-in tools that enable you to magnify portions of the display or have Windows read dialog boxes to you. You can turn on these options in PC Settings under Ease of Access (when you need help when Windows is already open) or right from the login screen (for quick help when logging in). To access these options from the login screen, before you fill in your password, click or tap the Ease of Access icon in the lower left corner of the screen to open the menu shown in Figure 17-13.

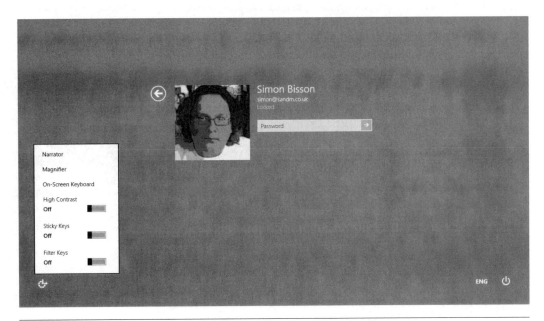

FIGURE 17-13   Ease of Access menu

There are six options you can set here:

- **Narrator**   Click or tap this option to have Windows read out any text that's displayed on the screen.
- **Magnifier**   Click or tap this option to enlarge an area of the screen to help you log in. If you need to use the Magnifier tool after you log in, you'll need to relaunch it from the All Apps screen to magnify running applications, as shown in Figure 17-14. You change the settings in the Magnifier window by clicking or tapping the minus-sign icon to make items on the screen smaller or the plus-sign icon to make those items larger. The default magnification is 200%.
- **On-Screen Keyboard**   If you find it hard to use a physical keyboard, you can choose this option to see a keyboard on screen that you can click or tap on, as shown in Figure 17-15. This is slightly different from the usual touch keyboard you get in Windows 8 if you have a touchscreen, and you can use it with a mouse even if you don't have a touchscreen.
- **High Contrast**   Switch this option to On if you want Windows to use high-contrast colors on the screen to make it easier to see text and some images.

FIGURE 17-14 Use the Magnifier window to make one part of the screen easier to read.

FIGURE 17-15 The onscreen keyboard

- **Sticky Keys**   Switch this option to On if you find it hard to hold down a key like CTRL or SHIFT while you press another key. Sticky Keys lets you type keyboard shortcuts like CTRL-S by pressing the CTRL key first and then pressing the s key, instead of having to press both keys at the same time.
- **Filter Keys**   Switch this option to On if you sometimes hit too many keys or press the same key too many times in quick succession. With Filter Keys turned on, Windows treats repeated key presses as a single keystroke and ignores when you press several keys at once (for example, if your hand knocks the keyboard).

The Ease of Access section of the Control Panel has a number of other accessibility settings that enable you to change the size of the cursor, change how long notifications are displayed for, make the arrow keys move the mouse pointer, set up text to speech, and configure other tools that are useful if you have a more pronounced disability. If you're not sure which tools would be useful to you, click or tap Let Windows Suggest Settings to answer a questionnaire about what's easy and difficult for you when you're using a computer. Windows will then offer you suggestions, which you can accept or decline.

18

Troubleshoot Problems in Windows 8

HOW TO...

- Monitor your system with Task Manager
- Use troubleshooters to find and fix problems
- View problem reports, system information, and system logs to trace errors
- Check for compatibility issues and make older software run happily
- Find troubleshooting information online
- Ask a friend for help via Remote Assistance
- Snapshot the problem for an expert with the Problem Steps Recorder
- Start and stop services
- Restart in Safe Mode
- Allow an app through Windows Firewall
- Solve hardware problems with Device Manager
- Diagnose memory failures

Even if you use the tips in the previous chapter to keep your system tuned up, things still go wrong on computers from time to time, whether it's a hardware failure, incompatible software, bugs in a new driver, confusing error messages, or even a complete system crash. If you're having trouble with your computer, Windows 8 has a set of tools to help you fix it, including troubleshooting wizards that try to repair problems automatically; problem reports that warn you when something is misconfigured or turned off; tools to view system information to help you diagnose the fault and fix it yourself, and utilities that gather information you can pass on to a professional so they can help you sort things out. In this chapter we'll show you how to use the key tools in Windows 8.

Monitor Your System with Task Manager

If one of your apps or programs isn't responding or your PC doesn't seem to be running as fast as it usually does, Task Manager is the place to start. This utility shows you which apps, programs, services, and processes are running in Windows so you can see how much CPU, memory, disk, or network bandwidth they're using and identify any that are using more resources than you expect. You can also check if your software is still responding to Windows, and shut it down if necessary. You can open Task Manager in several ways:

- From the Start screen, open the All Apps screen and then click or tap the Task Manager tile.
- Press CTRL-SHIFT-ESC.
- On the desktop, right-click or press and hold on any blank area in the taskbar and select Task Manager in the context menu that appears.
- Right-click or press and hold in the bottom left corner of your screen (or press WINDOWS-X) and choose Task Manager from the menu.
- Press CTRL-ALT-DELETE and select Task Manager from the screen that appears.

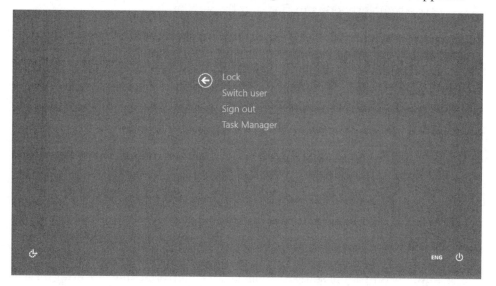

The first time the Task Manager window opens, it shows the Fewer Details view, with just a list of the Windows Store apps and desktop programs that are currently running. If you want to shut down one of the running apps or programs, select it in the list and then click or tap the End Task button. If you want to see more information about your system resources and a list that includes all the services, background tasks, and processes that are running currently, click or tap More Details.

The More Details view makes the Task Manager window larger and adds multiple tabs that show more in-depth information. The Processes tab, shown in Figure 18-1, lists all the software that's currently running, organized into three sections:

- **Apps**   Includes both Windows Store apps and desktop programs that you have open
- **Background processes**   Includes services from both Windows and your own software, as well as the tools you can open from the notification area of the taskbar
- **Windows processes**   Includes the programs that make up Windows itself, including Windows Defender

You can expand some of the processes to see another level of information; for a desktop program you might be able to see the windows and documents that are open. For system processes you can see any associated services or tools.

For each process, you can see what percentage of your CPU, memory, disk bandwidth, and network bandwidth it is using. If any of the processes have locked up or crashed, they'll be marked as Not Responding. The resource information is color coded; processes that are using more resources than others have their figures highlighted in darker yellow so that you can easily spot what is slowing down your system. You can also see the total resource usage at the top of each column. Again, this is a quick way to see why Windows might be running slowly.

   If the CPU, memory, disk, or network usage for your system looks unusually high, click or tap on the figure at the top of the column you're interested in to put the processes using the most of that resource at the top of the list. Click or tap the top of the Name column to go back to the usual view.

(3)

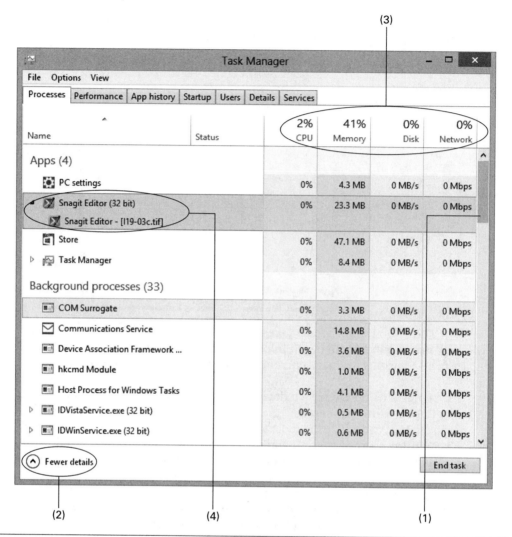

FIGURE 18-1 (1) Scroll down to view everything currently running on your computer. (2) Click or tap to switch back to the simpler view. (3) Click or tap a column heading to sort by resource use. (4) See the documents or windows open in a program.

Restart Explorer or Run a Process

The Windows Explorer process that you see in Task Manager is more than just File Explorer; it's actually the entire desktop environment, including the taskbar. If the Status for Windows Explorer is Not Responding, it may be a sign of a wider problem. The safest thing is to restart Windows, but you can also try restarting the Explorer process. When you select Windows Explorer in the list, the name of the button in the lower right corner of Task Manager changes from End Task to Restart. Click or tap Restart and wait while the desktop reloads (the taskbar may go blank for a brief period). If Explorer doesn't reload correctly, you can start it from Task Manager by choosing File | Run New Task and entering the process name, which is EXPLORER .EXE. If you know the name of any process, you can start it from Task Manager the same way.

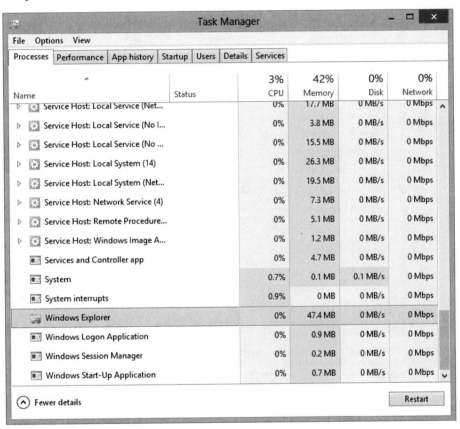

Manage Which Software Starts Automatically

If your PC is starting up more slowly than you expect, the problem might be either that you have too many programs set to start up automatically when you boot Windows, or that your system is having to wait for one specific startup program. The Startup tab of Task Manager lists all the tools and programs that Windows loads automatically, as well as what impact each of these has on how long it takes Windows to start (High, Medium, Low, None, or Not Measured for software Windows hasn't yet profiled). If you want to stop a program from loading automatically, select it in the list and click or tap the Disable button. You can reenable the program later if you change your mind or find that having it start up when Windows does is useful enough to justify the extra wait.

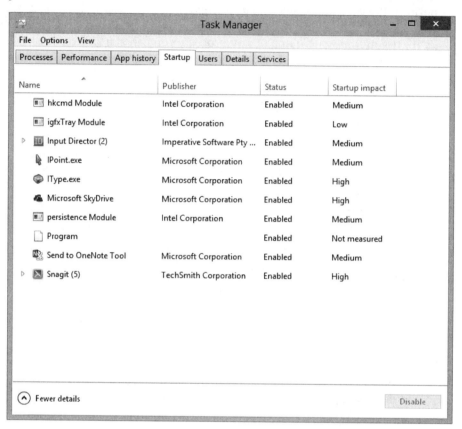

Programs that start automatically with Windows don't actually run until you open the Windows desktop, and the desktop doesn't start until you open its tile, so remember to open the desktop to make your startup programs run. To have Windows Store apps like Mail and Calendar run automatically so that you get messages and reminders, just make sure they're on the list of notification items on the Lock screen, as covered in Chapter 2, and they will run in the background.

Tip If the diagnostics that Windows runs automatically detect that startup is slow or that you have a lot of startup apps, you will see a message in Action Center (covered in Chapter 17) suggesting that you look at the startup list and turn off any that you don't need; click or tap the link to open the Startup tab in Task Manager.

View Your App History

The App History tab of Task Manager gives you some information about Windows Store apps that aren't currently running. It shows how much network bandwidth particular apps use, which is especially useful if you're using a metered network like a mobile broadband dongle or connecting using your smartphone. Because you might have to pay extra if you use a lot of data, it's a good idea to keep tabs on which apps are using your mobile data. If you want to see the same details for desktop programs and Windows processes as well, choose Options | Show History for All Processes.

Task Manager				
File Options View				
Processes Performance App history Startup Users Details Services				
Resource usage since 10/31/2012 for current user account. Delete usage history				
Name	CPU time	Network	Metered network	Tile updates
Adera	0:00:00	0 MB	0 MB	0 MB
ARMED!	0:00:00	0 MB	0 MB	0 MB
Astronomy Picture of th...	0:00:05	0.2 MB	0 MB	0 MB
Bing	0:00:00	0.8 MB	0 MB	0.1 MB
Browser Choice	0:00:00	0 MB	0 MB	0 MB
Calc4Win	0:00:00	0 MB	0 MB	0 MB
Camera	0:00:00	0 MB	0 MB	0 MB
CineTrailer	0:00:00	0 MB	0 MB	0 MB
Cut the Rope	0:00:00	0 MB	0 MB	0 MB
Doodle God Free	0:00:00	0 MB	0 MB	0 MB
Evernote	0:00:00	0 MB	0 MB	0 MB
Finance	0:00:00	0 MB	0 MB	0 MB
FineReader Touch	0:00:00	0 MB	0 MB	0 MB
Fewer details				

View More Details in Task Manager Tabs

If you can't solve your problem with the information on the Processes tab, you can get even more detail on the other tabs of Task Manager. Some of this information is very technical, but it might be useful to pass on to customer support to help them diagnose a problem.

- **Details**   Provides advanced technical information about the different processes that are running.
- **Services**   Provides more information about which Windows Services are currently running and which have stopped (Windows stops services that aren't needed, to save resources, but if a tool or program needs to use a service that's stopped, then you'll see problems). We'll cover starting and stopping services later in this chapter.

- **Performance**   Displays live graphs of how different system resources are being used. You can look back and see whether your PC has just slowed down because one program has starting using more CPU or the disk is busy. Select one of the small graphs to see more details (plus information about your hardware) and then look on the Processes tab to see which apps or programs are using the most CPU or disk bandwidth. If websites are loading slowly, select the network graph to see if network traffic is heavy. If it is, use the Network column on the Processes tab to see which other software is using the network and slowing down your browser.

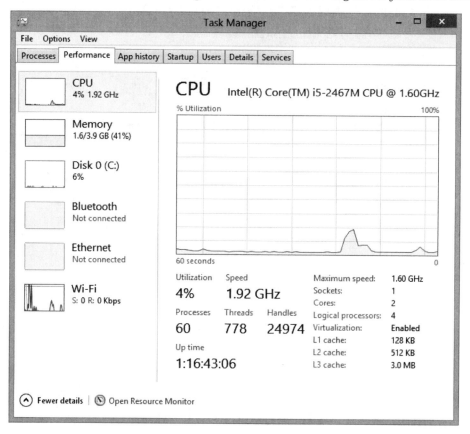

Which graphs you see on the Performance tab depends on which hardware you have. You'll always see CPU, Memory, and Disk graphs, and if you have Wi-Fi, Ethernet, and Bluetooth connections, you'll see graphs for those too.

 If you're looking for even more information, click or tap Open Resource Monitor at the bottom of the Performance tab.

- **Users**   If you share your PC with other users and they're logged in at the same time as you, this tab shows you which system resource are being consumed by the apps and programs that those users are running.

Find and Fix Problems

If closing processes, checking resources, and managing services in Task Manager doesn't solve your problems, there are many other tools in Windows to help you. Start with the built-in troubleshooting tools and the reports in Action Center (see Chapter 17) before digging into system information and looking at low-level options like services and the Windows Firewall.

These days, most malware is designed to run without drawing attention to itself by causing problems on your PC that you might notice, because if you look into those problems you might find and remove the malware. But if you're seeing unexplained behavior, heavy network traffic, applications crashing, or processes you don't recognize running in the background, it's possible that your system is infected with a virus. Run a full scan in Windows Defender (see Chapter 18 for details) or other antivirus software you have installed. If you find a virus, you may be able to remove it, but if it's very persistent, you may want to consider refreshing your PC to put Windows back the way it was when you installed it (without losing your files—we'll explain how this works in the next chapter).

Use the Troubleshooters

If you're experiencing a specific problem with your PC, like not being able to connect to Wi-Fi, your notebook battery not lasting long enough, or sound not working properly, you may be able to get Windows to fix it for you by running the troubleshooters you'll find in the Control Panel (click or tap Find and Fix Problems under System and Security or use the Troubleshooting link in Action Center).

Each *troubleshooter* is a wizard that helps you to solve common problems through a series of interactive steps, such as asking you questions about what you see on the screen. Based on your responses, the wizard then checks whether key settings are configured correctly and, if not, changes them for you.

There's a whole range of troubleshooters for different categories of problems that you can run from the Control Panel or Action Center. Some Windows tools have their own troubleshooters built in so you can get immediate help. For example, as described in Chapter 5, you can right-click or press and hold on the Network icon in the notification area of the taskbar and select Troubleshoot Problems to have Windows test and try to repair your network connection. Or if you are experiencing problems with your speakers, the volume icon in the notification area will have a red cross over it. Right-click or press and hold then select Troubleshoot Sound Problems.

You can also run troubleshooters directly from the Windows Help and Support tool, which is covered later in this chapter. Search for what you're having problems with, and you will often see a link to a troubleshooter in the explanation.

The Troubleshooting control panel is organized into four sections: Programs, Hardware and Sound, Network and Internet, and System and Security. Troubleshooters for the most common problems have links on this main page, but you can also open the individual sections to see all the wizards that are available in that section (which might include new troubleshooters that Microsoft has published on its support website).

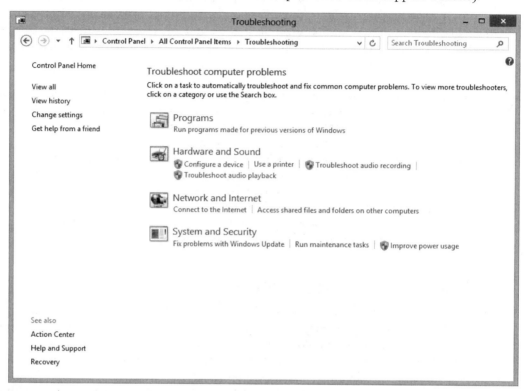

 If a troubleshooter has the yellow and blue User Account Control (UAC) shield next to its name, that means the troubleshooter needs to change some important Windows settings, so UAC might ask you to confirm that you want to run the troubleshooter or ask for an administrator password. Windows uses UAC to notify you when you're about to make major changes to your system, which helps make it more difficult for malware to make changes to your computer without your knowledge.

Troubleshooters work like any other wizards in Windows. Each page of the troubleshooter gives you information about what it does or asks you some questions about the problems you're having. Click or tap the Next button to move through the steps. After the troubleshooter has collected all the information it needs from you, it will check your Windows settings (and display the message Detecting Problems) and make changes to try and fix them (Resolving Problems). Some troubleshooters

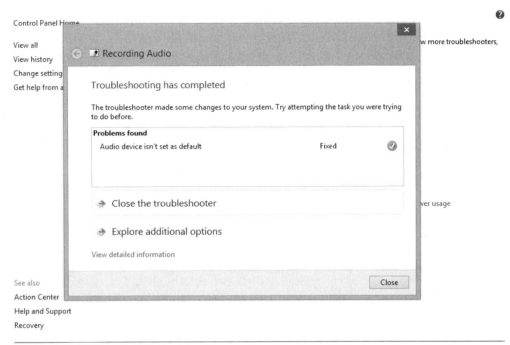

FIGURE 18-2   Scroll down the list to view the issues Windows found and some details about the troubleshooter itself.

can test to see if the problem is fixed, but usually the final page will ask you to check whether things are now working correctly, as shown in the example in Figure 18-2. Click or tap View Detailed Information in the lower left corner of the window to open the Troubleshooting report showing what problems were found and what tests Windows completed.

Ask a Friend for Help Using Remote Assistance

If the troubleshooter doesn't fix your problem, click or tap Explore Additional Options (refer to Figure 18-2) to get a list of ways you can get more help. This opens the Additional Information page of the Troubleshooting control panel, which has links to the Windows Help and Support section on your computer, where you can search for information, and to the Microsoft Community website, where you can check to see if anyone else has found a solution to a similar problem or ask for help. If you want to go straight to the Windows 8 Microsoft Community forum, click or tap the Online

Support button, which also has a link for the general Windows Support section on the Microsoft website, where you can search for related topics.

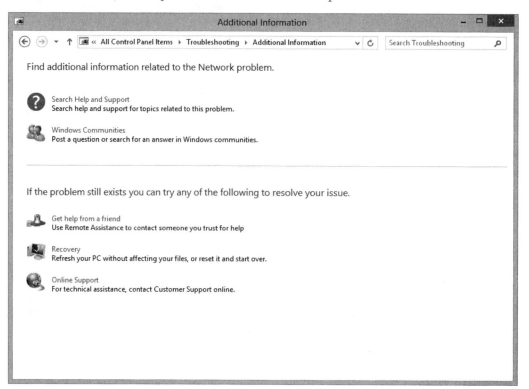

 You can also use the Search box in the Control Panel to search for another troubleshooting tool that might help.

If the problem is serious, click or tap the Recovery link on the Additional Information page to open the recovery tools and to reset Windows to the way it was when you first installed it.

If you have a knowledgeable friend who may be able to help you fix your computer, you can open the Remote Assistance tool, which will let them connect to your computer remotely to see your screen, make changes, or show you how to make the changes yourself.

 Because your friend will be able to see everything on your screen and even control your computer if you give them permission, it's a good idea to close any software or files that you don't want to share. They have to type in a password to get access to your PC, so that strangers can't try to take over your computer, but there are scams where you'll be asked to allow someone pretending to be a support expert to connect to your computer. Never let someone you don't know connect to your PC with Remote Assistance (and never accept technical support from companies who make unsolicited phone calls to tell you there are problems with your computer).

In the Remote Assistance window, click or tap Invite Someone You Trust to Help You and then choose whether you want to invite them via an email message or by using Microsoft's Easy Connect service. If you've asked the same person for help before, you'll see their name listed, so it's easy to invite them again. When they respond to your invitation, you'll see a dialog box asking you to let them connect. You can either chat in the Remote Assistance window or let them take control of your computer to make changes for you. You can click or tap Stop Sharing at any point to regain control.

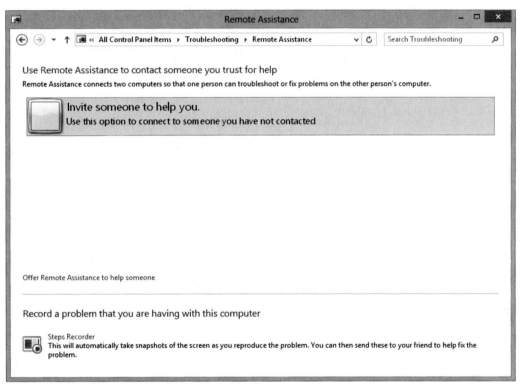

Use the Steps Recorder to Capture a Problem

If you're asking a friend for help or talking to customer support, it's always easier to show them the problem rather than describing it. If you don't want to let anyone connect to your PC (or if the problem is intermittent, so you can't be sure they will see it if they do connect), use the Steps Recorder to take snapshots of the screen (called *screenshots*) as you demonstrate the problem.

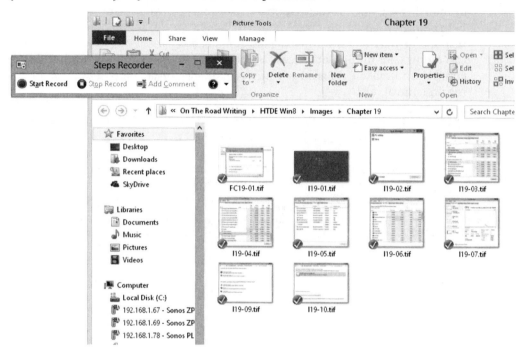

Open the Steps Recorder from the Windows Accessories section of the All Apps screen and then click or tap Start Record to begin taking screenshots. You can pause the recording if you need to do something you don't want recorded. Press CTRL-ALT-C if you want to add comments as you're recording. If you want to record screenshots for a Windows Store app, start Steps Recorder, switch to the app to record the steps, and then go back to the desktop and click or tap Stop Record when you're finished. Check that the screenshots show the problem, click or tap Add Comment if you want to describe or explain any of the steps, enter a name to describe the recording, and then click or tap Save. This creates a compressed Zip file that you can send to the person helping you.

Look Up Your Problem in Windows Help and Support

If the automated tools in the troubleshooters can't solve your problem, it's a good idea to find out a bit more about the feature you're having trouble with before you try anything else. Use the Help and Support area in Windows 8 to look for information;

often this includes links to tools that can help you solve problems. Windows Help and Support not only includes a database of information, but can also search the Microsoft website for more up-to-date information. Open Help and Support from the Windows System group on the All Apps screen.

 You can open Help and Support for information on a specific Windows feature by pressing F1 while you're using that feature.

The home page of Windows Help and Support has three sections you can open, as shown in Figure 18-3, or you can click or tap Browse Help to see a categorized list of help topics to explore. (For example, click or tap System Repair and File Recovery to see links explaining how to repair your system and recover your files.) For a specific problem, type the name of the feature into the Search box at the top of the window.

Check Reports in Action Center

Look in Action Center (introduced in Chapter 17) to see if there's a problem report that covers what you're trying to fix. If Windows has already found a solution, it will be listed at the top of the window. If not, open the Maintenance section and click or tap Check for Solutions under Check for Solutions to Problem Reports. Windows will check the list of problems it has detected; it may ask permission to send additional information about specific problems to Microsoft and if you agree, you'll have to wait for that to upload.

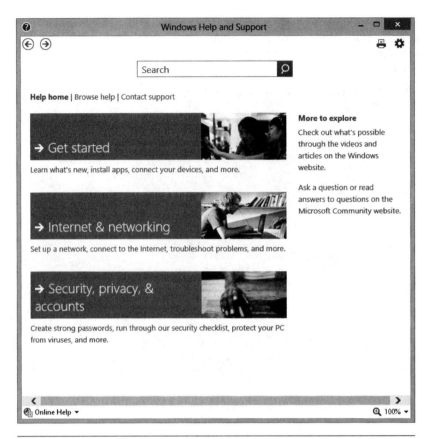

FIGURE 18-3   Click or tap the Windows Website link or the Microsoft Community Website link on the right side of the screen to visit the website and get more information.

If you can't find any problem reports or solutions that cover the issue you're having, click or tap View Archived Messages in the Action Center navigation pane to see if Windows has detected the problem and suggested a solution before.

Check Program Compatibility Settings

If you're running a program that was created for an older version of Windows, you can tell Windows 8 to pretend to be that earlier version of Windows so that the software works properly. You can use the Program Compatibility Troubleshooter to check

How to... **Check How Reliable Your PC Has Been**

If you're not sure how long your problems have been occurring, click or tap View Reliability History at the top of the Maintenance section, under Check for Solutions to Problem Reports, to open the Reliability Monitor. This shows a chart of how stable your system has been over recent days and weeks. If there have been problems with your software or with Windows itself, you can scroll back and select a day or week to see the details, as well as which software you installed and what changes you've made. If you can pinpoint what changed on your system just before a problem started, you may have found the cause.

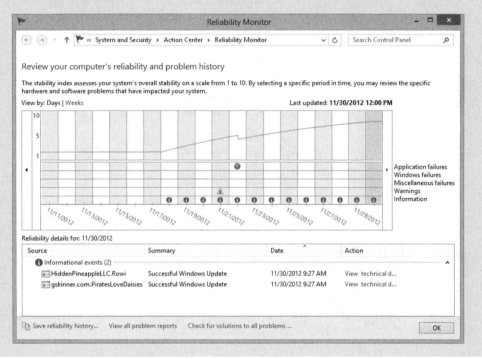

all the desktop programs you have installed to see whether any have compatibility issues. Open the Programs section in the Control Panel and, under the Programs and Features heading, click or tap Run Programs Made for Previous Versions of Windows.

If you're having problems installing or running a specific program and the troubleshooter doesn't fix the problem, you can run the troubleshooter for just that program or change its compatibility settings manually. Right-click or press and hold on the program icon (on the desktop or in File Explorer), choose Properties, and then open the Compatibility tab. Click or tap the Run Compatibility Troubleshooter button at the top to run the troubleshooter, or change the following settings:

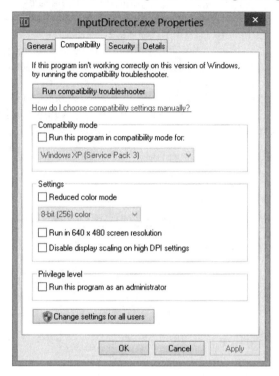

- **Run this program in compatibility mode for** If you know which version of Windows the program was designed for (or if you know it worked in a specific version of Windows), select this check box and choose that version of Windows from the drop-down menu.
- **Reduced-color mode** Some older programs work better if you limit them to fewer colors. When you select this check box you can choose a color mode from the drop-down menu.
- **Run in 640 × 480 screen resolution** If the graphics for the program look jagged or don't display correctly, select this check box to tell Windows to run the program in a smaller window.
- **Disable display scaling on high DPI settings** If you make the text on your screen larger using the high DPI settings in Windows 8 (instead of reducing the resolution), that can make older programs harder to read. This setting reduces that problem.
- **Run this program as an administrator** Often, older desktop programs expect you to be logged in as an administrator, and try to use privileges that aren't available when you're using a standard account. If you're comfortable with the security risk of running older software with administrator privileges and the program won't run otherwise, choose this setting.

Check Your System Information

If you're asking a friend for help or discussing your problem with other users in the Microsoft Community groups, they may ask you for more details about your PC. In Action Center, click or tap View Performance Information in the navigation pane to see the Windows Experience Index performance score for your system, like the score for this tablet PC, then click or tap View and Print Detailed Performance and System Information.

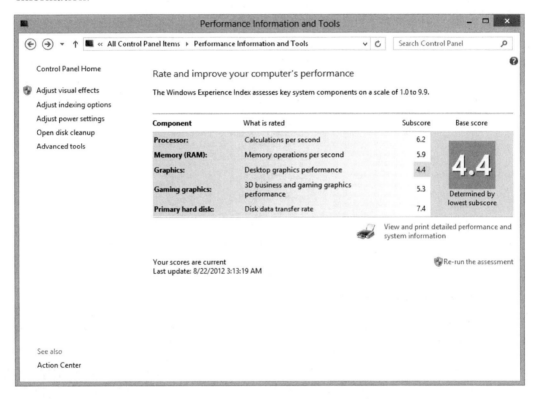

You can find out even more about your computer setup in the System Information tool. Click or tap Advanced Tools in the navigation pane of the Performance Information and Tools window and choose View Advanced System Details in System Information. The System Summary shows general info about your PC, like the make and name of your computer, which processor it has, and how much memory is installed. The rest of the information is intended for support professionals and covers your hardware, peripherals, and low-level Windows software tools.

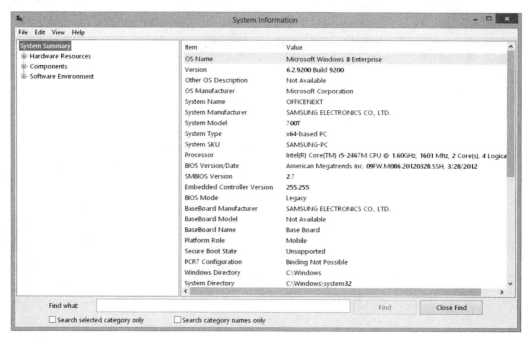

View System Events

Windows keeps logs of all significant events on your system, like Windows starting and shutting down, applications running, security errors, slow drivers, and other performance problems. If you run into a problem, you can review these logs to see what happened and when. Open Event Viewer by choosing Advanced Tools in the Performance Information and Tools window, or from the Advanced Tools menu that you open by pressing WINDOWS-X or by right-clicking or pressing and holding in the lower left corner of your screen.

The Event Viewer window is organized into three panes. The left pane contains a folder list of views and logs. Start by navigating to the System entry under Windows Logs to see recent events.

In the middle pane, shown in Figure 18-4, you can see a list of all system events, which includes the event level, the date and time the event occurred, the source of the event (such as Windows Update), and the event ID Windows assigned to the event. Event Viewer marks each system event as Information, Warning, Error, or Critical.

Click or tap an event in the list to view the details of the event.

The Actions pane on the right side of the window contains a list of commands. For example, under the Event section heading in the list, you can click or tap Event

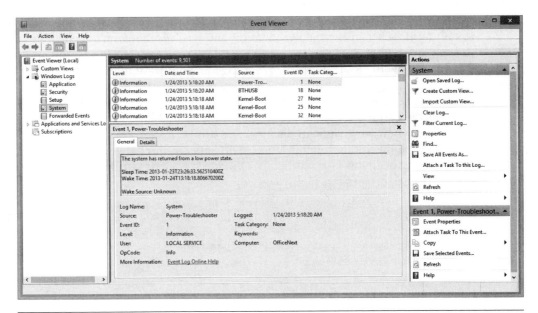

FIGURE 18-4 Looking at the most recent event from the System events list in Event Viewer

Properties to open an event in a larger window so the details are easier to read. Use Filter Current Log to narrow down the list of events—for example, by showing only errors.

Start and Stop Services

A Windows *service* is a small application that runs in the background to handle specific functions in Windows, like indexing files so you can search them or saving changes into File History. Some services are part of Windows, while others are part of different desktop programs like Adobe Acrobat (tools that check for updates usually run as a service).

You Can View Many Different Types of Logs

There are several categories of logs you can view in the Event Viewer window. In the folder list shown in Figure 18-4, you can also view Application, Security, Setup, and Forwarded Events logs within the Windows Logs folder. If you want to view logs for applications and services, double-click or double-tap the Applications and Services Logs folder.

Usually you don't need to worry about services, and generally it's not a good idea to stop services because Windows turns off any services that aren't needed. But there may be times when you'll need to stop a service because it isn't functioning properly, is interfering with other software, or is using too many system resources. Or if a service needed by a program isn't running, you may want to start it manually.

You can see a list of services, including whether they're running or stopped, in the Services tab of Task Manager. Right-click or press and hold on a service to open the menu, where you can start a service, or stop or restart a service that is already running. If you want to find out more about services or change whether a service starts automatically or is controlled by Windows, click or tap Open Services at the bottom of the Services tab.

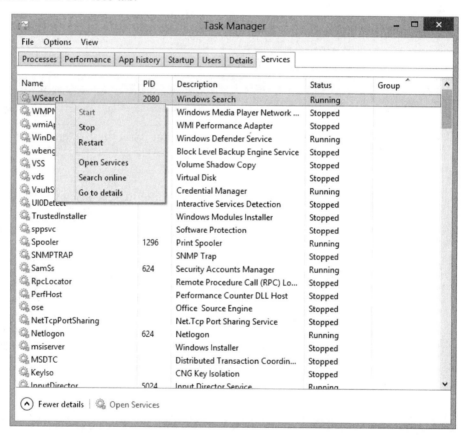

The Services window organizes detailed information about all the services on your system into the columns you can see in Figure 18-5:

- **Name**   The name of the service.
- **Description**   A brief description of what the service does.
- **Status**   If the service is active, it's labeled Running.

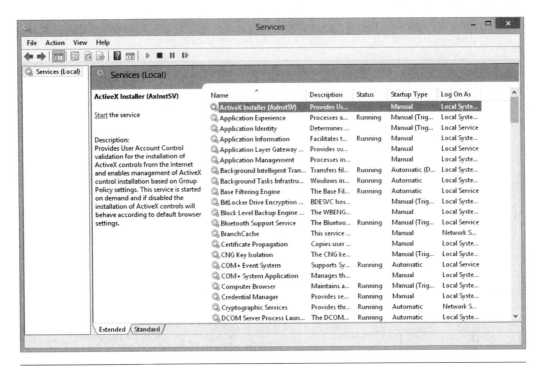

FIGURE 18-5   See which services are running and change how they start up if necessary.

- **Startup Type**   Some services are started automatically by Windows (Automatic), while others are started only if a program or another service needs them (Manual). Services that are not allowed to start are labeled Disabled. Both manual and automatic starts can be triggered by actions that you take. For example, the Device Install Service isn't started when Windows loads; it's started manually when it's needed, and only when it's triggered by you connecting a device that needs to be installed. Services that are labeled Delayed Start are still started automatically by Windows but not until after you've logged in and started using your PC, so you're not waiting for them when Windows first boots.
- **Log On As**   Which permissions a service gets depends on how it's logged in to Windows: as a Local System, as a Local Service, or as a Network Service.

When you select a service in the list, its complete description appears in the pane on the left. If the service is running, you will see a link to Stop or Restart the service. If it is not running, you will see a link to Start the service. The description of the service in the left pane may also include warnings about features that will stop working and other problems that may occur if the service is stopped or disabled. For example, if you stop the Print Spooler service, you won't be able to see your printers or print any files. Or, if you stop the Plug and Play service, your system won't be able to detect any devices you add or remove, and it might even crash when you unplug devices because it will carry on trying to use them. Right-click or press and hold on a service and choose Properties to see more details about how the service runs. On the Dependencies tab, you can see which other services must be running for this service to run correctly, as well as which services depend on this service. You can't use the fax features in Windows if the Print Spooler service isn't running, for example.

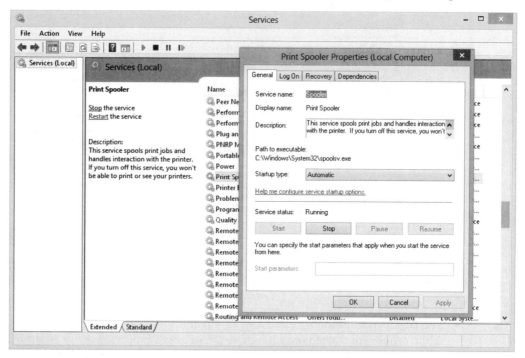

Changing how services start up usually isn't a good idea. Although you can do this on the General tab of Properties, if you're having a problem with a service, it's better to try to recover or refresh Windows (which we'll show you how to do later in this chapter).

Start in Safe Mode

If Windows is crashing and Reliability Monitor hasn't helped you track down what's making it unstable, you can try a process of elimination. Starting Windows in Safe Mode loads only the basic files, settings, and drivers needed to run Windows. If you still experience the problem while in Safe Mode, then the best option is to refresh Windows, because the problem is in Windows itself. If you don't experience the problem in Safe Mode, you can start the programs you use one by one until the problem starts happening again, helping you track which software is causing the problem.

To start in Safe Mode, open PC Settings, select the General section, and, under Advanced Startup, click or tap Restart Now. Choose Troubleshoot, then Advanced Options, and then Startup Settings. Click or tap the Restart button, and when you see the Startup Settings screen again, choose Safe Mode (you may be able to do that with your mouse or by touching your screen, or you may need to use the keyboard). Remember to sign in with an administrator account.

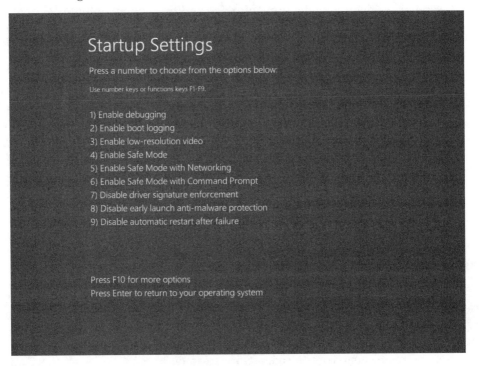

 If you refresh Windows, reinstall your apps and programs, and still encounter the same problems as before, then the problem is with either your hardware or some of the software you have installed (rather than in Windows itself). Refresh Windows again and install your applications one by one. When the problems start, the last app or program you installed is likely to be the problem.

If Windows isn't starting up correctly, the system may be able to repair itself: follow the same steps for starting in Safe Mode, but when you get to the Advanced Options screen, select Automatic Repair. Again, you will need the administrator password and you may be prompted to make choices during the repair. If Automatic Repair can fix the problem, your PC will restart normally; if not, you will see a message that Automatic Repair couldn't repair your PC. Choose Advanced Options to try again or Shut Down to turn your PC off.

Allow Applications Through Windows Firewall

If software you're trying to use doesn't seem to be working correctly, check whether it needs an online connection that's being blocked by Windows Firewall.

Many of the apps and programs on your system connect to online services to send and receive information. For example, Mail needs to download your messages, and your favorite games may download high-score leader boards. But malicious software also wants to send and receive data. A *firewall* is a tool that analyzes incoming and outgoing network traffic and determines if the packets of data that software wants to send or receive should be transmitted to and from your computer or not. Windows 8 has a built-in firewall, called Windows Firewall, that runs automatically when Windows starts up to protect your computer from attackers trying to gain access to Windows and to data stored on your computer, but its protection might also interfere with some legitimate programs.

While you're online, Windows Firewall is constantly checking all the data that comes into your computer, for example as you check your email or talk to friends on Skype. Unless incoming traffic is a response to a request from your PC, or on the list of traffic you always allow, then it will be blocked; so your messages arrive safely and your Skype calls get through, but commands from an attacker trying to control your computer can't get through.

There are plenty of apps and programs that you want to allow to send and receive information. For example, if you use the SkyDrive software to keep copies of documents in the cloud or if you want to get automatic updates for software you have installed, those programs need to be able to connect to the Internet. Most applications can connect without needing you to give them extra permissions to pass through Windows Firewall, but if you're having problems with software that requires a connection, you may need to set Windows Firewall to explicitly allow the connection.

 If an app or program tries to connect in a way that triggers Windows Firewall to block it, a message will warn you that the connection has been blocked. You can click on this message to see more details and choose whether to give the software more permissions to connect, if necessary.

Add Allowed Apps

You can open Windows Firewall either from the Start screen by searching for it in Settings or from the Control Panel. Under System and Security, click or tap Windows Firewall to see the current settings; you can also choose Allow an App Through Windows Firewall to see what's already allowed and add new apps and programs.

Windows Firewall Alone Isn't Enough Protection

Viruses and other malware can be merely irritating or very dangerous, interfering with your productivity by running programs you don't know about, sending sensitive data (like passwords and bank information) without your knowledge, and passing themselves on to other computers. While Windows Firewall gives you some protection, some attackers are very clever and persistent, and it's possible that malware and viruses will eventually get through Windows Firewall. That's why it's important to use the built-in Windows Defender antimalware protection (or other antivirus software) as well (see Chapter 17) and to check which applications are running on your computer.

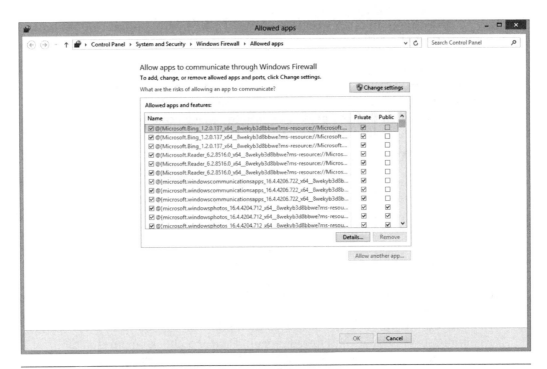

FIGURE 18-6   The list of allowed apps and features

In the Allowed Apps page, shown in Figure 18-6, you can scroll up and down the Allowed Apps and Features list to see all the Windows Store apps and desktop programs, plus some features of Windows itself, that are already allowed through the firewall, as well as those that don't have special permissions. For each app, program, or feature, you'll see details of what's allowed on the two different types of networks that Windows Firewall controls:

- **Private**   A check mark in the Private column indicates that Windows Firewall allows this software to connect to online services when you're connected to your private network, such as your company network or the Internet connection you have at home. These networks are considered to be more secure not only because you know and trust the people in your network and know more about how the networks are set up, but also because it's harder for an attacker to connect to a private network. You should still take precautions on a private network, in case someone else has malware on a computer that's connected to it.
- **Public**   A check mark in the Public column indicates that Windows Firewall allows this program to run on any network you use, including public networks such as Wi-Fi hotspots in a hotel or coffee shop. By default, Windows increases the security options for your computer when you're on a public network, because you don't know how the network is set up or who else is using it.

Some programs are allowed to connect on both kinds of network and you will see check marks in both columns.

 When you allow an app or program through Windows Firewall, you're allowing it to send and receive information. This could make your PC less secure, because an attacker or malware might be able to use that to attack your PC. Never allow an application that you don't recognize to communicate through the firewall. If you see an entry in the list for an app or feature that you're not familiar with, disable it and see if that causes problems.

Click or tap the Change Settings button to switch to working as an administrator so you can choose to give specific Windows Store apps or desktop programs permissions to go through the firewall. Select the app or program you want to allow (if you aren't certain you have the right one, click or tap the Details button to see the name and description). If you want the application to work only on more secure, private networks, click or tap the check box to the left of its name; the check box in the Private column will automatically be selected as well. If you want the software to be available on any network wherever you are, click or tap the check box in the Public column as well.

If you want to limit the access of an application that currently has permission to communicate through Windows Firewall, clear the check box in the Public or Private column to turn off access to public or private networks, respectively. If you clear both the Public and Private check boxes, then the check box by the name of the program is cleared as well. If you want Windows Firewall to block this application from connecting at all, you can just clear the check box by its name to turn off access on both kinds of network.

If the Windows Store app or desktop program you're looking for isn't already on the list, click or tap the Allow Another App button at the bottom of the page. In the Add an App dialog box, shown in Figure 18-7, you can see the other apps and programs you have installed.

If the app or program you want to allow through Windows Firewall isn't listed in the Add an App dialog box either, click or tap the Browse button to find the folder it's installed in. When you find the correct folder, click or tap the application file and then click or tap the Open button.

Again, you can choose which types of networks the application can communicate on by clicking or tapping the Network Types button; use the check boxes to select whether it can use private networks, public networks, or both.

When you finish adding the application, click or tap the Add button. Once you're finished making changes to the list, click or tap the OK button to save the changes and return to the Windows Firewall window. Now try launching the app or program you were having problems with and see if the problem has been solved.

 If you want to see how much a Windows Store app or desktop program uses your network connection, look in Task Manager.

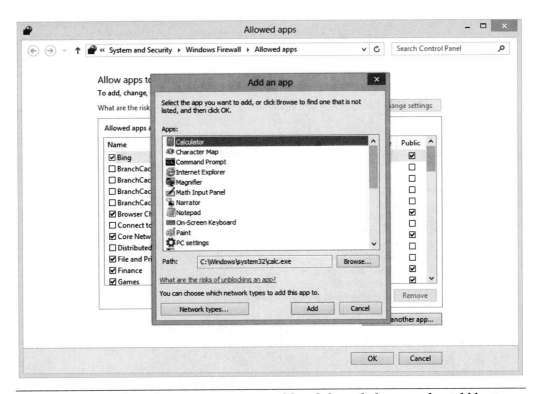

FIGURE 18-7   Select the app you want to add and then click or tap the Add button.

Solve Hardware Problems

If you're having problems with your PC hardware or a peripheral you're trying to use, some common problems are caused by hardware that isn't set up properly. Start by checking that everything is plugged in correctly and turned on.

If the tools we've looked at already can't help, or if the results point to your hardware, you need to find out whether the problem is that Windows isn't seeing the hardware device properly or whether it has a physical fault. Use these tools to find out.

Look in Devices and Printers

When you connect a peripheral like a scanner or printer to your PC, Windows looks in Windows Update for the correct driver to install. If it can't find it, your device won't work properly. Run the Hardware and Devices troubleshooter to look for devices that aren't correctly installed, or check the Devices and Printers control panel to see the status of a peripheral that isn't working properly.

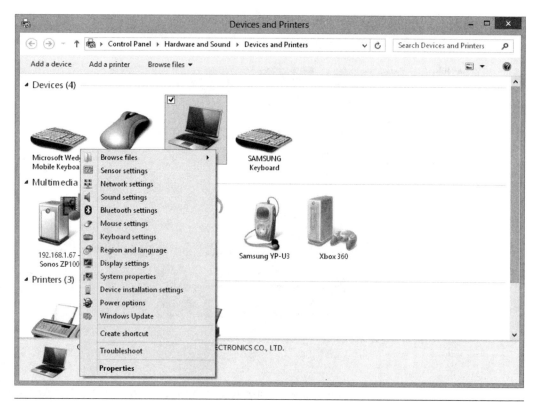

FIGURE 18-8 Devices and Printers shows your hardware and common functions.

To open Devices and Printers, in the Control Panel, click or tap View Devices and Printers under the Hardware and Sound heading. In Devices and Printers, right-click or press and hold the icon for your computer to see more options like Keyboard Settings and Sound Settings, as shown in Figure 18-8. If you do the same with a printer's icon, you can set print options or see the current print queue.

Any devices that Windows hasn't been able to install correctly will be marked with a yellow warning icon. Right-click or tap and hold on the device and choose Troubleshoot or Properties, if you want to see more technical details.

The Properties dialog box has two tabs; the General tab shows the make and model of your device, and the Hardware tab shows which functions the device has and whether it's working correctly. Click or tap Properties here as well to open a second dialog box with more options. Select the Driver tab to see which driver (if any) is installed. If you have a new driver from the manufacturer, click or tap Update Driver to install it or use Roll Back Driver to revert to a previous version. If Windows didn't detect the device correctly, click or tap Uninstall to remove the device so you can try setting it up again.

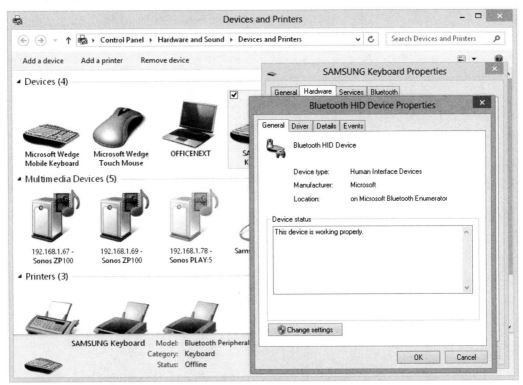

Diagnose Memory Problems

If Windows 8 detects problems with your PC that might indicate faults with the memory that's installed, it will display a message suggesting you run the Memory Diagnostics Tool. Click or tap Restart Now and Check for Problems, and then wait

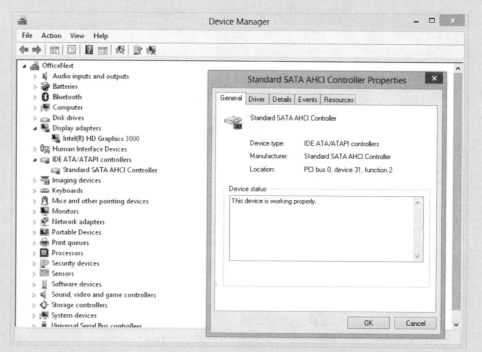

Did You Know?

You Can See More Hardware in Device Manager

You can see the same details for more devices in Device Manager, including your notebook battery, the CPU, and even USB ports and drive connections. In the Control Panel, choose Hardware and Sound, then click or tap Device Manager. Again, any devices that aren't working correctly will be marked with a yellow warning icon.

Choose View | Show Hidden Devices to see information about peripherals that you've used before but that aren't currently connected to your computer.

while your PC restarts and the tool checks the memory in your PC. If the tool reports errors, you should contact your PC maker for help because this usually means you have a hardware fault. If you suspect you have hardware problems but Windows hasn't asked to run this utility, you can search for it in the Control Panel and run it yourself.

19

Reset or Recover Your PC

HOW TO...

- Roll back changes with System Restore
- Refresh or reset your PC
- Make a recovery drive
- Boot from an external drive
- Transfer files and settings to a new computer

When you first get a new PC, it's usually faster because it has better hardware than you're used to, but it also comes with a new installation of Windows. As you install software, connect peripherals, and create files, you get extra features—but not all software is well written, and some of the things you install can slow down your system or cause configuration problems.

With Windows 8, there's no need to reinstall Windows to get that new PC feeling. If you run into problems, Windows 8 offers tools to refresh or restore your system to take you back to the setup you had when everything was working well. If the problem is with Windows and software and hardware you have installed, Windows 8 comes with several different recovery tools depending on how far back you need to go. And if you want to sell or give your PC to someone else, Windows 8 makes it easy to wipe your files and reset the PC to the way it was when you bought it.

 Note If you need an older version of a file after you've made changes to it that you don't want, or if you deleted a file and now realize you still want it, you can recover files using File History. Chapter 4 explains how to set up File History and recover your files with it.

- *Restoring* your PC (with the System Restore tool) is a way to undo recent changes to your system, like installing drivers or software, or changing configuration options.
- *Refreshing* your PC reinstalls Windows but keeps your personal files, many of your Windows settings, all the desktop programs and Windows Store apps that came with your PC when you bought it, and all the apps you've installed yourself from the

437

Windows Store (but not desktop programs you've installed yourself or the software drivers for hardware you've connected to your PC).

- *Resetting* your PC is a great way to clean it up if you want to sell it, donate it to charity, or pass it on to a family member. It's like rolling the PC back to the moment you unpacked it. Resetting your PC also reinstalls Windows and keeps any desktop programs and Windows Store apps that the PC maker put onto the system, but it deletes your files and settings and removes both the desktop programs and the Windows Store apps you've installed.

 Many PCs come with a recovery partition, which looks like another drive in File Explorer, with a name like TOOLS or RECOVERY (*partition* is the term for a separate section on a disk drive). If you look at this in Explorer, it may look as if the recovery partition is full, because it's just the right size for the files in it; you won't be adding any files to it, even when you use Windows Update, so don't worry about running out of space. Don't delete the recovery partition, because you will have problems refreshing, resetting, or reinstalling Windows without it.

We'll show you how to restore, refresh or reset your PC, as well as how to create a recovery drive and how to transfer your files and settings to a new PC.

Go Back in Time with System Restore

Sometimes you know exactly when your PC problems started and you can pinpoint that it was after you installed a new software package or downloaded a new hardware driver. Rather than trying to undo the changes by hand (because it's hard to be sure that you have changed everything back), you can restore your PC to the state it was in before you made the changes in the first place. That's called a *restore point*. Windows saves the details of your configuration as a restore point at regular intervals, and it makes a restore point every time you install new software, add new hardware device, or install an update from Windows Update.

 System Restore won't make any changes to your personal files, like documents and photos.

Run System Restore

You can open System Restore quickly from Action Center, which you can open either by clicking or tapping its icon in the notification area of the taskbar or by choosing Review Your Computer's Status under System and Security in the Control Panel. Click or tap the Recovery link in the lower right corner and choose Open System Restore. Click or tap Next after you've read the explanation of what will be changed.

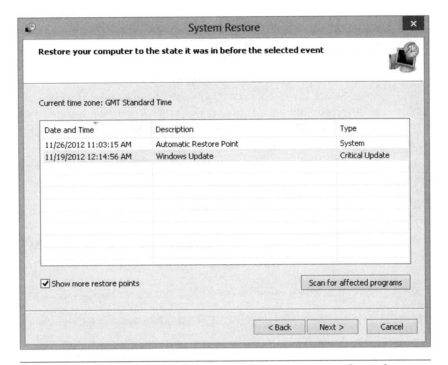

FIGURE 19-1   Click or tap the Next button to restore from the most recent restore point.

Usually, you'll want to undo just your most recent changes, so System Restore shows you just the most recent restore point, with a description of when the restore point was created and what you installed or changed to trigger it. If you want to go further back in time, select the Show More Restore Points check box (see Figure 19-1).

Select the restore point you want to roll back to, and then click or tap Next. You have to confirm that you want to roll back to this restore point, and the Confirm Your Restore Point page gives you another chance to see the date of the restore point, which disk you're restoring, and which programs and drivers this will affect.

Click or tap Finish, and then choose Yes when Windows warns you that System Restore can't be interrupted once you start. System Restore has to restart Windows to undo the changes that were made, so you will have to log back in. The next time you open the desktop, you'll see a notification from System Restore that it has completed the rollback successfully.

Configure System Restore

You can't change any settings in the main System Restore window. Instead, click or tap the Recovery link in Action Center to open the Advanced Recovery tools page, and then choose Configure System Restore to open the System Protection tab in the System Properties dialog box.

How to... Preview the Changes System Restore Will Make

Before you run System Restore, you can check to see what changes it will make. Select the restore point you want to use, and then click or tap Scan for Affected Programs. It may take a few seconds for System Restore to check your system, after which you'll see the following dialog box, which first lists the programs and drivers that will be deleted if you roll back to this restore point, and then lists the programs and drivers that will be restored. Scroll down each of the lists to see complete information. Click or tap Close to return to the main System Restore window.

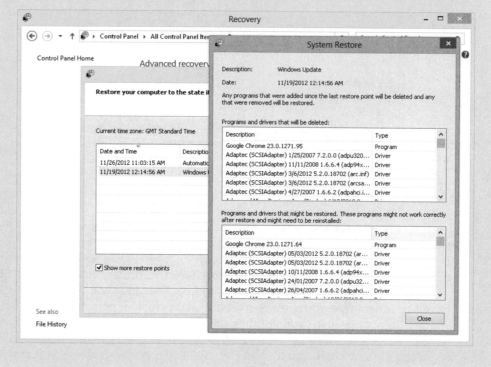

You can see which of your drives are protected by System Restore. If you're experimenting with the way Windows is configured, you can click or tap Create to save a restore point (although many changes will trigger Windows to save a restore point automatically). And if you want to choose how much disk space to use for System Restore, click or tap the Configure button to open the System Protection dialog box, as you can see in Figure 19-2.

By default, System Restore uses 5% of the space on the drive it's protecting. You can see how much disk space that takes up (and change it if you want, by moving the Max Usage slider) in the Disk Space Usage area. When System Restore fills up that space, the oldest restore point is deleted to make room for the newest restore point.

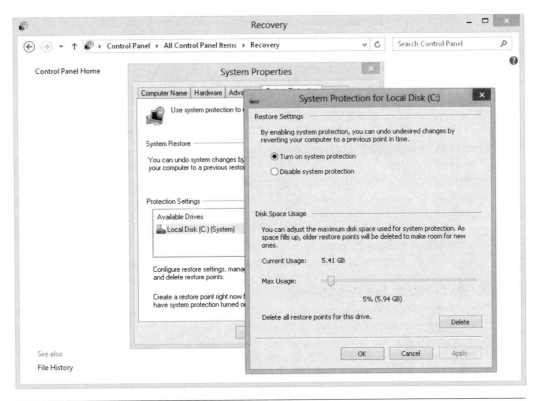

FIGURE 19-2   Set how much disk space is allocated for your restore points.

If you want to keep restore points for longer, move the slider to the right to reserve more space.

 If your PC is short on space, you can set System Restore to use less disk space, but that means you won't be able to undo as many changes to your system.

When you're finished making changes, click or tap the OK button to return to the System Properties window.

Refresh Your PC

Often, you don't know what changes caused problems on your PC, and sometimes rolling back to your oldest System Restore point doesn't fix your issues. Sometimes there isn't a specific problem but you just feel that your PC isn't performing as well as it used to. Refreshing your PC gives you a fresh copy of Windows without deleting any of your personal files.

When you refresh your PC, you also get to keep some—but not all—of your Windows settings. The settings that aren't retained are those that are often the source of problems, so keeping them could give you the same problems you're trying to fix. You keep all the settings that are synced with your Microsoft account, like your personalization options for the Start screen color and design, the Lock screen image, your desktop background, and the details for your wireless network connections. You also retain settings from your PC, like language settings, drive letters, and mobile broadband connections. However, display settings, Windows Firewalls settings, and file type associations aren't carried over.

A refresh doesn't keep your desktop programs (unless they were preinstalled by your PC maker and you have either the recovery disc that came with the PC or a recovery partition created by the PC maker), so keeping the association of a file type with a particular program wouldn't be useful. There are several reasons for not keeping all your software when you refresh. First, a specific program is probably causing the problems you're trying to fix, but it's hard to tell which one. Second, if the problem is a virus or other malware, or some software you didn't actually intend to install that came with another program you did want, you don't want to keep that either. Finally, it's difficult to restore programs and make sure they work in the same way and still get a clean copy of Windows; the order in which you install desktop software matters (you have to install your email software before you install add-ins for it, for example).

Refreshing your PC automatically reinstalls your Windows Store apps, because it is able to get them from the Store. After the refresh you will also find a file on your desktop listing the desktop programs that were installed previously, so you can refer to that to make sure you reinstall everything.

To refresh your PC, open the General section in PC Settings and, under Remove Everything and Reinstall Windows, tap or click Get Started. Windows shows you the following warning about the desktop programs and settings that will be removed. Click or tap Next, then choose Refresh on the next screen.

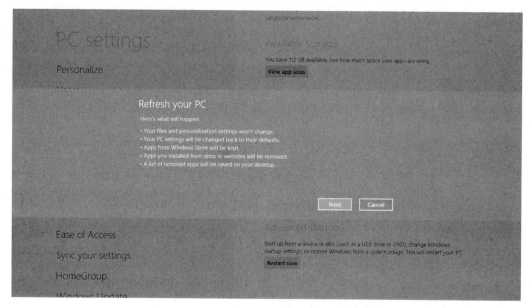

If your PC came with a set of recovery discs, keep them handy as Windows may ask for them or for the media you installed Windows 8 from: the message will tell you that some files are missing. (If your PC didn't come with a recovery disc, you might have created your own when you first set up your PC.) If your PC came with Windows 8 installed and it has a recovery partition created by the PC maker, Windows will use the information in there.

If you're refreshing a notebook or tablet, Windows 8 will remind you to plug it in before you start the refresh in case your battery runs out. The process takes about as long as installing Windows 8 in the first place (it uses the same setup system) but, because it keeps your settings, you won't need to answer questions or fill in your Microsoft account details the way you did when you first set up Windows 8. When the refresh finishes, you can log in to Windows and start reinstalling your desktop programs.

Reset Your PC

If you want a completely fresh start with your PC (or if you want to wipe all your files off it because you're giving it away or selling it), use the Reset tool. In PC Settings, open the General section and, under Remove Everything and Reinstall Windows, tap or click Get Started. Windows shows you the following warning that you'll lose your files, programs, and settings; click or tap Next. As with refreshing your PC, Windows might ask for your recovery or setup media.

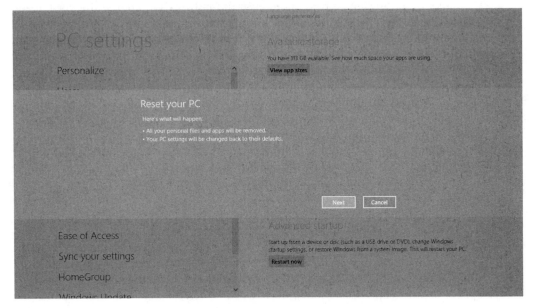

Resetting your PC deletes all your files. Make sure you have a copy of them before you do the reset. If you're using File History (see Chapter 4), that will have copies of everything in your libraries, but check for important files in other folders as well and back them up (or move them into a library).

If your PC has more than one drive, Windows will ask if you want to remove files on all of your drives or just the drive where Windows is installed. If you're passing your PC on to someone else, you'll probably want to delete all the files; if you just want a fresh start, you can keep them without affecting the reset. Windows will also ask whether you want to erase your data quickly or thoroughly. Choose Just Remove My Files if you don't want to wait, but be aware that someone with special recovery tools might be able to recover some of your files. If you have any important information (like downloaded bank statements or other personal documents) on your PC, select Clean the Drive Fully. Finally, click or tap Reset and wait while Windows removes your files, settings, apps, and programs and reinstalls itself.

Create a Recovery Drive

If Windows isn't starting up at all (so you can't refresh or reset your PC to fix the problems), you can start your PC from an external drive or a bootable CD or DVD. It's a good idea to make one of these when you first start using Windows so that you have it in case you need it. Windows also puts some system recovery tools on the recovery drive that might let you fix your startup problems without refreshing.

Open Action Center from its icon in the notification area of the taskbar (or by choosing Review Your Computer's Status under System and Security in the Control Panel) and click or tap Recovery at the bottom of the page. Choose Create a Recovery Drive to open the Recovery Media Creator wizard (see Figure 19-3). You might have to click or tap the Yes button in the User Account Control prompt, or type in the password for an administrator account.

If your PC has a recovery partition installed by your PC maker (and the drive you're using for the recovery drive is large enough), you can check the box to copy this onto the recovery drive. Click or tap Next. If you haven't yet plugged in the drive you want to use, the Recovery Drive wizard will ask you to connect a USB drive that can hold at least 256MB of data. If you want to burn a recovery drive onto a CD or DVD, click or tap Create a System Repair Disc with a CD or DVD Instead. When the Create a System Repair Disc window appears, select your CD or DVD burner from the Drive drop-down list then click or tap Create Disc.

When you plug in a USB drive, a File Explorer window might open to show you the drive (depending on what you've told Windows to do when you plug in USB drives); close the window and go back to the Recovery Drive wizard, where you will see the drive (along with any other USB drives that are plugged in and large enough to use). Click or tap Next. Windows will warn you that any files on the drive will be deleted, to give you a chance to make copies of anything you need to keep. Click or tap Create to delete all files on the drive and set it up as a recovery drive. When the drive is ready, click or tap the Finish button. Remove the drive and store it in a safe place.

FIGURE 19-3   Create a recovery drive on a removable drive or on a CD or DVD.

How to... Boot from an External Storage Device

If your PC came with Windows 8 already installed, then you might have a Windows DVD that came with the computer. If you downloaded the files to upgrade to Windows 8 rather than buying a copy on DVD, during the download process you were given a choice to make a copy of it on either a DVD or a USB drive. You can restart your computer and boot from that installation DVD or USB drive if you ever need to reinstall Windows (and you don't want to use the options in PC Settings to refresh or reset your PC).

You will also need to boot from an external drive if you want to use your recovery drive to try to fix startup problems, or if you want to refresh or reset your PC but Windows won't start up normally. Refer to the manual that came with your computer to learn how to change your computer's startup sequence so it will start from your DVD or USB drive instead of from your

(Continued)

hard drive. Or if you have a newer PC, you can choose to use an external drive from inside Windows 8. Plug in your bootable drive, open the General section in PC Settings, and click or tap Restart Now under Advanced Startup. On the Choose an Option screen, select Use a Device, and then click or tap USB Drive. Your PC will shut down and then restart from the bootable drive. (If you don't have a bootable drive connected, your PC will just reboot.)

Move to a New PC

Chapter 4 explains how to protect your documents with the built-in File History utility, and if you move to a new PC, you can connect your File History drive and restore all your personal files from that (as long as you make sure all your files are in libraries, so that they're saved in File History). If you also sync your settings by logging in with a Microsoft account (also covered in Chapter 4), moving to a new PC (or reinstalling Windows on the same PC) is much less disruptive.

This also works when you're getting a clean start on your existing PC by resetting it, or reinstalling Windows. It's faster and less complicated than trying to restore from a backup, and if the problems were caused by a specific desktop program, a virus, or a problem with your Windows settings, you're not transferring that to the new system.

Here are the steps for getting started on a new PC using the new Windows 8 tools:

1. Set up your new PC (or reset your old PC, use the recovery drive you made earlier to restore Windows on your old PC, or reinstall Windows).
2. Connect to your Microsoft account.
3. Make your PC trusted to sync your passwords along with your other settings.
4. Go to the Windows Store and reinstall your apps.
5. Reinstall your desktop programs.
6. Connect your old File History drive and restore everything to copy all your personal files across.

Transfer Files and Settings to Another Computer

If you want to take more of your settings to a new PC or if you haven't been using File History, you can also back up files, user accounts, and other settings to another computer using the Windows Easy Transfer wizard. You'll find this tool on the All Apps screen in the Windows System group.

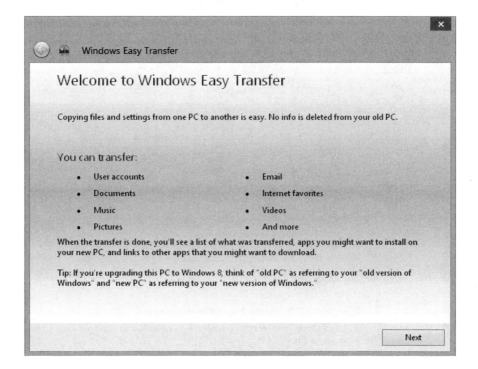

 It can take some time to save and transfer your files and settings. If you're using a notebook or tablet, the Windows Easy Transfer wizard will suggest you plug it in before you start.

The Easy Transfer wizard takes you step by step through transferring your files. Click or tap Next on the first screen and choose how you want to move the files to your new computer: over a special Easy Transfer USB cable or a network connection (if you are moving to a different computer and you have access to both PCs at once) or by saving a file onto a removable drive (if you don't want to have both PCs running at once, or if you're going to reinstall Windows on the same PC).

In the next step, specify whether the computer you're using is the new PC (that you're moving files and settings to) or the old PC (the computer that has the files and settings you want to transfer).

If you want to use a cable or network to copy the files and settings across, you have to have both PCs turned on and running Windows Easy Transfer. First, run the wizard on the old PC and note down the Windows Easy Transfer key that's displayed when you select This Is My Old PC. Next, connect the cable (if necessary), run Windows Easy Transfer on the new computer, and select This Is My New PC and type in the key. Windows Easy Transfer will connect to the other computer and walk you through copying your files and settings across.

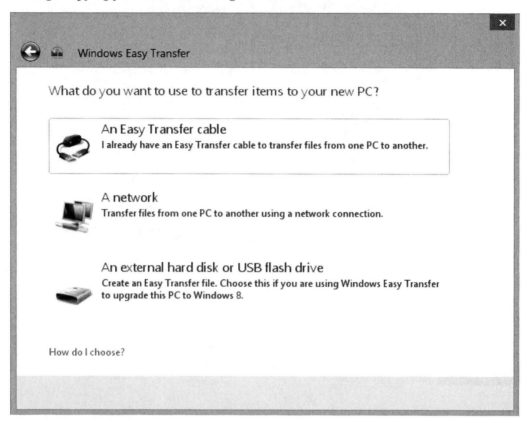

If you want to use a removable drive, you don't have to connect the two systems. Select This Is My Old PC to collect your information. Windows Easy Transfer scans your computer to find files and settings for each account. Tap or click Customize to see what will be copied, and clear the check boxes for any file types or settings you don't need (you can see how much disk space each group of files needs). Choose Next, decide whether you want to protect the transfer file with a password, and then choose Save to export your files and settings (see Figure 19-4).

For each account you want to transfer files and settings from using Windows Easy Transfer, click or tap Customize and choose which files and settings to keep.

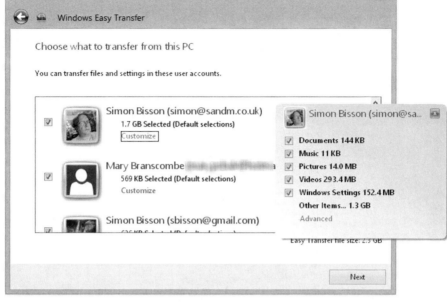

FIGURE 19-4   You can choose which files and settings to transfer to your new PC.

Plug the removable drive into your new PC (or the same PC once you've reinstalled Windows), run Windows Easy Transfer, and select This Is My New PC so you can select the removable drive that has the transfer file and import the files and settings. If you have a lot of files, transferring them can take time, but then you'll have a new PC that feels exactly like the one you were using before.

Index